T0331588

Effective Big Data Management and Opportunities for Implementation

Manoj Kumar Singh
Adama Science and Technology University, Ethiopia

Dileep Kumar G.
Adama Science and Technology University, Ethiopia

A volume in the Advances in Data Mining and
Database Management (ADMDM) Book Series

Published in the United States of America by
Information Science Reference (an imprint of IGI Global)
701 E. Chocolate Avenue
Hershey PA, USA 17033
Tel: 717-533-8845
Fax: 717-533-8661
E-mail: cust@igi-global.com
Web site: http://www.igi-global.com

Library of Congress Cataloging-in-Publication Data

Names: Singh, Manoj Kumar, editor. | Kumar G., Dileep, 1982- editor.
Title: Effective big data management and opportunities for implementation / Manoj Kumar Singh and Dileep Kumar G, editors.
Description: Hershey : Information Science Reference, 2016. | Includes bibliographical references and index.
Identifiers: LCCN 2016004454| ISBN 9781522501824 (hardcover) | ISBN 9781522501831 (ebook)
Subjects: LCSH: Big data. | Database management.
Classification: LCC QA76.9.D3 E335 2016 | DDC 005.7--dc23 LC record available at https://lccn.loc.gov/2016004454

This book is published in the IGI Global book series Advances in Data Mining and Database Management (ADMDM) (ISSN: 2327-1981; eISSN: 2327-199X)

British Cataloguing in Publication Data
A Cataloguing in Publication record for this book is available from the British Library.

All work contributed to this book is new, previously-unpublished material. The views expressed in this book are those of the authors, but not necessarily of the publisher.

For electronic access to this publication, please contact: eresources@igi-global.com.

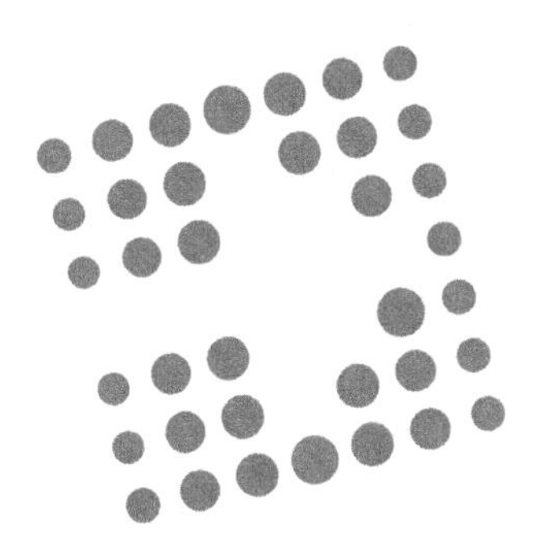

Advances in Data Mining and Database Management (ADMDM) Book Series

David Taniar
Monash University, Australia

ISSN: 2327-1981
EISSN: 2327-199X

Mission

With the large amounts of information available to organizations in today's digital world, there is a need for continual research surrounding emerging methods and tools for collecting, analyzing, and storing data.

The **Advances in Data Mining & Database Management (ADMDM)** series aims to bring together research in information retrieval, data analysis, data warehousing, and related areas in order to become an ideal resource for those working and studying in these fields. IT professionals, software engineers, academicians and upper-level students will find titles within the ADMDM book series particularly useful for staying up-to-date on emerging research, theories, and applications in the fields of data mining and database management.

Coverage

- Database Security
- Profiling Practices
- Association Rule Learning
- Text Mining
- Quantitative Structure–Activity Relationship
- Sequence Analysis
- Data warehousing
- Web mining
- Customer Analytics
- Neural Networks

IGI Global is currently accepting manuscripts for publication within this series. To submit a proposal for a volume in this series, please contact our Acquisition Editors at Acquisitions@igi-global.com or visit: http://www.igi-global.com/publish/.

The Advances in Data Mining and Database Management (ADMDM) Book Series (ISSN 2327-1981) is published by IGI Global, 701 E. Chocolate Avenue, Hershey, PA 17033-1240, USA, www.igi-global.com. This series is composed of titles available for purchase individually; each title is edited to be contextually exclusive from any other title within the series. For pricing and ordering information please visit http://www.igi-global.com/book-series/advances-data-mining-database-management/37146. Postmaster: Send all address changes to above address.

Titles in this Series

For a list of additional titles in this series, please visit: www.igi-global.com

Intelligent Techniques for Data Analysis in Diverse Settings
Numan Celebi (Sakarya University, Turkey)
Information Science Reference • copyright 2016 • 353pp • H/C (ISBN: 9781522500759) • US $195.00 (our price)

Managing and Processing Big Data in Cloud Computing
Rajkumar Kannan (King Faisal University, Saudi Arabia) Raihan Ur Rasool (King Faisal University, Saudi Arabia) Hai Jin (Huazhong University of Science and Technology, China) and S.R. Balasundaram (National Institute of Technology, Tiruchirappalli, India)
Information Science Reference • copyright 2016 • 307pp • H/C (ISBN: 9781466697676) • US $200.00 (our price)

Handbook of Research on Innovative Database Query Processing Techniques
Li Yan (Nanjing University of Aeronautics and Astronautics, China)
Information Science Reference • copyright 2016 • 625pp • H/C (ISBN: 9781466687677) • US $335.00 (our price)

Handbook of Research on Trends and Future Directions in Big Data and Web Intelligence
Noor Zaman (King Faisal University, Saudi Arabia) Mohamed Elhassan Seliaman (King Faisal University, Saudi Arabia) Mohd Fadzil Hassan (Universiti Teknologi PETRONAS, Malaysia) and Fausto Pedro Garcia Marquez (Campus Universitario s/n ETSII of Ciudad Real, Spain)
Information Science Reference • copyright 2015 • 500pp • H/C (ISBN: 9781466685055) • US $285.00 (our price)

Improving Knowledge Discovery through the Integration of Data Mining Techniques
Muhammad Usman (Shaheed Zulfikar Ali Bhutto Institute of Science and Technology, Pakistan)
Information Science Reference • copyright 2015 • 391pp • H/C (ISBN: 9781466685130) • US $225.00 (our price)

Modern Computational Models of Semantic Discovery in Natural Language
Jan Žižka (Mendel University in Brno, Czech Republic) and František Dařena (Mendel University in Brno, Czech Republic)
Information Science Reference • copyright 2015 • 335pp • H/C (ISBN: 9781466686908) • US $215.00 (our price)

Mobile Technologies for Activity-Travel Data Collection and Analysis
Soora Rasouli (Eindhoven University of Technology, The Netherlands) and Harry Timmermans (Eindhoven University of Technology, The Netherlands)
Information Science Reference • copyright 2014 • 325pp • H/C (ISBN: 9781466661707) • US $225.00 (our price)

www.igi-global.com

701 E. Chocolate Ave., Hershey, PA 17033
Order online at www.igi-global.com or call 717-533-8845 x100
To place a standing order for titles released in this series, contact: cust@igi-global.com
Mon-Fri 8:00 am - 5:00 pm (est) or fax 24 hours a day 717-533-8661

Table of Contents

Detailed Table of Contents

With the advent of Internet of Things (IoT) and Web 2.0 technologies, there has been a tremendous growth in the amount of data generated. This chapter emphasizes on the need for big data, technological advancements, tools and techniques being used to process big data. Technological improvements and limitations of existing storage techniques are also presented. Since the traditional technologies like Relational Database Management System (RDBMS) have their own limitations to handle big data, new technologies have been developed to handle them and to derive useful insights. This chapter presents an overview of big data analytics, its application, advantages, and limitations. Few research issues and future directions are presented in this chapter.

The homogeneous data structure 'train' and the heterogeneous data structure 'atrain' are the fundamental, very powerful dynamic and flexible data structures, being the first data structures introduced exclusively for big data. Thus 'Data Structures for Big Data' is to be regarded as a new subject in Big Data Science, not just as a new topic, considering the explosive momentum of the big data. Based upon the notion of the big data structures train and atrain, the author introduces the useful data structures for the programmers working with big data which are: homogeneous stacks 'train stack' and 'rT-coach stack', heterogeneous stacks 'atrain stack' and 'rA-coach stack', homogeneous queues 'train queue' and 'rT-coach queue', heterogeneous queues 'atrain queue' and 'rA-coach queue', homogeneous binary trees 'train binary tree' and 'rT-coach binary tree', heterogeneous binary trees 'atrain binary tree' and 'rA-coach binary tree', homogeneous trees 'train tree' and 'rT-coach tree', heterogeneous trees 'atrain tree' and 'rA-coach tree', to enrich the subject 'Data Structures for Big Data' for big data science.

N. G. Bhuvaneswari Amma, Indian Institute of Information Technology Srirangam, India

Big data is a term used to describe very large amount of structured, semi-structured and unstructured data that is difficult to process using the traditional processing techniques. It is now expanding in all science and engineering domains. The key attributes of big data are volume, velocity, variety, validity, veracity, value, and visibility. In today's world, everyone is using social networking applications like Facebook, Twitter, YouTube, etc. These applications allow the users to create the contents for free of cost and it becomes huge volume of web data. These data are important in the competitive business world for making decisions. In this context, big data mining plays a major role which is different from the traditional data mining. The process of extracting useful information from large datasets or streams of data, due to its volume, velocity, variety, validity, veracity, value and visibility is termed as Big Data Mining.

Wen-Chen Hu, University of North Dakota, USA
Naima Kaabouch, University of North Dakota, USA
Hongyu Guo, University of Houston – Victoria, USA
Hung-Jen Yang, National Kaohsiung Normal University, Taiwan

Relational databases have dominated the database markets for decades because they perform extremely well for traditional applications like electronic commerce and inventory systems. However, the relational databases do not suit some of the contemporary applications such as big data and cloud computing well because of various reasons like their low scalability and unable to handle a high volume of data. NoSQL (not only SQL) databases are part of the solution for developing those newer applications. The approach they use is different from the one used by relational databases. This chapter discusses NoSQL databases by using an empirical instead of theoretical approach. Other than introducing the types and features of generic NoSQL databases, practical NoSQL database programming and usage are shown by using MongoDB, a NoSQL database. A summary of this research is given at the end of this chapter.

Nigel McKelvey, Letterkenny Institute of Technology, Ireland
Kevin Curran, Ulster University, UK
Luke Toland, Letterkenny Institute of Technology, Ireland

Data cleansing is a long standing problem which every organisation that incorporates a form of data processing or data mining must undertake. It is essential in improving the quality and reliability of data. This paper presents the necessary methods needed to process data at a high quality. It also classifies common problems which organisations face when cleansing data from a source or multiple sources while evaluating methods which aid in this process. The different challenges faced at schema-level and instance-level are also outlined and how they can be overcome. Currently there are tools which provide data cleansing, but are limited due to the uniqueness of every data source and data warehouse. Outlined are the limitations of these tools and how human interaction (self-programming) may be needed to ensure vital data is not lost. We also discuss the importance of maintaining and removing data which has been stored for several years and may no longer have any value.

The population of humanity has become more than seven billion. Daily used devices, machines, and equipment, are also increasing quicker than the human population. The number of mobile devices in use like phones, tablets and IoT devices already passed the two billion barrier and even more than one billion as vehicles are also on the roads. Combining these two will make the one of the biggest Big Data Environment about the daily life of human beings after the use of internet and social applications. For the newly manufactured vehicles, internet operated entertainment and information Systems are becoming a standard equipment delivering such an information to the manufacturers but most of the current vehicles do not have a system like that. This chapter explains the combined version of IoT and vehicles to create a V2C vehicle to cloud system that will create the big data for environmental sustainability, energy and traffic management by different technical and political views and aspects.

Recent advances in acquisition technologies, such as LIDAR and photogrammetry, have brought back to popularity 3D point clouds in a lot of fields of application of Computer Graphics: Civil Engineering, Architecture, Topography, etc. These acquisition systems are producing an unprecedented amount of geometric data with additional attached information, resulting in huge datasets whose processing and storage requirements exceed usual approaches, presenting new challenges that can be addressed from a Big Data perspective by applying High Performance Computing and Computer Graphics techniques. This chapter presents a series of applications built on top of Point Cloud Manager (PCM), a middleware that provides an abstraction for point clouds with arbitrary attached data and makes it easy to perform out-of-core operations on them on commodity CPUs and GPUs. Hence, different kinds of real world applications are tackled, showing both real-time and offline examples, and render-oriented and computation-related operations as well.

Many organizations are beginning to feel frustrated by the limited progress of their companies with the application of new technologies to date. At the same time is convenient to remember that this is something that always happens when new technologies are introduced, companies must accept the challenge of self-assessment and measure the barriers that threaten to prevent them from reaching to get the maximum potential derived from big data and analytics In financial services, there are significant opportunities to obtain benefits by applying technologies and methodologies of big data and analytics. Regulatory pressure has forced many businesses, particularly in banking, to invest in areas such as risk management, compliance and operations. This has accelerated the trend toward enterprise data management.

Preface

In recent years, volumes of data produced by a variety of heterogeneous sources have increased around the world. As a result, both Information Technology and business users need to efficiently collect and process this huge amount of data in real time to discover relevant situations which will allow driving successful business decisions or actions. In this regard, big data management is an approach which helps to process this huge amount of data and is a reality for an increasing number of organizations in many areas and represents a set of challenges involving big data modeling, storage and retrieval, analysis and visualization. However, technological resources, people and processes are crucial to facilitate the management of big data in any kind of organization, allowing information and knowledge from a large volume of data to support decision-making. Big data management can be supported by these three dimensions: technology, people and processes. It normally focuses on database Management system of Big Data.

The main aim of this publication is to collect and compile the most representative approaches in current research which tackle the different faces of big data management. In this regard, readers will be able to acquire a panoramic overview of existing solutions for dealing with big amounts of data in real time in different development scopes. In this sense, the book would have a twofold purpose, not only as background reading on big data management, but also as a reference book in the search for dealing with big data management solutions to managing massive datasets problems.

ORGANIZATION OF THE BOOK

This book consists of 15 peer-reviewed invited chapters authored by several international researchers around the world.

Chapters

Chapter 1: Big Data – Challenges, Opportunities and Realities

This chapter discusses the emerging technology of modern era: Big Data with detailed description of the three Vs (Variety, Velocity and Volume). Further sections of this chapter will enable to understand the concepts of big data analytics, its application, advantages and limitations how this large amount of data is increasing rapidly as compared to the advancement in computing resources and which new technologies and architectures are needed to extract value from it by capturing and analysis processes. The chapter also raised few research issues and future directions about Big Data.

Chapter 2: Introducing Data Structures for Big Data

This chapter covers very important and new aspects so called data structures for Big Data and to be regarded as a new subject in Big Data Science, not just as a new topic, considering the explosive momentum of the big data. Based upon the notion of the big data structures train and atrain, this chapter introduces the useful data structures for the programmers working with big data which are: homogeneous stacks 'train stack' and 'rT-coach stack', heterogeneous stacks 'atrain stack' and 'rA-coach stack', homogeneous queues 'train queue' and 'rT-coach queue', heterogeneous queues 'atrain queue' and 'rA-coach queue', homogeneous binary trees 'train binary tree' and 'rT-coach binary tree', heterogeneous binary trees 'atrain binary tree' and 'rA-coach binary tree', homogeneous trees 'train tree' and 'rT-coach tree', heterogeneous trees 'atrain tree' and 'rA-coach tree', to enrich the subject 'Data Structures for Big Data' for implementation of Big Data Management.

Chapter 3: Big Data Mining

This chapter explores various schemes that have been used to tackle the big databases. In this context, this chapter present big data mining plays a major role which is different from the traditional data mining as well as providing the process of extracting useful information from large datasets or streams of data, due to its volume, velocity, variety, validity, veracity, value and visibility. This chapter also discusses the big data mining tools and applications issues concerning big data Management.

Chapter 4: An Empirical Study of NoSQL Databases for Big Data

This chapter provides a demonstration of the ways in which author introduce NoSQL databases by using an empirical approach with MongoDB. The chapter is organized as follows:It starts with an introduction followed by Features and types of NoSQL Databases, big data management, technologies, and applications, big data generation, capturing, and collection, Big Data Storage and Preservation, Big Data Analytics, Management, Visualization, and Sharing. It also discusses the practical implementation of MongoDB database to manage Big Data Management.

Chapter 5: The Challenges of Data Cleansing with Data Warehouses

This chapter describes how data cleansing methods and related technologies can be used to which every organisation that incorporates a form of data processing or data mining. The chapter also discusses the necessary methods needed to process data at a high quality. It also classifies common problems which organisations face when cleansing data from a source or multiple sources while evaluating methods which aid in this process. Second, the new and different challenges faced at schema-level and instance-level are also explained and how they can be overcome. The chapter also introduces tools which provide data cleansing, but are limited due to the uniqueness of every data source and data warehouse. Outlined are the limitations of these tools and how human interaction (self-programming) may be needed to ensure vital data is not lost as well as discussing the importance of maintaining and removing data which has been stored for several years and may no longer have any value in perspectives of big data management.

Chapter 6: Big Data Analysis – Big Data Analysis Pipeline and Its Technical Challenges

This chapter presents a new approach in order to analyze the big data. By this approach a new class of systems had to be designed and implemented, giving rise to the new phenomenon of "Big Data". It discusses how the data-driven world has the potential to improve the efficiencies of enterprises and improve the quality of our lives and also there are a number of challenges that addressed to allow exploiting the full potential of Big Data. This chapter also highlights the key technical challenges of Big Data.

Chapter 7: Possibilities, Impediments, and Challenges for Network Security in Big Data

This chapter presents an analytical approach regarding possibilities, impediments and challenges for network security in Big Data. This chapter covers big data security management from concepts to real-world issues. It identifies the major challenges, industry trends, security management framework, Possibilities for Network Security in Big Data, Impediments for Network Security in Big Data, Existing tools and Techniques best for Big Data Security solutions in solving security problems, current research results, and future research issues.

Chapter 8: Mastering Big Data in the Digital Age

This chapter explains the overview of big data; the volume, velocity, variety, veracity, and variability of big data; the privacy and security of big data applications; big data and multimedia utilization; the concept of MapReduce; the concept of Hadoop; big data and data mining; big data and cloud computing; the applications of big data in health care industry; the applications of big data analytics in tourism and hospitality industry; and the challenges and implications of big data in the digital age. The chapter also discusses that how big data has the potential to increase organizational performance and gain sustainable competitive advantage in the digital age.

Chapter 9: Legal Responses to the Commodification of Personal Data in the Era of Big Data – The Paradigm Shift from Data Protection towards Data Ownership

The chapter presents a succinct overview of the legal ownership of big data by examining the key players in control of the information at each stage of the processing and managing of big data. This chapter also covers and describes the current legislative framework with regard to data protection and addition, techno-legal solutions offered to complement the law of big data in this respect.

Chapter 10: Big Data and Business Decision Making

This chapter analyzes the possibilities of big data to improve the services offered by companies and the customer experience and increase the efficiency of these companies. It also examines some special aspects associated with the use of big data such as the issues of data privacy and compliance with the regulations on the use of the information.

Chapter 11: Using Big Data to Improve the Educational Infrastructure and Learning Paradigm

This chapter proposes a generic model that uses the techniques of educational data mining to explore and analyze Big Data being generated by the educational sector. This chapter also examines and discusses the various questions that can be answered using educational data mining methods and how the discovered patterns can be used to enrich the learning experience of a student as well as help teachers make pedagogical decisions.

Chapter 12: Vehicle to Cloud – Big Data for Environmental Sustainability, Energy, and Traffic Management

This chapter explains the combined version of IoT and vehicles to create a V2C vehicle to cloud system that will create the big data for environmental sustainability, energy and traffic management by different technical and political views and aspects. There is a need to elaborate about the characteristics of IoT based data to find out the available and applicable solutions. Such kind of study also directs to realize the need of new techniques to cope up with such challenges.

Chapter 13: Point Cloud Manager – Applications of a Middleware for Managing Huge Point Clouds

This chapter presents a series of applications built on top of Point Cloud Manager (PCM), a middleware that provides an abstraction for point clouds with arbitrary attached data and makes it easy to perform out-of-core operations on them on commodity CPUs and GPUs. The chapter covers different kinds of real world applications are tackled, showing both real-time and offline examples, and in addition, render-oriented and computation-related operations as well.

Chapter 14: Big Data Management in Financial Services

This chapter discusses and provides a demonstration of big data management in financial services. The chapter is organized as follows: introduction, benefit of Big Data for financial institutions, main challenges for implementation of Big Data, smart data, storage and processing, the risks of Big Data.

Chapter 15: Recommender System in the Context of Big Data – Implementing SVD-Based Recommender System using Apache Hadoop and Spark

This chapter surveys the literature of RSs, reviews the current state of RSs with the main concerns surrounding them due to Big Data, investigates thoroughly SVD and provides an implementation to it using Apache Hadoop and Spark. This chapter also intended to validate the applicability of, existing contributions to the field of, SVD-based RSs as well as validated the effectiveness of Hadoop and spark in developing large-scale systems. The results proved the scalability of SVD-based RS and its applicability to Big Data.

Manoj Kumar Singh
Adama Science and Technology University, Ethiopia

Dileep Kumar G.
Adama Science and Technology University, Ethiopia

Acknowledgment

We would like to acknowledge and thank all of those involved in the development of this book. It is always a major undertaking but most importantly, a great encouragement and somehow a reward and an honor when seeing the enthusiasm and eagerness of people willing to advance their discipline by taking the commitment to share their experiences, ideas, and visions towards the evolvement of collaboration like the achievement of this book. Without their support the book could not have been satisfactory completed.

First, we would like to thank each one of the authors for their contributions. Our sincere gratitude goes to the chapter's authors who contributed their time and expertise to this book. The team of reviewers deserves special attention as they very generously provided their time and expertise to ensure a high-quality review process. Often the work associated with chapter review is underestimated and forgotten–thanks to all of you for your great work.

Second, we wish to gratefully acknowledge that we were fortunate to work closely with an outstanding team at IGI Global. Specifically and with no particular order, I wish to thank Jan Travers, Rachel Ginder, Katherine Shearer, and Erin Wesser who were everything someone should expect from a publisher: professional, efficient, and a delight to work with. Thanks are also extended to all those at IGI Global who have taken care with managing the design and the timely production of this book. The editor wishes to apologize to anyone whom they have forgotten.

Finally, we are deeply indebted to our family for their love, patience, and support throughout this rewarding experience.

Manoj Kumar Singh
Adama Science and Technology University, Ethiopia

Dileep Kumar G.
Adama Science and Technology University, Ethiopia

Chapter 1
Big Data:
Challenges, Opportunities, and Realities

Abhay Kumar Bhadani
Indian Institute of Technology Delhi, India

Dhanya Jothimani
Indian Institute of Technology Delhi, India

ABSTRACT

With the advent of Internet of Things (IoT) and Web 2.0 technologies, there has been a tremendous growth in the amount of data generated. This chapter emphasizes on the need for big data, technological advancements, tools and techniques being used to process big data. Technological improvements and limitations of existing storage techniques are also presented. Since the traditional technologies like Relational Database Management System (RDBMS) have their own limitations to handle big data, new technologies have been developed to handle them and to derive useful insights. This chapter presents an overview of big data analytics, its application, advantages, and limitations. Few research issues and future directions are presented in this chapter.

INTRODUCTION

With digitization of most of the processes, emergence of different social network platforms, blogs, deployment of different kind of sensors, adoption of hand-held digital devices, wearable devices and explosion in the usage of Internet, huge amount of data are being generated on continuous basis. No one can deny that Internet has changed the way businesses operate, functioning of the government, education and lifestyle of people around the world. Today, this trend is in a transformative stage, where the rate of data generation is very high and the types of data being generated surpass the capability of existing data storage techniques. It cannot be denied that these data carry a lot more information than ever before due to the emergence and adoption of Internet.

Over the past two decades, there is a tremendous growth in data. This trend can be observed in almost every field. According to a report by International Data Corporation (IDC), a research company claims that between 2012 and 2020, the amount of information in the digital universe will grow by 35 trillion

DOI: 10.4018/978-1-5225-0182-4.ch001

gigabytes (1 gigabyte equivalent to 40 (four-drawer) file cabinets of text, or two music CDs). That's on par with the number of stars in the physical universe! (Forsyth, 2012).

In the mid-2000s, the emergence of social media, cloud computing, and processing power (through multi-core processors and graphics processing unit (GPUs)) contributed to the rise of big data (Manovich, 2011; Agneeswaran, 2012). As of December 2015, Facebook has an average of 1.04 billion daily active users, 934 million mobile daily active users, available in 70 languages, 125 billion friend connections, 205 billion photos uploaded every day, 30 billion pieces of content, 2.7 billion likes, and comments are being posted and 130 average number of friends per Facebook user (Facebook, 2015). This has created new pathways to study social and cultural dynamics.

Making sense out of the vast data can help the organizations in informed decision making and provide competitive advantage. Earlier, organizations used transaction-processing systems that inherently used Relational Data Base Management Systems (RDBMS) and simple data analysis techniques like Structured Query Language (SQL) for their day-to-day operations that helped them in their decision making and planning. However, due to the increase in the size of data especially the unstructured form of data (for example, customer reviews of their Facebook pages or tweets), it has become almost impossible to process these data with the existing storage techniques and plain queries.

In this chapter, an overview of big data including its sources to dimensions is given. The limitations of existing data processing approaches; need for big data analytics and development of new approaches for storing and processing big data are briefed. The set of activities ranging from data generation to data analysis, generally termed as Big Data Value Chain, is discussed followed by various applications of big data analytics. The chapter concludes by discussing the limitations of big data analytics and provides direction to open issues for further research.

BACKGROUND AND NEED FOR BIG DATA ANALYTICS

Storage and retrieval of vast amount of data within a desirable time lag is a challenge. Some of these limitations to handle and process vast amount of data with the traditional storage techniques has led to the emergence of the term "Big Data". Though big data has gained attention due to the emergence of the Internet, but it cannot be compared with it. It is beyond the Internet, though Web makes it easier to collect and share knowledge as well data in raw form. Big Data Analytics (BDA) is all about how these data can be stored, processed, and comprehended such that it can be used for predicting the future course of action with a great precision and acceptable time delay.

Marketers focus on target marketing, insurance providers focus on providing personalized insurance policies to their customers, and healthcare providers focus on providing quality and low-cost treatment to patients. Despite the advancements in data storage, collection, analysis and algorithms related to predicting human behavior; it is important to understand the underlying driving as well as the regulating factors (market, law, social norms and architecture), which can help in developing robust models that can handle big data and yet yield high prediction accuracy (Boyd & Crawford, 2011).

The current and emerging focus of big data analytics is to explore traditional techniques such as rule-based systems, pattern mining, decision trees and other data mining techniques to develop business rules even on the large data sets efficiently. It can be achieved by either developing algorithms that use distributed data storage, in-memory computation or by using cluster computing for parallel computation.

Earlier these processes were carried out using grid computing, which was overtaken by cloud computing in recent days.

Grid Computing

Grid computing is a means of allocating the computing power in a distributed manner to solve problems that are typically vast and require lots of computational time and power. It works on the principle of voluntary basis, where the users share their computing and memory resources to be used by others. In this setting, the goal is to access computers only when needed and to scale the problems in such a manner that even small computers can make a contribution to the grid. Every computer that is connected to the Internet and wants to become a part of the grid is considered to be a node in an extremely large computing machine. The main advantage of this computing technique is that it offers an opportunity to harness unused computing power. In the grid environment, the problem is divided and distributed to thousands or even millions of computers to obtain a solution in a cost effective manner. There are a number of applications which use this technology, for instance, weather, astronomy, medicine, multi-player gaming, etc. Typically grid computing works on two dominant models: Commercial Model and Social Model (Smith, 2005).

- **Commercial Model:** It works on the principle that this technology can be used for the commercial purpose by creating large processing centers and sell its capabilities to the users on hourly basis and charge money. The advantage of this model is that Quality of Service (QoS) is maintained and is a trusted way of computation.
- **Social Model:** It works with a concept that these resources should be harnessed for the good of society. Grid computing concept is implemented through software that follows Open Grid Service Architecture (OGSA). Globus toolkit is popular software that implements OGSA and is used in grid computing environment.

The important components of a grid computing system are Computing Element (CE), a number of Storage Elements (SE) and Worker Nodes (WN). The CE helps to establish a connection with other GRID networks and dispatches jobs on the Worker Nodes using a Workload Management System. The Storage Element is in charge with the storage of the input and the output of the data needed for the job execution. Garlasu et al. (2013) proposed a framework for processing big data using grid technologies. By introducing a framework for managing big data, it paves a way to implement it around grid architecture.

Grid computing suffers from several drawbacks, including financial, social, legal and regulatory issues. Distributing a commercial project across these volunteered machines also raises the issues related to ownership of the results. Given the aggressiveness with which hackers have created e-mail viruses and cheats for computer games create uninvited problems along with the benefits associated with the grid computing.

Cloud Computing

Cloud computing has become a recent buzzword, however, it is not completely a new concept. It has its roots from grid computing and other related areas like utility computing, cluster computing and distributing systems, in general. Cloud computing refers to the concept of computing at a remote location with control at the users' end through a thin client system, computer or even mobile phones. Processing, memory, and storage will be done at the service providers' infrastructure (Figure 1). Users need to connect to the virtual system residing at some remote location, which might run several virtual operating systems on physical servers with the help of virtualization. It supports all sorts of fault tolerant features like live migration, scalable storage, and load balancing (Bhadani & Chaudhary, 2010). It provides the flexibility of scaling the computational power, memory as well as storage dynamically on the fly. It works on "pay as you go" concept and is driven by economies of scale. To some extent, cloud computing is similar to the commercial model of grid computing. Primarily, cloud computing works on three different levels, namely, *Infrastructure as a Service (IaaS), Platform as a Service (PaaS)* and *Software as a Service (SaaS)* (Bhadani, 2011; Assuncao et al., 2015).

Cloud computing suffers from similar drawbacks of grid computing like data location, data replication, data segregation, security threats, regulatory compliances, recovery issues, long-term viability, high dependency on the Internet for accessing the remote virtual machine, different laws of different countries, investigative support, etc.

No technology is full proof, however, given the benefits and drawbacks of grid computing or cloud computing, it might prove useful to process a huge amount of data that need to be processed for analysis of big data or live stream data (Foster et al., 2008).

BIG DATA: DEFINITION, DIMENSIONS, AND SOURCES

Definition

Recently, the word "Big Data" has become a buzzword. It is being used by almost everyone including academicians and industry experts. There are various definitions available in the literature. But the concept of big data dates back to the year 2001, where the challenges of increasing data were addressed with a 3V model by Laney (2001). 3Vs, also known as the dimensions of big data, represent the increasing

Figure 1. Basic model of cloud computing

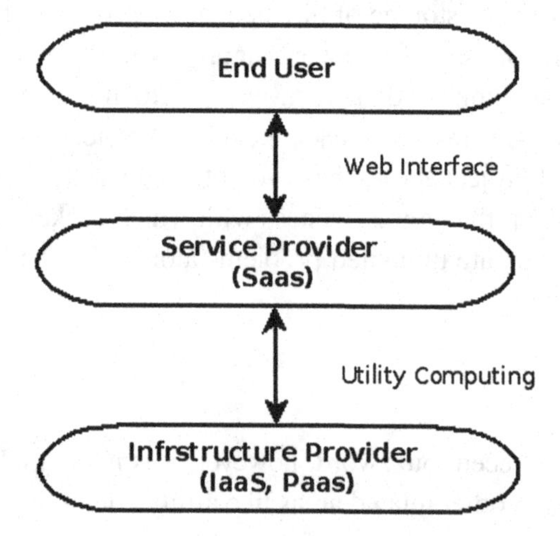

Volume, Variety, and Velocity of data (Assunção et al., 2015). The model was not originally used to define big data but later has been used eventually by various enterprises including Microsoft and IBM to define the same (Meijer, 2011).

In 2010, Apache Hadoop defined big data as "datasets, which could not be captured, managed, and processed by general computers within an acceptable scope" (p.173, Chen et al., 2014). Following this, in 2011, McKinsey Global Institute defined big data as "datasets whose size is beyond the ability of typical database software tools to capture, store, manage, and analyze" (p.1, Manyika et al., 2011). International Data Corporation (IDC) defines "big data technologies as a new generation of technologies and architectures, designed to economically extract value from very large volumes of a wide variety of data, by enabling high-velocity capture, discovery, and/or analysis" (p. 6, Gantz & Reinsel, 2011).

Academicians define big data as huge size of data produced by high-performance heterogeneous group of applications that spans from social network to scientific computing applications. The datasets range from a few hundred gigabytes to zetabytes that it is beyond the capacity of existing data management tools to capture, store, manage and analyze (Cuzzocrea et al., 2011; Qin et al., 2012; Agneeswaran, 2012).

Though big data has been defined in various forms but there is no specific definition. Few have defined what it does while very few have focused on what it is. The definition of the big data on the basis of 3Vs is relative. What is defined as big data today may not be the same tomorrow. For instance, in future, with the advancements in the storage technologies, the data that is deemed as big data today might be captured. In addition to defining big data, there is a need to understand how to make the best use of this data to obtain valuable information for decision making.

Dimensions of Big Data

Initially, big data was characterized by the following three dimensions, which were, often, referred as 3V model:

- **Volume:** Volume refers to the magnitude of the data that is being generated and collected. It is increasing at a faster rate from terabytes to petabytes (1024 terabytes) (Zikopoulos et al., 2012; Singh & Singh, 2012). With increase in storage capacities, what cannot be captured and stored now will be possible in the future. The classification of big data on the basis of volume is relative with respect to the type of data generated and time. In addition, the type of data, which is often referred as Variety, defines "big" data. Two types of data, for instance, text and video of same volume may require different data management technologies (Gandomi & Haider, 2015).
- **Velocity:** Velocity refers to the rate of generation of data. Traditional data analytics is based on periodic updates- daily, weekly or monthly. With the increasing rate of data generation, big data should be processed and analyzed in real- or near real-time to make informed decisions. The role of time is very critical here (Singh & Singh, 2012; Gandomi & Haider, 2015). Few domains including Retail, Telecommunications and Finance generate high-frequency data. The data generated through Mobile apps, for instance, demographics, geographical location, and transaction history, can be used in real-time to offer personalized services to the customers. This would help to retain the customers as well as increase the service level.
- **Variety:** Variety refers to different types of data that are being generated and captured. They extend beyond structured data and fall under the categories of semi-structured and unstructured data (Zikopoulos et al., 2012; Singh & Singh, 2012; Gandomi & Haider, 2015). The data that can be

organized using a pre-defined data model are known as structured data. The tabular data in relational databases and Excel are examples of structured data and they constitute only 5% of all existing data (Cukier, 2010). Unstructured data cannot be organized using these pre-defined model and examples include video, text, and audio. Semi-structured data that fall between the categories of structured and unstructured data. Extensible Markup Language (XML) falls under this category.

Later, few more dimensions have been added, which are enumerated below:

- **Veracity:** Coined by IBM, veracity refers to the unreliability associated with the data sources (Gandomi & Haider, 2015). For instance, sentiment analysis using social media data (Twitter, Facebook, etc.) is subject to uncertainty. There is a need to differentiate the reliable data from uncertain and imprecise data and manage the uncertainty associated with the data.
- **Variability:** Variability and Complexity were added as additional dimensions by SAS. Often, inconsistency in the big data velocity leads to variation in flow rate of data, which is referred to as variability (Gandomi & Haider, 2015). Data are generated from various sources and there is an increasing complexity in managing data ranging from transactional data to big data. Data generated from different geographical locations have different semantics (Zikopoulos et al., 2012; Forsyth, 2012).
- **Low-Value Density:** Data in its original form is unusable. Data is analyzed to discover very high value (Sun and Heller, 2012). For example, logs from websites cannot be used in its initial form to obtain business value. It must be analyzed to predict the customer behavior.

Sources of Big Data

Having understood what big data is and their dimensions, here various sources of big data are briefed. Digitization of content by industries is the new source of data (Villars et al., 2011). Advancements in technology also lead to high rate of data generation. For example, one of the biggest surveys in Astronomy, Sloan Digital Sky Survey (SDSS) has recorded a total of 25TB data during their first (2000-2005) and second surveys (2005-2008) combined. With the advancements in the resolution of the telescope, the amount of data collected at the end of their third survey (2008-14) is 100 TB. Use of "smart" instrumentation is another source of big data. Smart meters in the energy sector record the electricity utilization measurement every 15 minutes as compared to monthly readings before.

In addition to social media, Internet of Things (IoT) has, now, become the new source of data. The data can be captured from agriculture, industry, medical care, etc of the smart cities developed based on IoT.

Table 1 summarizes the various types of data produced in different sectors.

BIG DATA VALUE CHAIN

Value Chain, the concept introduced by Porter (1980), refers to a set of activities performed by a firm to add value at each step of delivering a product/service to its customers. In a similar way, data value chain refers to the framework that deals with a set of activities to create value from available data. It can be divided into seven phases: data generation, data collection, data transmission, data pre-processing, data storage, data analysis and decision making (Figure 2).

Table 1. Various sources of data

Sector	Data Produced	Use
Astronomy	Movement of stars, satellites, etc.	To monitor the activities of asteroid bodies and satellites
Financial	News content via video, audio, twitter and news report	To make trading decisions
Healthcare	Electronic medical records and images	To aid in short-term public health monitoring and long-term epidemiological research programs
Internet of Things (IoT)	Sensor data	To monitor various activities in smart cities
Life Sciences	Gene sequences	To analyze genetic variations and potential treatment effectiveness
Media/Entertainment	Content and user viewing behavior	To capture more viewers
Social Media	Blog posts, tweets, social networking sites, log details	To analyze the customer behavior pattern
Telecommunications	Call Detail Records (CDR)	Customer churn management
Transportation, Logistics, Retail, Utilities	Sensor data generated from fleet transceivers, RFID tag readers and smart meters	To optimize operations
Video Surveillance	Recordings from CCTV to IPTV cameras and recording system	To analyze behavioral patterns for service enhancement and security

Figure 2. Big data value chain

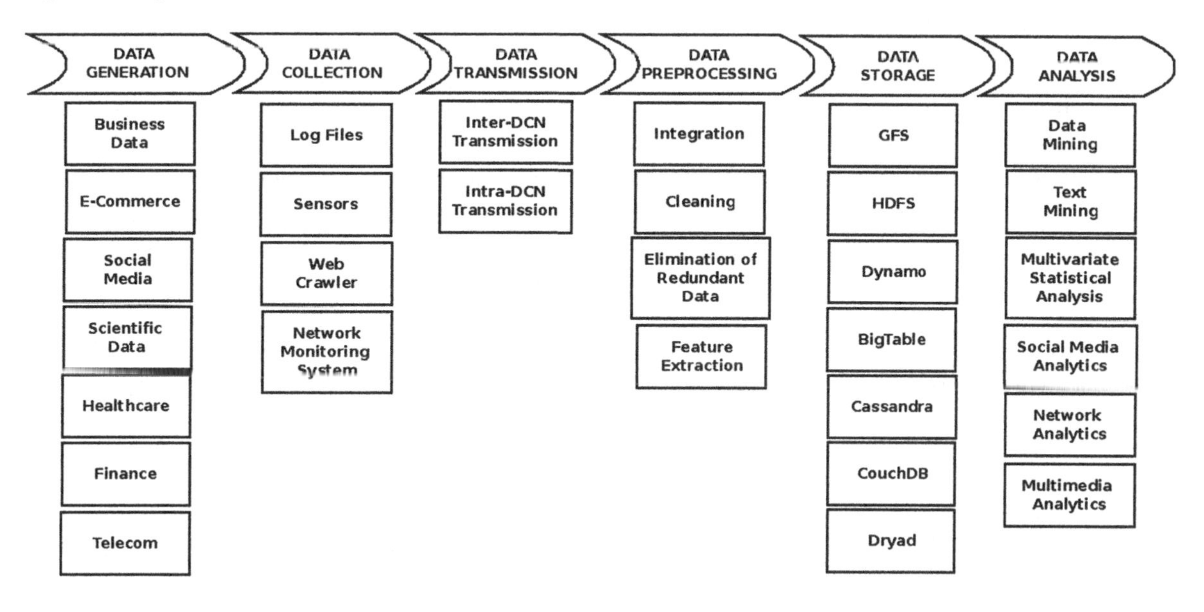

1. **Data Generation:** The first and foremost step in the big data value chain is the generation of data. As discussed in the previous section, data is generated from various sources that include data from Call Detail Records (CDR), blogs, Tweets and Facebook Page.
2. **Data Collection:** In this phase, the data is obtained from all possible data sources (Miller and Mork, 2013; Chen et al., 2014). For instance, in order to predict the customer churn in Telecom, data can be obtained from CDRs and opinions/complaints of the customers on Social Networking Sites such

as Twitter (in the form of tweets) and Facebook (opinions shared on the company's Facebook page). The most commonly used methods are log files, sensors, web crawlers and network monitoring software (Chen et al., 2014).

3. **Data Transmission:** Once the data is collected, it is transferred to a data storage and processing infrastructure for further processing and analysis. It can be carried out in two phases: Inter-Dynamic Circuit Network (DCN) transmission and Intra-DCN transmissions. Inter-DCN transmission deals with the transfer of data from the data source to the data center while the latter helps in the transfer within the data center. Apart from storage of data, data center helps in collecting, organizing and managing data.
4. **Data Pre-Processing:** The data collected from various data sources may be redundant, noisy and inconsistent; hence, in this phase, the data is pre-processed to improve the data quality required for analysis. This also helps to improve the accuracy of the analysis and reduce the storage expenses. The data can be pre-processed with the help of following steps:
    a. **Integration:** The data from various sources are combined to provide a unified and uniform view of the available data. Data federation and data warehousing are the two commonly used traditional methods. Data warehousing executes the Extract, Transform, and Load (ETL) process. During extract process, the data is selected, collected, processed and analyzed. The process of converting the extracted data to a standard format is called Transformation process. In Loading, the extracted and transformed data is imported into a storage infrastructure. In order to make data integration dynamic, data can be aggregated from various data sources using a virtual database. It does not contain any data but the details regarding the information related to original data or metadata can be obtained (Miller and Mork, 2013; Chen et al., 2014).
    b. **Cleaning:** The data is checked for accuracy, completeness and consistency. During this process, the data may be deleted and modified to improve the data quality. The general process followed includes these five sub-processes: error types are defined and determined, errors are identified from the data, errors are corrected, error types and corresponding examples are documented, and data entry procedure may be modified to avoid future errors (Maletic and Marcus, 2000).
    c. **Elimination of Redundant Data:** Many datasets have surplus data or data repetitions and are known as data redundancy. This increases the storage cost, leads to data inconsistency and affects the quality of data. In order to overcome this, various data reduction methods such as data filtering and compression, are used. The limitation of these data reduction techniques is that they increase the computational cost. Hence, a cost-benefit analysis should be carried before using data reduction techniques.
5. **Data Storage:** The big data storage systems should provide reliable storage space and powerful access to the data. The distributed storage systems for big data should consider factors like consistency (C), availability (A) and partition tolerance (P). According to the CAP theory proposed by Brewer (2000), the distributed storage systems could meet two requirements simultaneously, that is, either consistency and availability or availability and partition tolerance or consistency and partition tolerance but not all requirements simultaneously (Gilbert & Lynch, 2002). Considerable research is still going on in the area of big data storage mechanism. Little advancements in this respect are Google File System (GFS), Dynamo, BigTable, Cassandra, CouchDB, and Dryad.

6. **Data Analysis:** Once the data is collected, transformed and stored, the next process is data exploitation or data analysis, which is enumerated using the following steps:
    a. **Define Metrics:** Based on the collected and transformed data, a set of metrics is defined for a particular problem. For instance, to identify a potential customer who is going to churn out, the number of times he/she contacted the company (be it through a voice call, tweets or complaints on Facebook page) can be considered. (Miller & Mork, 2013).
    b. **Select Architecture Based on Analysis Type:** Based on the timeliness of analysis to be carried out, suitable architecture is selected. Real-time analysis is used in the domain where the data keeps on changing constantly and there is a need for rapid analysis to take actions. Memory-based computations and parallel processing systems are the existing architectures. Fraud detection in retail sectors and telecom fraud are the examples of real-time analysis. The applications that do not require high response time are carried out using offline analysis. The data can be extracted, stored and analyzed relatively later in time. Generally used architecture is Hadoop platform (Chen et al., 2014).
    c. **Selection of Appropriate Algorithms and Tools:** One of the most important steps of data analysis is selection of appropriate techniques for data analysis. Few traditional data analysis techniques like cluster analysis, regression analysis and data mining algorithms, still hold good for big data analytics. Cluster analysis is an unsupervised technique that groups objects based on some features. Data mining techniques help to extract unknown, hidden and useful information from a huge data set. The 10 most powerful data mining algorithms were short-listed and discussed in Wu et al. (2007). Various tools are available for data analysis including open source softwares and commercial softwares. Few examples of open source softwares are R for data mining and visualization, Weka/Pentaho for machine learning and RapidMiner for machine learning and predictive analysis.
    d. **Data Visualization:** The need for inspecting details at multiple scales and minute details gave rise to data visualization. Visual interfaces along with statistical analysis and related context help to identify patterns in large data over time (Fisher et al., 2012). Visual Analytics (VA) is defined as "the science of analytical reasoning facilitated by visual interactive interfaces" (Thomas & Cook, 2005). Few visualization tools are Tableau, QlikView, Spotfire, JMP, Jaspersoft, Visual Analytics, Centrifuge, Visual Mining and Board. A comparison of various visualization tools based on their data handling functionality, analysis methods and visualization techniques has been discussed in Zhang et al. (2012).
7. **Decision Making:** Based on the analysis and the visualized results, the decision makers can decide whether and how to reward a positive behavior and change a negative one. The details of a particular problem can be analyzed to understand the causes of the problems, take informed decisions and plan for necessary actions (Miller & Mork, 2013).

Having discussed about how value can be extracted from big data, an industry regardless of sector should consider three criteria before implementing big data analytics: can useful information be obtained in addition to those obtained from the existing systems?, will there be any improvement in the accuracy of information obtained using big data analytics? and finally, will implementation of big data analytics help in improving the timeliness of response? (Villars et al., 2011).

TOOLS FOR COLLECTING, PREPROCESSING AND ANALYZING BIG DATA

Advancements in computing architecture are required to handle both data storage requirements and heavy server processing required for analyzing large volumes and variety of data economically (Villars et al., 2011). This section gives an overview of the technologies adopted to analyze big data.

With the availability of high computational capacity at a relatively inexpensive cost allows researchers to explore the underlying opportunities of big data with the field of data science. Increasingly, data are not solely being captured for record keeping, but to explore them with intelligent systems to derive new insights, which may not have been envisioned at the time of collecting the data. By initiating interesting questions and refining them without experts' intervention, it becomes capable of discovering new information on its own (Dhar, 2013). For instance, if an information can be derived that a specific group of people are prone to cancer and also gives other information such as their diets, daily habits and nature of drugs causing this effect. It would be amazing to develop these kinds of models, which may look like a fiction story at this point of time.

Tools that are being used to collect data encompass various digital devices (for example, mobile devices, camera, wearable devices, and smart watches) and applications that generate enormous data in the form of logs, text, voice, images, and video. In order to process these data, several researchers are coming up with new techniques that help better representation of the unstructured data, which makes sense in big data context to gain useful insights that may not have been envisioned earlier.

Not Only Structured Query Languages (NoSQL)

Relational Database Management System (RDBMS) is the traditional method of managing structured data. RDBMS uses a relational database and schema for storage and retrieval of data. A data warehouse is used to store and retrieve large datasets. Structured Query Language (SQL) is most commonly used database query language. The data is stored in a data warehouse using dimensional approach and normalized approach (Bakshi, 2012). In dimensional approach, data are divided into fact table and dimension table which supports the fact table. In normalized approach, data is divided into entities creating several tables in a relational database.

Due to Atomicity, Consistency, Isolation and Durability (ACID) constraint, scaling of a large volume of data is not possible. RDBMS is incapable of handling semi-structured and unstructured data (Qin et al., 2012; Mukherjee et al., 2012; Zikopoulos et al., 2012). These limitations of RDBMS led to the concept of NoSQL.

NoSQL stores and manages unstructured data. These databases are also known as "schema-free" databases since they enable quick upgradation of structure of data without table rewrites. NoSQL supports document store, key value stores, BigTable and graph database. It uses looser consistency model than the traditional databases. Data management and data storage functions are separate in NoSQL database (Bakshi, 2012). It allows the scalability of data. Few examples of NoSQL databases are HBase, MangoDB, and Dynamo.

Hadoop

In 2005, an open source Apache Hadoop project was conceived and implemented on the basis of Google File System (GFS) and Map Reduce programming paradigm (Prekopcsàk et al., 2011; Bakshi, 2012; Minelli et al., 2013).

Hadoop Distributed File System (HDFS)

Hadoop Distributed File System (HDFS) is a fault-tolerant, scalable, highly configurable distributed storage system for a Hadoop cluster. Data in the Hadoop cluster is broken down into pieces by HDFS and are distributed across different servers in the Hadoop cluster. A small chunk of the whole data set is stored on the server.

Hadoop MapReduce

MapReduce is a software framework for distributed processing of vast amounts of data in a reliable, fault-tolerant manner. The two distinct phases of MapReduce are:

1. **Map Phase:** In Map phase, the workload is divided into smaller sub-workloads. The tasks are assigned to Mapper, which processes each unit block of data to produce a sorted list of (key, value) pairs. This list, which is the output of mapper, is passed to the next phase. This process is known as shuffling.
2. **Reduce:** In Reduce phase, the input is analyzed and merged to produce the final output which is written to the HDFS in the cluster.

Table 2 summarizes the big data capabilities and the available primary technologies (Sun and Heller, 2012).

Table 2. Big data capabilities and their primary technologies

Big Data Capability	Primary Technology	Features
Storage and management capability	Hadoop Distributed File System (HDFS)	Open source distributed file system, Runs on high-performance commodity hardware, Highly scalable storage and automatic data replication
Database capability	Oracle NoSQL	Dynamic and flexible schema design, Highly scalable multi-node, multiple data center, fault tolerant, ACID operations, High-performance key-value pair database
	Apache HBase	Automatic failover support between Region servers, Automatic and configurable sharding of tables
	Apache Cassandra	Fault tolerance capability for every node, Column indexes with the performance of log-structured updates and built-in caching
	Apache Hive	Query execution via MapReduce, Uses SQL-like language HiveQL, Easy ETL process either from HDFS or Apache HBase
Processing capability	MapReduce	Distribution of data workloads across thousands of nodes, Breaks problem into smaller sub-problems
	Apache Hadoop	Highly customizable infrastructure, Highly scalable parallel batch processing, Fault tolerant
Data integration capability	Oracle big data connectors, Oracle data integrator	Exports MapReduce results to RDBMS, Hadoop, and other targets, Includes a Graphical User Interface
Statistical analysis capability	R and Oracle R Enterprise	Programming language for statistical analysis

Limitations of Hadoop

In spite of Hadoop's advantages over RDBMS, it suffers from the following limitations (ParAccel, 2012):

1. **Multiple Copies of Data:** Inefficiency of HDFS leads to creation of multiple copies of the data (minimum 3 copies).
2. **Limited SQL Support:** Hadoop offers a limited SQL support and they lack basic functions such as sub-queries, "group by" analytics etc.
3. **Inefficient Execution:** Lack of query optimizer leads to inefficient cost-based plan for execution thus resulting in larger cluster compared to similar database.
4. **Challenging Framework:** Complex transformational logic cannot be leveraged using the MapReduce framework.
5. **Lack of Skills:** Knowledge of algorithms and skills for distributed MapReduce development are required for proper implementation.

One of the biggest challenges is to have a computing infrastructure that can analyze high-volume and varied (structured and unstructured) data from multiple sources and to enable real-time analysis of unpredictable content with no apparent schema or structure (Villars et al., 2011).

SOFTWARE TOOLS FOR HANDLING BIG DATA

There are many tools that help in handling big data and help data scientists to process data for analyzing them. Processes involved in big data analysis are shown in Figure 3. Few popular tools are discussed below:

- **R:** is an open-source statistical computing language that provides a wide variety of statistical and graphical techniques to derive insights from the data. It has an effective data handling and storage facility and supports vector operations with a suite of operators for faster processing. It has all the features of a standard programming language and supports conditional arguments, loops, and user-defined functions. R is supported by a huge number of packages through Comprehensive R Archive Network (CRAN). It is available on Windows, Linux, and Mac platforms. It has a strong documentation for each package. It has a strong support for data munging, data mining and machine learning algorithms along with a good support for reading and writing in distributed envi-

Figure 3. Big data processes illustration

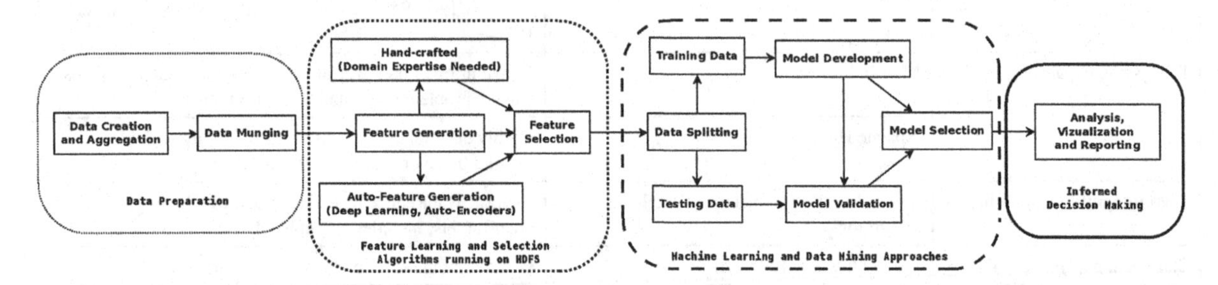

ronment, which makes it appropriate for handling big data. However, the memory management, speed, and efficiency are probably the biggest challenges faced by R. R Studio is an Integrated Development Environment (IDE) that is developed for programming in R language. It is distributed for standalone Desktop machines as well as it supports client-server architecture, which can be accessed from any browser.

- **Python:** is yet another popular programming language, which is open source and is supported by Windows, Linux and Mac platforms. It hosts thousands of packages from third-party or community contributed modules. NumPy, Scikit, and Pandas support some of the popular packages for machine learning and data mining for data preprocessing, computing and modeling. NumPy is the base package for scientific computing. It adds support for large, multi-dimensional arrays and matrices with Python. Scikit supports classification, regression, clustering, dimensionality reduction, feature selection, and preprocessing and model selection algorithms. Pandas help in data munging and preparation for data analysis and modeling. It has strong support for graph analysis with its NetworkX library and nltk for text analytics and Natural language processing. Python is user-friendly and great for quick and dirty analysis on a problem. It also integrates well with Spark through the PySpark library.
- **Scala**: is an object-oriented language and is an acronym for "Scalable Language". The object and every operation in Scala is a method-call, just like any object-oriented language. It requires java virtual machine environment. Spark, an in-memory cluster computing framework is written in Scala. Scala is becoming popular programming tool for handling big data problems.
- **Apache Spark:** is an in-memory cluster computing technology designed for fast computation, which is implemented in Scala. It uses Hadoop for storage purpose as it has its own cluster management capability. It provides built-in APIs for Java, Scala, and Python. Recently, it has also started supporting R. It comes with 80 high-level operators for interactive querying. The in-memory computation is supported with its Resilient Distributed Data (RDD) framework, which distributes the data frame into smaller chunks on different machines for faster computation. It also supports Map and Reduce for data processing. It supports SQL, data streaming, graph processing algorithms and machine learning algorithms. Though Spark can be accessed with Python, Java, and R, it has a strong support for Scala and is more stable at this point of time. It supports deep learning with sparkling water in H2O.
- **Apache Hive:** is an open source platform that facilitates querying and managing large datasets residing in distributed storage (for example, HDFS). It is similar to SQL and it is called as HiveQL. It uses Map Reduce for processing the queries and also supports developers to plug in their custom mapper and reducer codes when HiveQL lacks in expressing the desired logic.
- **Apache Pig:** is a platform that allows analysts to analyze large data sets. It is a high-level programming language, called as Pig Latin for creating MapReduce programs that require Hadoop for data storage. The Pig Latin code is extended with the help of User-Defined Functions that can be written in Java, Python and few other languages. It is amenable to substantial parallelization, which in turns enables them to handle very large data sets.
- **Amazon Elastic Compute Cloud (EC2)**: is a web service that provides compute capacity over the cloud. It gives full control of the computing resources and allows developers to run their computation in the desired computing environment. It is one of the most successful cloud computing platforms. It works on the principle of the pay-as-you-go model.

Few other frameworks that support big data are MongoDB, BlinkDB, Tachyon, Cassandra, CouchDB, Clojure, Tableau, Splunk and others.

APPLICATION OF BIG DATA ANALYTICS

The concept of big data analytics has left no sector untouched. Few sectors like Telecommunication, Retail and Finance have been early adopters of big data analytics, followed by other sectors (Villars et al., 2011). The applications of big data analytics in various sectors are discussed as follows:

Healthcare

Data analysts obtain and analyze information from multiple sources to gain insights. The multiple sources are electronic patient record; clinical decision support system including medical imaging, physician's written notes and prescription, pharmacy and laboratories; clinical data; and machine generated sensor data (Raghupathi & Raghupathi, 2014). The integration of clinical, public-health and behavioural data helps to develop a robust treatment system, which can reduce the cost and at the same time, improve the quality of treatment (Brown et al., 2011). Rizzoli Orthopedic Institute in Bologna, Italy analyzed the symptoms of individual patients to understand the clinical variations in a family. This helped to reduce the number of imaging and hospitalizations by 60% and 30%, respectively (Raghupathi & Raghupathi, 2014).

Obtaining information from external sources such as social media helps in early detection of epidemics and precautionary efforts. After the earthquake in Haiti in January 2010, analysis of tweets helped to track the spread of Cholera in the region (Raghupathi & Raghupathi, 2014). The data from the sensors are monitored and analyzed for adverse event prediction and safety monitoring (Mukherjee et al., 2012).

Artemis, a system developed by Blount et al. (2010), monitors and analyzes the physiological data from sensors in the intensive care units to detect the onset of medical complications, especially, in the case of neo-natal care. The real-time analysis of a huge number of claims requests can minimize fraud.

Telecommunication

Low adoption of mobile services and churn management are few of the most common problems faced by the mobile service providers (MSPs). The cost of acquiring new customer is higher than retaining the existing ones. Customer experience is correlated with customer loyalty and revenue (Soares, 2012a,b). In order to improve the customer experience, MSPs analyze a number of factors such as demographic data (gender, age, marital status, and language preferences), customer preferences, household structure and usage details (CDR, internet usage, value-added services (VAS)) to model the customer preferences and offer a relevant personalized service to them. This is known as targeted marketing, which improves the adoption of mobile services, reduces churn, thus, increasing the revenue of MSPs. Ufone, a Pakistan-based MSP, reduced the churn rate by precisely marketing the customized offers to their customers (Utsler, 2013). The company analyzes the CDR data to identify the call patterns to offer different plans to customers. The services are marketed to the customers through a call or text message. Their responses are recorded for further analysis.

Telecom companies are working towards combating telecom frauds. Often, traditional fraud management systems are poor at detecting new types of fraud. Even if they detect the occurrence of fraud lately, by then fraudsters would have changed their strategy. In order to overcome the limitations of traditional fraud management system, MSPs are analyzing real-time data to minimize the losses due to fraud. Mobileum Inc., one of the leading telecom analytics solution providers, is working towards providing a real-time fraud detection system using predictive analytics and machine learning (Ray, 2015).

Network Analytics is the next big thing in Telecom, where MSPs can monitor the network speed and manage the entire network. This helps to resolve the network problems within few minutes and helps to improve the quality of service and the customer experience. With the diffusion of Smartphones, based on analysis of real-time location and bevioural data, location-based services/context-based services can be offered to the customers when requested. This would increase the adoption of mobile services.

Financial Firms

Currently, capital firms are using advanced technology to store huge volumes of data. But increasing data sources like Internet and Social media require them to adopt big data storage systems. Capital markets are using big data in preparation for regulations like EMIR, Solvency II, Basel II etc, anti-money laundering, fraud mitigation, pre-trade decision-support analytics including sentiment analysis, predictive analytics and data tagging to identify trades (Verma & Mani, 2012). The timeliness of finding value plays an important role in both investment banking and capital markets, hence, there is a need for real-time processing of data.

Retail

Evolution of e-commerce, online purchasing, social-network conversations and recently location-specific smartphone interactions contribute to the volume and the quality of data for data-driven customization in retailing (Brown et al., 2011). Major retail stores might place CCTV not only to observe the instances of theft but also to track the flow of customers (Villars et al., 2011). It helps to observe the age group, gender and purchasing patterns of the customers during weekdays and weekends. Based on the purchasing patterns of the customers, retailers group their items using a well-known data mining technique called Market Basket Analysis (proposed by (Agrawal and Srikant, 1994)), so that a customer buying bread and milk might purchase jam as well. This helps to decide on the placement of objects and decide on the prices (Brown et al., 2011; Villars et al., 2011). Nowadays, e-commerce firms use market basket analysis and recommender systems to segment and target the customers. They collect the click stream data, observe behavior and recommend products in the real time.

Analytics help the retail companies to manage their inventory. For example, Stage stores, one of the brand names of Stage Stores Inc. which operates in more than 40 American states, used analytics to forecast the order for different sizes of garments for different geographical regions (Meek, 2015).

Law Enforcement

Law enforcement officials try to predict the next crime location using past data i.e., type of crime, place and time; social media data; drone and smartphone tracking. Researchers at Rutgers University developed an app called RTM Dx to prevent crime and is being used by police department at Illinois, Texas, Arizona, New Jersey, Missouri and Colorado. With the help the app, the police department could measure the spatial correlation between the location of crime and features of the environment (Mor, 2014).

A new technology called facial analytics that examines images of people without violating their privacy. Facial analytics is used to check child pornography. This saves the time of manual examination. Child pornography can be identified by integration of various technologies like Artemis and PhotoDNA by comparing files and image hashes with existing files to identify the subject as adult or child. It also identifies the cartoon based pornography (Ricanek & Boehnen, 2012).

Marketing

Marketing analytics helps the organizations to evaluate their marketing performance, to analyze the consumer behavior and their purchasing patterns, to analyze the marketing trends which would aid in modifying the marketing strategies like the positioning of advertisements in a webpage, implementation of dynamic pricing and offering personalized products (Soares, 2012a).

New Product Development

There is a huge risk associated with new product development. Enterprises can integrate both external sources, i.e., Twitter and Facebook page and internal data sources, i.e., customer relationship management (CRM) systems to understand the customers' requirement for a new product, to gather ideas for new product and to understand the added feature included in a competitor's product. Proper analysis and planning during the development stage can minimize the risk associated with the product, increase the customer lifetime value and promote brand engagement (Anastasia, 2015). Ribbon UI in Microsoft 2007 was created by analyzing the customer data from previous releases of the product to identify the commonly used features and making intelligent decisions (Fisher et al., 2012).

Banking

The investment worthiness of the customers can be analyzed using demographic details, behavioral data, and financial employment. The concept of cross-selling can be used here to target specific customer segments based on past buying behavior, demographic details, sentiment analysis along with CRM data (Forsyth, 2012; Coumaros et al., 2014).

Energy and Utilities

Consumption of water, gas and electricity can be measured using smart meters at regular intervals of one hour. During this interval, a huge amount of data is generated and analyzed to change the patterns of power usage (Brown et al., 2011). The real-time analysis reveals energy consumption pattern, instances of electricity thefts and price fluctuations.

Insurance

Personalized insurance plan is tailored for each customer using updated profiles of changes in wealth, customer risk, home asset value, and other data inputs (Brown et al., 2011). Recently, driving data of customers such as miles driven, routes driven, time of day, and braking abruptness are collected by the insurance companies by using sensors in their cars. Comparing individual driving pattern and driver risk with the statistical information available such as peak hours of drivers on the road develops a personalized insurance plan. This analysis of driver risk and policy gives a competitive advantage to the insurance companies (Soares, 2012a; Sun & Heller, 2012).

Education

With the advent of computerized course modules, it is possible to assess the academic performance real time. This helps to monitor the performance of the students after each module and give immediate feedback on their learning pattern. It also helps the teachers to assess their teaching pedagogy and modify it based on the students' performance and needs. Dropout patterns, students requiring special attention and students who can handle challenging assignments can be predicted (West, 2012). Beck and Mostow (2008) studied the student reading comprehension using intelligent tutor software and observed that reading mistakes reduced considerably when the students re-read an old story instead of a new story.

Other sectors

With increasing analytics skills among the various organizations, the advantage of big data analytics can be realized in sectors like construction and material sciences (Brown et al., 2011).

TECHNOLOGICAL GROWTH AND TECHNOLOGICAL LIMITATIONS

Advantages and applications of big data analytics are being realized in various sectors. The development of distributed file systems (eg., HDFS), Cloud computing (eg., Amazon EC2), in-memory cluster computing (eg., Spark), parallel computing (eg., Pig), emergence of NoSQL frameworks, advancement in machine learning algorithms (eg., Support Vector Machines, Deep Learning, Auto-Encoders, Random Forest) have made big data processing a reality.

Despite the growth in these technologies and algorithms to handle big data, there are few limitations, which are discussed in this section.

1. **Scalability and Storage Issues:** The rate of increase in data is much faster than the existing processing systems. The storage systems are not capable enough to store these data (Chen et al., 2014; Li & Lu, 2014; Kaisler et al., 2013; Assunção et al., 2015). There is a need to develop a processing system that not only caters to today's needs but also future needs.
2. **Timeliness of Analysis:** The value of the data decreases over time. Most of the applications like fraud detection in telecom, insurance and banking, require real time or near real time analysis of the transactional data (Chen et al., 2014; Li & Lu, 2014).
3. **Representation of Heterogeneous Data:** Data obtained from various sources are heterogeneous in nature. Unstructured data like images, videos and social media data cannot be stored and processed using traditional tools like SQL. Smartphones now record and share images, audios and videos at an incredibly increasing rate, forcing our brains to process more. However, the process for representing images, audios and videos lacks efficient storage and processing (Chen et al., 2014; Li & Lu, 2014; Cuzzocrea et al., 2011).

4. **Data Analytics System:** Traditional RDBMS are suitable only for structured data and they lack scalability and expandability. Though non-relational databases are used for processing unstructured data, but there exist problems with their performances. There is a need to design a system that combines the benefits of both relational and non-relational database systems to ensure flexibility (Chen et al., 2014; Li & Lu, 2014;).
5. **Lack of Talent Pool:** With the increase in amount of (structured and unstructured) data generated, there is a need for talent. The demand for people with good analytical skills in big data is increasing. Research says that by 2018, as many as 140,000 to 190,000 additional specialists in the area of big data may be required (Brown et al., 2011).
6. **Privacy and Security:** New devices and technologies like cloud computing provide a gateway to access and to store information for analysis. This integration of IT architectures will pose greater risks to data security and intellectual property. Access to personal information like buying preferences and call detail records will lead to increase in privacy concerns (Kaisler et al., 2013; Benjamins, 2014). Researchers have technical infrastructure to access the data from any data source including social networking sites, for future use whereas the users are unaware of the gains that can be generated from the information they posted (Boyd & Crawford, 2012). Big data researchers fail to understand the difference between privacy and convenience.
7. **Not Always Better Data:** Social media mining has attracted researchers. Twitter has become the new popular source. Twitter users do not represent the global population. Big data researchers should understand the difference between big data and whole data. The tweets containing references to pornography and spam are eliminated resulting in the inaccuracy of the topical frequency. There is a redundancy in number of twitter users and twitter accounts; one account accessed by multiple people and multiple accounts created by single user. There are active users and passive users who just sign in to listen. There are two types of accounts public and protected or private. Public tweets can be accessed through API. Few companies and start-ups have access to fire hose (containing all public tweets posted and excludes private or protected tweets) while others have access to a garden hose (roughly 10 percent public tweets) and a spritzer (roughly 1 percent of public tweets). Further, researchers have very limited access to fire hose. Hence it does not provide the accuracy of the sample size of the dataset and interpretation obtained from analysis (Fisher et al., 2012; Boyd & Crawford, 2012, 2011).
8. **Out of Context:** Data reduction is one of common ways to fit into a mathematical model. Retaining context during data abstraction is critical. Data that are out of context lose meaning and value. There is an obsession for 'social graph' with the rise of social networking sites. Big data introduces two types of social networks: 'articulated networks' and 'behavioral network'. Articulated networks are those resulting from specifying contacts through mediating technology. "Friends", "Acquaintances" in Facebook, "Follow" is twitter and "Best Friends", "Friends" and other circles in Google+ are examples of articulated network. Articulated networks are created to have separate group for friends, colleagues, and friends of friends and filter the content that each group can view. Behavioral networks are obtained from social media interactions and communication patterns. But communication patterns necessarily need not reveal tie strength. Boss and a subordinate have large communication patterns compared to those with family members. Though the analysis of both articulated and behavioral networks reveals important insights but they are not equivalent to personal networks (Boyd & Crawford, 2012, 2011).

9. **Digital Divide:** Gaining access to big data is one of the most important limitations. Data companies and social media companies have access to large social data. Few companies decide who can access data and to what extent. Few sell the right to access for high fees while others offer a portion of data sets to researchers. This results in "Digital Divide" in the realm of big data: Big Data rich and Big Data poor. There are three types of people and organization in this big data realm. First, people those who create data and this includes entire community who use web, mobile or other technologies. Second, people those who collect data and this group is small. Third, people who can analyze the data. This group is the smallest and the most privileged. Limited access to large social data explains the difficulty of conducting contemporary data-oriented social sciences and contemporary data-oriented humanities research (Boyd & Crawford, 2012, 2011; Manovich, 2011).
10. **Data Errors:** With increase in the growth of information technology, huge amount of data is generated. With advent of cloud computing for storage and retrieval of data, there is a need to utilize the big data. Large datasets from internet sources are prone to errors and losses, hence unreliable. The sources of the data should be understood to minimize the errors caused while using multiple datasets. The properties and limits of the dataset should be understood before analysis to avoid or explain the bias in the interpretation of data (Boyd & Crawford, 2011). For instance, consider the analysis of first-party and third-party pages in Social media, where the content in the first-party pages is verified whereas it is not the case in the latter (Kaisler et al., 2013).

RESEARCH AREAS WITH TECHNOLOGICAL ENHANCEMENTS

Big data analytics is gaining so much attention these days but there are a number of research problems that still need to be addressed.

1. **Storage and Retrieval of Images, Audios and Videos:** Multidimensional data should be integrated with analytics over big data hence array-based in-memory representation models can be explored. Integration of multidimensional data models over big data requires the enhancement of query language HiveQL with multidimensional extensions (Cuzzocrea et al., 2011). With the proliferation of smart phones images, audios and videos are being generated at an unremarkable pace. However, storage, retrieval and processing of these unstructured data require immense research in each dimension.
2. **Life-Cycle of Data:** Most application scenarios require real-time performance of the big data analytics. There is a need to define the life cycle of the data, the value it can provide and the computing process to make the analytics process real time, thus, increasing the value of the analysis (Chen et al., 2014). Big data is always not always better, hence proper data filtering techniques can be developed to ensure correctness in the data (Boyd & Crawford, 2012). Another big issue is related to the availability of data that is complete and reliable. In most of the cases, data are sparse and do not show clear distribution, yielding misleading conclusions. A method to overcome these problems needs proper attention and sometimes handling of unbalanced data sets leads to biased conclusion (We et al., 2014).
3. **Big Data Computations:** Apart from current big data paradigms like Map-Reduce, other paradigms such as YarcData (Big Data Graph Analytics) and High-Performance Computing cluster (HPCC explores Hadoop alternatives), are being explored (Agneeswaran, 2012).

4. **Visualization of High-Dimensional Data:** Visualization aids in decision analysis at each and every step of the data analysis. Visualization issues are still part of data warehousing and OLAP research. There is a scope for visualization tools for high-dimensional data (Cuzzocrea et al., 2011; Chen et al., 2014; Li & Lu, 2014).
5. **Development of Algorithms for Handling Domain Specific Data:** Machine learning algorithms are developed to meet general requirements for processing data. However, it cannot replace the domain specific requirements and specific algorithms will be needed to gain insights from the desired discipline.
6. **Real Time Processing Algorithms:** The pace at which data is being generated and the expectations from these algorithms may not be met, if the time delay in producing results is high.
7. **Efficient Storage Devices:** The demand for storing digital information is increasing continuously. Purchasing and using available storage devices cannot meet this demand (Khan et al., 2014). Research towards developing efficient storage device that can replace the need for HDFS systems that is fault tolerant can improve the data processing activity and replace the need for software management layer.
8. **Social Perspectives Dimensions:** It is important to understand that any technology can yield faster results however, it is upto the decision makers to use it wisely. These results may have several social and cultural implications and sometimes leading to cynicism towards online platforms (Jothimani et al., 2015). There are few questions whether large-scale search data would help in creating better tools and services or will it usher in privacy incursions and invasive marketing; whether data analytics would help in understanding the online behavior, communities and political movements or will it be used to track protesters and suppress freedom of speech (Boyd & Crawford, 2012).

CONCLUSION

This chapter gave an overview of big data, processed involved in big data analytics and discussed various tools and techniques to process big data. Different platforms for addressing big data storage, tools for handling big data, different libraries and packages have been highlighted. An overview of different languages used to handle big data has been covered. Different application domains where big data can play a significant role in improving the services have been discussed. Technological growth, limitations and direction for future research in improving big data have been highlighted.

REFERENCES

Agneeswaran, V. (2012). Big-data - Theoretical, engineering and analytics perspective. In Big Data Analytics (LNCS), (vol. 7678, pp. 8-15). Springer Berlin Heidelberg.

Agrawal, R., & Srikant, R. (1994). Fast algorithms for mining association rules in large databases. In *Proceedings of the 20th International Conference on Very Large Data Bases* (VLDB '94). Morgan Kaufmann Publishers Inc.

Anastasia. (2015). *Big data and new product development.* Entrepreneurial Insights. Retrieved from http://www.entrepreneurial-insights.com/big-data-new-product-development/

Assunção, M. D., Calheiros, R. N., Bianchi, S., Netto, M. A. S., & Buyya, R. (2015). Big Data computing and clouds: Trends and future directions. *Journal of Parallel and Distributed Computing*, *79–80*(May), 3–15. doi:10.1016/j.jpdc.2014.08.003

Bakshi, K. (2012). *Considerations for big data: Architecture and approach.* Big Sky, MT: IEEE Aerospace Conference.

Beck, J., & Mostow, J. (2008). How who should practice: Using learning decomposition to evaluate the efficacy of different types of practice for different types of students. In *Proceedings of the 9th International Conference on Intelligent Tutoring Systems.* doi:10.1007/978-3-540-69132-7_39

Benjamins, V. R. (2014). Big data: From hype to reality? In *Proceedings of the 4th International Conference on Web Intelligence, Mining and Semantics (WIMS14).* ACM.

Bhadani, A. (2011). Cloud Computing and Virtualization. Saarbrucken: VDM Verlag Dr. Muller Aktiengesellschaft & Co. KG.

Bhadani, A., & Chaudhary, S. (2010). Performance evaluation of web servers using central load balancing policy over virtual machines on cloud. In *Proceedings of the Third Annual ACM Conference*. Bangalore: ACM. doi:10.1145/1754288.1754304

Blount, M., Ebling, M., Eklund, J., James, A., McGregor, C., Percival, N., & Sow, D. et al. (2010). Real-time analysis for intensive care: Development and deployment of the Artemis analytic system. *IEEE Engineering in Medicine and Biology Magazine*, *29*(2), 110–118. doi:10.1109/MEMB.2010.936454 PMID:20659848

Boyd, D., & Crawford, K. (2011). Six provocations for big data. In *A Decade in Internet Time: Symposium on the Dynamics of the Internet and Society.*

Boyd, D., & Crawford, K. (2012). Critical questions for big data. *Information Communication and Society*, *15*(5), 662–679. doi:10.1080/1369118X.2012.678878

Brewer, E. A. (2000). Towards robust distributed systems (abstract). In *Proceedings of the Nineteenth Annual ACM Symposium on Principles of Distributed Computing (PODC '00).* ACM. doi:10.1145/343477.343502

Brown, B., Chui, M., & Manyika, J. (2011). Are you ready for the era of big data? *McKinsey Quarterly*. Retrieved from http://www.mckinsey.com/insights/strategy/areyoureadyfortheeraofbigdata

Chen, M., Mao, S., & Liu, Y. (2014). Big data: A survey. *Mobile Networks and Applications*, *19*(2), 171–209. doi:10.1007/s11036-013-0489-0

Coumaros, J., de Roys, S., Chretien, L., Buvat, J., Clerk, V., & Auliard, O. (2014). *Big data alchemy: How can banks maximize the value of their customer data?* Capgemini Consulting White Paper. Retrieved from https://www.capgemini.com/resources/big-data-customer-analytics-in-banks

Cukier, K. (2010). Data, data everywhere: A special report on managing information. *The Economist*. Retrieved 15 June 2015 from: http://www.economist.com/node/15557443

Cuzzocrea, A., Song, I.-Y., & Davis, K. C. (2011). Analytics over large-scale multidimensional data: the big data revolution! In *Proceedings of the ACM 14th International workshop on Data Warehousing and OLAP* (DOLAP '11). ACM. doi:10.1145/2064676.2064695

Dhar, V. (2013). Data science and prediction. *Communications of the ACM*, *56*(12), 64–73. doi:10.1145/2500499

Facebook. (2015). Retrieved 20 February 2016 from: http://www.statisticbrain.com/facebook-statistics/

Fisher, D., DeLine, R., Czerwinski, M., & Drucker, S. (2012). Interactions with big data analytics. *Interaction*, *19*(3), 50–59. doi:10.1145/2168931.2168943

Forsyth, C. (2012). *For big data analytics there's no such thing as too big*. Cisco White paper. Retrieved 20 February 2015 from: http://www.cisco.com/en/US/solutions/ns340/ns517/ns224/big data wp.pdf

Foster, I., Zhao, Y., Raicu, I., & Lu, S. (2008). Cloud computing and grid computing 360-degree compared. In Grid Computing Environments Workshop, 2008 (GCE '08).

Gandomi, A., & Haider, M. (2015). Beyond the hype: Big data concepts, methods, and analytics. *International Journal of Information Management*, *35*(2), 137–144. doi:10.1016/j.ijinfomgt.2014.10.007

Gantz, J., & Reinsel, D. (2011). *Extracting value from chaos. Tech. rep.* IDC.

Garlasu, D., Sandulescu, V., Halcu, I., Neculoiu, G., Grigoriu, O., Marinescu, M., & Marinescu, V. (2013). A big data implementation based on grid computing. In *11th Roedunet International Conference (RoEduNet)*. Sinaia. doi:10.1109/RoEduNet.2013.6511732

Gilbert, S., & Lynch, N. (2002). Brewer's conjecture and the feasibility of consistent, available, partition-tolerant web services. *SIGACT News*, *33*(2), 51–59. doi:10.1145/564585.564601

Jin, X., Wah, B. W., Cheng, X., & Wang, Y. (2015). Significance and challenges of big data research. *Big Data Research*, *2*(2), 59–64. doi:10.1016/j.bdr.2015.01.006

Jothimani, D., Bhadani, A. K., & Shankar, R. (2015). Towards Understanding the Cynicism of Social Networking Sites: An Operations Management Perspective. *Procedia: Social and Behavioral Sciences*, *189*, 117–132. doi:10.1016/j.sbspro.2015.03.206

Kaisler, S., Armour, F., Espinosa, J., & Money, W. (2013). Big data: Issues and challenges moving forward. In *46th Hawaii International Conference on System Sciences (HICSS)*. doi:10.1109/HICSS.2013.645

Khan, N., Yaqoob, I., & Hashem, I. A. T. (2014). Big Data: Survey, Technologies, Opportunities, and Challenges. The Scientific World Journal.

Laney, D. (2001). *3D data management: Controlling data volume, velocity and variety*. Tech. Rep. 949. META Group.

Li, H., & Lu, X. (2014). Challenges and trends of big data analytics. In *Ninth International Conference onP2P, Parallel, Grid, Cloud and Internet Computing* (3PGCIC). doi:10.1109/3PGCIC.2014.136

Maletic, J., & Marcus, A. (2000). Data cleansing: Beyond integrity analysis. In *Proceedings of the Conference on Information Quality (IQ2000)*.

Manovich, L. (2011). Trending: the promises and the challenges of big social data. In *Debates in the Digital Humanities*. The University of Minnesota Press. Retrieved 15 July 2015 from: http://www.manovich.net/DOCS/Manovich_trending_paper.pdf

Manyika, J., Chui, M., Brown, B., Bughin, J., Dobbs, R., Roxburgh, C., & Byers, A. H. (2011). *Big data: The next frontier for innovation, competition, and productivity*. McKinsey Global Institute.

Meek, T. (2015). Big data in retail: How to win with predictive analytics. *Forbes*. Retrieved 27 May 2015 from: http://www.forbes.com/sites/netapp/2015/02/18/big-data-in-retail/

Meijer, E. (2011). The world according to LINQ. *ACM Communications*, *54*(10), 45–51. doi:10.1145/2001269.2001285

Miller, H. G., & Mork, P. (2013). From data to decisions: A value chain for big data. *IT Professional*, *15*(1), 57–59. doi:10.1109/MITP.2013.11

Minelli, M., Chambers, M., & Dhiraj, A. (2013). Big Data, Big Analytics: Emerging Business Intelligence and Analytic Trends for Today's Businesses. Wiley Publishing.

Mor, Y. (2014). Big data and law enforcement: Was 'minority report' right? *Wired*. Retrieved from http://www.wired.com/2014/03/big-data-law-enforcement-minority-report-right/

Mukherjee, A., Pal, A., & Misra, P. (2012). Data analytics in ubiquitous sensor-based health information systems. In *6th International Conference on Next Generation Mobile Applications, Services and Technologies (NGMAST)*. doi:10.1109/NGMAST.2012.39

ParAccel. (2012). *Hadoops limitations for big data analytics*. ParAccel White Paper. Retrieved from: http://www.paraccel.com/resources/Whitepapers/Hadoop-Limitations-for-Big-Data-ParAccel-Whitepaper.pdf

Porter, M. (1980). *Competitive Strategy: Techniques for Analyzing Industries and Competitors*. New York: The Free Press.

KEY TERMS AND DEFINITIONS

Big Data: refers to a huge amount of both structured and unstructured data that cannot be stored and analyzed using traditional database management techniques.

Big Data Analytics: is the process of obtaining, storing and analyzing high voluminous structured and unstructured data to obtain insights from the data.

Cloud Computing: is a process that provides infrastructure at a remote location using the Internet for storing and processing the data following a principle of pay-as-you-go model.

Data Value Chain: refers to the framework that deals with a set of activities to create value from the available data. It includes entire processes of data analysis including data generation, data collection, data transmission, data preprocessing, data storage and data analysis.

Grid Computing: is a distributed computing technology that allocates computing power that may require huge computational resources and is not available at the users' end. It works on a voluntary basis where users donate memory and compute power of their computers so that other users can get benefitted.

Hadoop: is a Java-based framework that uses distributed computing environment to process a large amount of data.

High Dimensional Data: Data in which the number of variables is larger than the sample size.

MapReduce: is a software framework for processing a large dataset in a distributed manner in Hadoop clusters and uses Hadoop distributed file system.

Chapter 2
Introducing Data Structures for Big Data

Ranjit Biswas
Jamia Hamdard University, India

ABSTRACT

The homogeneous data structure 'train' and the heterogeneous data structure 'atrain' are the fundamental, very powerful dynamic and flexible data structures, being the first data structures introduced exclusively for big data. Thus 'Data Structures for Big Data' is to be regarded as a new subject in Big Data Science, not just as a new topic, considering the explosive momentum of the big data. Based upon the notion of the big data structures train and atrain, the author introduces the useful data structures for the programmers working with big data which are: ***homogeneous stacks 'train stack' and 'rT-coach stack', heterogeneous stacks 'atrain stack' and 'rA-coach stack', homogeneous queues 'train queue' and 'rT-coach queue', heterogeneous queues 'atrain queue' and 'rA-coach queue', homogeneous binary trees 'train binary tree' and 'rT-coach binary tree', heterogeneous binary trees 'atrain binary tree' and 'rA-coach binary tree', homogeneous trees 'train tree' and 'rT-coach tree', heterogeneous trees 'atrain tree' and 'rA-coach tree', to enrich the subject 'Data Structures for Big Data' for big data science.***

INTRODUCTION

The present world of big data are expanding very fast in 4Vs: Volume, Varity, Velocity and Veracity, and also in many more directions. How to deal with explosive momentum of big data, how to process big data in an efficient way within limited resources, etc. are of major concern to the computer scientists now-a-days. For a detailed study about big data, one could see (Berman, 2013; Feinleib, 2013; Needham, 2013; Viktor Mayer-Schönberger, 2013). Big data has variable mass of 4Vs in various directions, and in this sense it is to be philosophically regarded as a vector, or rather as a tensor. The existing data structures of computer science are neither appropriate nor sufficient to deal with the big data. Big data in most of the cases are of heterogeneous type. The homogeneous data structure 'r-Train' and the heterogeneous data structure 'r-Atrain' for big data are the first attempt to introduce any exclusive data structures (Biswas, 2011, 2012, 2013b, 2015a) for big data.

DOI: 10.4018/978-1-5225-0182-4.ch002

It is obvious that the 'Data Structures for Big Data' is to be regarded as a new subject in big data science, not just as a new topic, considering the explosive momentum of the big data in a new universe. One could view big data with philosophical eyes as a tensor of increasing order. The data structures 'train' and 'atrain' on the platform of infinitely scalable architecture of a new type of distributed system ADS (Biswas, 2015a) designed exclusively for big data, and the new mathematical models: 'solid matrix/latrix', 'solid hematrix/helatrix', to store big data of any big amount of any datatype have opened easy gates to the world giant organizations and their developers to deal with big data. In this chapter we introduce few very useful data structures for big data which are : homogeneous stacks 'train stack' and 'rT-coach stack'; heterogeneous stacks 'atrain stack' and 'rA-coach stack'; homogeneous queues 'train queue' and 'rT-coach queue'; heterogeneous queues 'atrain queue' and 'rA-coach queue'; homogeneous binary trees 'train binary tree' and 'rT-coach binary tree'; heterogeneous binary trees 'atrain binary tree' and 'rA-coach binary tree'; homogeneous trees 'train tree' and 'rT-coach tree'; heterogeneous trees 'atrain tree' and 'rA-coach tree'; to enrich the subject 'Data Structures for Big Data' with the extended notion of the architecture of the data structures r-atrain and r-train for big data. All these data structures, homogeneous or heterogeneous, are designed in compatible with the architecture of a new distributed system ADS (Biswas, 2015a) proposed exclusively for big data of any 4V and infinitely scalable.

PRELIMINARIES OF THE DATA STRUCTURE r-ATRAIN FOR BIG DATA

The data structure **'**r-Train' ('train', in short) where r is a natural number is a new kind of powerful robust data structure which can store homogeneous big data dynamically in a flexible way. However, the heterogeneous data structure **'**r-Atrain' ('atrain', in short) where r is a natural number is a new kind of powerful robust data structure which can store heterogeneous big data of any 4V dynamically in a flexible way. In (Biswas, 2015a) a detailed study of the two fundamental big data structures train and atrain is available with the detailed description of the distributed system ADS for big data, an infinitely scalable architecture to deal with big data of any 4Vs. However, for the sake of preliminaries of this chapter, the heterogeneous data structure r-atrain for big data is reproduced in brief from (Biswas, 2015a), before we start for the actual content here. For details of train and atrain, one could see (Biswas, 2015a).

The heterogeneous big data structure 'atrain' can store heterogeneous data (by the term heterogeneous data, we mean here data of various datatypes). The classical data structures viz. array, linked list, etc. can store and handle with homogeneous data only, not heterogeneous data. The data structure 'r-Atrain' ('atrain', in short) is one of the most useful, most powerful and most appropriate data structures in the field of Computer Science considering the application potential of it by the programmers programming with any computer languages. This advanced data structure 'r-Atrain' ('atrain', in short) is logically almost analogous to the homogeneous data structure r-train (train) but with an advanced level of construction to accommodate any variety of heterogeneous big data. The data structure train can be viewed as a special case of the data structure atrain. It is important to note that none of these two new big data structures train and atrain is a competitor of the other, but they are the basic and most fundamental data structures for big data. By default, any heterogeneous data structure can work as a homogeneous data structure too. For working with homogeneous big data, train is more suitable than atrain. However, for working with heterogeneous big data, atrain is suitable while train can not be applicable even. The natural number r is to be suitably predecided and fixed by the programmer depending upon the problem under consideration and also upon the organization/industry for which the big data problem is posed.

In a homogeneous data structure the data elements considered are all of the same datatype, like in array, linked list, r-train, etc. In a heterogeneous data structure data elements are of various datatypes as in a 'structure'. In this section an upgradation of the homogeneous data structure r-Train is introduced which is a new but heterogeneous data structure 'r-Atrain'. The term "Atrain" stands for the phrase '*Advanced train*', because in the construction of r-Atrain we incorporate few advanced features (not available in r-train) which make it suitable to deal with heterogeneous data, in particular while there are a large volume of heterogeneous data. This data structure is developed with the thought about a reality. In railways transport system we see that in most of the trains one or more coaches are created for pantry, one or more coaches are for accommodating postal mails, one or more are for accommodating booked luggage, one or more are for accommodating goods, one or more exclusively for ladies, etc. and most of the coaches are for accommodating passengers. Different coaches are there for accommodating different types of contents, i.e. for accommodating heterogeneous types of contents. With this real example, it is encouraged to develop a new data structure 'r-Atrain' where coaches may accommodate data of various datatypes, but no coach is allowed to accommodate data of different datatypes. The datatype in a r-atrain may vary from coach to coach (unlike in r-train), but in a coach all data must be homogeneous i.e. of identical datatype. Thus each coach is homogeneous although the atrain is heterogeneous.

Code of a Datatype and CD-Table

A table is to be created by the concerned organization to fix integer code for each datatype under use in the organization. This is not an absolute set of codes to be followed universally by every organization, but it is a local document for the concerned organization. For different organizations, this table could be different. But once it is fixed by an organization it should not be altered by this organization, except that addition of new datatypes and corresponding codes may be decided and be incorporated in the table at any stages later retaining the existing records. This table is called Code of Datatype Table or *CD-Table* (Biswas, 2015a). An example CD-Table of a hypothetical organization is shown in Table 1.

It may be noted that for the datatypes character, integer, Boolean, etc. the space requirement is known to us as it is absolutely fixed, whereas for the datatype string (appearing twice in this case) the space requirement has been fixed at 20 bytes for one kind and 12 bytes for another kind, fixed by the choice of the concerned organization (developers).

A r-Atrain in Memory

For the sake of a preliminary idea before we go for the actual content, the following example and the concept of few fundamental operations (Biswas, 2015a) are important to understand.

Refer to the example of CD-Table presented earlier. Consider the data: 9.2, 2.4, 5.8, CALCUTTA, DELHI, BOMBAY, t, +, *, 6, 7 which are stored in the Data Segment of the 8086 memory using the data structure 3-atrain, as shown below starting from START = 0A02h. This is a 3-atrain T = < [10A5h, (2,0)], [BA98h, (3,0)], [00ADh, (0,0)], [E49Bh, (1,1)] > which is of length 4 where the coach C_1 begins from the address 10A5h, the coach C_2 begins from the address BA98h, the coach C_3 begins from the address 00ADh, the coach C_4 begins from the address E49Bh. Here START = 0A02h, i.e. the pilot of this 3-atrain is stored at the address 0A02h. Also in this example, the pilot is implemented as an array, not using linked list. However, for a big size pilot linked list representation may be preferred (Table 2).

Table 1. A hypothetical example of a CD-Table of an organization

Sr. No.	Datatype	Space required in bytes (n)	Code of Datatype (c)
1	Character	1	0
2	Integer	2	1
3	Real	4	2
4	String-1	10	3
5	String-2	20	4
6	String-3	50	5
7	File-1	100 KB	6
8	File-2	1 MB	7
9	File-3	10 MB	8
10	File-4	25 MB	9
11	....	....	....
12	....	....	....

FUNDAMENTAL OPERATIONS ON THE DATA STRUCTURE 'r-ATRAIN'

The two fundamental operations (Biswas, 2015a) on the data structure r-atrain (atrain) are 'insertion' and 'deletion' which are defined below:

Insertion

There are three types of insertion operation in the data structure r-atrain:

i. Insertion (addition) of a new coach in a r-atrain.
ii. Insertion of a data element (passenger) in a given coach of a r-atrain.
iii. Insertion of a data element (passenger) in a r-atrain.

i. Insertion of a New Coach in a r-Atrain

Insertion of a new coach can be done at the end of the pilot, nowhere else. The first job is to decide about the datatype of the coach which is required now to be inserted.

Consider the r-atrain $T = < [C_1, s_{C1}], [C_2, s_{C2}], [C_3, s_{C3}], \ldots, [C_k, s_{Ck}] >$, with k number of coaches, where the coach $C_i = (A_i, e_i)$ for i = 1, 2, 3, ..., k.

After insertion of a new additional coach, the updated r-atrain immediately becomes the following r-atrain:

$$T = < [C_1, s_{C1}], [C_2, s_{C2}], [C_3, s_{C3}], \ldots, [C_k, s_{Ck}], [C_{k+1}, r] >.$$

Initially at the time of insertion, we create C_{K+1} as an empty coach with status = (c,r) where c is the code of the intended datatype of the coach and since the new coach is empty therefore the number of

Table 2. A r-Atrain in memory

Address	Memory Content	Size
	X (an invalid Address)	2 bytes
	ε	2 bytes
	7	2 bytes
E49Bh	6	2 bytes
	00AD h	2 bytes
	BOMBAY	20 bytes
	DELHI	20 bytes
BA98h	CALCUTTA	20 bytes
	BA98 h	2 bytes
	5.8	4 bytes
	2.4	4 bytes
10A5h	9.2	4 bytes
	1	2 bytes
	1	2 bytes
0A0Dh	C_4 = E49b h	2 bytes
	0	2 bytes
	0	2 bytes
C_3 – 0A0Ah	C_3 = 00AD h	2 bytes
	0	2 bytes
	3	2 bytes
0A06h	C_2 = BA98 h	2 bytes
	0	2 bytes
	2	2 bytes
START = 0A02h	C_1 = 10A5 h	2 bytes
	E49B h	2 bytes
	*	1 byte
	+	1 byte
00ADh	T	1 byte

available space is r at this time, but the coach is likely to get filled-up with non-ε passengers (data) later on with time.

For insertion of a new coach C_{K+1} in a r-atrain, we need to do the following steps:

1. Read the CD-Table for the code c of the datatype of the new coach intended for insertion. If the code c is not available in the CD-Table, expand CD-Table accordingly.
2. Update the pilot (linked list).
3. $\mathbf{e_k}$ in C_k is to be updated and to be made equal to the address $C_{K+1.}$
4. Set $e_{k+1,\,j} = \varepsilon$ for j = 1, 2, ….., r
5. Set $\mathbf{e_{k+1}}$ = an invalid address.
6. Set $s_{Ck+1} = (c,r)$.

ii. Insertion of an Element x Inside the Coach Ci = (A_i, e_i) of a r-Atrain

Insertion of an element (a new passenger) x inside the coach C_i is feasible if x is of same datatype (like other passengers of the coach C_i) and if there is an empty space available inside the coach C_i. If the availability-status n of C_i is greater than 0 then data can be stored successfully in this coach, otherwise insertion operation fails here at this moment of time. For insertion of x, we can replace the lowest indexed passenger ε of C_i with x.

After each successful insertion, the availability-status n of the coach is to be updated by doing n = n–1, and thus by updating the status $S_{Ci} = (c,n)$ by its new value given by $S_{Ci} = (c,n\text{-}1)$.

iii. Insertion of an Element x in a r-Atrain

In this case too, the code c (with reference to the CD-Table) corresponding to the datatype of the data x plays an important role in the process of insertion. An initial search is done for the coaches (starting from C_1 onwards) which are having the same code c in their status. Suppose that, the array of the code-matched coaches so extracted from the pilot is

$$Z = (Ç_1, Ç_2, Ç_3, \dots, Ç_t).$$

If the array Z is a null array or if the availability-status is zero for each and every member of Z, then the insertion operation is to be done by inserting a new coach C_μ first of all, and then by performing the insertion operation.

Otherwise we find out the coach $Ç_k$ in Z with lowest index k for which the availability-status n is > 0, and then perform the insertion operation.

Deletion

There are two types of deletion operation in the data structure r-atrain:

i. Deletion of a data element ($\neq\varepsilon$) from any coach of the r-atrain.
ii. Deletion of the last coach C_i, if it is an empty coach, from a r-atrain.

i. Deletion of a Data e_{ij} ($\neq \varepsilon$) from the Coach C_i of a r-Atrain

Deletion of e_i from the coach C_i is not allowed as it is the link. But we can delete a data element e_{ij} from the coach C_i. Deletion of a data (passenger) from a coach means replacement of the data by an ε element (of same datatype). Consequently, if $e_{ij} = \varepsilon$, then the question of deletion does not arise. Here it is pre-assumed that e_{ij} is a non-ε member element of the coach C_i .

For j = 1, 2, ..., r, deletion of e_{ij} is done by replacing it by the null element ε, and updating the availability-status n by doing n = n+1. Deletion of a data element (passenger) does not affect the size r of the coach.

For example, consider the tagged coach $[C_i, (c_i,m)]$ where

$C_i = < e_{i1,}\ e_{i2,}\ e_{i3,}\ e_{i4}, ..., e_{ir} >$.

If we delete e_{i3} from the coach $C_{i,}$ then the updated tagged coach will be

$[\ C_i, (c_i, m+1)\ ]$

where $C_i = < e_{i1}, e_{i2}, \varepsilon, e_{i4}, ..., e_{ir} >$.

(ii) Deletion of the Last Coach C_i from a r-Atrain

Deletion of coaches from a r-atrain is allowed from the last coach only and in backward direction, one after another. An interim coach cannot be deleted. Advertently, we avoid here any kind of deletion of interim coach. The last coach C_i can be deleted if it is an empty coach, as shown in Table 3.

If the last coach is not empty, it cannot be deleted unless its all the passengers are deleted to make it empty.

To delete the empty last coach $C_{i,}$ of a r-atrain, we have to do the following actions:

1. Update e_{i-1} of the coach C_{i-1} by storing an invalid address in it.
2. Delete $[C_i, (c_i,r)]$ from the r-atrain $T = < [C_1, s_{C1}], [C_2, s_{C2}], [C_3, s_{C3}], ..., [C_{i-1}, s_{Ci-1}], [C_i, (c_i,r)] >$, and get the updated r-atrain $T = < [C_1, s_{C1}], [C_2, s_{C2}], [C_3, s_{C3}], ..., [C_{i-1}, s_{Ci-1}] >$.
3. Update the pilot.

Searching for a Data x in a r-Atrain T of Length k

Searching for a data x in a r-atrain T is very easy. If we know in advance the coach number Ci of the passenger x, then by visiting the pilot we can enter into the coach Ci of the r-atrain directly and then can

Table 3.

ε	ε	ε	ε
invalid address			ε
ε	ε	ε	ε

read the data-elements e_{i1}, e_{i2}, …, e_{ir} of the larray Ai for a match with x. Otherwise, the code c (with reference to the CD-Table) of the datatype of the data x plays an important role in the process of searching. The initial search is done for the coaches (starting from C_1 onwards) which are having the same code c in their status. Suppose that the array of the code-matched coaches so extracted is Z = ($Ç_1$, $Ç_2$, $Ç_3$, ..., $Ç_{t-1}$, $Ç_t$). If the array Z is a null array, the search fails. Otherwise we start searching inside, beginning from the coach $Ç_1$ onwards till the last coach $Ç_t$ of Z. The search may lead to either success or failure. We need not go back to the pilot for any help during the tenure of our searching process. Here lies an important dominance of the data structure r-atrain over the data structure HAT.

In case of multi-processor system the searching can be done in parallel very fast, which is obvious from the architecture of the data structure r-atrain.

r-TRAIN STACK AND r-ATRAIN STACK

While processing big data using the homogeneous data structure r-train or the heterogeneous data structure r-atrain in an atrain distributed system (ADS), the programmer may need to store many files in a stack/queue/tree/binary tree and many images in a stack/queue/tree/binary tree and many arrays or tables in a stack/queue/tree/binary tree and also many linked lists in a stack/queue/tree/binary tree, many networks using graphs/multigraphs, etc. There is no data structure for processing such complex storing systems in big data. There are some situations where we need to create an entirely new type of data structure of generalized nature, and creating such a new but simple data structure is not always a straightforward task. The next requirement to the computer scientists is to develop a new but simple big data language called by "ADSL" (Atrain Distributed System Language) which can easily be used by any laymen user at the PC of an ADS to answer any query, be it arithmetical or statistical or relational query. As a step towards developing the ADSL, in this section we introduce two new data structures for big data:

1. 'r-train stack' or 'train stack' in short, and
2. 'r-atrain stack' or 'atrain stack' in short.

(The natural number r is suitably predecided and fixed by the programmer depending upon the problem of Big Data under consideration and also upon the organization/industry for which the problem is posed. We do not feel it appropriate to propose r in a r-train or in a r-atrain as a variable).

First of all we define few terminologies.

Coach of a 'Train Stack'

The term coach here is coined from the notion of the data structures train and atrain for big data. By a coach C in a train stack we mean a non-empty larray (however, it could be a null larray) containing data of homogeneous data type.

Table 4 shows a coach of a 7-train in a '7-train stack' as a larray.

Table 4. A coach of a train in a 7-train stack

69.37	5.75	0.48	95.26	732.03	0.40	571.86	e

Suppose that the larray C has m number of elements in it. If each element of C is of size x bytes, then to store the coach C in memory exactly m.x number of consecutive bytes are required.

Status of a Coach and Tagged Coach (TC) of a Train Stack

The *status* s of a coach is a non-negative integer variable which is equal to the number of ε elements present in it (i.e. in its larray) at this point of time. Therefore, $0 \leq s \leq r$. The significance of the variable s is that it informs us about the exact number of free spaces available in the coach at this point of time. If there is no ε element in the larray of the coach C, then the value of s is 0 at this point of time.

If C is a coach, then the corresponding *tagged coach* (TC) is denoted by the notation (C,s) where s is the status of the coach. This means that C is a coach tagged with an information on the total amount of available free space (here it is termed as ε elements) inside it at this time.

For example, consider the coach C in Table 4. Clearly its corresponding TC will be denoted by (C,0) as shown in Table 5.

Consider the following coach H in a train of a 7-train stack represented as a larray in Table 6.Clearly its corresponding TC will be denoted by (H,2) as shown in Table 7.

INTRODUCING r-TRAIN STACK (TRAIN STACK)

A 'r-train stack' (or, train stack) is a crisp stack of r-trains containing data of homogeneous data type in the whole stack. For a given r-train stack, the value of the natural number r is fixed throughout. For different r-train stacks, the value of r could be different. The r-train stack is thus a linear data structure in which a r-train may be added or removed only at the end, called the TOP of the train stack in LIFO manner as in classical stack. If TOP = 0 (Null), it implies that the train stack is an empty train stack (Figure 1).

Thus a train stack T (see Figure 1) may be written as an array of trains as

$$T : T_1, T_2, T_3, \ldots, T_n$$

Table 5. The tagged coach of the coach C in a train of a 7-train stack

69.37	5.75	0.48	95.26	732.03	0.40	571.86	e

Table 6. A coach of a train in a 7-train stack

1037	875	0	ε	3	ε	61	e

Table 7. The tagged coach of the coach H

1037	875	0	ε	3	ε	61	2	e

Figure 1. A train stack

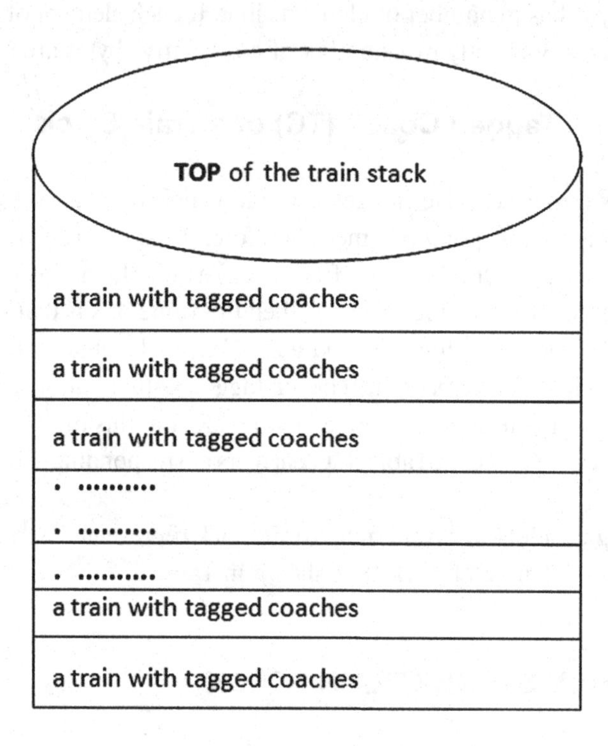

with the implication that the rightmost element is the top element (train T_n). In a train stack, all the trains contain data of identical data type, and so a train stack is to be regarded as a homogeneous data structure.

Insertion and deletion can occur only at the top of the train stack. Two basic operations associated with train stacks are:

i. **"PUSH"** (to insert a new train into a train stack)
ii. **"POP"** (to delete a train from a train stack)

The train stack has the following two important operations too, which can be easily implemented using PUSH and POP multiple times, and the properties of the data structure larray:

iii. **"c-PUSH"** for pushing a coach. (to insert a tagged coach in a given train of the train stack)
iv. **"c-POP"** for popping a coach. (to delete a tagged coach from a given train of the train stack)

rT-Coach Stack (or Coach Stack)

A 'rt-coach stack' (or, coach stack in short) is a special case of r-train stack where every train consists of one coach only. For a given rT-coach stack, the value of the natural number r is fixed throughout. For different rT-coach stacks, the value of r could be different. Thus a rT-coach stack is a crisp stack of tagged coaches containing data of homogeneous data type. It is a linear data structure in which a tagged coach may be added or removed only at the end, called the TOP of the train stack in LIFO manner as in classical stack. If TOP = 0 (Null), it implies that the coach stack is an empty coach stack. (The term 'rT-coach' signifies that it is a coach of a r-Train) (Figure 2).

Thus a rT-coach stack T (see Figure 3) may be written as an array of TCs as

$$T : (C_1,s_1), (C_2,s_2), (C_3,s_3), (C_4,s_4), \ldots, (C_r,s_r)$$

with the implication that the rightmost element is the top element (tagged coach). In a rT-coach stack all the coaches contain data of identical data type, and so a rT-coach stack is to be regarded as a homogeneous data structure.

Insertion and deletion can occur only at the top of the rT-coach stack.

Two basic operations associated with rT-coach stacks are:

i. **"c-PUSH"** (to insert a new tagged coach into a rT-coach stack)
ii. **"c-POP"** (to delete a tagged coach from a rT-coach stack)

The rT-coach stack has the following two important operations too, which can be easily implemented using PUSH, POP, c-PUSH, and c-POP operations multiple times, and the properties of the data structure larray:

iii. **"e-PUSH"** for pushing an element. (to insert an element into a tagged coach (TC) of a rT-coach stack where status s is not 0, i.e. at least 1).

Figure 2. A rT-coach stack

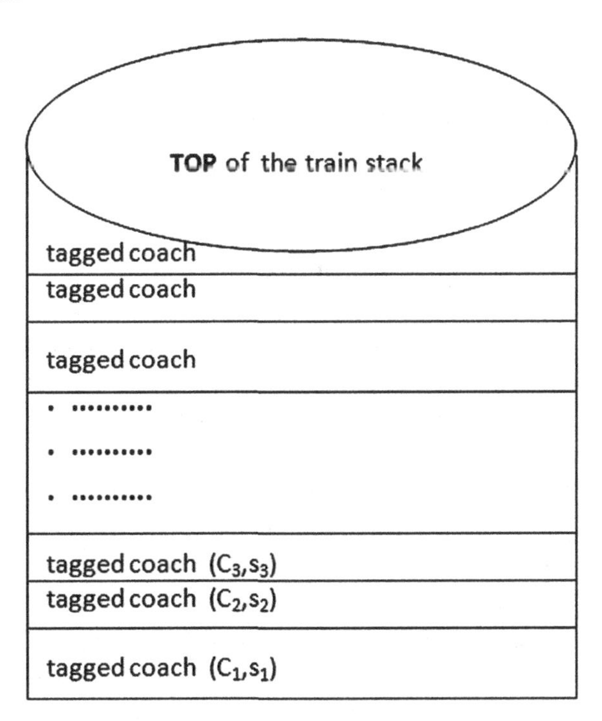

Insertion of an element (a new passenger) x inside the coach C_i is feasible if x is of same datatype (like other passengers of the coach) and if there is an empty space available inside the coach C_i.

```
If status of Cj is greater than 0 then data can be stored successfully in the
coach, otherwise insertion operation fails here. After each successful inser-
tion, the status s of the coach is to be updated by doing s = s - 1.
```

For insertion of x, we can replace the lowest indexed passenger ε of C_i with x.

iv. **"e-POP"** for popping an element. (to delete an element from a tagged coach of a rT-coach stack, retaining the tagged coach in the memory adjusting its status s by doing s ← s+1).

We can delete a data element e_{ij} from the coach C_i. Deletion of a data (passenger) from a coach means replacement of the data by an ε element (of same datatype). Consequently, if $e_{ij} = \varepsilon$, then the question of deletion does not arise. Here it is pre-assumed that e_{ij} is a non-ε member element of the coach C_i . Thus deletion of e_{ij} is done by replacing it by the null element ε, and updating the status s by doing s = s+1. Deletion of a data element (passenger) does not effect the size r of the coach.

For example, consider the tagged coach (C_i, m) where

$$C_i = < e_{i1,} e_{i2,} e_{i3,} e_{i4}, ..., e_{ir}> .$$

If we delete e_{i3} from the coach $C_{i,}$ then the updated tagged coach will be (C_i, m+1) where

$$C_i = < e_{i1,} e_{i2}, \varepsilon, e_{i4}, ..., e_{ir}>.$$

INTRODUCING r-ATRAIN STACK (ATRAIN STACK)

Before proceeding to introduce 'r-atrain stack', few terminologies need to be defined:

Code of a Datatype and CD-Table for an Atrain Stack

The concept of CD-Table in atrain stack is analogous to that of the CD-Table introduced in case of r-atrain (atrain). A table is to be created by the user (i.e. by the concerned organization) to fix unique integer code for each datatype which are under use in the organization. This is not an absolute set of codes to be followed universally by every organization, but it is a local document for the concerned organization. For different organizations, this table could be different. But once it is fixed by an organization it should not be altered by this organization, except that addition of new datatypes and corresponding codes may be decided and be incorporated in the table at any stages later retaining the existing records. This table is called *Code of Datatype Table* or *CD-Table* (in short). A sample CD-Table of a hypothetical organization is shown in Table 1 for the sake of understanding. It may be noted that for any organization, for the datatypes character, integer, boolean, etc. the individual space requirement respectively are absolutely fixed. But for a particular organization, for the datatypes String-1, String-2 and String-3 (String type appearing thrice in this case) the space requirement in the Table 1 has been fixed at 10 bytes for one kind, 20 bytes for another and 50 bytes for another kind. Similarly there are four types of file: File-1, File-2, File-3 and File-4, in the CD-Table and the space requirement for them have been fixed at 100 KB, 1 MB, 10 MB and 25 MB respectively, fixed by choice of the concerned organization (developers).

Coach of an Atrain Stack

As seen earlier, all the coaches in a train stack contain data of homogeneous datatype across the train. In an atrain stack although a coach stores homogeneous data only (not heterogeneous data), but different coaches of an atrain stack store data elements of different datatypes. Thus the data structure atrain stack is a kind of heterogeneous data structure. For constructing a coach for an atrain stack in an organization, we must know in advance the datatype of the data to be stored in it. For this we have to look at the CD-Table of the organization, and reserve space accordingly for r number of data.

Suppose that the larray A has r number of elements in it of a given datatype. If each element of A is of size x bytes (refer to CD-Table) then to store the coach C in memory exactly r.x number of consecutive bytes are required, and accordingly the coach be created by the programmer (concerned organization). In our discussion henceforth, by the phrase "datatype of a coach" we shall always mean the datatype of the data elements of the coach. A coach stores and can store only homogeneous data (i.e. data of identical datatype), but datatype may be different for different coaches in an atrain stack.

By a coach C in an atrain stack we mean a non-empty larray (however, it could be a null larray) containing data of homogeneous data type. Tables 8 and 9 show two coaches C_1 and C_2 of an atrain stack T.

Status of a Coach and Tagged Coach (TC) of an Atrain Stack

The *status* s of a coach in an atrain stack is a pair of information (c, n), where c is a non-negative integer variable which is the code of datatype (with reference to the concerned CD-Table) of the data to be stored in this coach and n is a non-negative integer variable which is equal to the number of ε elements present in it (i.e. in its larray) at this point of time. Therefore, $0 \leq n \leq r$. In the status s = (c, n) of a coach, the information c is called the "*code-status*" of the coach and the information n is called the "*availability-status*" of the coach at this time. The significance of the variable n is that it informs us about the exact number of free spaces available in the coach at this point of time. If there is no ε element at this time in the larray of the coach C, then the value of n is 0. Thus, without referring the CD-Table, the status of a coach can not be and should not be fixed.

Table 8. A coach C1 of a 7-atrain stack T

69.37	5.75	0.48	95.26	732.03	0.40	571.86	e

Table 9. Another coach C2 of the 7-atrain stack T

#	*	@	ε	&	ε	#	e

If C is a coach in an atrain stack, then the corresponding tagged coach (TC) is denoted by the notation [C,s], where s = (c, n) is the status of the coach. This means that C is a coach tagged with the following two information:

1. One signifying the datatype of the data of the coach.
2. The other reflects the total amount of available free spaces (here it is termed as ε elements) inside the coach at this time.

(Thus the concept of TC for atrain stack is slightly different from the concept of TC for train stack).

For example, consider Table 8 and Table 9 of two coaches C_1 and C_2 respectively of the atrain stack T. Then Table 10 and Table 11 shows the two tagged coaches C_1 and C_2 of the atrain stack T.

r-Atrain Stack (Atrain Stack)

An 'atrain stack' is a crisp stack of r-atrains containing data of heterogeneous data type. Here, each coach is homogeneous internally containing data of identical data type, but different coaches have data of different data types. For a given r-atrain stack, the value of the natural number r is fixed throughout. For different r-atrain stacks, the value of r could be different. The datatype in an atrain stack may vary from coach to coach (unlike in train stacks), but in a coach all data must be homogeneous i.e. of identical datatype. Thus each coach is homogeneous, although the atrain stack is heterogeneous. In this sense, 'atrain stack' is regarded as a heterogeneous data structure. (In a homogeneous data structure the data elements considered are all of the same datatype, like in array, linked list, train, etc., but in a heterogeneous data structure data elements are of various datatypes as in atrain).

Analogous to the notion of a train stack, an atrain stack is also a linear data structure in which an atrain may be added or removed only at the end, called the TOP of the atrain stack in LIFO manner as in classical stack (see Figure 8). If TOP = 0 (Null), it implies that the atrain stack is an empty atrain stack (Figure 3).

Thus an atrain stack T (see Figure 3) may be written as an array of atrains as

$$T : T_1, T_2, T_3, \ldots, T_n$$

with the implication that the rightmost element is the top element (atrain T_n).

Insertion and deletion can occur only at the top of the atrain stack. Two basic operations associated with atrain stacks are:

Table 10. The tagged coach of the coach C1 in the 7-atrain stack T

69.37	5.75	0.48	95.26	732.03	0.40	571.86	e, (2,0)

Table 11. The tagged coach of the coach C2 in the 7-atrain stack T

#	*	@	ε	&	ε	#	e, (0,2)

Figure 3. An atrain stack

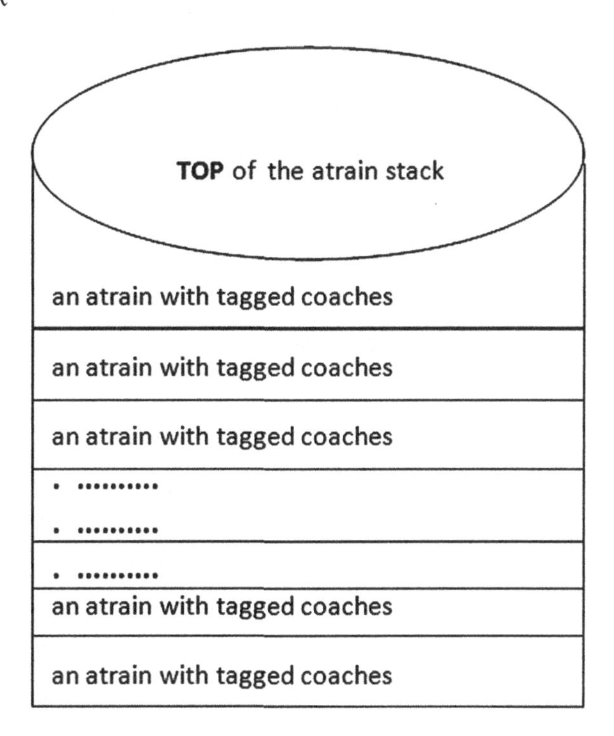

i. **"PUSH"** (to insert a new atrain into an atrain stack)
ii. **"POP"** (to delete an atrain from an atrain stack)

The atrain stack has the following two important operations too, which can be easily implemented using PUSH and POP multiple times, and the properties of the data structure larray:

iii. **"c-PUSH"** for pushing a coach. (to insert a tagged coach in a given atrain of the atrain stack)
iv. **"c-POP"** for popping a coach. (to delete a tagged coach from a given atrain of the atrain stack)

It is important to note that in this heterogeneous data structure atrain stack, the size of coaches in bytes are not same, although each coach accommodates r number of data elements (including ε which is of same data). It depends upon the code from the CD-Table. Therefore, each time we push a new atrain in an atrain stack (assuming that there is no overflow), the TOP gets updated accordingly in a dynamic way. Similarly, each time we POP an atrain from an atrain stack, the TOP gets updated accordingly.

rA-Coach Stack (or Coach Stack)

A 'rA-coach stack' (or, coach stack in short) is a special case of r-atrain stack where every atrain consists of one coach only. For a given rA-coach stack, the value of the natural number r is fixed throughout. For different rA-coach stacks, the value of r could be different. Thus a rA-coach stack is a crisp stack of tagged coaches (of atrain) containing data of heterogeneous data type. It is a linear data structure in which a tagged coach may be added or removed only at the end, called the TOP of the rA-coach stack in LIFO manner as in classical stack. If TOP = 0 (Null), it implies that the rA-coach stack is an empty rA-coach stack. (The term 'rA-coach' signifies that it is a coach of a r-Atrain) (Figure 4).

Thus a rA-coach stack T(see Figure 4) may be written as an array of TCs as

$$T : (C_1,s_1), (C_2,s_2), (C_3,s_3), (C_4,s_4), \ldots\ldots.., (C_r,s_r)$$

$$\text{i.e. as } T : (C_1,(c_1,s_1)), (C_2,(c_2,s_2)), (C_3,(c_3,s_3)), (C_4,(c_4,s_4)), \ldots.., (C_r,(c_r,s_r)),$$

with the implication that the rightmost element is the top element (TC).

Insertion and deletion can occur only at the top of the rA-coach stack. Two basic operations associated with rA-coach stacks are:

i. **"c-PUSH"** (to insert a new tagged coach into a rA-coach stack)
ii. **"c-POP"** (to delete a tagged coach from a rA-coach stack)

The rA-coach stack has the following two important operations too, which can be easily implemented using PUSH, POP, c-PUSH, and c-POP operations multiple times, and the properties of the data structure larray:

iii. **"e-PUSH"** for pushing an element. (to insert an element into a tagged coach (TC) of a rA-coach stack where status s is not 0, i.e. at least 1).

Figure 4. a rA-coach stack

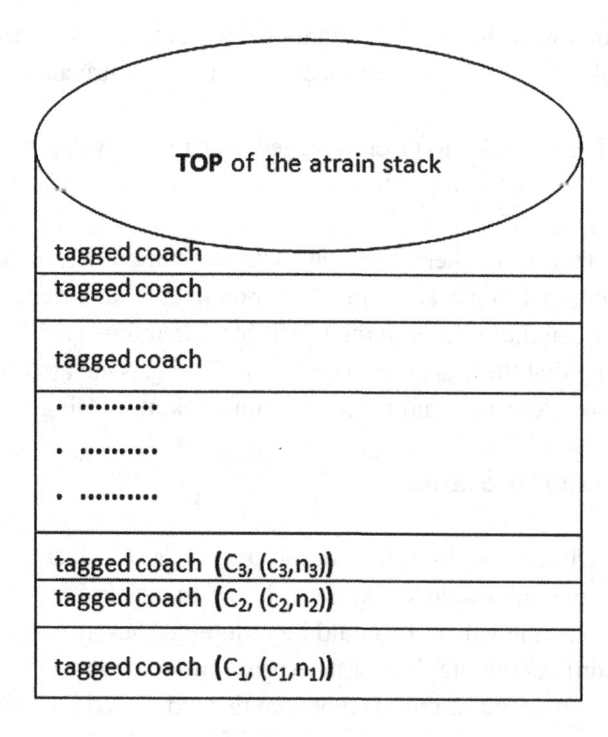

Insertion of an element (a new passenger) x inside the coach C_i is feasible if x is of same datatype (like other passengers of the coach) and if there is an empty space available inside the coach C_i.

```
If status of Cj is greater than 0 then data can be stored successfully in the
coach, otherwise insertion operation fails here. After each successful inser-
tion, the status s of the coach is to be updated by doing s = s - 1.
```

For insertion of x, we can replace the lowest indexed passenger ε of C_i with x.

iv. **"e-POP"** for popping an element. (to delete an element from a tagged coach of a rA-coach stack, retaining the tagged coach in the memory adjusting its status s by doing s $\leftarrow$ s+1).

We can delete a data element e_{ij} from the coach C_i. Deletion of a data (passenger) from a coach means replacement of the data by an ε element (of same datatype). Consequently, if $e_{ij} = \varepsilon$, then the question of deletion does not arise. Here it is pre-assumed that e_{ij} is a non-ε member element of the coach C_i in the atrain stack.

For j = 1, 2, ..., r, deletion of e_{ij} is done by replacing it by the null element ε, and updating the availability-status n by doing n = n+1. Deletion of a data element (passenger) does not affect the size r of the coach.

For example, consider the tagged coach $[C_i, (c_i,m)]$ where

$C_i = < e_{i1}, e_{i2}, e_{i3}, e_{i4}, \ldots\ldots, e_{ir} >$.

If we delete e_{i3} from the coach C_i, then the updated tagged coach will be $[C_i, (c_i, m+1)]$ where

$C_i = < e_{i1}, e_{i2}, \varepsilon, e_{i4}, \ldots\ldots, e_{ir} >$.

It can be noted that the data structure rT-coach stack is a special case of the data structure r-train stack, the data structure rA-coach stack is a special case of the data structure r-atrain stack. The classical stack (in Computer Science) is a '1A-coach stack', special case of the data structures rA-coach stack for r = 1.

r-TRAIN QUEUE AND r-ATRAIN QUEUE

In this section we introduce two new data structures for big data:

1. 'r-train queue' or 'train queue' in short, and
2. 'r-atrain queue' or 'atrain queue' in short.

The concept of the terminologies: coach, status and tag in a train queue are similar to those of a coach in a train stack. The concept of the terminologies: coach, status, tag, CD-table in an atrain queue are similar to those of a coach in an atrain stack.

A 'r-train queue' (or, train queue) is a crisp queue of r-trains containing data of homogeneous data type across the whole queue. It is a linear data structure in which deletion of a train can take place only at one end called the 'front' and insertion of a train can take place only at the other one end called the 'rear', in the manner of FIFO list, as shown in Figure 5.

In the larray of a train queue, there are two pointer variables: FRONT and REAR. The FRONT contains the location of the front TC and the REAR contains the location of the rear TC. If FRONT = Null, then the train queue is empty. Whenever a TC is deleted from the train queue, the value of FRONT gets incremented by 1. Similarly, whenever a TC is added to the train queue, the value of REAR gets incremented by 1.

A 'rT-coach queue' is a crisp queue of tagged coaches (of trains) containing data of homogeneous data type. It is a linear data structure in which deletion of tagged coach can take place only at one end called the 'front' and insertion of a tagged coach can take place only at the other one end called the 'rear', in the manner of FIFO list, as shown in Figure 6.

A 'r-atrain queue' (or, atrain queue) is a crisp queue of r-atrains containing data of heterogeneous data type, where each coach is homogeneous in itself. Datatypes of different coaches are different. Thus it is a linear data structure in which deletion of an atrain can take place only at one end called the 'front' and insertion of an atrain can take place only at the other one end called the 'rear', in the manner of FIFO list, as shown in Figure 7.

The datatype in an atrain queue may vary from coach to coach (unlike in train queue), but in a coach all data must be homogeneous i.e. of identical datatype. Thus each coach is homogeneous, although the atrain queue is heterogeneous. In this sense, 'atrain queue' is regarded as a heterogeneous data structure.

A 'rA-coach queue' is a crisp queue of tagged coaches containing data of heterogeneous data type (see Figure 8).

Figure 5. A train queue

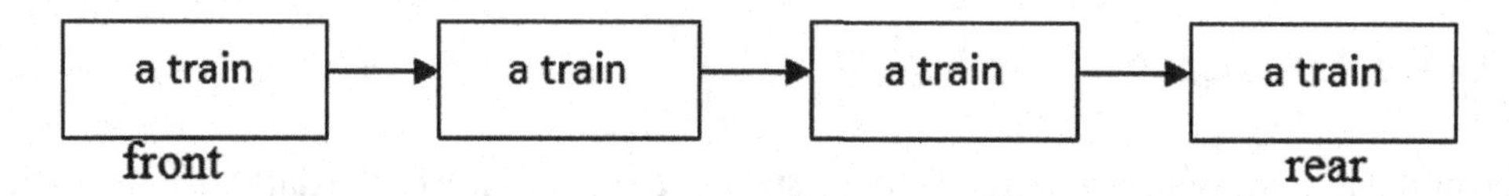

Figure 6. A rT-coach queue

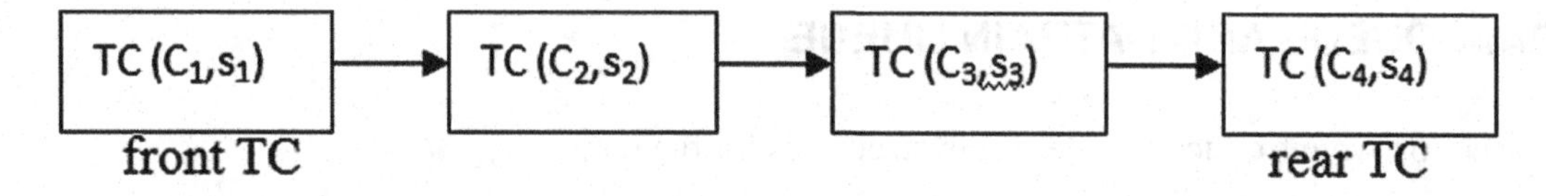

Figure 7. An atrain queue

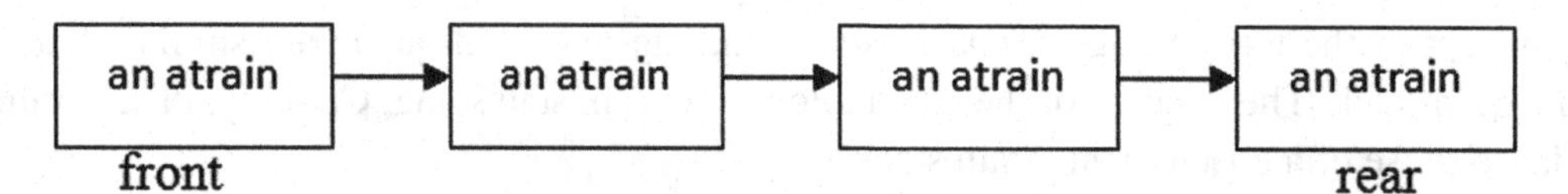

Figure 8. A rA-coach queue

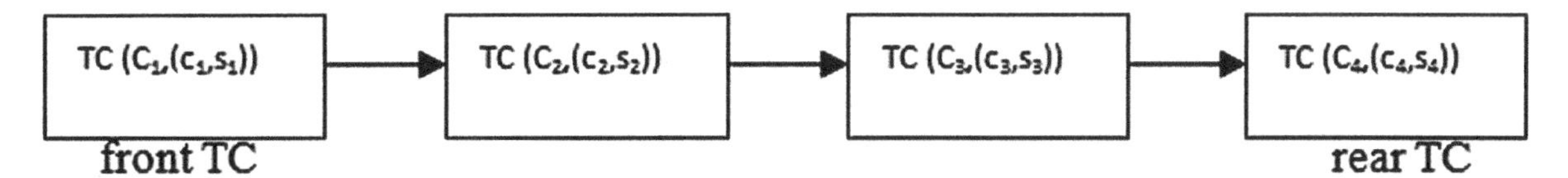

In an atrain queue or rA-coach queue, different TCs are of different sizes depending upon the CD-table concerned.

It can be noted that the data structure rT-coach queue is a special case of the data structure r-train queue, the data structure rA-coach queue is a special case of the data structure r-atrain queue. The classical queue is a special case of the data structures r-train queue and r-atrain queue.

r-TRAIN BINARY TREE AND r-ATRAIN BINARY TREE

In this section we introduce two new non-linear data structures for big data:

1. 'r-train binary tree' or 'train binary tree' in short, and
2. 'r-atrain binary tree' or 'atrain binary tree' in short.

They are basically extension of the notion of classical binary tree, and are defined in a similar way in the context of train-atrain architecture for big data.

The concept of the terminologies: coach, status and tag in a train binary tree or train tree are similar to those of a coach in a train stack. The concept of the terminologies: coach, status, tag, CD-table in an atrain binary tree or atrain tree are similar to those of a coach in an atrain stack.

A r-train binary tree (or train binary tree, in short) T is defined as a finite set of r-trains called *train-nodes* such that:

a. T is empty (called the *null tree* or *empty tree*), or
b. T contains a distinguished train-node R called the *root-train* of T, and the remaining train-nodes of T form an ordered pair of disjoint train binary trees T_1 and T_2.

If T does contain a root-train R, then the two train binary trees T_1 and T_2 are called respectively *left train subtree* and *right train subtree* of the train binary tree R. If T_1 is non-empty then its root-train is called the left successor of R and if T_2 is non-empty then its root-train is called the right successor of R (see Figure 9). The concept of left child train, right child train, parent train, sibling trains, etc. can also be visualized in a classical way.

A rT-coach binary tree T is defined as a finite set of tagged train coaches called *coach-nodes* such that:

a. T is empty (called the *null tree* or *empty tree*), or
b. T contains a distinguished coach-node R called the *root-coach* of T, and the remaining coach-nodes of T form an ordered pair of disjoint rT-coach binary trees T_1 and T_2 (see Figure 10).

Figure 9. A train binary tree

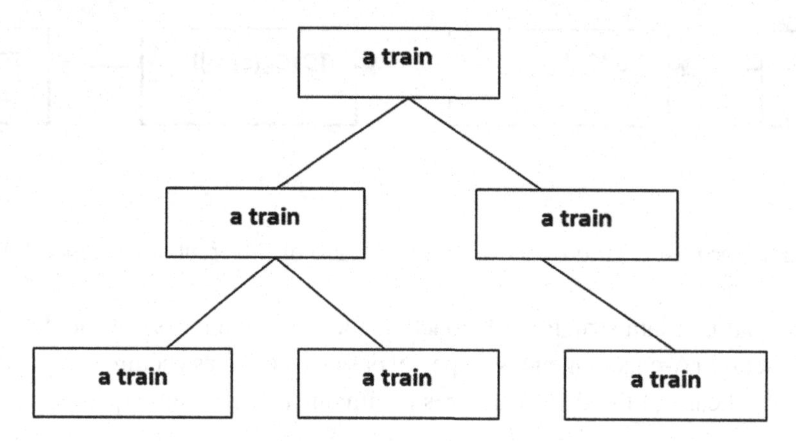

Figure 10. A rT-coach binary tree

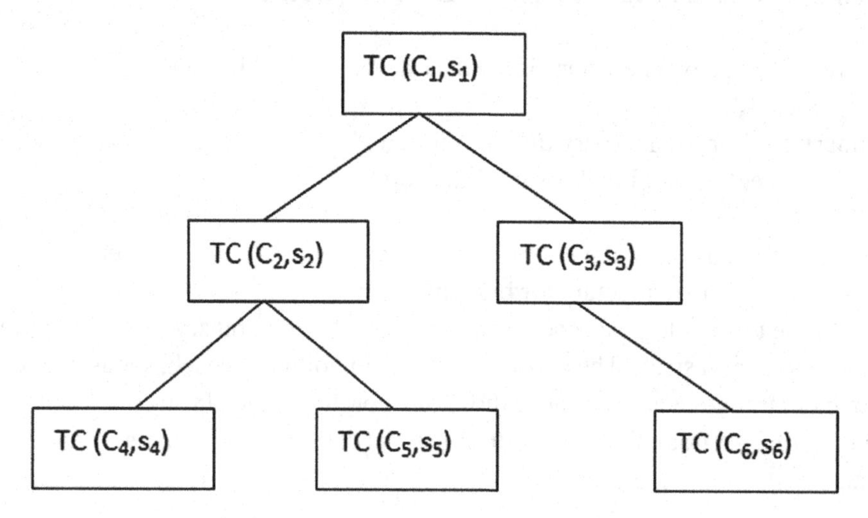

A r-atrain binary tree (or, atrain binary tree, in short) can also be defined in an analogous way (see Figure 11) with tagged coaches.

A rA-coach binary tree T is defined as a finite set of tagged atrain coaches called *coach-nodes* such that:

a. T is empty (called the *null tree* or *empty tree*), or
b. T contains a distinguished coach-node R called the *root-coach* of T, and the remaining coach- nodes of T form an ordered pair of disjoint rA-coach binary trees T_1 and T_2 (see Figure 12).

A r-train tree (or train tree in short) T is defined as a non-empty finite set of r-trains called *train-nodes* such that:

a. T contains a distinguished train-node R called the *root-train* of T, and
b. the remainingtrain-nodes of T form an ordered collection of zero or more number of disjoint train trees T_1, T_2, …, T_m.

Figure 11. An atrain binary tree

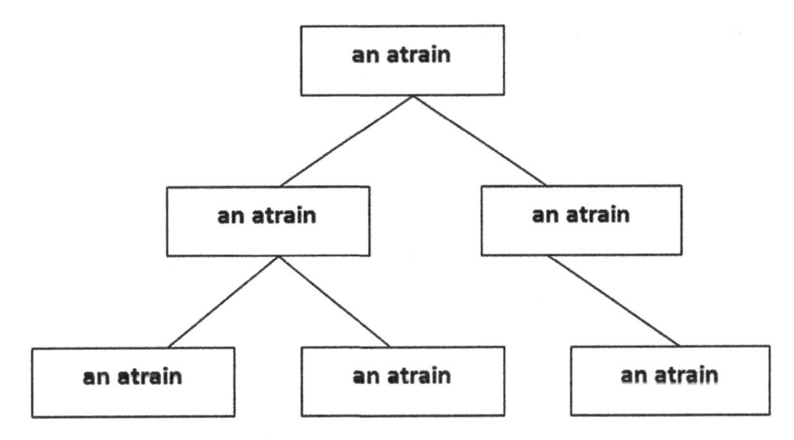

Figure 12. A rA-coach binary tree

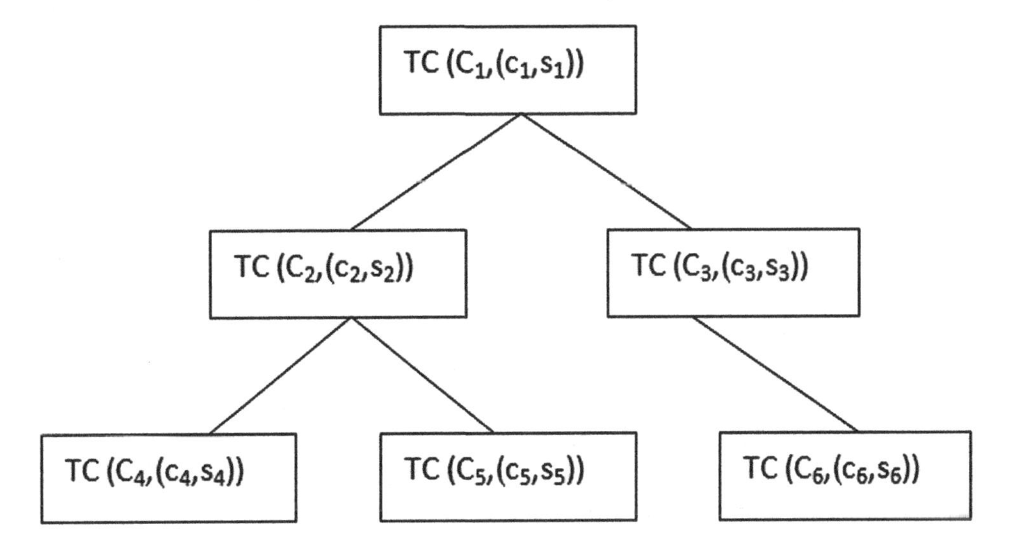

The train trees T_1, T_2, …, T_m are called train subtrees of the *root-train* R, and the root-trains of T_1, T_2, …, T_m are called successors of R. The concept of a children trains, parent train, sibling trains, etc. can be visualized in a classical way.

A r-atrain tree (or atrain tree, in short), rT-coach tree and rA-coach tree can be defined in an analogous way. The data structures r-train, r-atrain, r-train tree, and r-atrain tree should not be confused with any of the data structures (basically for multidimensional data) of the group: X-tree, R-tree, R+-trees, R*-trees, M-tree, KD-tree, PQ-tree, SPQR-tree, Hilbert R-tree, etc.

It may be noted that the data structure rT-coach binary tree is a special case of the data structure r-train binary tree, the data structure rA-coach binary tree is a special case of the data structure r-atrain binary tree. The classical binary tree is a special case of the data structures r-train binary tree and r-atrain binary tree. Similarly the classical tree is a special case of the data structures r-train tree and r-atrain tree. The ADS (unitier or multitier) with the new type of network topologies 'Multi-horse Cart Topology' and

'Cycle Topology' is the appropriate distributed system to implement atrain tree for big data of any 4Vs of any momentum as the ADS is scalable upto any desired extent both in breadth and depth.

EMPIRICAL ANALYSIS

Today's supercomputer or multiprocessor system can provide huge parallelism to the computer programmers. It is fact that in most of the giant organizations, the corresponding systems have to deal with heterogeneous big data for which the data structures of the existing literature cannot be helpful in any way because of their huge limitations in particular while working upon distributed storage architecture. The very common and frequent operations like Insertion, deletion, searching, etc. are required to be much faster for heterogeneous big data. The situations of big data explosions cannot be controlled by the simple rudimentary data structures such as arrays, linked lists, hash tables, binary search trees, dictionary, etc. Obviously, there is a genuine need of a dash of creativity of a new heterogeneous data structure which at the same time must be of rudimentary in nature. The heterogeneous data structure r-atrain (atrain) is the only data structure available in the literature for heterogeneous big data. It is also a reasonably space efficient data structure although memory space is not costly nowadays. But faster execution of operations contribute a lot to the growth of the organizations, especially of those who are giants. The most important merit is that parallel processing will be very easier for heterogeneous big data if stored and processed using the data structure r-atrain in ADS (Biswas, 2015a).

One of the major topic in Big Data Science is the "*Big Data Statistics*" recently introduced in (Biswas, 2016, 2014c). If the populations (R-populations or *NR-populations*) be massive in size then such kind of Statistics (R-Statistics and *NR-Statistics*) are to be called by "*Big Data Statistics*". The "Big Data Statistics" is a major subject for the future Statisticians where there will be many real populations consisting of big data expanding very fast in 4Vs, unlike the Statistics of past. It is observed that the existing volume of the giant subject Statistics is actually 'R-Statistics', being one side of the coin. The other side of the coin is *NR-Statistics*, and thus the giant subject Statistics has been now reshaped in (Biswas, 2016, 2014c) as the physical union of two siblings R-Statistics and NR-Statistics. This work (Biswas, 2016) is a major breakthrough in the giant subject Statistics. The "Big Data Statistics", be it in R-Statistics or in *NR-Statistics*, cannot be studied without an appropriate data structure for it. Otherwise the subject will remain in hibernation to the statisticians, or at best can progress with some growth but theoretically just. The Big Data Statistics cannot be well studied without any heterogeneous data structure for big data. Consequently the big data structures train and atrains, alongwith its family members: homogeneous stacks 'train stack' and 'rT-coach stack', heterogeneous stacks 'atrain stack' and 'rA-coach stack', homogeneous queues 'train queue' and 'rT-coach queue', heterogeneous queues 'atrain queue' and 'rA-coach queue', homogeneous binary trees 'train binary tree' and 'rT-coach binary tree', heterogeneous binary trees 'atrain binary tree' and 'rA-coach binary tree', homogeneous trees 'train tree' and 'rT-coach tree', heterogeneous trees 'atrain tree' and 'rA-coach tree', etc. can play a huge role to the present-day statisticians in the area of 'Big Data Statistics', in due time.

Shifting our focus of attention from precise crisp data to imprecise data, it can be observed that the amount of fuzzy data in our real life environment is also knocking the computer scientists and the soft-computing experts to a case of a new type of big data which we call by *Big Soft Data* (Biswas, 2016). In fact, if there is no debate, one can realize that big soft data are more in volume than the crisp big data in our real life scenario. The big soft data in most of the cases are modeled using fuzzy numbers for soft computing and computer programming. The most popular fuzzy numbers for soft computing with soft big data are triangular fuzzy numbers and trapezoidal fuzzy numbers. Unfortunately, a major failure of triangular fuzzy numbers and trapezoidal fuzzy numbers have been recently unearthed in (Biswas, 2015c), where it has been rigorously justified that the drawbacks are due to the practical reasons that there is no existing data structures in Computer Science which can support the basic operations of triangular fuzzy numbers and trapezoidal fuzzy numbers (for instance, the product of two triangular fuzzy numbers is not in general a triangular fuzzy number, and consequently the data structure used for the operands by a programmer cannot be a suitable or compatible one to store the resultant fuzzy number). This deficit has been leading to the programmers, mathematicians, statisticians, scientists, engineers, and academicians to a paralyzed situation in most of the cases of their soft computing analysis, in particular while dealing with big soft data. For details about the fact of non-compatibility of the notion of the triangular fuzzy numbers and trapezoidal fuzzy numbers with any existing data structures, one could view (Biswas, 2015c). In fact, considering the drawbacks of the notion of fuzzy numbers studied in (Biswas, 2015c), it is obvious that the new notion of fuzzy numbers called by 'Z Numbers' introduced by Zadeh in (Zadeh, 2011) does also carry multiple faults because of the reason that a Z-number is an ordered pair of fuzzy numbers where both the fuzzy numbers are in most of the cases triangular fuzzy numbers (or, trapezoidal fuzzy numbers). In our future work we will deal with the revised notion of fuzzy number called by T-fuzzy numbers and Z-fuzzy numbers introduced in (Biswas, 2015c) which can be well exercised with the help of our data structures train or atrain (and also with their family members), while dealing with big soft data. It may be noted that Z-numbers and Z-fuzzy numbers are two different notions.

On the issue of large or big data, another important issue has been recently unearthed. Since the inception of fuzzy theory (Zadeh, 1965) whose 50 years has been recently celebrated in 2015 by the world scientists, an important path-breaking result of Soft Computing is reported in (Biswas, 2015b) which justifies that 'Fuzzy Theory' is not appropriate for large size fuzzy problems if we are in quest of good and reliable results, and consequently Big Soft Data needs to be dealt with a very careful choice of an appropriate soft-computing theory by the concerned decision makers. Although a huge volume of literature have been published by a large number of scientists in a large number of journals/books during the last five decades, but the fact established in (Biswas, 2015b) cannot be ignored, in particular if it is the case of big soft data. However, there are few cases (Biswas, 2015b, 2015d), not of soft big data or soft large data, where Fuzzy Theory can play dominantly compared to any other theory of soft computing.

FUTURE RESEARCH DIRECTION

The existing data structures, network topologies and type of distributed system are not sufficiently rich to deal with big data. The existing network topologies like tree topology or bus/ring/star/mesh/hybrid topologies seem to be weak topologies for big data processing. For a success, there is no other way but to develop 'new data structures', 'new type of distributed systems' having a very fast and tremendous extent of mutual compatibility and mutual understanding with the new data structures, 'new type of network topologies' to support the new distributed system, and of course 'new mathematical/logical theory' models. Needless to mention that the next important issue is how to integrate all these 'new' to make ultimately a single and simple scalable system to the laymen users

The architecture of a new type of distributed system 'Atrain Distributed System' (ADS) is exclusively designed for processing big data (Biswas, 2015a). The huge merit of ADS stands on the fact that both the data structures train and atrain are 100% compatible with the new distributed system 'ADS' for processing big data, in particular to coup easily with 4Vs of any momentum. The strong merit of the atrain distributed system (ADS) is that it is an infinitely scalable architecture (along breadth and depth both) of distributed system for processing big data of any momentum of 4Vs. It is so constructed that it has 100% compatibility with the data structure atrain (and train) exclusively discovered for big data. The data structures train tree and atrain tree can be well implemented in atrain distributed systems for big data. Although big data is explosively expanding with 4Vs, the subject has not been growing in the same pace. One of the reasons is that the existing data structures are not the appropriate data structures for big data. The first attempt to introduce a data structure for big data is the discovery of the data structures atrain (and train), with the distributed system ADS of new type of network topologies 'Multi-horse Cart Topology' and 'Cycle Topology'. An important problem to the computer scientists is to develop a new but simple big data language called by "ADSL" (Atrain Distributed System Language) which can easily be used by any laymen user at the PC of an ADS to download unlimited amount of relevant big data of any heterogeneous datatype (if not of homogeneous datatype) from the cyberspace, to upload unlimited amount of big data of any heterogeneous datatype (or homogeneous datatype) in the cyberspace, to store the downloaded big data online in the coaches of PC/DCs of ADS in an organized way of atrain (train) architecture, to answer any query be it arithmetical or statistical or relational query or imprecise query on big data.

The next work could also be to study these big data structures with sufficient examples, to introduce the data structures 'train graph' and 'atrain graph' considering the big data in the topologies of communication network, in particular while a large number of communication networks logically merge together to form a singly network and to work efficiently as a single network as it seems to the laymen users.

The "Big Data Universe" needs intensive attention not only just for finding solutions to the present problem of explosive expansion, but also for the tremendous future expansion. It is fact that the present 4Ns are lagging behind the present 4Vs. Everyday's big data is bigger than the previous day's big data in the big data universe. The data structure atrain for big data and the distributed system ADS for big data can deal with any amount of 4Vs because of its scalability property upto any desired amount both in breadth and depth. However, for the future big data of the 'Big Data Universe', the train/atrain data structures can be further extended embedded with the families of data structures proposed in this chapter to create new big data structures viz. m-train of r-trains, m-atrain of r-atrains, m-train of r-train stacks, m-atrain of r-atrain stacks, m-train of r-train queues, m-atrain of r-atrain queues, m-train of r-train binary trees, m-atrain of r-atrain binary trees, etc. depending upon the 4Vs of future big data. Consequently, the corresponding distributed system EADS ('Extended ADS') of several designs can be created by developing new methods on how to integrate multiple ADSs to make an EADS, designing new type of Hybrid Topologies of 'Multi-horse Cart Topology', 'Cycle Topology' and other existing classical topologies.

CONCLUSION

To begin this chapter and its main content, we initially presented the preliminaries of two basic and fundamental data structures (Biswas, 2015a) for storing big data. The data structure 'r-train' (or 'train' in short) is a homogeneous data structure which can deal with a big data of homogeneous datatype efficiently, as used in (Alam, 2013) for fast computing of multiplication of large matrices. The data structure r-atrain (or, atrain) is a robust kind of dynamic heterogeneous data structure which encapsulates the merits of the arrays and of the linked lists, but are different from them and can deal with big data of heterogeneous datatype. Today's supercomputer or multiprocessor system which can provide huge parallelism has become the dominant computing platform (through the proliferation of multi-core processors), and the term has come to stand for highly flexible advanced level of data structures that can be accessed by multiple threads which may actually access heterogeneous data simultaneously, that can run on different processors simultaneously. In most of the giant business organizations, the system has to deal with a large volume of heterogeneous data for which the data structures of the existing literature cannot always lead to the desired optimal satisfaction. The very common and frequent operations like Insertion, deletion, searching, etc. are required to be much faster even if the data are huge in number, even if the data are of heterogeneous types. Such situations require some way or some method which work more efficiently than the simple rudimentary data structures such as arrays, linked lists, hash tables, binary search trees, dictionary, etc. Obviously, there is a need of a dash of creativity of a new or better performed heterogeneous data structure which at the same time must be of rudimentary in nature. The data structure r-atrain (atrain) is neither a dynamic array nor a HAT. It is reasonably space efficient as well. Parallel processing will be easier for huge amount of heterogeneous data if stored using the data structure r-atrain. The pilot of a atrain is, in general, a linked list. But, if we are sure that there will be no requirement of any extra coach in future, then it is better to implement pilot as an array. Although the notion of r-atrain is closely analogous to that of r-train, but none conflicts the interest of other in application areas. Coaches in a r-train can store homogeneous data only, not heterogeneous data. But in a r-atrain the coaches accommodate heterogeneous data (although the data of a coach are always homogeneous and cannot be heterogeneous). In r-train, all coaches are of common datatype. For working with homogeneous data train is suitable, not atrain. However, for working with heterogeneous data, atrain is suitable while train cannot be applicable. The introduction of CD-Table is a pre-requisite to create any r-atrain for an organization. But addition of new datatypes and corresponding codes can be decided and incorporated at any later stages on retaining all the existing records in the table. The CD-Table is a kind of local document which may vary from organization to organization. The 'status' of a coach at any moment of time in a train reveals only one information which is about the availability of seat inside this coach at that time, whereas the 'status' of a coach in a r-train reveals two information about the coach one of which is same as in the case of a train i.e. about the availability of seat inside this coach at that time, and the other is about the Code of the datatype (as per CD-Table) of the valid contents of the coach. The natural number r is suitably predecided and fixed by the programmer depending upon the problem under consideration and also upon the organization/industry for which the problem is posed. We do not feel it appropriate to propose r in a r-train or in a r-atrain as a variable. Both the notion of r-train and r-atrain can be made much more flexible if r is made to vary from coach to coach. But, if we do so, the overhead cost/complexity over the totality of the implementation task may dominate the extra benefit of flexibility expected to be exploited. Making r a variable is in fact not required because it is alternatively equivalent to opening new empty coaches whenever required; and opening a new coach is an easy task here in a r-train or in a r-atrain. An undesirable situation apparently seems to happen if we have to open a new empty coach just for storing one or two or very less number of data elements, in particular while r is not a small integer. But in giant organizations of todays fast and very dynamic business trends around the world, such situations in general will surely remain for temporary tenure only, and hence of minor concern or of no concern at all to those organizations. Nowadays memory space is not costly, but faster execution of operations contribute a lot to the growth of the organizations, especially of those who are giants.

The 'Data Structures for Big Data' is to be regarded as a new subject, not just as a new topic in Big Data Science, considering the explosive momentum of the big data. A programmer, while dealing with big data, may need to store millions of files using stacks, millions of images using queues, millions of tables using binary trees, millions of networks using graphs/multigraphs, etc. Consequently, in this chapter we introduce new useful data structures for big data which are: homogeneous stacks 'train stack' and 'rT-coach stack', heterogeneous stacks 'atrain stack' and 'rA-coach stack', homogeneous queues 'train queue' and 'rT-coach queue', heterogeneous queues 'atrain queue' and 'rA-coach queue', homogeneous binary trees 'train binary tree' and 'rT-coach binary tree', heterogeneous binary trees 'atrain binary tree' and 'rA-coach binary tree', homogeneous trees 'train tree' and 'rT-coach tree', heterogeneous trees 'atrain tree' and 'rA-coach tree', to enrich the new subject 'Data Structures for Big Data' with the extended notion of the architecture of the data structures r-atrain (atrain) and r-train (train) for big data. The natural number r is fixed for a stack / queue / binary tree or tree, but could be different for different stacks / queues / binary trees or trees. The potential of these big data structures lies in the fact that they are well applicable in case of structured data like: record, file, relational database and spreadsheet, etc. or semi-structured data like XML, other markup languages, email, etc. or even unstructured data like: books, journals, documents, metadata, health records, audio, video, analog data, images, files, and unstructured text such as the body of an e-mail message, web page, or word-processor document, etc. All these big data structures can be well implemented in the distributed system ADS (Biswas, 2015a) which is exclusively designed for big data on infinitely scalable architecture to deal with any 4Vs.

REFERENCES

Alam, B. (2013). Matrix Multiplication using r-Train Data Structure, 2013 AASRI Conference on Parallel and Distributed Computing Systems. *AASRI Procedia*, *5*, 189-193.

Berman, J. J. (2013). Principles of Big Data: Preparing, Sharing, and Analyzing Complex Information. Morgan Kaufmann (Elsevier) Publisher.

Biswas, R. (2011). r-Train (Train): A New Flexible Dynamic Data Structure. *Information: An International Journal (Japan)*, *14*(4), 1231–1246.

Biswas, R. (2012). Heterogeneous Data Structure "r-Atrain". *Information: An International Journal (Japan)*, *15*(2), 879–902.

Biswas, R. (2013a). Theory of Solid Matrices & Solid Latrices, Introducing New Data Structures MA, MT: For Big Data. *International Journal of Algebra*, *7*(16), 767–789.

Biswas, R. (2013b). *Heterogeneous Data Structure "r-Atrain". In Global Trends in Knowledge Representation and Computational Intelligence*. IGI Global.

Biswas, R. (2014a). Processing of Heterogeneous Big Data in an Atrain Distributed System (ADS) Using the Heterogeneous Data Structure r-Atrain. *International Journal of Computing and Optimization*, *1*(1), 17–45.

Biswas, R. (2014b). Data Structures for Big Data, *Int. Journal of Computing and Optimization*, *1*, 73–93.

Biswas, R. (2014c). Introducing Soft Statistical Measures. *The Journal of Fuzzy Mathematics*, *22*(4), 819–851.

Biswas, R. (2015a). Atrain Distributed System (ADS): An Infinitely Scalable Architecture for Processing Big Data of Any 4Vs. In Computational Intelligence for Big Data Analysis Frontier Advances and Applications. Springer International Publishing.

Biswas, R. (2015b). *Is 'Fuzzy Theory' An Appropriate Tool For Large Size Problems?* Heidelberg, Germany: Springer.

Biswas, R. (2015c). *Is 'Fuzzy Theory' An Appropriate Tool For Large Size Decision Problems? In Imprecision and Uncertainty in Information Representation and Processing*. Heidelberg, Germany: Springer.

Biswas, R. (2015d). "Theory of CESFM": A Proposal to FIFA & IFAB for a new 'Continuous Evaluation Fuzzy Method' of Deciding the WINNER of a Football Match that Would Have Otherwise been Drawn or Tied after 90 Minutes of Play. *The Journal of Fuzzy Mathematics*, *23*(4), 991–1008.

Biswas, R. (2016in Press). Introducing 'NR-Statistics': A New Direction in "Statistics". In S. J. John (Ed.), *Generalized and Hybrid Set Structures and Applications for Soft Computing*. IGI Global. doi:10.4018/978-1-4666-9798-0.ch023

Feinleib, D. (2013). Big Data Demystified: How Big Data Is Changing The Way We Live, Love And Learn. The Big Data Group Publisher, LLC.

Mayer-Schönberger, V., & Cukier, K. (2013). BIG DATA: A Revolution That Will Transform How We Live, Work, and Think, Eamon Dolan/Houghton Mifflin Harcourt Publisher.

Needham, J. (2013). *Disruptive Possibilities: How Big Data Changes Everything*. O'Reilly Publisher.

Zadeh, L. A. (1965). Fuzzy Sets. *Information and Control*, *8*(3), 338–353. doi:10.1016/S0019-9958(65)90241-X

Zadeh, L. A. (2011). A Note on Z-numbers. *Information Sciences*, *181*(14), 2923–2932. doi:10.1016/j.ins.2011.02.022

KEY TERMS AND DEFINITIONS

Atrain: It is the heterogeneous and dynamic data structure to deal with big data in any 4Vs.

Atrain Binary Tree: A binary tree where each node contains an atrain.

Atrain Distributed System (ADS): A special designed distributed system with an infinitely scalable architecture for processing big data of any 4Vs.

Atrain Queue: A queue of atrains storing heterogeneous big data.

Atrain Stack: A stack of atrains storing heterogeneous big data.

Atrain Tree: A tree where each node contains an atrain.

Code of Datatype (CD) Table: A table created by the concerned organization to fix integer code for each datatype under use in the organization. This is not an absolute set of codes to be followed universally by every organization, but it is a local document for the concerned organization. For different organizations, this table could be different.

Coach: By a coach C of a train or atrain we mean a pair (A,**e**) where A is a non-empty larray (could be a null larray) and **e** is an address in the memory. Here **e** is basically a kind of link address. Its significance is that it says the address of the next coach, and thus it links two coaches in the train or atrain.

Cycle Topology: A network topology for storing big data in ADS looking like a cycle.

Larray: Larray stands for "Like ARRAY". A larray is like an array of elements of identical datatype, where zero or more number of elements may be null element (i.e. no element or empty).

Multi-Horse Cart Topology: A network topology for storing big data in the distributed system ADS looking like a multi-horse cart.

Pilot: It is the linked list of an atrain (train).

rA-Coach Binary Tree: A binary tree where each node contains an atrain coach.

rA-Coach Queue: A queue of atrain coaches storing heterogeneous big data.

rA-Coach Stack: A stack of atrain coaches storing heterogeneous big data.

rA-Coach Tree: A tree where each node contains an atrain coach.

rT-Coach Binary Tree: A binary tree where each node contains a train coach.

rT-Coach Queue: A queue of train coaches storing homogeneous big data.

rt-Coach Stack: A stack of train coaches storing homogeneous big data.

rT-Coach Tree: A tree where each node contains a train coach.

Train: It is the homogeneous data structure to deal with big data in any 4Vs.

Train Binary Tree: A binary tree where each node contains a train.

Train Queue: A queue of trains storing homogeneous big data.

Train Stack: A stack of trains storing homogeneous big data.

Train Tree: A tree where each node contains a train.

Chapter 3
Big Data Mining

N. G. Bhuvaneswari Amma
Indian Institute of Information Technology Srirangam, India

ABSTRACT

Big data is a term used to describe very large amount of structured, semi-structured and unstructured data that is difficult to process using the traditional processing techniques. It is now expanding in all science and engineering domains. The key attributes of big data are volume, velocity, variety, validity, veracity, value, and visibility. In today's world, everyone is using social networking applications like Facebook, Twitter, YouTube, etc. These applications allow the users to create the contents for free of cost and it becomes huge volume of web data. These data are important in the competitive business world for making decisions. In this context, big data mining plays a major role which is different from the traditional data mining. The process of extracting useful information from large datasets or streams of data, due to its volume, velocity, variety, validity, veracity, value and visibility is termed as Big Data Mining.

1. INTRODUCTION

Big Data is originated due to the fact that huge amount of data is created every day like Google has more than 1 billion queries per day, Twitter has more than 250 million tweets per day, Facebook has more than 800 million updates per day, and YouTube has more than 4 billion views per day etc. These data are produced in the order of zetabytes, and it is growing around 40% every year (Wei & Albert, 2012). The need for Big Data Mining (BDM) is to extract useful information from large datasets because companies like Google, Apple, Facebook, Yahoo, Twitter are started to look carefully to these data to find useful patterns to improve their user experience. With the help of BDM, one can find useful pattern from mobile data too such as what the users do with the mobile.

1.1 Dimensions of Big Data

Big data differs from other data in seven dimensions such as Volume, Velocity, Variety, Validity, Veracity, Value and Variability. Table 1 shows the seven dimensions of big data with the characteristic of all the seven Vs. The data used in BDM must be based on the seven Vs.

DOI: 10.4018/978-1-5225-0182-4.ch003

Table 1. Dimensions of big data

S.No	Dimensions	Characteristics
1	Volume	Data at rest
2	Velocity	Data in motion
3	Variety	Data in many forms
4	Validity	Data in live
5	Veracity	Data in doubt
6	Value	Data to make decisions
7	Variability	Data in change

1.2 Need for BDM

The main objective of BDM is knowledge extraction from big data which is used in the process of Business Intelligence (BI). Figure 1 shows the steps in BI. It consists of four steps namely Data Acquisition, Information Conversion, Knowledge Extraction, and Actionable Plans.

1.2.1 Data to Information

The process of determining what data is to be collected and managed and in what context.

1.2.2 Information to Knowledge

The process which involves the analytical components such as data warehousing, online analytical processing, data profiling, business rule analysis, and data mining.

Figure 1. Steps in business intelligence

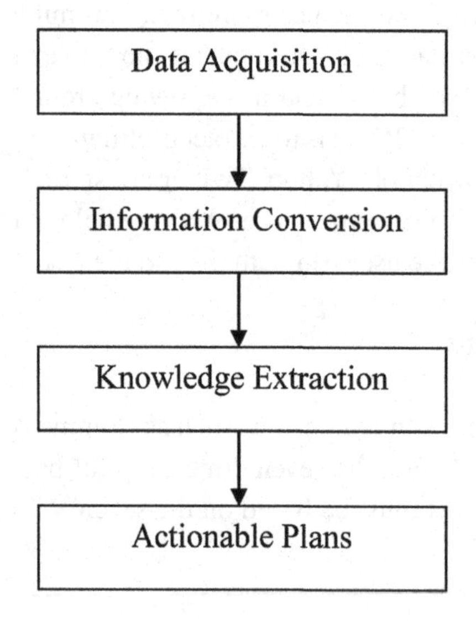

1.2.3 Knowledge to Actionable Plans

It is an important aspect in a BI process because based on the extracted knowledge the organization has to make decisions and execute the plans for the growth of the organization.

2. BIG DATA MINING ENVIRONMENT

In order to tackle data mining tasks, the mining procedure requires high computing units for data analysis and knowledge extraction. Therefore a computing platform is required to effectively access the data and computing processors. To handle small scale data mining tasks, a single desktop computer is sufficient to fulfill the goals. But for big data mining tasks, a single desktop computer is not sufficient because data is scaled far beyond the capacity of a single computer. So, big data mining platform rely on cluster computers with high performance computing platform (Xindong, Xingquan, Gang & Wei, 2014). Parallel programming tools like Map Reduce and Cloud Computing platform of big data services for the public are used to handle large number of clusters.

3. BIG DATA MINING TOOLS

This section deals with the tools that are used in BDM. The term big data is more or less related to the open source software revolution. Companies such as Facebook, Yahoo!, Twitter, LinkedIn contributed and benefitted a lot through open source software. The following are the BDM tools used nowadays:

3.1 Apache Hadoop

Apache Hadoop is an open source software for data-intensive distributed applications (Ghoting & Pednault, 2009). It is scalable, fault tolerant virtual grid operating system architecture for data storage and processing. It runs on commodity hardware. It is based on Map Reduce programming model and distributed file system called Hadoop Distributed File System (HDFS) which is fault tolerant and clustered storage architecture. It allows applications to process large amounts of data in parallel on large clusters of computing nodes. Map Reduce (Gillick, Faria &DeNero, 2006) is a job that divides the input dataset into independent subsets that are processed by map tasks in parallel. This step of mapping is then followed by a step of reducing tasks. These reduce tasks use the output of the maps to obtain the final result of the job. The projects in Apache Hadoop are Apache Pig, Apache Hive, Apache HBase, Apache ZooKeeper, Apache Cassandra etc.

3.2 Apache S4

Apache S4 is a platform for processing continuous data streams. It is designed specifically for managing data streams. The applications in S4 are designed by combining streams and processing elements in real time.

3.3 Storm

Storm is a software for streaming data-intensive distributed applications. It is similar to S4. It was developed by Nathan Marz at Twitter.

3.4 Apache Mahout

Apache Mahout is a scalable machine learning and data mining open source software based on Hadoop. It is used for implementing wide range of machine learning and data mining algorithms like classification, clustering, filtering and pattern mining.

3.5 R

R is a open source programming language and software environment designed for statistical computing and visualization. It is also used for statistical analysis of very large data sets.

3.6 MOA

MOA is a stream data mining open source software to perform data mining in real time. It is used for classification, regression, clustering, frequent item set mining and frequent graph mining. The stream framework provides an environment for defining and running stream processes using simple XML based definitions and is able to use MOA, Android and Storm. SAMOA is a new upcoming software project for distributed stream mining that will combine S4 and Storm with MOA.

3.7 Pegasus

Pegasus is a big graph mining system built on top of Map Reduce. It is used to find patterns and anomalies in massive real-world graphs.

3.8 GraphLab

GraphLab is a high-level graph parallel system built without using Map Reduce. GraphLab computes over dependent records which are stored as vertices in a large distributed graph. Algorithms in GraphLab are expressed as vertex programs which are executed in parallel on each vertex and can interact with neighboring vertices (Chang, Bai & Zhu, 2009).

4. CHALLENGES IN BIG DATA MINING

There are many important challenges in BDM that arise from the nature of data: large, diverse, and evolving (Puneet & Sanchita, 2013). The following are some of the challenges that researchers and practitioners have to deal with:

4.1 Architecture Analytics

It is not clear yet how an optimal architecture of an analytical system should be constructed to deal simultaneously with historic data and real time data. An interesting proposal is the Lambda architecture of Nathan Marz (Wei & Albert, 2012). The Lambda Architecture solves the problem of computing arbitrary functions on arbitrary data in real time by decomposing the problem into three layers: the batch layer, the serving layer, and the speed layer. It combines in the same system as Hadoop for the batch layer, and Storm for the speed layer. The properties of the system are: robust and fault tolerant, scalable, general, extensible, allows ad hoc queries, minimal maintenance, and debuggable.

4.2 Evaluation

It is important to achieve significant statistical results, and not be fooled by randomness. It is easy to go wrong with huge data sets and thousands of questions to answer at once. Also, it will be important to avoid the trap of a focus on error or speed.

4.3 Distributed Mining

Many data mining techniques are not trivial to paralyze. To have distributed versions of some methods, a lot of research is needed with practical and theoretical analysis to provide new methods.

4.4 Time Evolving Data

Data may be evolving over time, so it is important that the Big Data mining techniques should be able to adapt and in some cases to detect change first. For example, the data stream mining field has very powerful techniques for this task.

4.5 Compression

The quantity of space needed to store is very relevant while dealing with BDM. There are two main approaches: compression where nothing is lost, or sampling where the choose data is more representative. Compression takes more time and less space, so it can be considered as a transformation from time to space. Sampling losses information, but the gains in space may be in orders of magnitude.

4.6 Visualization

A main task of BDM is how to visualize the results. As the data is so big, it is very difficult to find user-friendly visualizations. New techniques, and frameworks tell and show stories will be needed, as for example the photographs, infographics and essays in the beautiful book "The Human Face of Big Data".

4.7 Hidden Big Data

Large quantities of useful data are getting lost since new data is largely untagged file- based and unstructured data. The 2012 IDC study on Big Data explains that in 2012, 23% (643 exabytes) of the digital universe would be useful for Big Data if tagged and analyzed. However, currently only 3% of the potentially useful data is tagged, and even less is analyzed.

5. APPLICATIONS OF BIG DATA MINING

The following are the applications of BDM:

1. **Data Analysis Streaming**: Streaming data in real time is becoming the fastest and most efficient way to obtain useful knowledge from what is happening now, allowing organizations to react quickly when problems appear or to detect new trends helping to improve their performance (Domingos & Hulten, 2000).
2. **Business**: Costumer personalization, churn detection.
3. **Technology**: Reducing process time from hours to seconds.
4. **Health**: Mining DNA of each person, to discover, monitor and improve health aspects of 5. every one.
5 **Smart cities**: Cities focused on sustainable economic development and high quality of life, with wise management of natural resources.

These applications will allow people to have better services, better costumer experiences, and also be healthier, as personal data will permit to prevent and detect illness much earlier than before.

6. CONCLUSION

Nowadays big data is an emerging trend and mining big data is one of the very challenging tasks and it is needed in all science and engineering domains. In order to support big data mining, high performance cluster computing platforms are required. Many BDM tools are available and they play a major role in mining big data. The future challenges and applications of BDM are also discussed. Extracting knowledge from big data provides more market value for the upcoming generation because optimal decisions should be made in an efficient manner.

REFERENCES

Chang, E. Y., Bai, H., & Zhu, K. (2009). Parallel Algorithms for Mining Large Scale Rich Media Data. *ACM International Conference on Multimedia*. doi:10.1145/1631272.1631451

Domingos, P., & Hulten, G. (2000). Mining High Speed Data Streams.*ACM SIGKDD International Conference on Knowledge Discovery and Data Mining*.

Duggal, P. S., & Paul, S. (2013). Big Data Analysis: Challenges and Solutions.*International Conference on Cloud, Big Data and Trust*.

Fan, W., & Bifet, A. (2012). Mining Big Data: Current Status, and Forecast to the Future. *SIGKDD Explorations*, *14*(2), 1–5. doi:10.1145/2481244.2481246

Ghoting, A., & Pednault, E. (2009). Hadoop-ML: An Infrastructure for the Rapid Implementation of Parallel Reusable Analytics.*Proc. Large Scale Machine Learning Workshop*.

Gillick, D., Faria, A. & DeNero, J. (2006). *MapReduce: Distributed Computing for Machine Learning*. Academic Press.

Wu, X., Zhu, X., Wu, G. Q., & Ding, W. (2014). Data Mining with Big Data. *IEEE Transactions on Knowledge and Data Engineering*, *26*(1), 97–107. doi:10.1109/TKDE.2013.109

Chapter 4
An Empirical Study of NoSQL Databases for Big Data

Wen-Chen Hu
University of North Dakota, USA

Hongyu Guo
University of Houston – Victoria, USA

Naima Kaabouch
University of North Dakota, USA

Hung-Jen Yang
National Kaohsiung Normal University, Taiwan

ABSTRACT

Relational databases have dominated the database markets for decades because they perform extremely well for traditional applications like electronic commerce and inventory systems. However, the relational databases do not suit some of the contemporary applications such as big data and cloud computing well because of various reasons like their low scalability and unable to handle a high volume of data. NoSQL (not only SQL) databases are part of the solution for developing those newer applications. The approach they use is different from the one used by relational databases. This chapter discusses NoSQL databases by using an empirical instead of theoretical approach. Other than introducing the types and features of generic NoSQL databases, practical NoSQL database programming and usage are shown by using MongoDB, a NoSQL database. A summary of this research is given at the end of this chapter.

INTRODUCTION

Much of current data processing requires horizontal scaling, faster speed, and processing different kinds of data and relational databases are not able to meet the requirements adequately. A NoSQL database is to meet the needs by providing a simple and efficient mechanism for data storage and retrieval. The approach it uses is different from the one used by a relational database. An RDBMS (relational database management system) is a general-purpose data store, whereas a NoSQL database is normally a key-value store for simple insertion and retrieval operations. This chapter discusses the NoSQL databases by using an empirical approach. A NoSQL database, MongoDB, is used to show how to program and use NoSQL databases.

DOI: 10.4018/978-1-5225-0182-4.ch004

Importance of Big Data

In the information age, data is generated explosively. For example, everyday there are 230 million tweets sent, 294 billion emails delivered, and 100 terabytes of data uploaded to Facebook according to IDC (2012). Important and useful information such as crime prevention and customer buying patterns could be buried inside the huge amount of unstructured data. How to effectively manage and use the big data is a big headache for organizations. Many IT researchers and scholars and organizations start working on this problem. Even the Obama Administration (The White House, 2012) announced a "Big Data Research and Development Initiative." Several US Federal departments and agencies have pledged more than $200 million for this big data initiative. The departments and agencies and their big data themes include

- Together National Science Foundation (NSF) and the National Institutes of Health (NIH): *Core Techniques and Technologies for Advancing Big Data Science & Engineering*,
- National Science Foundation (NSF): Including funding the big data solicitations, keeping with its focus on basic research, and implementing a comprehensive, long-term big data strategy,
- Department of Defense (DOD): *Data to Decisions*,
- National Institutes of Health (NIH): *1000 Genomes Project Data Available on Cloud*,
- Department of Energy (DOE): *Scientific Discovery Through Advanced Computing*, and
- US Geological Survey (USGS): *Big Data for Earth System Science.*

Big data is everywhere now and valuable information is hiding in it. In the past, this information was simply ignored and opportunities were missed. Realizing the great importance of big data, organizations scramble to find hidden information buried in big data and try to make the best use of it.

Features of NoSQL Databases

Many of contemporary applications require the features of being generic, distributed, open-source, and scalable. The features are also some of the benefits of NoSQL databases including (Han, E, Le, & Du, 2011):

- NoSQL databases are able to handle structured, semi-structured, and unstructured data, not just semi-structured data for relational databases.
- Compared to relational databases, NoSQL databases are simple and therefore are faster.
- Most NoSQL databases allow object-oriented programming, which is the most popular programming paradigm.
- NoSQL databases include the feature of horizontal scalability, which is the ability to connect multiple NoSQL databases so that they work as a single logical unit.

Relational databases can no longer meet the requirements of some of the mobile-age applications, which desire simple, efficient, and scalable databases. The emergence of NoSQL databases is to meet the needs of newer applications. However, from the history of databases, none of other databases has successfully replaced relational databases, which have the greatest advantages of easy-to-use. NoSQL databases do not intend to replace relational databases. Instead, they are a great complement to relational databases.

Types of NoSQL Databases

Unlike relational databases using tables, NoSQL databases do not use a standard data structure. There are several types of NoSQL databases including (Zaki, 2014):

- **Document Databases** (e.g., MongoDB), which pair each key with a document (a document could be collections, tags, metadata, or directory hierarchies).
- **Graph Stores** (e.g., Neo4J and HyperGraphDB), which are best for storing network (such as social networks) information.
- **Key-Value Stores** (e.g., Riak and Oracle NoSQL Database), which are the simplest NoSQL databases, where each item includes a pair, key and value, like associative arrays.
- **Wide-Column Stores** (e.g., Cassandra and HBase), which store columns (instead of rows) of data (the size of the data is usually higher than the size of the relational databases' row data).

Chapter Organization

This chapter discusses the next generation databases, NoSQL databases, for big data by using MongoDB databases. The rest of this chapter is organized as follows. The next section discusses the current status of big data. Section 3 shows how to download and install a MongoDB database. MongoDB shell interface is explained in Section 4. Sections 5 and 6 discuss how to connect Java and ASP.NET to MongoDB databases, respectively. A summary of these discussions is given in the final section.

BIG DATA MANAGEMENT, TECHNOLOGIES, AND APPLICATIONS

Big data covers a wide variety of subjects and methods. This section tries to introduce essential big data management, technologies, and applications by using the following steps: (i) big data generation, capturing, and collection, (ii) big data storage and preservation, (iii) big data analytics, management, visualization, and sharing, and (iv) big data applications and other related topics as shown in Figure 1. Each step is explained next.

Current Status of Big Data

Nowadays the growth of information size is not linear, but exponential. For example, at least one million web pages are added to the Internet every day, a massive amount of genetic data is created from various genome projects, or vast astronomical data is recorded after studying numerous galaxies. Big data is one of the hottest IT topics these days because many opportunities and great revenue are behind it based on the following reports:

- Big data is a major driver of IT spending these days; for example, $232 billion will be spent on IT including information management and analytics infrastructure from 2012 through 2016 according to Gartner (Beyer, Lovelock, Sommer, & Adrian, 2012).
- IDC (2012) predicted the worldwide market of big data technology and services will grow from $3.2 billion in 2010 to $16.9 billion in 2015, which represents a CAGR (compound annual growth

Figure 1. A flowchart of generic big data management

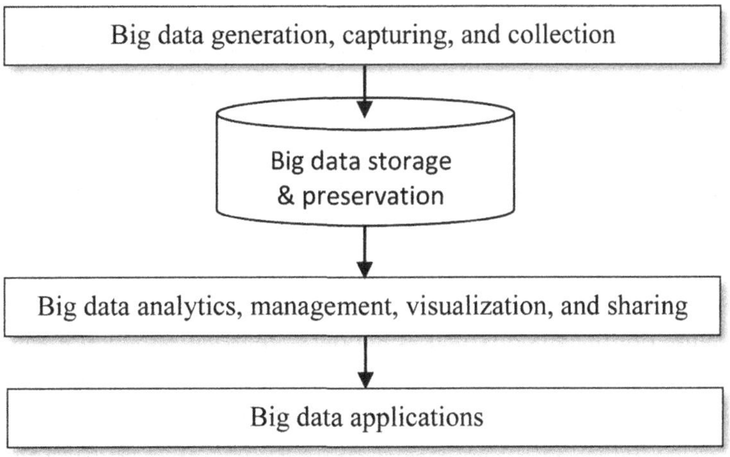

Big data generation, capturing, and collection

Big data storage & preservation

Big data analytics, management, visualization, and sharing

Big data applications

rate) of 40%. For example, it reported big data storage had the strongest growth rate, growing at 61.4% annually.

- Two observations from Kelly, Floyer, Vellante, & Miniman (2013) are (i) factory revenue generated by the sale of big data-related hardware, software, and services growing by 59% in 2012 over 2011, and (ii) the total big data market having an average 31% CAGR over the five-year period from 2012 ($11.4 billion) to 2017 ($47 billion).

Though the future of big data is bright, traditional IT technologies such as files and relational databases are not able to handle this kind of data anymore because of its vast size, constant changes, and high complication. Other technologies have to be created or used to manage big data, which is complex, unstructured, or semi-structured.

Big Data Generation, Capturing, and Collection

This is the first step of big data management including three actions: big data generation, capturing, and collection, which are briefly introduced as follows:

- **Big Data Generation:** During the time when computers were not popular, big data was rare. Since the number of (embedded) computers was greatly increased in the '80s, data is generated explosively. Big data can be generated from many sources; for example, all kinds of sensors, customer purchasing data, astronomical data, and texting messages.
- **Big Data Capturing:** Big data may be generated continuously (like steady satellite image transmission) or abruptly (during the peak hours). Compared to continuously generated big data, capturing abruptly generated big data is a challenge.
- **Big Data Collection:** Not all captured data is worth collection because of limited storage and processing power. For example, the size of videos of traffic monitor could be huge. Instead of saving the whole videos, specific video frames are selected and saved.

Big Data Storage and Preservation

After collecting big data, the next step is to store and preserve it. Because of its high volume, velocity, and variety, it is not a trivial task of storing and preserving big data. Big data storage and preservation are shortly explained below:

- **Big Data Storage:** The size of big data is huge and large scalable storage is required for storing it. Many times datacenters and warehousing are used and data structures are tailored for specific big data.
- **Big Data Preservation:** Big data has three key features: large volume, great variety, and high velocity. The feature of high velocity makes big data preservation volatile and complicated.

Big Data Analytics, Management, Visualization, and Sharing

Before big data can be put into use, it might need to be processed first. Various big data processing methods are available. Four major ones are analytics, management, visualization, and sharing introduced as follows:

- **Big Data Analytics:** It is to examine big data and uncover its hidden information. Examples of using the uncovered information include weather forecasts and economic indicators. Tools for big data analytics include NoSQL databases, Hadoop, and MapReduce.
- **Big Data Management:** After big data is collected, it needs to be well managed and maintained. There are many kinds of big data management methods. Some of them are organizing, searching, processing, mining big data.
- **Big Data Visualization:** Reading big data item by item is not feasible. Visualization tools or functions must be provided so data can be searched, viewed, and managed easily and collectively.
- **Big Data Sharing:** Many issues, like privacy and security, are related to big data sharing. Additionally, big data sharing is considered a hard problem because of its huge size. Cloud computing may relieve this problem.

Big Data Applications and Other Related Issues

Results of big data processing can be applied to many areas like businesses and sciences and can be used in many ways like increasing revenue and inventing new drug. Other related critical big data issues worth mentioning such as privacy and security are given as follows:

- **Big Data Applications:** Most data-intensive areas could be the candidates for big data applications. Some of the examples are:
  - Data from various sensors for weather forecasts,
  - Data from numerous traffic monitors for transportation control, and
  - Customer purchasing patterns for revenue discovery.
- **Big Data Privacy and Security:** Without rigorous privacy and security control, big data could not flourish. Strict privacy encourages big data collection and high security assures the safety of big data.

- **Big Data Standards, Policies, and Benchmarks:** Big data is a fairly new research subject. Therefore, its standards, policies, and benchmarks are still developing and investigated.
- **Cloud, Green, and Mobile Computing for Big Data:** Many newest computing paradigms could be used by big data. Among them are:
  - Cloud computing for sharing big data,
  - Green computing for saving time and energy, and
  - Mobile computing for accessing big data from anywhere and anytime.

MONGODB DATABASE DOWNLOAD AND INSTALLATION

Several NoSQL databases are available on the market and each one is not significantly different from the others. This study picks the MongoDB databases (MongoDB, Inc., n.d.) because of their simplicity and high efficiency. This section discusses the steps of how to download and install a MongoDB database as follows:

a. **Download a MongoDB Database**. Download the NoSQL database MongoDB at MongoDB Downloads (http://www.mongodb.org/downloads). The one the authors downloaded is Windows 64-bit mongodb-win32-x86_64-2008plus-2.4.8.zip .
b. **Install the MongoDB database**. Unzip the zip file mongodb-win32-x86_64-2008plus-2.4.8.zip and it will create a folder mongodb-win32-x86_64-2008plus-2.4.8, which again includes one folder: bin, and three files:
   i. README,
   ii. THIRD-PARTY NOTICES, and
   iii. GNU-AGPL-3.0.
c. **Download a Java SE (Java Platform, Standard Edition)**. Download a Java SE at Java SE Downloads (http://www.oracle.com/technetwork/java/javase/downloads). The one the authors downloaded is Java SE Development Kit 7u45 for Windows x86 jdk-7u45-windows-i586.exe .
d. **Install the Java SE**. Doubly click the file jdk-7u45-windows-i586.exe and it will start installing the Java SE for you. After installation, it creates a folder such as C:\Program File (x86)\Java, which again includes two folders:
   i. jdk1.7.0_45, where the JDK (Java Development Kit) includes a complete JRE plus tools for developing, debugging, and monitoring Java applications, and
   ii. jre7, where the JRE (Java Runtime Environment) contains everything required to run Java applications on your system.
e. **Download an Eclipse IDE** *for Java Developers*. Download an Eclipse IDE for Java Developers at Eclipse IDE for Java Developers. The one the authors downloaded is eclipse-java-europa-winter-win32.zip .
f. **Install the Eclipse IDE for Java Developers**. Unzip the zip file eclipse-java-europa-winter-win32.zip and it will create a folder eclipse, which again includes four folders:
   i. Configuration,
   ii. Features,
   iii. Plugins, and
   iv. Readme.

g. **Download a Mongo Java Driver**. Download a Mongo Java driver at Mongo Java driver. The one the authors downloaded is mongo-2.10.1.jar, which is put into the folder of Mongo DB such as C:\MongoDB-SDK\bin .

THE MONGODB SHELL INTERFACE

The MongoDB shell is an interface for systems administrators as well as a way for developers to test queries and operations directly with the MongoDB databases. This section discusses various MongoDB shell commands (Seguin, 2013).

Starting up a MongoDB Database Server

In order to use a MongoDB database, a single MongoDB database server must be activated by using the following three steps:

a. Create a folder C:\data\db,
b. cd (change directory) into the bin folder of the Mongo DB directory such as C:\MongoDB\bin to start the MongoDB database server, and
c. Enter the command mongod, which is used to start up a MongoDB database server.

Figure 2 shows a screenshot of starting up a MongoDB database server.

Activating Mongo and Entering MongoDB Commands

From another system prompt, start the MongoDB by issuing the mongo command. mongo is an interactive JavaScript shell interface to MongoDB database. It allows the system administrators and developers

Figure 2. A screenshot showing starting up a MongoDB Database server

```
Administrator: Command Prompt - mongod

C:\>cd MongoDB-SDK\bin

C:\MongoDB-SDK\bin>mongod
mongod --help for help and startup options
Fri Feb 21 19:44:08.999 [initandlisten] MongoDB starting : pid=1016 port=27017 d
bpath=\data\db\ 64-bit host=M140349-SH212
Fri Feb 21 19:44:08.999 [initandlisten] db version v2.4.8
Fri Feb 21 19:44:09.000 [initandlisten] git version: a350fc38922fbda2cec8d5dd842
237b984cafc14
Fri Feb 21 19:44:09.000 [initandlisten] build info: windows sys.getwindowsversio
n(major=6, minor=1, build=7601, platform=2, service_pack='Service Pack 1') BOOST
_LIB_VERSION=1_49
Fri Feb 21 19:44:09.000 [initandlisten] allocator: system
Fri Feb 21 19:44:09.001 [initandlisten] options: {}
Fri Feb 21 19:44:09.014 [initandlisten] journal dir=\data\db\journal
Fri Feb 21 19:44:09.014 [initandlisten] recover : no journal files present, no r
ecovery needed
Fri Feb 21 19:44:09.155 [initandlisten] waiting for connections on port 27017
Fri Feb 21 19:44:09.155 [websvr] admin web console waiting for connections on po
rt 28017
```

to communicate with the database directly. Figure 3 shows a screenshot of a list of MongoDB (shell) commands entered. The MongoDB commands are

```
> db.createCollection("persons")
> db.persons.insert({ personID: "P1", name: "Poke Mon" })
> db.persons.insert({ personID: "P2", name: "Digi Mon" })
> db.persons.insert({ personID: "P3", name: "Sponge Bob" })
>
> db.createCollection("passwords")
> db.passwords.insert({ pID: "P1", password: "secret" })
> db.passwords.insert({ pID: "P2", password: "hush" })
> db.passwords.insert({ pID: "P3", password: "secret" })
```

which create the collections persons and passwords and enter three documents for each.

After connecting to the database server, which runs as mongod, the developers can start using the mongo shell to manage their databases. Table 1 shows some common MongoDB shell commands.

CONNECTING JAVA TO MONGODB

Other than managing the MongoDB databases via the shell interface, developers can also use various languages to manage them. This section discusses the steps of connecting a Java program to a MongoDB database.

Figure 3. A screenshot showing a list of MongoDB (Shell) commands and system responses

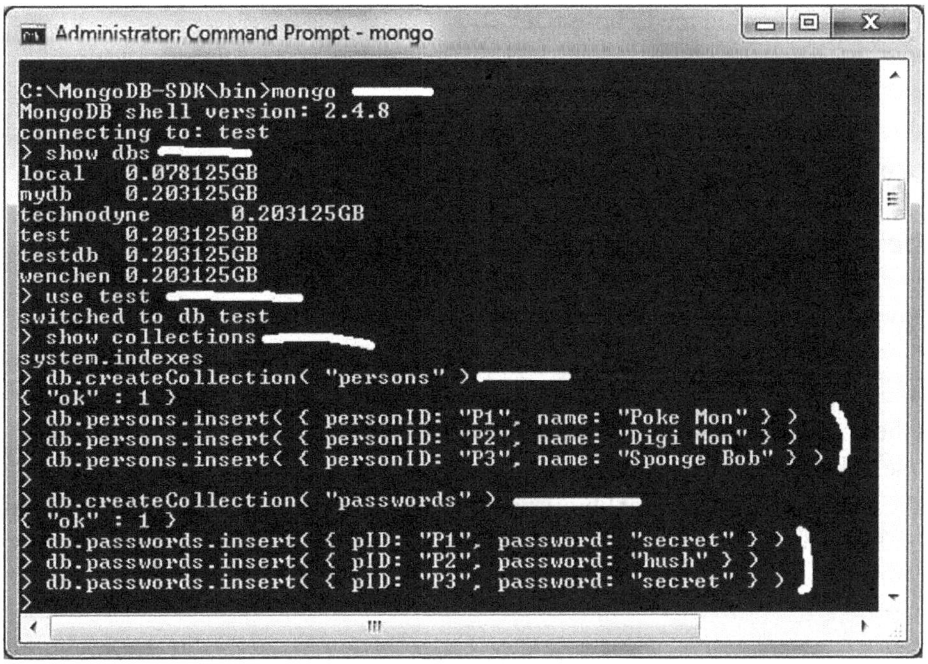

```
Administrator: Command Prompt - mongo
C:\MongoDB-SDK\bin>mongo
MongoDB shell version: 2.4.8
connecting to: test
> show dbs
local   0.078125GB
mydb    0.203125GB
technodyne      0.203125GB
test    0.203125GB
testdb  0.203125GB
wenchen 0.203125GB
> use test
switched to db test
> show collections
system.indexes
> db.createCollection( "persons" )
{ "ok" : 1 }
> db.persons.insert( { personID: "P1", name: "Poke Mon" } )
> db.persons.insert( { personID: "P2", name: "Digi Mon" } )
> db.persons.insert( { personID: "P3", name: "Sponge Bob" } )
>
> db.createCollection( "passwords" )
{ "ok" : 1 }
> db.passwords.insert( { pID: "P1", password: "secret" } )
> db.passwords.insert( { pID: "P2", password: "hush" } )
> db.passwords.insert( { pID: "P3", password: "secret" } )
>
```

Table 1. Some MongoDB Shell commands and their explanations (Mongo, Inc., n.d.)

Command	Description
Db	Reports the name of the current database.
db.help()	Help on db methods
db.mycoll.help()	Help on collection methods
DBQuery.shellBatchSize = x	Sets default number of items to display on shell.
exit	Quits the mongo shell.
help admin	Administrative help
help connect	Connecting to a db help
help keys	Key shortcuts
help misc	Miscellaneous things to know
help mr	Mapreduce
it	Result of the last line evaluated; use to further iterate
rs.help()	Replica set helpers
sh.help()	Sharding helpers
show collections	Shows collections in current database.
show dbs	Shows database names.
show logs	Shows the accessible logger names.
show profile	Shows most recent system.profile entries with time ≥ 1 ms.
show users	Shows users in current database.
use <db_name>	Sets current database.

Creating a Java Project

Select the following options in the Eclipse IDE:

```
File ⇒ New ⇒ Java Project
```

and enter the project name such as com.userid.mongo.

Adding the Mongo Java Driver Library

Take the following steps to add the Mongo Java driver library:

a. Go to the Libraries tab and click the button Add Libraries.
b. Select the option User Library and click the button Next.
c. Click the button User Libraries.
d. Click the button New, enter a user library name such as java-driver, and click the button Add JARs....
e. Add the JAR such as C:\MongoDB\bin\mongo-2.10.1.jar and click the button OK.

Starting Developing the Application

Take the following steps on the Eclipse IDE. Point to the project in the left pane of Package Explorer, right click the mouse, select the options New and Class, enter the class name such as App, and click the button Finish. Complete the class such as the one shown in Program 1.

Program 1. src/com/wenchen/mongo/App.java

```
package com.userid.mongo;
import java.net.UnknownHostException;
import java.util.Date;
import com.mongodb.BasicDBObject;
import com.mongodb.DB;
import com.mongodb.DBCollection;
import com.mongodb.DBCursor;
import com.mongodb.MongoClient;
import com.mongodb.MongoException;

/**
 * Java + MongoDB Hello World Example
 *
 */
public class App {
  public static void main(String[] args) {
    try {
      /**** Connect to MongoDB ****/
      // Since 2.10.0, uses MongoClient
      MongoClient mongo = new MongoClient("localhost", 27017);

      /**** Get database ****/
      // If database doesn't exist, MongoDB will create it for you.
      DB db = mongo.getDB("testdb");

      /**** Get collection / table from 'testdb' ****/
      // If collection doesn't exist, MongoDB will create it for you.
      DBCollection table = db.getCollection("user");

      /**** Insert ****/
      // Create a document to store key and value.
      BasicDBObject document = new BasicDBObject();
      document.put("name", "Pokemon");
      document.put("age", 30);
      document.put("createdDate", new Date());
```

continued on following page

Program 1. Continued

```
      table.insert(document);

      /**** Find and display ****/
      BasicDBObject searchQuery = new BasicDBObject();
      searchQuery.put("name", "Pokemon");

      DBCursor cursor = table.find(searchQuery);

      while (cursor.hasNext())
        System.out.println(cursor.next());

      /**** Update ****/
      // Search document where name="Pokemon" and update it with new values.
      BasicDBObject query = new BasicDBObject();
      query.put("name", "Pokemon");

      BasicDBObject newDocument = new BasicDBObject();
      newDocument.put("name", "Digimon");

      BasicDBObject updateObj = new BasicDBObject();
      updateObj.put("$set", newDocument);

      table.update(query, updateObj);

      /**** Find and display ****/
      BasicDBObject searchQuery2
        = new BasicDBObject().append("name", "Digimon");

      DBCursor cursor2 = table.find(searchQuery2);

      while (cursor2.hasNext())
        System.out.println(cursor2.next());

      /**** Done ****/
      System.out.println("Done");
    }
    catch (UnknownHostException e) {
      e.printStackTrace();
    }
    catch (MongoException e) {
      e.printStackTrace();
    }
  }
}
```

Building and Running the Project

Select the following options of the Eclipse IDE to build the project:

```
Project ⇒ Build Project
```

and then select the following options to run the project:

```
Run ⇒ Run
```

The output is then displayed in the Console tab of the Eclipse as shown in Figure 4.

CONNECTING ASP.NET TO MONGODB

The previous section shows how to run a MongoDB database by using Java in an Eclipse environment. Nevertheless, these days many databases are connected to the Web. This section discusses how to connect ASP.NET (Microsoft, n.d.) to a MongoDB database step by step (Shovan, 2013).

Figure 4. A screenshot showing the results from Program 1

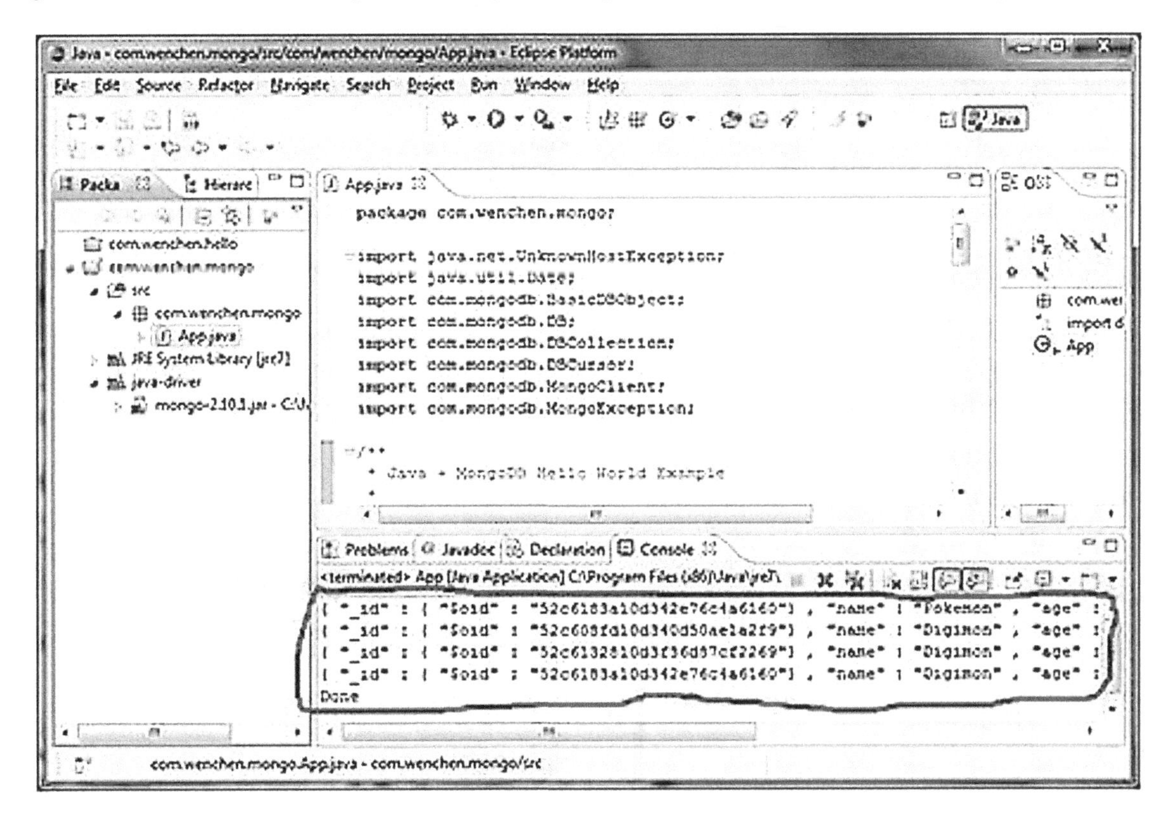

Starting the Visual Studio

Select the following Windows options to start the Microsoft Visual Studio:

```
Start ⇒ All Programs ⇒ Visual Studio 2013
      ⇒ Visual Studio 2013
```

Creating a New Project

The new project is an ASP.NET Web Application, instead of Website, in C#. Add mongocsharpdriver from nuget using package manager console by selecting the following options:

```
TOOLS ⇒ NuGet Package Manager
      ⇒ Package Manager Console
```

and enter the following command:

```
PM> Install-Package mongocsharpdriver
```

The connection string for MongoDB server has to be defined. Because the MongoDB database server runs on the port 27017 by default, add the following code to the web.config file inside <configuration> </configuration>:

```
<appSettings>
  <add key="connectionString" value="Server=localhost:27017" />
</appSettings>
```

Starting the ASP.NET Programming

This simple ASP.NET application contains create.aspx page with a textbox, a button, and a label. The application displays the users' passwords based on the name entered from the Web. Figure 5 shows the web interfaces before and after entering a query.

Figure 5. A screenshot showing the results from Program 1

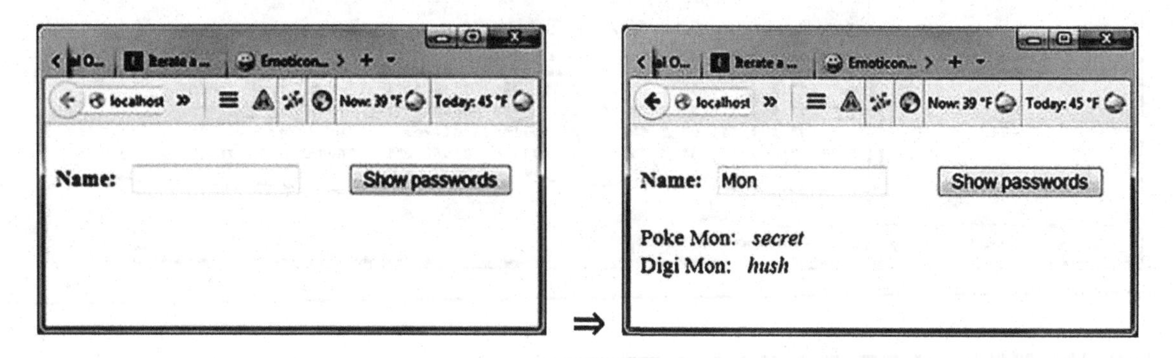

The corresponding code is shown in Programs 2, 3, and 4. Program 2 is the code for web interface, Program 3 is the C# code for implementing the web interface, and two classes are defined in Program 4.

SUMMARY

Big data has existed for a long time, but it did not catch great attention until recently because it did not prevail. However, owing to the high popularity of computers and great IT advancements, big data is everywhere nowadays. Tremendous amount of data is generated every day, everywhere, from fields

Program 2. C:\AspWithMongo\Create.aspx

```
<%@ Page Language="C#" AutoEventWireup="true" CodeBehind="Create.aspx.cs"
Inherits="AspWithMongo.Create" %>
<!DOCTYPE html>
<html xmlns="http://www.w3.org/1999/xhtml">
 <head runat="server">
  <title>ASP.NET with Mongo</title>
 </head>
 <body>
  <form id="form1" runat="server">
   <asp:TextBox ID="name1" runat="server" Width="120px">
   </asp:TextBox>
   <asp:Button  ID="showButton" runat="server" Text="Show passwords"
                OnClick="showButton_Click" />
   <asp:Label ID="pLabel" runat="server"></asp:Label>
  </form>
 </body>
</html>
```

Program 3. C:\AspWithMongo\Create.aspx.cs

```
using MongoDB;
using MongoDB.Driver;
using MongoDB.Driver.Builders;
using System;
using System.Collections.Generic;
using System.Configuration;
using System.Linq;
using System.Web;
using System.Web.UI;
using System.Web.UI.WebControls;
```

continued on following page

Program 3. Continued

```
namespace AspWithMongo {
 public partial class Create: System.Web.UI.Page {
  string pwords = "";
  protected void Page_Load(object sender, EventArgs e) {
  }
  protected void showButton_Click(object sender, EventArgs e) {
   MongoServer server = MongoServer.Create(
     ConfigurationManager.AppSettings["connectionString"]);
   MongoDatabase myDB = server.GetDatabase("test");
   MongoCollection<Info> Persons = myDB.GetCollection<Info>("persons");
   MongoCollection<Info1> Passwords = myDB.GetCollection<Info1>("passwords");
   foreach (Info Aperson in Persons.Find(
     Query.Matches("name", name1.Text))) {
    foreach (Info1 Apword in Passwords.Find(
      Query.EQ("pID", Aperson.personID)))
     pwords = pwords + " " + Aperson.name + ": " + Apword.password ;
    pLabel.Text = pwords;
   }
  }
 }
}
```

Program 4. C:\AspWithMongo\Info.cs

```
using MongoDB.Bson;
using System;
using System.Collections.Generic;
using System.Linq;
using System.Web;
namespace AspWithMongo {
  public class Info {
    public ObjectId _id { get; set; }
    public string personId { get; set; }
    public string name { get; set; }
  }
  public class Info1 {
    public ObjectId _id { get; set; }
    public string pID { get; set; }
    public string password { get; set; }
  }
}
```

such as businesses, research, and sciences. Big data exists in a wide variety of data-intensive areas such as atmospheric science, genome research, astronomical studies, and network traffic monitor. The high volume, velocity, and variety of data cause a great headache to people because the traditional methods are no longer working for this kind of data. Though relational databases have its limitations, they have dominated the database markets for decades, during which several databases like object-oriented databases tried to replace them, but failed. However, the emergence of new applications such as big data and cloud computing makes the shortcomings of relational databases like low scalability and agility become unbearable (Khan, 2014). The creation of NoSQL databases is to mitigate the problems of relational databases and facilitate the development of contemporary applications. This chapter discusses the NoSQL databases by using an empirical approach, which uses the MongoDB databases as practical examples. Readers learn how to program for the MongoDB, a NoSQL database, by studying this chapter.

REFERENCES

Apache Software Foundation. (n.d.a). *Cassandra*. Retrieved January 28, 2016, from http://cassandra.apache.org/

Apache Software Foundation. (n.d.b). *HBase*. Retrieved February 08, 2016, from http://hbase.apache.org/

Basho Technologies. (n.d.). *Riak*. Retrieved December 12, 2015, from http://basho.com/riak/

Beyer, M. A., Lovelock, J.-D., Sommer, D., & Adrian, M. (2012, October 12). *Big Data Drives Rapid Changes in Infrastructure and $232 Billion in IT Spending Through 2016*. Retrieved June 12, 2013, from http://www.gartner.com/id=2195915

Han, J. E. H., Le, G., & Du, J. (2011). Survey on NoSQL database. *The 6th International Conference on Pervasive Computing and Applications (ICPCA 2011)*, (pp. 363-366).

IDC. (2012, March 7). *IDC Releases First Worldwide Big Data Technology and Services Market Forecast, Shows Big Data as the Next Essential Capability and a Foundation for the Intelligent Economy*. Retrieved May 4, 2013, from http://www.idc.com/getdoc.jsp?containerId=prUS23355112

Kelly, J., Floyer, D., Vellante, D., & Miniman, S. (2013, April 17). *Big Data Vendor Revenue and Market Forecast 2012-2017*. Retrieved May 22, 2013, from http://wikibon.org/wiki/v/Big_Data_Vendor_Revenue_and_Market_Forecast_2012-2017

Khan, H. (2014, December). NoSQL: A database for cloud computing. *International Journal of Computer Science and Network*, *3*(6), 498–501.

Kobrix Software. (n.d.). *HyperGraphDB*. Retrieved February 14, 2016, from http://hypergraphdb.org/index

Microsoft. (2015). *ASP.NET*. Retrieved February 13, 2016, from http://www.asp.net

mongoDB, Inc. (n.d.). *mongoDB*. Retrieved October 07, 2015, from http://www.mongodb.org/

Neo4j Technology Inc. (n.d.). *Neo4j*. Retrieved January 22, 2016, from http://neo4j.com/download/

Oracle Corporation. (n.d.). *Oracle NoSQL Database*. Retrieved from November 03, 2015, from http://www.oracle.com/technetwork/database/database-technologies/nosqldb/overview/index.html

Seguin, K. (2013). *The Little MongoDB Book*. Retrieved January 08, 2016, from http://openmymind.net/mongodb.pdf

Shovan, P. (2013, October 23). *Connecting MongoDB with ASP.NET*. Retrieved November 03, 2015, from http://www.codeproject.com/Chapters/656093/Connecting-MongoDB-with-ASP-NET

The White House. (2012, March 29). *Obama Administration Unveils "Big Data" Initiative: Announces $200 Million in New R&D Investments*. Retrieved February 13, 2013, from http://www.whitehouse.gov/sites/default/files/microsites/ostp/big_data_press_release_final_2.pdf

Zaki, A. K. (2014, May). NoSQL databases: New millennium database for big data, big users, cloud computing and its security challenges. *International Journal of Research in Engineering and Technology, 3*(3), 403–409.

KEY TERMS AND DEFINITIONS

Big Data Analytics: It is to examine big data and uncover its hidden information. Examples of using the uncovered information include weather forecasts and economic indicators. Tools for big data analytics include NoSQL databases, Hadoop, and MapReduce.

Big Data: Big data is complex, unstructured or semi-structured data of which the size is huge. Conventional methods can no longer be applied to it because of its vast size and high complication and volatile.

Document Databases: They are a kind of databases and are one kind of data stores used by the NoSQL databases. They pair each key with a document (a document could be collections, tags, metadata, or directory hierarchies).

Eclipse IDE (Integrated Development Environment): Eclipse is a multi-language software development environment, which is used to facilitate application development in various languages (such as C++ and Java) by installing appropriate plug-ins.

Graph Stores: They are a kind of databases and are one kind of data stores used by the NoSQL databases. They are best for storing network (such as social networks) information.

Key-Value Stores: They are a kind of databases and are one kind of data stores used by the NoSQL databases. They are the simplest NoSQL databases, where each item includes a pair, key and value, like associative arrays.

NoSQL Databases: Much of current data processing requires horizontal scaling, faster speed, and processing different kinds of data. A NoSQL database is to meet the requirements by providing a simple and efficient mechanism for data storage and retrieval. The approach it uses is different from the one used by a relational database. An RDBMS (relational database management system) is a general-purpose data store, whereas a NoSQL database is normally a key-value store for simple insertion and retrieval operations.

Wide-Column Stores: They are a kind of databases and are one kind of data stores used by the NoSQL databases. They store columns (instead of rows) of data (the size of the data is usually higher than the size of the relational databases' row data).

Chapter 5
The Challenges of Data Cleansing with Data Warehouses

Nigel McKelvey
Letterkenny Institute of Technology, Ireland

Kevin Curran
Ulster University, UK

Luke Toland
Letterkenny Institute of Technology, Ireland

ABSTRACT

Data cleansing is a long standing problem which every organisation that incorporates a form of data processing or data mining must undertake. It is essential in improving the quality and reliability of data. This paper presents the necessary methods needed to process data at a high quality. It also classifies common problems which organisations face when cleansing data from a source or multiple sources while evaluating methods which aid in this process. The different challenges faced at schema-level and instance-level are also outlined and how they can be overcome. Currently there are tools which provide data cleansing, but are limited due to the uniqueness of every data source and data warehouse. Outlined are the limitations of these tools and how human interaction (self-programming) may be needed to ensure vital data is not lost. We also discuss the importance of maintaining and removing data which has been stored for several years and may no longer have any value.

1. INTRODUCTION

Processing and analysing data has become increasingly important to organisations in recent years. As companies are growing and adapting, the ability to retrieve current and correct data is of key importance. Data cleansing, cleaning or scrubbing is the process of identifying and removing or modifying incorrect entries or inconsistencies in a dataset to improve the overall quality (Rahm et al, 2000). Data

DOI: 10.4018/978-1-5225-0182-4.ch005

warehousing is the concept of storing data in a relational database which is designed for query and analysis rather than transaction processes (Docs.oracle.com, 2014). It is also referred to as an organisation's "single source of truth". It is designed to provide management with a large amount of data from multiple sources within the organisation, which is vital in strategic decision making. For data to be stored in a data warehouse, it is crucial that it is cleansed. This process becomes more difficult as retrieving data from multiple sources increases the amount of "dirty data" and may also introduce an inconsistency in the way in which the data is represented.

Figure 1 describes the typical flow and layout of a data warehouse. Extraction, Transformation and Loading is the process reliable for the initial loading and refreshing the contents of the data warehouse. The probability of this data being incomplete or incorrect is quite high as it has been retrieved from multiple sources, therefore the data is processed through a number of methods, which include instance extraction and transformation, instance matching and integration, filtering and aggregation. Data cleansing is normally performed in a separate area before data is loaded into the data warehouse. The sheer volume of data being processed means that writing a successful tool to complete this task is very difficult.

2. DATA QUALITY

Data auditing is the first step in the data cleansing process. Its purpose is to process through the data and outline any data anomalies that are found (Muller et al, 2003). Using statistical and parsing methods, this process derives information such as value range, frequency of values, variance, uniqueness, occurrence of null values, typical string patterns, also detecting any functional dependencies and association rules in the complete data collection (Muller et all, 2003). Data quality refers to the standard, reliability and

Figure 1. Data warehouse model

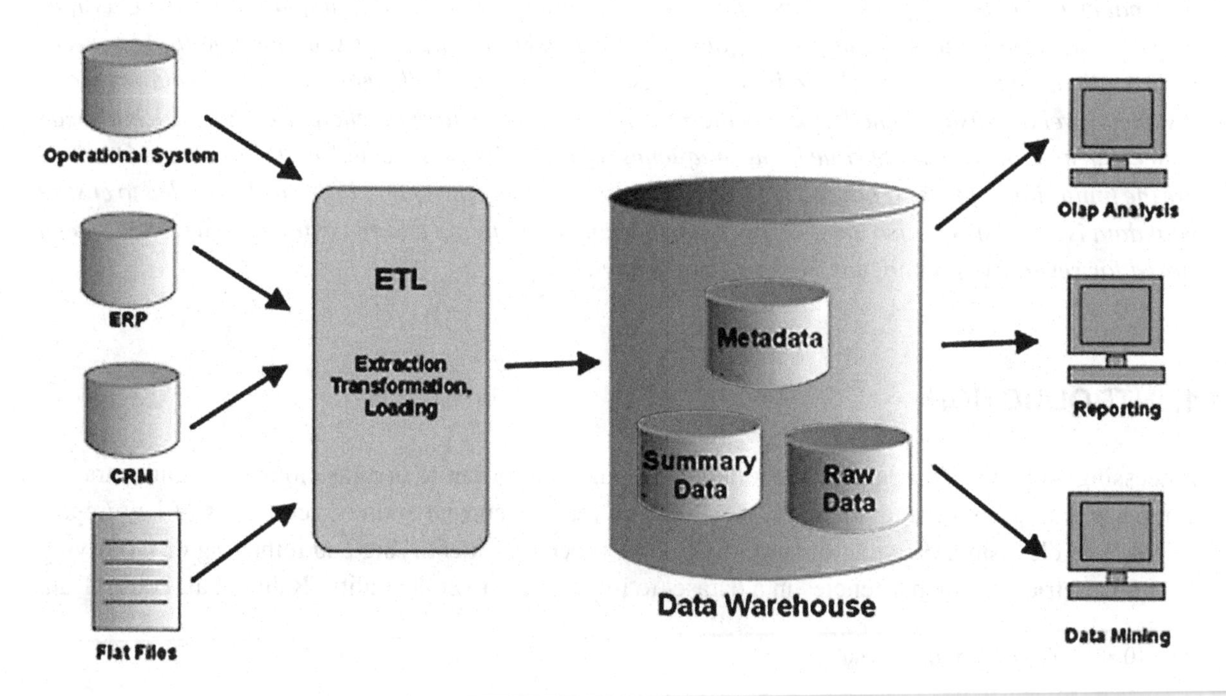

efficiency of data to inform and evaluate decisions (Karr et al, 2003). For data to be processed as fast and efficiently as possible, data must adhere to a certain standard. Data which adheres to this standard is said to be of high quality. To measure the quality of a data collection, scores are assessed. The result of these scores will identify the need to data cleanse and to which level of data cleansing is performed.

Before data is entered into a database, it usually is passed through a number of phases which include human interaction and computation. Naturally, data errors will occur through typographic or formatting errors or misunderstanding of the data source. To ensure data quality, during its lifespan, certain data will undertake iterative processes involving collection, transformation, storage, auditing, cleaning and analysis. This may be spread across multiple organisations and or agencies, potentially over large amounts of time. On average, U.S organizations believe that 25% of their data is inaccurate (Qas.com, 2014). Quality assurance is a major part of a data warehouse model. Ensuring that data is kept to a high standard when stored in a data warehouse is a time consuming and expensive task. Using processes such as Extraction, Transformation and Loading (ETL) can keep content current and correct. Data cleansing is executed in the data staging area. After data is collected from its source, it is gathered in this area and prepared for analysing. ETL and staging are considered to be the most important sequence of events to occur in the data warehouse (Singh et al, 2010). It is an important area for tracking down errors and undertaking audits to validate data quality.

3. PROBLEMS

Data cleansing in a data warehouse is a problematic task. Each data warehouse and each source can be unique in its own way. This means that each source can create a new conflict, which may not have been planned or foreseen. The degree to which each problem occurs is largely based on the schema level and instance level assigned to each data source. This section will explore the problems associated with both sourcing methods. Due to data cleansing being an expensive and time consuming task, it is just as important to reduce the cleaning problem before analysing data.

3.1. Semantic Complexity

Semantic complexity is described as the user's representation of what data represents in a given database. This is a common problem as different users may have different conceptions of what the data represents. For example, a two databases containing a list of drivers and their cars are to be merged. There may be a data conflict where by a user will use the driver's licence number as a primary key and the other user may use the driver's social security number as a primary key. This can lead to an occurrence of missing values, meaning any data that is requested may be incorrect.

3.2. Multi-Source Problems

Problems which may be present at single-source level are only more emphasised at multi-source. Data from each source may contain certain attributes which may be represented differently and can overlap or contradict. This may be because each source is developed uniquely and could be tailored to suit different applications, and when combining several sources this results in a large degree of heterogeneity.

At schema level, the main issues are schema translation and schema integration, specifically being naming conventions and structural conflicts in the databases. Naming conflicts arise when attributes in different databases are assigned the same name and represent the same object in different sources. Structural conflicts arise when there are variations in the representation of data in different sources. Due to these conflicts, data is merged from different sources may be entered more than once creating duplicate entries and contradicting records.

In an ideal scenario, data from different sources would complement each other without overlapping or creating "dirty data". Thus, the main challenge of cleaning data retrieved from different sources is identifying the overlapping data. This problem is often referred to as object identify problem, the merge/purge problem, or the duplicate problem (Hernandez et al, 1998). Although this problem can be overcome, there are a few issues which may arise:

- The dataset may be too large to reside in main memory at a single time. Therefore, the main dataset may have to exist in external memory allowing as few pass overs as possible to solve the problem.
- The incoming data may be corrupted which makes it difficult to compare matches.

In a multiple source scenario, each source may also have different platforms. As an example, IBM mainframe may contain files on a server using an Oracle database, while another IBM mainframe may contain files on a server using SQL. The exact amount of sources needed for a data warehouse are based on the needs of the organisation and the specifics of the implementation.

3.3. Single-Source Problems

Since data warehouses are mostly built using multiple sources, single-source problems are uncommon, but may still arise. At instance level, errors that occur are largely similar to errors which occur at instance level from multiple sources; entry errors, misspellings, duplicate entries. At schema level, problems facing data cleansing are slightly different to multiple source problems. Some of which are poor schema design, referential integrity and lack of integrity constraints.

3.4. Data Transformation

Data transformation is the process of converting the format of one data set into another dataset (Techopedia2.com, 2014). It is usually carried out after the data to be transformed has been verified. Verification ensures that the data to be transformed is evaluated to ensure that it will be necessary to cleanse.

There are currently many tools which are available to complete this task, but are expensive and can be ineffective. For these reasons it is vital that the organization has a working knowledge of their data sources. This method is also used to refresh current information in the data warehouse to ensure it is of high data quality.

3.5. Data Maintenance and Improving Performance

After data has been cleansed, it is important to ensure that it is being managed and updated/refreshed on a regular basis. In an ideal situation, a data warehouse would be able to retain an organisation's information for several years, but in order to retain the system's performance a portion of the data is going to have to be extracted. Data purging is a term that is commonly used to describe methods that permanently erase and remove data from a storage space (Techopedia.com, 2014). Typically organisations will come to a decision on the data to be removed from the data warehouse.

Purging a database can be executed by a program which will use circular buffer methodology, meaning the oldest data must make way for the newest data. This is an inefficient method as the importance of data should not be ranked on its age but rather its use to the organisation. Therefore, it can be better practice to manually purge a database. This will involve a single or several administrators manually selecting data to be removed from the database, ensuring that important data is retained.

4. CONCLUSION

Data cleansing is a fundamental process in every data warehouse. Data cleansing can be defined as a list or sequence of operations which improve overall data quality. Data warehouses can supply organisations with endless information and statistical observations. Therefore, to retrieve the most current and correct information each data collection should be cleansed before it is entered into the data warehouse. In this paper, the author has provided a rough description of the problems associated with data cleansing from multiple and single sources while trying to provide a focus on schema-level and instance-level problems. We have discussed the importance of maintaining already cleansed data, specifically the benefits to manually reviewing data to be removed over automatically removing data using a tool. It has also become evident that creating a tool to cleanse a data source is a tough task. Data is represented in many different formats, and a single tool may not be efficient in cleansing a number of data sources. It has become clear that although these tools can prove useful in a number of areas, such as removing duplicates, some human intervention may be needed to review data and users may need to self-program these tools to suit the circumstances.

REFERENCES

Bradji, L., & Boufaida, M. (2011). Open User Involvement in Data Cleaning for Data Warehouse Quality. *International Journal of Digital Information and Wireless Communications*, *1*(2), 536–544.

Docs.oracle.com. (2014). *Data Warehousing Concepts*. Retrieved from: http://docs.oracle.com/cd/B10500_01/server.920/a96520/concept.htm

Helfert, M. & Herrmann, C. (2002). *Proactive data quality management for data warehouse systems*. Academic Press.

Hernandez, M. & Stolfo, S. (1995). *The merge/purge problem for large databases*. Academic Press.

Hernandez, M., & Stolfo, S. (1998). Real-world data is dirty: Data cleansing and the merge/purge problem. *Data Mining and Knowledge Discovery*, *2*(1), 9–37. doi:10.1023/A:1009761603038

Karr, A., Sanil, A. & Banks, D. (2003). *Data Quality: A Statistical Perspective*. Academic Press.

Lee, M., Lu, H., Ling, T., & Ko, Y. (1999). Cleansing data for mining and warehousing. Academic Press.

Monge, A., Elkan, C., & Associates. (1996). The Field Matching Problem: Algorithms and Applications. Academic Press.

Muller, H., & Freytag, J. (2003). *Problems*. Methods, and Challenges in Comprehensive Data Cleansing.

Qas.com. (2014). *Contact Data Management Software and Services | Experian Data Quality*. Retrieved from: http://Qas.com

Rahm, E., & Do, H. (2000). Data cleaning: Problems and current approaches. *IEEE Data Eng. Bull.*, *23*(4), 3–13.

Singh, R., & Singh, K. et al. (2010). A descriptive classification of causes of data quality problems in data warehousing. *International Journal of Computer Science Issues*, *7*(3), 41–50.

Techopedia2.com. (2014b). *What is Data Transformation? - Definition from Techopedia*. Retrieved from: http://www.techopedia.com/definition/6760/data-transformation

Techopedia.com. (2014a). *What is Data Purging? - Definition from Techopedia*. Retrieved from: http://www.techopedia.com/definition/28042/data-purging

Chapter 6
Big Data Analysis:
Big Data Analysis Pipeline and Its Technical Challenges

Rajanala Vijaya Prakash
S. R. Engineering College, India

ABSTRACT

The data management industry has matured over the last three decades, primarily based on Relational Data Base Management Systems (RDBMS) technology. The amount of data collected and analyzed in enterprises has increased several folds in volume, variety and velocity of generation and consumption, organizations have started struggling with architectural limitations of traditional RDBMS architecture. As a result a new class of systems had to be designed and implemented, giving rise to the new phenomenon of "Big Data". The data-driven world has the potential to improve the efficiencies of enterprises and improve the quality of our lives. There are a number of challenges that must be addressed to allow us to exploit the full potential of Big Data. This article highlights the key technical challenges of Big Data.

1. INTRODUCTION

Big Data has the potential to revolutionize much more than just research. Google's works on Google File System, MapReduce, and Hadoop, have led to arguably the most extensive development and adoption of Big Data technologies. They have become the indispensable foundation for applications ranging from Web search to content recommendation and computational advertising. There have been persuasive cases made for the value of Big Data for Healthcare - through home based continuous monitoring and through integration across providers (CCCc, 2011) Urban planning - through fusion of high fidelity geographical data, Intelligent transportation - through analysis and visualization of live and detailed road network data, Environmental modelling - through sensor networks ubiquitously collecting data (CCCd, 2011), Energy saving - through unveiling patterns of use, Smart materials - through the new materials genome initiative (National Science and Technology 2011), Machine translation between natural languages - through analysis of large corpora, Education - particularly with online courses (CCCb, 2011), Computational

DOI: 10.4018/978-1-5225-0182-4.ch006

social sciences - a new methodology growing fast in popularity because of the dramatically lowered cost of obtaining data (Lazar, D. et al. 2009), Systemic risk analysis in finance - through integrated analysis of a web of contracts to find dependencies between financial entities (Flood Jagadish, H.V., Kyle, A., Olken, F. And Raschid, 2011), Homeland security - through analysis of social networks and financial transactions of possible terrorists, Computer security - through analysis of logged events, known as Security Information and Event Management, or SIEM).

While the potential benefits of Big Data are real and significant, and some initial successes have already been achieved. There remain many technical challenges that must be addressed to fully realize this potential. The sheer size of the data is a major challenge, and is the one most easily recognized. Industry analysis companies like to point out there are challenges not just in *Volume*, but also in *Variety* and *Velocity* (Gartner Group 2011), and those companies should not focus on just the first of these. Variety refers to heterogeneity of data types, representation, and semantic interpretation. Velocity denotes both the rate at which data arrive and the time frame in which they must be acted upon. While these three are important, this short list fails to include additional important requirements. Several additions have been proposed by various parties, such as *Veracity*. Other concerns, such as privacy and usability, still remain. The analysis of Big Data is an iterative process, each with its own challenges, that involves many distinct phases.

2. BACKGROUND

Practically everything on the Internet is recorded. When you search on Google or Bing, your queries and subsequent clicks are recorded. When you shop on Amazon or eBay, not only every purchase, but every click is captured and logged. When you read a newspaper online, watch videos, or track your personal finances, your behaviour is recorded. The recording of individual behaviour does not stop with the Internet: text messaging, cell phones and geo locations, scanner data, employment records, and electronic health records are all part of the data.

Consider the data collected by retail stores. A few decades ago, stores might have collected data on daily sales, and it would have been considered high quality if the data was split by products or product categories. Nowadays, scanner data makes it possible to track individual purchases and item sales, capture the exact time at which they occur and the purchase histories of the individuals, and use electronic inventory data to link purchases to specific shelf locations or current inventory levels. Internet retailers observe not just this information, but can trace the consumer's behaviour around the sale, including his or her initial search query, items that were viewed and discarded, recommendations or promotions that were shown, and subsequent product or seller reviews. And in principle these data could be linked to demographics, advertising exposure, social media activity, offline spending, or credit history.

There has been a parallel evolution in business activity. Firms have moved their day to day operations to computers and then online, it has become possible to compile rich data sets of sales contacts, hiring practices, and physical shipments of goods. Increasingly, there are also electronic records of collaborative work efforts, personnel evaluations, and productivity measures. The same story also can be told about the public sector, in terms of the ability to access and analyze tax fi lings, social insurance programs, government expenditures, and regulatory activities.

The data management industry has matured over the last three decades, primarily based on Relational Data Base Management Systems (RDBMS) technology. Even today, RDBMS systems power a majority of backend systems for online digital media, financial systems, insurance, health care, transportation, and telecommunication companies. The amount of data collected and analyzed in enterprises has increased several folds in volume, variety and velocity of generation and consumption, organizations have started struggling with architectural limitations of traditional RDBMS architecture. As a result a new class of systems had to be designed and implemented, giving rise to the new phenomenon of "Big Data".

Industry analyst firm Gartner (CCCa, 2011) defines Big Data as "Big data is high-volume, high-velocity, and high-variety information assets that demand cost effective, innovative forms of information processing for enhanced insight and decision-making.

The data that is generated in digital form by humankind, will double every two years, and will reach 40,000 Exabyte's by 2020. A major driving factor behind this data growth is ubiquitous connectivity via rapidly growing reach of mobile devices, constantly connected to the networks or Internet.

A vast amount of data will be created not by human users, but about humans by the digital universe, and it will be stored, managed, and analyzed by the enterprises, such as Internet service providers, and cloud service providers of all varieties like Infrastructure-as-a-service, platform-as-a-service, and Software-as-a-service.

Around us there is a rapid growth of data generation in the online world. Facebook has grown from one million users in 2004, to more than one billion in 2012, a thousand-fold increase in less than eight years. More than 60% of these users access Facebook from mobile phones today. The value generated by a social network is proportional to the number of contacts between users of the social network, rather than the number of users. According to the Metcalf's Law (CCCb, 2011), the number of contacts for N users is proportional to NlogN. Thus, the growth of contacts, and therefore the interactions within a social network, results in data generation, is non-linear with respect to number of users. As the world gets more connected, one can expect the number of interactions to grow, resulting in even more accelerated data growth.

Litrature Review

Works of this nature have recently been undertaken through the lens of big data investment impact on company productivity, (Brynjolfsson et al. 2011), (Tambe P 2014), Bakhshi et al. (2014). The seminal study by (Brynjolfsson, et al. 2011), leveraged survey collection at corporate level by McKinsey & Company, to document a 5–6% increase in global productivity from leveraging data-driven analytics, over the non-big data-friendly company. Using similar approaches, (Bakhshi et al. 2014) confirmed a productivity effect of 8% for UK firms.

Strictly speaking, though, the above studies may have scope and bias issues, leading to an overly optimistic effect of big data on productivity measures. Regarding scope, most of the quoted studies concentrate on the effect from "data" analytics, rather than on the more focused domain of big data. (Bakhshi et al. 2014) mention that big data techniques (in their study, text- or data-mining techniques) are used for only half of the companies in their sample.

The recent work by (Tambe P 2014) on US firms goes a long way towards limiting such biases. Correcting for them as diligently as possibly, (Tambe P 2014) shows that US companies that have hired IT labour with specific Hadoop/no SQL skills have achieved labour productivity that is 3% higher than the average. This effect is lower, but likely to be more robust than in other studies. Further, (Tambe P 2014) shows that the big data effect is not universal: it is statistically significant only for firms established in data-intensive industries, such as IT-related or financial services, where data is a key strategic production input, and for the various firms that were geographically located in a Hadoop intensive labour market, so as to secure a large enough pool of complementary talents for investment in big data projects.

3. PHASES IN THE BIG DATA LIFE CYCLE

Many people unfortunately focus just on the analysis/modelling step—while that step is crucial, it is of little use without the other phases of the data analysis pipeline. For example, in data analysis approaches the question of what data to record from the perspective that data is valuable. Potentially analyst cannot fully anticipate the data, and derive value from data that is imperfectly and incompletely captured. Doing so raises the need to track provenance and to handle uncertainty and error. As another example, when the same information is represented in repetitive and overlapping fashion, it allows analyst to bring statistical techniques to bear on challenges such as data integration and entity/relationship extraction. This is likely to be a key to successfully leveraging data that is drawn from multiple sources (for example, related experiments reported by different labs, crowd sourced traffic information, data about a given domain such as entertainment, culled from different websites).

In the rest of this article begin by considering the five stages in the Big Data pipeline, along with challenges specific to each stage. In this paper there are six crosscutting challenges.

Data Acquisition

Big Data does not arise in a vacuum: it is a record of some underlying activity of interest. For example, consider the ability to sense and observe the world around us, from the heart rate of an elderly citizen, to the presence of toxins in the air we breathe, to logs of user activity on a website or event-logs in a software system. Sensors, simulations and scientific experiments can produce large volumes of data today. For example, the planned square kilometer array telescope will produce up to one million terabytes of raw data per day. Much of this data can be filtered and compressed by orders of magnitude without compromising the ability to reason about the underlying activity of interest. One challenge is to define these "on-line" filters in such a way they do not discard useful information. The raw data is often too voluminous to even allow the option of storing it all. For example, the data collected by sensors most often are spatially and temporally correlated (such as traffic sensors on the same road segment). Suppose one sensor reading differs substantially from the rest. This is likely to be due to the sensor being faulty. Furthermore, loading of large datasets is often a challenge, especially when combined with on-line filtering and data reduction, and it needs efficient incremental ingestion techniques. These might not be enough for many applications, and effective insight processing has to be designed.

Information Extraction and Cleaning

Frequently, the information collected will not be in a format ready for analysis. For example, consider the collection of electronic health records in a hospital, comprised of transcribed dictations from several physicians, structured data from sensors and measurements (possibly with some associated uncertainty), image data such as X-rays, and videos from probes. This cannot leave the data in this form and still effectively analyze it. Rather, it requires an information extraction process that pulls out the required information from the underlying sources and expresses it in a structured form suitable for analysis. Doing this correctly and completely is a continuing technical challenge. Such extraction is often highly application dependent. For example, the required data pull out from a MRI is very different than the tug of a picture of the stars, or a surveillance photo. Productivity concerns require the emergence of declarative methods to precisely specify information extraction tasks, and then optimizing the execution of these tasks when processing new data.

Most data sources are notoriously unreliable, like sensors can be faulty, humans may provide biased opinions, and remote websites might be stale, and so on. Understanding and modelling these sources of error is a first step toward developing data cleaning techniques. Unfortunately, much of this is data source and application dependent.

Data Integration, Aggregation, and Representation

Effective large-scale analysis often requires the collection of heterogeneous data from multiple sources. For example, obtaining the 360-degrees health view of a patient benefits from integrating and analyzing the medical health record, along with this, environmental data available from Internet and readings from multiple types of meters (for example, glucose meters, heart meters, accelerometers, among others3). A set of data transformation and integration tools helps the data analyst to resolve heterogeneities in data structure and semantics. This heterogeneity resolution leads to integrated data that is uniformly interpretable within a community, as they fit its standardization schemes and analysis needs. However, the cost of full integration is often formidable and the analysis needs shift quickly, so recent "pay-as-you-go" integration techniques provide an attractive "relaxation", doing much of this work on the fly in support of ad hoc exploration.

It is notable that the massive of data is available on the Internet. Integration and analysis tools that allow for the production of derived data, lead to yet another kind of data proliferation, which is not only a problem of data volume, but also a problem of tracking the provenance of such derived data.

Even for simpler analyses that depend on only one dataset, there usually are many alternative ways of storing the same information, with each alternative incorporating certain trade-offs. Witness, for instance, the tremendous variety in the structure of bioinformatics databases with information about substantially similar entities, such as genes. Database design is today an art, and is carefully executed in the enterprise context by highly paid professionals. We must enable other professionals, such as domain scientists, to create effective data stores, either through devising tools to assist them in the design process or through forgoing the design process completely and developing techniques so datasets can be used effectively in the absence of intelligent database design.

Modelling and Analysis

Methods for querying and mining Big Data are fundamentally different from traditional statistical analysis on small samples. Big Data is often noisy, dynamic, heterogeneous, inter-related, and untrustworthy. Nevertheless, even noisy Big Data could be more valuable than tiny samples because general statistics obtained from frequent patterns and correlation analysis usually overpower individual fluctuations and often disclose more reliable hidden patterns and knowledge. In fact, with suitable statistical care, one can use approximate analyses to get good results without being overwhelmed by the volume.

Interpretation

Ultimately, a decision-maker, provided with the result of analysis, has to interpret these results. Usually, this involves examining all the assumptions made and retracing the analysis. Furthermore, there are many possible sources of error: computer systems can have bugs, models almost always have assumptions, and results can be based on erroneous data. For all of these reasons, no responsible user will cede authority to the computer system. Rather, she will try to understand, and verify, the results produced by the computer. The computer system must make it easy for her to do so. This is particularly a challenge with Big Data due to its complexity. There are often crucial assumptions behind the data recorded. Analytical pipelines can involve multiple steps, again with assumptions built in. The recent mortgage-related shock to the financial system dramatically underscored the need for such decision-maker diligence—rather than accept the stated solvency of a financial institution at face value, a decision-maker has to examine critically the many assumptions at multiple stages of analysis. In short, it is rarely enough to provide just the results. Rather, one must provide users with the ability both to interpret analytical results obtained and to repeat the analysis with different assumptions, parameters, or datasets to better support the human thought process and social circumstances.

The net result of interpretation is often the formulation of opinions that annotate the base data, essentially closing the pipeline. It is common that such opinions may conflict with each other or may be poorly substantiated by the underlying data. In such cases, communities need to engage in a conflict resolution "editorial" process (the Wikipedia community provides one example of such a process). A novel generation of data workspaces is needed where community participants can annotate base data with interpretation metadata, resolve their disagreements and clean up the dataset, while partially clean and partially consistent data may still be available for inspection.

4. CHALLENGES IN BIG DATA ANALYSIS

Having described the multiple phases in the Big Data analysis pipeline, we now turn to some common challenges that underlie many, and sometimes all, of these phases, due to the characteristics of Big Data. These are shown as six boxes in the lower part of Figure 1.

Heterogeneity

When humans consume information, a great deal of heterogeneity is comfortably tolerated. In fact, the nuance and richness of natural language can provide valuable depth. However, machine analysis algorithms expect homogeneous data, and are poor at understanding nuances. In consequence, data must be carefully structured as a first step in (or prior to) data analysis. An associated challenge is to automatically generate the right metadata to describe the data recorded. For example, in scientific experiments, considerable detail regarding specific experimental conditions and procedures may be required in order

Figure 1. Big data analysis pipeline. Top is the major steps in the analysis of big data and bottom is the big data characteristics.

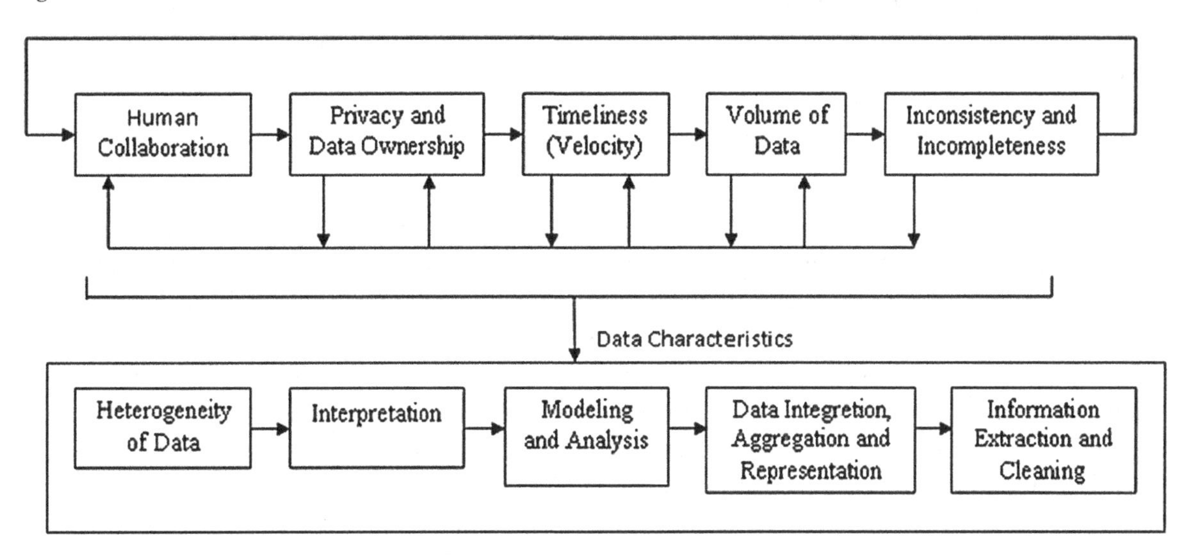

to interpret the results correctly. Metadata acquisition systems can minimize the human burden in recording metadata. Recording information about the data at its birth is not useful unless this information can be interpreted and carried along through the data analysis pipeline. This is called data provenance. For example, a processing error at one step can render subsequent analysis useless; with suitable provenance, we can easily identify all subsequent processing that depends on this step. Therefore, this needs data systems to carry the provenance of data and its metadata through data analysis pipelines.

Inconsistency and Incompleteness

Big Data increasingly includes information provided by increasingly diverse sources, of varying reliability. Uncertainty, errors, and missing values are endemic, and must be managed. The volume and redundancy of Big Data can often be exploited to compensate for missing data, to crosscheck conflicting cases, to validate trustworthy relationships, to disclose inherent clusters, and to uncover hidden relationships and models.

Similar issues emerge in crowd sourcing. While most such errors will be detected and corrected by others in the crowd, needs technologies to facilitate this. As humans can look at reviews of a product, some of which are gushing and others negative, and come up with a summary assessment based on which can decide whether to buy the product. The issues of uncertainty and error become even more pronounced in a specific type of crowd sourcing called participatory sensing. In this case, every person with a mobile phone can act as a multi-modal sensor collecting various types of data instantaneously like picture, video, audio, location, time, speed, direction, acceleration. The extra challenge here is the inherent uncertainty of the data collection devices. The fact that collected data is probably spatially and temporally correlated can be exploited to better assess their correctness. When crowd sourced data is obtained for hire, such as with Mechanical Turks, the varying motivations of workers give rise to yet another error model.

Even after error correction has been applied, some incompleteness and some errors in data are likely to remain. This incompleteness and these errors must be managed during data analysis. Doing this correctly is a challenge. Recent work on managing and querying probabilistic and conflicting data suggests one way to make progress.

Scale

The first thing anyone thinks of with Big Data is its size. Managing large and rapidly increasing volumes of data has been a challenging issue for many decades. In the past, this challenge was mitigated by processors getting faster, following Moore's Law. But there is a fundamental shift under way now: data volume is increasing faster than CPU speeds and other compute resources.

Due to power constraints, clock speeds have largely stalled and processors are being built with increasing numbers of cores. In short, one has to deal with parallelism within a single node. Unfortunately, parallel data processing techniques that were applied in the past for processing data across nodes do not directly apply for intra-node parallelism, since the architecture looks very different.

Another dramatic shift under way is the move toward cloud computing, which now aggregates multiple disparate workloads with varying performance goals into very large clusters. This level of sharing of resources on expensive and large clusters stresses grid and cluster computing techniques from the past, and requires new ways of determining how to run and execute data processing jobs to meet the goals of each workload cost effectively, and to deal with system failures, which occur more frequently when operate on larger and larger systems.

This leads to a need for global optimization across multiple users' programs, even those doing complex machine learning tasks. Reliance on user driven program optimizations is likely to lead to poor cluster utilization, since users are unaware of other users' programs, through virtualization. System-driven holistic optimization requires programs to be sufficiently transparent. In fact, if users are to compose and build complex analytical pipelines over Big Data, it is essential they have appropriate high-level primitives to specify their needs.

In addition to the technical reasons for further developing declarative approaches to Big Data analysis, there is a strong business imperative as well. Organizations typically will outsource Big Data processing. Declarative specifications are required to enable meaningful and enforceable service level agreements. The point of outsourcing is to specify precisely what task will be performed without going into details of how to do it.

Timeliness

As data grow in volume needs real-time techniques to summarize and filter the data, since in many instances it is not economically viable to store the raw data. This gives rise to the acquisition rate challenge described earlier, and a timeliness challenges. For example, if a fraudulent credit card transaction is suspected, it should ideally be flagged before the transaction is completed potentially preventing the transaction from taking place at all. Obviously, a full analysis of a user's purchase history is not likely to be feasible in real time. Rather, needs to develop partial results in advance so that a small amount of incremental computation with new data can be used to arrive at a quick determination. The fundamental challenge is to provide interactive response times to complex queries at scale over high volume event streams.

Another common pattern is to find elements in a very large dataset that meet a specified criterion. In the course of data analysis, this sort of search is likely to occur repeatedly. Scanning the entire dataset to find suitable elements is obviously impractical. Rather, index structures are created in advance to find qualifying elements quickly. For example, consider a traffic management system with information regarding thousands of vehicles and local hot spots on roadways. The system may need to predict potential congestion points along a route chosen by a user, and suggest alternatives. Doing so requires evaluating multiple spatial proximity queries working with the trajectories of moving objects. This needs to devise new index structures to support a wide variety of such criteria.

Privacy and Data Ownership

The privacy of data is another huge concern, and one that increases in the context of Big Data. For electronic health records, there are strict laws governing what data can be revealed in different contexts. For other data, regulations, particularly in the U.S., are less forceful. However, there is great public fear regarding the inappropriate use of personal data, particularly through linking of data from multiple sources. Managing privacy effectively is both a technical and a sociological problem, which must be addressed jointly from both perspectives to realize the promise of Big Data.

Consider, for example, data gleaned from location based services, which require a user to share his/her location with the service provider. There are obvious privacy concerns, which are not addressed by hiding the user's identity alone without hiding user location. An attacker location based server can infer the identity of the query source from its subsequent location information. For example, a user may leave "a trail of packet crumbs" that can be associated with a certain residence or office location, and thereby used to determine the user's identity. Several other types of surprisingly private information such as health issues for example, presence in a cancer treatment centre can also be revealed by just observing anonymous users' movement and usage patterns over time. In general, it has been shown there is a close correlation between people's identities and their movement patterns (González, M.C., Hidalgo, C.A. and Barabási, 2008). But with location based services, the location of the user is needed for a successful data access or data collection, so doing this right is challenging.

Another issue is that many online services share private information like Facebook applications, but record level access control does not understand what it means to share data, how the shared data can be linked, and how to give users fine grained control over this sharing. In addition, real data are not static but get larger and change over time; none of the prevailing techniques results in any useful content being released in this scenario.

Privacy is but one aspect of data ownership. In general, as the value of data is increasingly recognized, the value of the data owned by an organization becomes a central strategic consideration. Organizations are concerned with how to leverage this data, while retaining their unique data advantage, and questions such as how to share or sell data without losing control are becoming important. These questions are not unlike the Digital Rights Management (DRM) issues faced by the music industry as distribution shifted from sales of physical media such as CDs to digital purchases; we need effective and flexible Data DRM approaches.

The Human Perspective: Visualization and Collaboration

In ranking and recommendation algorithms can help identify the most interesting data for a user, taking into account of users preferences. However, especially when these techniques are being used for scientific discovery and exploration, special care must be taken to not imprison end users. Interesting discoveries come from detecting and explaining outliers from data similar to what they have already seen in the past (Pariser, 2011).

In spite of the tremendous advances made in computational analysis, there remain many patterns that humans can easily detect but computer algorithms have a difficult time finding. For example, CAPTCHAs exploit precisely this fact to tell human Web users apart from computer programs. Ideally, analytics for Big Data will not be all computational rather it will be designed explicitly to have a human in the loop. The new subfield of visual analytics is attempting to do this, at least with respect to the modelling and analysis phase in the pipeline. There is similar value to human input at all stages of the analysis pipeline.

In today's complex world, it often takes multiple experts from different domains to really understand what is going on. A Big Data analysis system must support input from multiple human experts, and shared exploration of results. These multiple experts may be separated in space and time when it is too expensive to assemble an entire team together in one room. The data system must accept this distributed expert input, and support their collaboration. Technically, this requires us to consider sharing more than raw datasets are considered to enable sharing algorithms and artefacts such as experimental results.

Systems with a rich palette of visualizations can be quickly and declaratively created, become important in conveying to the users the results of the queries in ways that are best understood in the particular domain and are at the right level of detail. Whereas early business intelligence systems'users were content with tabular presentations, today's analysts need to pack and present results in powerful visualizations that assist interpretation, and support user collaboration. Furthermore, with a few clicks the user should be able to drill down into each piece of data and understands its provenance. This is particularly important since there is a growing number of users who have data and wish to analyze it.

A popular new method of harnessing human ingenuity to solve problems is through crowd sourcing. Wikipedia, the online encyclopaedia, is perhaps the best known example of crowd sourced data. Social approaches to Big Data analysis hold great promise. As it makes a broad range of data centric artifacts sharable, such as rating of artifacts, leader-boards, and induced reputations of algorithms and experts.

CONCLUSION

Many sectors of economy are now moving to a data driven decision making model where the core business relies on analysis of large and diverse volumes of data that are continually being produced. This data-driven world has the potential to improve the efficiencies of enterprises and improve the quality of our lives. However, there are a number of challenges that must be addressed to allow us to exploit the full potential of Big Data. This article highlighted key technical challenges that must be addressed, and acknowledge there are other challenges, such as economic, social, and political, that are not covered in this article but must also be addressed. Not all of the technical challenges discussed here arise in all application scenarios. But many do. Also, the solutions to a challenge may not be the same in all situations. But again, there often are enough similarities to support cross-learning. As such, the broad range of challenges described here make good topics for research across many areas of computer science. Further reading at http://db.cs.pitt.edu/bigdata/resources. These are a few dozen papers we have chosen on account of their coverage and importance, rather than a comprehensive bibliography, which would comprise thousands of papers.

REFERENCES

CCC. (2011a). *Computing Community Consortium. Advancing Discovery in Science and Engineering*. CCC.

CCC. (2011b). *Computing Community Consortium. Advancing Personalized Education*. CCC.

CCC. (2011c). *Computing Community Consortium. Smart Health and Wellbeing*. CCC.

CCC. (2011d). *Computing Community Consortium. A Sustainable Future*. CCC.

Flood, M., Jagadish, H. V., Kyle, A., Olken, F., & Raschid, L. (2011). Using data for systemic financial risk management. In *Proc. 5th Biennial Conf. InnovativeData Systems Research*. Gartner Group. Retrieved from http://www.gartner.com/it/page.jsp?id=1731916

González, M. C., Hidalgo, C. A., & Barabási, A.-L. (2008). A-L.Understanding individual human mobility patterns. *Nature*, *453*(7196), 779–782. doi:10.1038/nature06958 PMID:18528393

Lazar, D., et al. (2009). Computational social science. *Science, 323*(5915), 721–723.

National Science and Technology. (2011). *Council*. Materials Genome Initiative for Global Competitiveness.

Pariser, E. (2011). *The Filter Bubble: What the Internet Is Hiding From You*. Penguin Press.

Brynjolfsson, E., Hitt, L., & Kim, H. H. (2011). Strength in numbers: how does data-driven decision making affect firm performance? MIT - Sloan School of Management.

Tambe, P. (2014). Big data investment, skills and firm value. *Management Science*, *60*(6), 1452–1469. doi:10.1287/mnsc.2014.1899

Bakhshi, H., Bravo-Biosca, A., & Mateos-Garcia, J. (2014). *Inside the datavores: how data and online analytics affect business performance*. Nesta.

Chapter 7
Possibilities, Impediments, and Challenges for Network Security in Big Data

Anuj Kumar Dwivedi
Govt. Vijay Bhusan Singh Deo Girls Degree College, India

O. P. Vyas
Indian Institute of Information Technology Allahabad, India

ABSTRACT

With the time, Big Data became the core competitive factor for enterprises to develop and grow. Some enterprises such as, information industrial enterprises will put more focus on the technology or product innovation for solving the challenges of big data, i.e., capture, storage, analysis and application. Enterprises like, manufacturing, banking and other enterprises will also benefit from analysis and manage big data, and be provided more opportunities for management innovation, strategy innovation or marketing innovation. High performance network capacity provides the backbone for high end computing systems. These high end computing systems plays vital role in Big Data. Persistent and Sophisticated targeted network attacks have challenged today's enterprise security teams. By exploring each aspect of high performance network capacity, the major objective of this book chapter is to present fundamental theoretical aspects in analytical way with deep focus on possibilities, impediments and challenges for network security in Big Data.

1. INTRODUCTION

Since it is an era of information (The Economist, 2011). In this era, due to continuous development in field of electronics and IT, the computational devices and storage becomes inexpensive. With this growing computational capabilities, data is generated from everywhere. These data are stored in databases for future references/decisive purposes. The term Big Data is used for these massive data having varieties, generated with velocity and measured in term of Tera, Peta, Exa, Zetta, Yotta Bytes (Sagiroglu &

DOI: 10.4018/978-1-5225-0182-4.ch007

Sinanc, 2013). As per the Oracle (Dijcks, 2013), big data typically refer these types of data: traditional enterprise data, machine-generated /sensor data, and social data.

With the time, Big Data became the core competitive factor for enterprises to develop and grow. In the age of Big Data (Lohr, 2012), data is generated from everywhere, some enterprises such as, information industrial enterprises will put more focus on the technology or product innovation for solving the challenges of big data, i.e., capture, storage, analysis and application. Enterprises like, manufacturing, banking and other enterprises will also benefit from analysis and manage big data, and be provided more opportunities for management innovation, strategy innovation or marketing innovation. High performance network capacity provides the backbone for high end computing systems. These high end computing systems plays vital role in Big Data. Persistent and Sophisticated targeted network attacks have challenged today's enterprise security teams.

Big Data analytics promises major benefits to the enterprises. Enterprises need to enable secure access to data for analytics, in order to extract maximum value from gathered information, but these initiatives can be a cause for big prospective risks. Handling massive amounts of data increases the risk with magnitude of prospective data breaches. Sensitive data are goldmines for criminals, data can be theft/ exposed, it can violate compliance and data security regulations, aggregation of data across borders can break data residency laws. Thus secure solutions for sensitive data, yet enable analytics for meaningful insights, is necessary for any Big Data initiative (Voltage Security, n.d). Big data analytics will play a crucial role in future for detecting crime and security breaches (Gartner-Research Firm, n.d.).

2. PRIOR RESEARCH WORKS ON NETWORK SECURITY FOR BIG DATA

Enterprises awash in flood of unstructured, semi structured and structured data, which introduced a multitude of security and privacy issues for organizations to contend with. Today's enterprise security teams focused and searching for the root causes of the attack often feels like looking for a needle in a haystack, but as per a white paper (White Paper, n.d.), getting valuable information in context of big data is more than "looking for the needles", security is a serious business and it is "eliminating the hay from the haystack". Security has traditionally been all about the defense. The term network security means providing security when data is on fly, i.e. over network.

Network traffic monitoring remains a decisive component of any enterprise's security strategy, but gaining context into the gigantic amounts of data collected from network, in a timely fashion, is still a hurdle for many enterprise security teams. Incident responders are eventually looking for possible ways to definitively identify threats for evaluating risk of infection and to take the necessary steps to remediate (Arbor Networks Blog, 2014).

A new generation of methods and architectures designed specifically for big data technologies are needed that extract value from gigantic amounts of different data types through high-velocity capture, discovery and analysis. In its review, authors (Matti & Kvernvik 2012) illustrates efficient extraction of value from data and through a figure correlate three associated things: analytics, cloud-based distributed environment/deployment, and Networked Society, and these will be inextricably linked.

It is observed that data generated by the many devices having spatial and temporal characteristics, are part of the networked society. The emergence of complex networks and networks within networks are today's reality (Hurlburt & Voas 2014). When network society, cloud computing and different phases associated with big data are correlated and viewed in a single sleeve, these two figures (Figure 1 and Figure 2) are originated in current and future context, because networking is currently in a transition phase, from layer-based approaches to layer-less approaches.

So from network security point of view focus should be assessed from current scenario to future requirements/aspects. Getting oneself abreast of current literature on Big Data and their idiosyncrasies with respect to security and privacy issues of/in Big Data is totally dependent on three Vs (variety, velocity and volume). Since a proliferation of data which is being generated by multitude of devices, users, and generated traffic, with incredible volume, velocity, and variety ("Big security for big data," 2012). Authors of a research paper discussed characteristics, architecture and framework for Big Data (Tekiner & Keane, 2013). As per authors of same research paper, a big data framework consists several layers, such as system layer, data collection layer, processing layer, modelling/statistical layer, service/query/access layer, visualization/presentation layer etc.

Authors of a paper (Cardenas et al. 2012) highlights that traditional security approaches are inadequate since they are tailored to secure small-scale static data. The three Vs of Big Data demands ultra-fast response times from security and privacy solutions/products. In same paper, authors highlights that these are the top 10 Big Data security and privacy challenges from Big Data point of view: needs secure computations in distributed programming frameworks, non-relational data stores demands best security practices, required security at data storage and transactions logs, validation/filtering is required at input end-points, real time security/compliance monitoring is required, scalable and composable privacy preserved data mining and analytics required, access control and secure communication must be cryptographically enforced, demands granular access control, required granular audits, and data provenance.

Figure 1. Big data aspects in current networking scenario

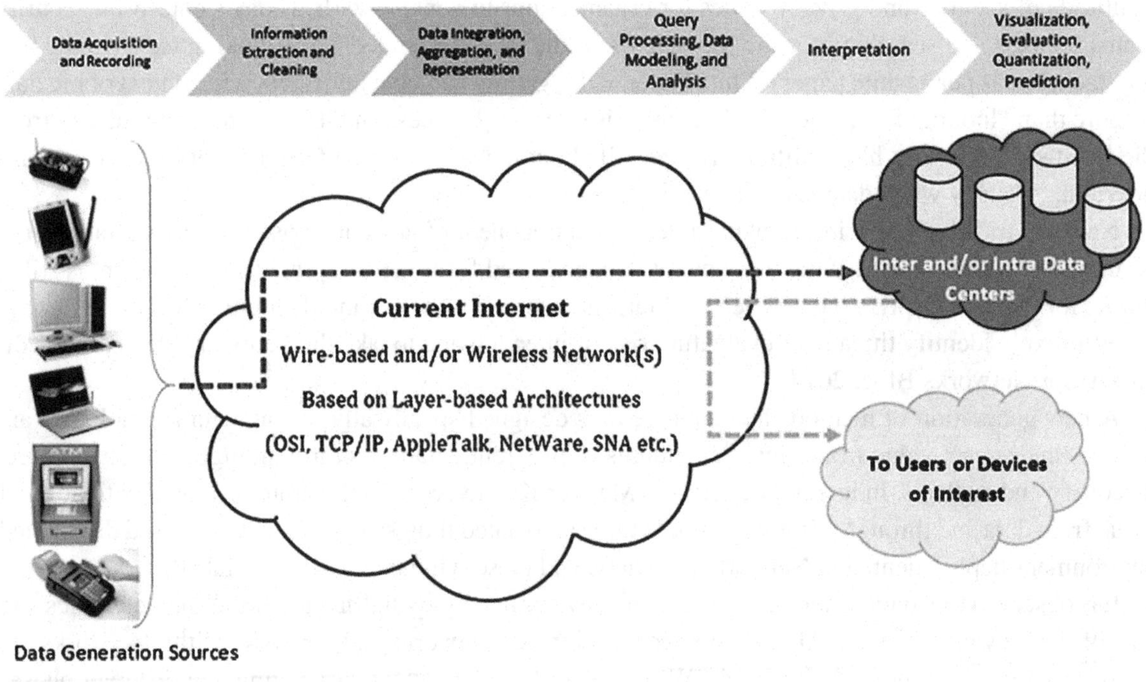

Figure 2. Big data aspects in future networking consequence

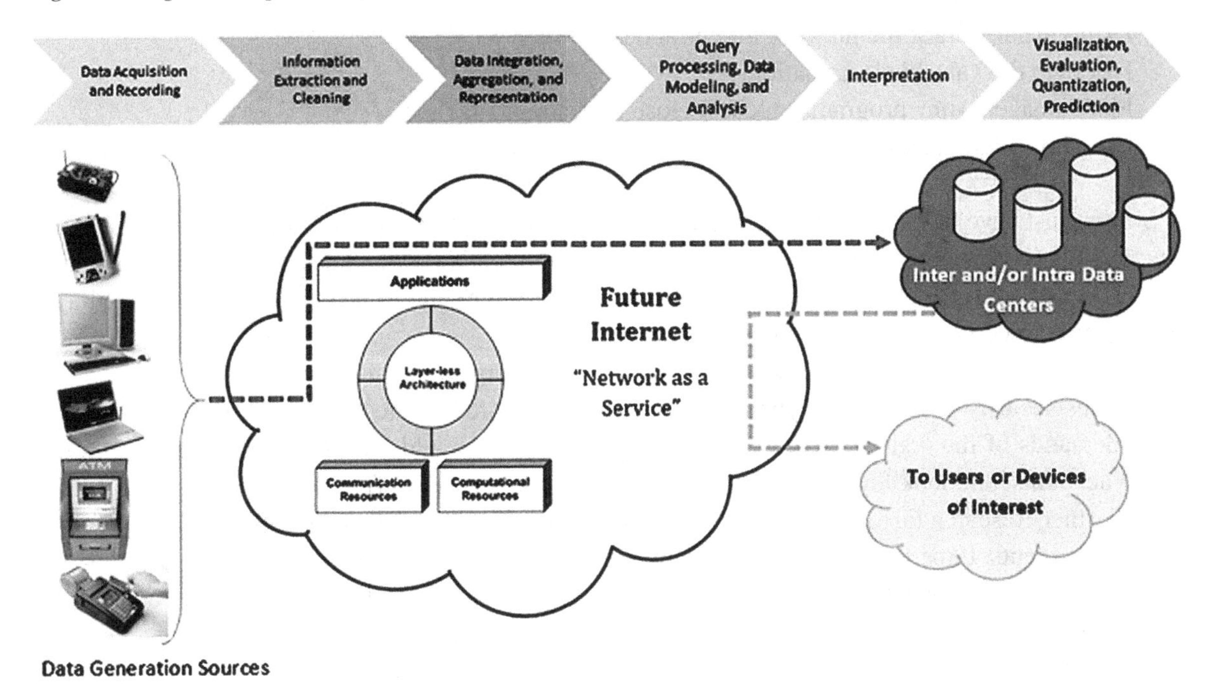

Due to dependency on Big Data and criticalness of data/information/knowledge in terms of human lives, there is a need to rethink particularly from a security viewpoint. Big Data breaches will be big too, with the potential for even more serious reputational damage and legal repercussions than at present. Security and privacy issues must be magnified by three Vs of Big Data. Diversity of data sources, streaming nature of data acquisition, distinct data formats, large scale heterogeneous networking environment, proprietary technologies/software are the big causes that why there is a need to think beyond traditional security and privacy solutions.

In a white paper (Curry, et al 2013), author focuses on intelligence-driven security for big data and states that rapid and massive growth information related to security creates new competencies to defend against the unknown threats.

Authors of another white paper ("Big security for big data," 2012), focuses that intelligence is necessary for tackling security and privacy issues related to big data. In the same paper authors suggested that these four steps are required for security intelligence: Data collection, Data integration, Data analytics and Intelligent threat and risk detection (which includes real-time threat detection/evaluation, pattern matching, statistical correlation, security analysis, and log data management, i.e. monitor and respond with the help of sophisticated correlation technologies).

3. POSSIBILITIES FOR NETWORK SECURITY IN BIG DATA

Threats or malicious cyber events typically cross multiple channels and use multiple attack trajectories. Traditionally data theft involve five steps:

1. Identify target and a way to enter network,
2. Drill/Partially crack the network for entrance,
3. Discover the valuable information,
4. Plant an agent (tiny programs/patches) close to desired data, and
5. Data/Information leak out.

So we must have binaries involved in an attack or file hashes, log data, command and control infrastructure, host ownership, location, actor meta-data, etc. for identification of treats in real-time. The best way for security during data on fly is fastest data transfer between source and destination with multilayer strongly encrypted wrapping of data packets.

As per as a research firm (Gartner-Research Firm, n.d.), organizations/enterprises should align the capabilities security in a holistic cyber security strategy tailored to the threats and the risks specific to the demands of the organization. Organizations/enterprises should look for users or other entities, profile accounts, and look for anomalous transactions against those profiles. As per the same research firm (Gartner-Research Firm, n.d.), big data demands will soon change the currently available security products/concepts. Experts believe the growth of big data analytics may provide new tools in combating cyber security threats, but an integrated prevention approaches is the best option against treats.

Since threat landscape is growing simultaneously with the three Vs of big data and showing same characteristics as well, if threat detection/countermeasures mechanisms are weak, the result will be inadequate (Figure 3).

As per the authors of another white paper ("Addressing Big Data Security Challenges," 2012), the right combination of mechanisms/methodologies, an expert understanding of the threat landscape, human insight and quick-witted and fast processing of big data to create actionable intelligence. Thus a good understanding and intelligence is required to correlate how data is collected and where, how to organized them, how to analyze complex relationships with the help of specialized search algorithms and employing need based custom models are the main critical components to achieve security/privacy in big data.

Due to the massive availability of available data in/from public domain, data leak-out can be costly and data hackers become more damaging (Schmitt, et al 2013). Passwords and controlled access via permissions, Two-factor (or multi-factor) authentication, Firewalls, Data Leakage Prevention (DLP) Technology are basic available existing technological approaches that are already relatively mature with time but inadequate to tackle and fulfill demands of big data.

Figure 3. A simultaneous growth in big data and threats

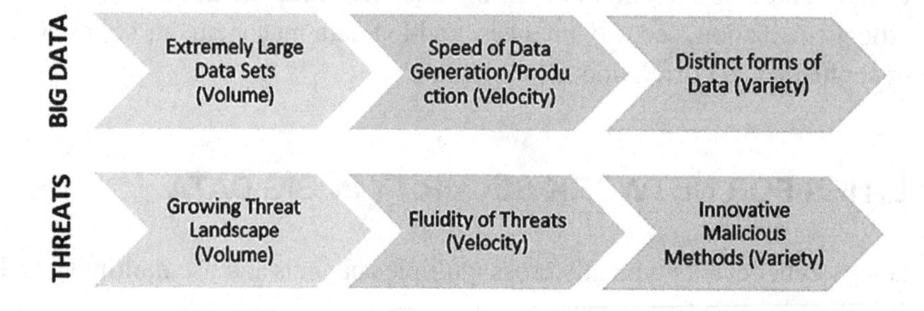

Since confidentiality, authentication and integrity are the basic security primitives, for these and other specific needs for big data one integrated solution from a holistic point of view rather than solving the security and privacy issues on requirement basis. Due to gigantic and variety of data the traditional cryptography based security mechanism are not sufficient, to resolve this. Authors of a research paper (Huang & Du 2014) proposes an image data privacy in hybrid cloud. Since with the hybrid cloud sensitive cloud can be stored in private clouds whereas no-sensitive data can be store in public clouds.

By bringing the security related data together at single centralized place, analysis can be performed that wasn't possible previously. This provides a competitive advantage over previous approaches here additional data sets can be correlated in different ways with existing data and new relationships will be found which was previously unimaginable.

Validation and assurance of end-to-end security, application specific security model, message-level security, policy oriented security, and security as a service are some security solutions and can be fruitful when shifted from current context to future context.

4. IMPEDIMENTS FOR NETWORK SECURITY IN BIG DATA

Highly distributed, redundant, and elastic data repositories makes big data architecture so critical. In current context and with future requirements, security challenges from big data point of view can be categorized at different level, such as:

1. Data level,
2. Authentication level,
3. Network level, and
4. Rest of the generic issues.

These are the some identified impediments discussed by an author (Chauhan, n.d.) for network security in big data:

1. Vulnerability at the data collection end in term of different devices, insecure software, dishonest employees.

Information leak out, data corruption and D.o.S. (denial of service) are some identified treats at data collection end. Sensitive data can be accessed, can corrupt the data leading to incorrect results, and can perform D.o.S. leading to financial/creditable losses.

2. Input validation and data filtering problem during data collection process.

A clear hallucination/strategy is needed during input about trusted data/data sources, trust parameters, untrusted data/data sources as well as there should be clear mechanisms for filtering rogue or malicious data.

3. Data are partitioned replicated and distributed in thousands of nodes (mobility, outsourcing, virtualization, and cloud computing) for performance and business initiative reasons.

Heartbleed vulnerability (The Heartbleed Bug, 2014) in the OpenSSL library was a biggest event/ challenge for Security Industry in year 2014. For good security more attention is needed on vulnerabilities, exposure and de-identification issues as well.

As per the authors of a white paper ("The Big Data Security Gap" 2013), open source technologies, was not created with security in mind, they support few security features but this is inadequate in current context.

5. CHALLENGES FOR NETWORK SECURITY IN BIG DATA

In new context of complex, social and nested networks, ubiquitous computing environment, privacy and personal security are increasingly at stake (Hurlburt & Voas 2014).

Traditional network perimeters are thawing as businesses reshape their organizations around emerging technologies such as clouds, social media, handheld computing devices, big data etc. - these sending risks escalating sky high and making it more difficult to defend against the increasing frequency and impact of attacks and ensure the safety of people tapping into data and applications.

Traditional security tools for example firewalls are good enough and mature but offers no protection from breaches which originate from within the firewall perimeter. Thus regular awareness and training for staffs are required on security and privacy issues with do's and don'ts.

While security solutions are emerging/enhanced prepared for the big data, but security teams may not. Data analysis is also an area where internal knowledge of the staff may be lacking.

As per the authors of a research paper (Lu et al, 2013), a serious attention is needed in term of security on ICT supply chain (all hardware and software involve in different phases of big data from production, storage and application) which is the carrier of big data.

As well as, from network point of view small and midsize businesses may not have adequate expertise and resources to concentrate on security issues related to networks. Therefore, they like to get it as a service from a third party which can be suspicious in many time.

6. EXISTING TOOLS AND TECHNIQUES BEST FOR BIG DATA SECURITY SOLUTIONS

As per the authors of a white paper (White Paper, n.d.), big data can play a vital role in security management as well, security management foundational concepts involve three aspects:

- An agile "scale out" infrastructure must be able to retort and fit for scalable infrastructure and evolving security threats.
- Analytics and visualization tools to support security professionals. It includes from basic event identification with supporting details, trending of key metrics in addition to high-level visualization, reconstruction of suspicious files with tools to automate testing of these files, and full reconstruction of all log and network information about a session to determine precisely what happened.
- Threat intelligence to correlate causes/pattern/impact of treats visible inside organization with the currently available information about threats outside the organization.

With the help of a comprehensive enterprise information architecture strategy that incorporates both cybersecurity and big data, proper classification of risks/risk levels, enough and regular investment on emerging tools business houses/companies mitigate risks.

There are several steps that must be normally taken before deciding on a treat tackling tool for each use case. First, search for different currently popular solutions and do a survey regarding general pros and cons for each tool. Second, narrow the list down to few (two/three) candidate tools for each use case based on the fit between the tools' strengths and own specific requirements. Third, conduct a complete benchmarking and comparison test among the candidate tools using own data sets and use cases to decide which one fits on needs best. Usually, after these three steps, we found the best available tools to tackle the threats.

Big data will have great impact that will change most of the product categories in the field of computer security including solutions/network monitoring/authentication and authorization of users/identity management/fraud detection, and systems of governance, risk and compliance. Big data will change also the nature of the security controls as conventional firewalls, anti-malware and data loss prevention. Techniques such as attribute based encryption may be useful and necessary to protect sensitive data and apply access controls. In coming years, the tools of data analysis will evolve further to enable a number of advanced predictive capabilities and automated controls in real time.

Organizations should ensure that the continued investment in security products promote technologies that use approaches agile-based analysis, not static signature-based tools to threats or on the edge of the network.

Some commercial/proprietary products are available to tackle emerging threats associated with/for Big data, few of them are addressed as follows:

- IBM Threat Protection System (IBM, n.d.), is a robust and comprehensive set of tools and best practices that are built on a framework that spans hardware, software and services to address intelligence, integration and expertise required for Big data security and privacy issues.
- HP ArcSight ("Big security for big data," 2012), another product that can strengthen security intelligence able to delivers the advanced correlation, application protection, and network defenses to protect today's hybrid IT infrastructure from sophisticated cyber threats.
- Another set of products (Identity-Based Encryption, Format-Preserving Encryption and many more) provided by Voltage Security Inc. (Voltage Security, n.d.), provides new powerful methods to protect data across its full lifecycle.
- RSA Security Management Portfolio (White Paper, n.d.), for Infrastructure, Analytics, and Intelligence can be another good option.
- Cisco's Threat Research, Analysis, and Communications (TRAC) tools (Gundert, 2013) is also a good option in this category.

Except above mentioned tools a multitude of vendors play in this space with their respective tools.

An updated and good list of Network Monitoring platforms/tools (Cottrell, n.d.) and vulnerability management tool (TechTarget, n.d.) currently in use are available with open source and proprietary classification. These tools can be useful for some fruitful context.

7. CONCLUSION AND FUTURE DIRECTIONS

Numerous literatures/white papers are available that focused/discussed on security and privacy issues associated with Big data. It is also observed that security professionals/companies apply most controls at the very edges of the network. Though, if attackers infiltrate security perimeter, they will have full and unrestricted access to sensitive big data. Some literatures/white papers/technical report suggest that placing controls as close as possible to the data store and the data itself, in order to create a more effective line of defense. Traditional security and privacy tools and techniques are even mature but unable to tackle new issues specifically associated with big data. An additional intelligence regarding pattern identification, layer based security, event based security, identification based security etc. is required parallel with traditional security approaches. As with the time detecting and preventing advanced persistent threats may be concretely answered by using Big Data style analysis. Tools and techniques will continuously demand enhancement with time as well. This book chapter present an analytical approach regarding possibilities, impediments and challenges for network security in Big Data and will be fruitful for individuals focusing on this emerging area of research.

REFERENCES

Addressing Big Data Security Challenges: The Right Tools for Smart Protection. (2012, September). White Paper. Trend Micro Incorporated. Retrieved from www.trendmicro.com

Arbor Networks Blog. (2014). *Next Generation Incident Response, Security Analytics and the Role of Big Data*. Retrieved from http://www.arbornetworks.com/corporate/blog/5126-next-generation-incident-response-security-analytics-and-the-role-of-big-data-webinar

Big security for big data. (2012, December). Business White Paper. HP.

Cardenas, A., Chen, Y., Fuchs, A., Lane, A., Lu, R., Manadhata, P., . . . Sathyadevan, S. (2012, November). *Top Ten Big Data security and Privacy Challenges*. White Paper, Cloud Security Alliance. Retrieved from http://www.cloudsecurityalliance.org/

Chauhan, J. (n.d.). *Penetration Testing, Web Application Security*. Available at: http://www.ivizsecurity.com/blog/penetration-testing/top-5-big-data-vulnerability-classes/

Cottrell, L. (2016). *Network Monitoring Tools*. Retrieved from: http://www.slac.stanford.edu/xorg/nmtf/nmtf-tools.html

Curry, Kirda, Sy, Stemberg, Schwartz, Stewart, & Yoran. (2013, January). *Big Data Fuels Intelligence-driven Security*. RSA Security Brief.

Dijcks, J. (2013, June). *Big Data for the Enterprise*. Oracle White Paper. Oracle Corporation.

Gartner-Research Firm. (n.d.). Retrieved from https://www.gartner.com

Gundert, L. (2013). *Big Data in Security – Part I: TRAC Tools*. Retrieved from: *http*://blogs.cisco.com/security/big-data-in-security-part-i-trac-tools/

Huang, X., & Du, X. (2014). Achieving Big Data Privacy via Hybrid Cloud. In *Proceedings of IEEE INFOCOM Workshop on Security and Privacy in Big Data*, (pp. 512-517). doi:10.1109/INFCOMW.2014.6849284

Hurlburt, G. F., & Voas, J. (2014). Big Data, Networked Worlds. *Computer*, (April): 84–87.

IBM. (n.d.). *SPSS Statistics*. Retrieved from: http://www.ibm.com/software/security/

Lohr, S. (2012, February 11). The Age of Big Data. *New York Times*. Retrieved from http://www.nytimes.com/2012/02/12/sunday-review/big-datasimpact-in-the-world.html

Lu, T., Guo, X., Xu, B., Zhao, L., Peng, Y., & Yang, H. (2013). Next Big Thing in Big Data: the Security of the ICT Supply Chain. In *Proceedings of the IEEE SocialCom/PASSAT/BigData/EconCom/BioMedCom*, (pp. 1066-1073). doi:10.1109/SocialCom.2013.172

Matti, M., & Kvernvik, T. (2012). *Applying Big-data technologies to Network Architecture*. Ericsson Review.

Paper, W. (n.d.). *Gettting Real About Security Management And Big Data: A Roadmap for Big Data in Security Analytics*. White Paper, RSAs and EMC Corporation. Retrieved from www.EMC.com/rsa

Sagiroglu, S., & Sinanc, D. (2013). Big Data. *RE:view*, 42–47. PMID:23577548

Schmitt, C., Shoffner, M., Owen, P., Wang, X., Lamm, B., Mostafa, J., . . . Fecho, K. (2013, November). *Security and Privacy in the Era of Big Data*. White Paper. ARENCI/National Consortium for Data Science. ARENCI White Paper Series.

Security, V. (n.d.). *Big Data, Meet Enterprise Security*. White Paper. Retrieved from http://www.voltage.com/solution/enterprise-security-for-big-data/

TechTarget. (n.d.). *Commercial and open source vulnerability management tools*. Retrieved from: *http://*searchitchannel.techtarget.com/feature/Commercial-and-open-source-vulnerability-management-tools

Tekiner, F., & Keane, J. A. (2013). Big Data Framework. In *Proceedings of IEEE International Conference on Systems, Man, and Cybernetics.*

The Big Data Security Gap: Protecting the Hadoop Cluster. (2013). A White Paper. Zettaset Company.

The Economist. (2011). *Drowning in numbers – Digital data will flood the planet and help us understand it better*. Retrieved from http://www.economist.com/blogs/dailychart/2011/11/big-data-0

The Heartbleed Bug. (2014). Retrieved from: http://heartbleed.com/

Chapter 8
Mastering Big Data in the Digital Age

Kijpokin Kasemsap
Suan Sunandha Rajabhat University, Thailand

ABSTRACT

This chapter explains the overview of big data; the volume, velocity, variety, veracity, and variability of big data; the privacy and security of big data applications; big data and multimedia utilization; the concept of MapReduce; the concept of Hadoop; big data and data mining; big data and cloud computing; the applications of big data in health care industry; the applications of big data analytics in tourism and hospitality industry; and the challenges and implications of big data in the digital age. Big data is the large volumes of data of high velocity and their variety requiring information processing to add value to the information in the future. The chapter argues that applying big data has the potential to increase organizational performance and gain sustainable competitive advantage in the digital age.

INTRODUCTION

Technology industry is experiencing its dramatic changes in the amount of data that requires the effective management and the sufficient place that data can be stored (Park, Kim, Jeong, Hong, & Kang, 2016). The pervasiveness of computers and the Internet can increase the availability of digital data in terms of volume and variety (Bantouna, Poulios, Tsagkaris, & Demestichas, 2014). The variety and veracity that are related to big data introduce a degree of uncertainty that has to be handled in addition to the volume and velocity requirements (López, del Río, Benítez, & Herrera, 2015). Big data can be utilized in science, technology, economics, and social studies (Guo, Wang, Chen, & Liang, 2014). The emergence of big data offers unprecedented opportunities for not only accelerating scientific advances, but also enabling the new modes of discovery (Honavar, 2014).

The advancements in telecommunications and computer technologies and the associated reductions in costs have led to an exponential growth and availability of data, both in structured and unstructured patterns (Kshetri, 2014). Due to the increase in the volume and types of data processed in the cloud

DOI: 10.4018/978-1-5225-0182-4.ch008

computing environments, methods that allow easy access to big data stored in the heterogeneous devices in the different network environments are in demand (Jeong & Shin, 2015). Processing big data presents an important approach to the existing computation platforms and hardware (Yang & Fong, 2015). Contemporary discussions concerning big data have been technologically biased and industry-oriented, toward the technical aspects of its design (Boyd & Crawford, 2012).

In recent years, big data has been an important item on the national agenda and is considered as a crucial element of technological infrastructure (Esposti, 2014). The design and analysis of big data-related technologies should be based on contextual understanding, that is, a context-based evaluation that determines the usefulness of a technology within a specific context (Shin, 2014). Big data becomes more popular because it widely exists in many applications, such as social network and astronomy (Li, Chen, Jin, Zhang, & Zhou, 2014). Big data goes beyond the critical data that companies traditionally used to make business decisions (Fanning & Grant, 2013). Big data is generated from recent social network services, and distributed processing techniques have been studied to analyze it (Park, Kim, Jeong, & Lee, 2014).

This chapter aims to bridge the gap in the literature on the thorough literature consolidation of big data. The extensive literature of big data provides a contribution to practitioners and researchers by describing the theory and applications of big data in order to maximize the business impact of big data in the digital age.

BACKGROUND

The quantity of data is exploding worldwide, and the ability to analyze large data sets, also known as big data, is a significant factor for competitiveness that is underpinning the new waves of productivity, growth, and innovation (Kitchin, 2014). The advancements in big data analysis offer the cost-effective opportunities for the improvements in the critical decision-making development areas, such as health care, employment, economic productivity, crime, security, natural disasters, and resource management (Tinati, Halford, Carr, & Pope, 2014). Big data technology revolutionizes commerce and society. The unlimited potential of a data-driven economy is widely recognized, and there is an increasing enthusiasm for the notion of big data (Shin & Choi, 2015).

Big data is an emerging paradigm applied to the large data sets whose size is beyond the ability of commonly used software tools to capture, manage, and process the data within a tolerable elapsed time (Wigan & Clarke, 2013). The collection and aggregation of large data sets and the development of analytical tools by which to study these data is part of cutting-edge efforts across scientific disciplines, with social, behavioral, and economic sciences (White & Breckenridge, 2014). With the rapid development of group-oriented services over big data, it needs the technological solutions to ensure the security of big data (Hsu, Zeng, & Zhang, 2014).

The data generated through mobile applications on smartphones represents one of the most interesting and valuable shares of big data (Buck, Horbel, Kesseler, & Christian, 2014). Business knowledge is as important as technical skills for working on big data initiatives (Debortoli, Müller, & vom Brocke, 2014). The characteristics of big data are tightly linked to data privacy, security, and effects on consumer welfare, thus attracting the attentions of practitioners, policymakers, and researchers (Kshetri, 2014). Big data requires a shift in traditional computing architecture (Chen, Lu, Xiao, & Liu, 2014).

THEORY AND APPLICATIONS OF BIG DATA IN THE DIGITAL AGE

This section emphasizes the overview of big data; the volume, velocity, variety, veracity, and variability of big data; the privacy and security of big data applications; big data and multimedia utilization; the concept of MapReduce; the concept of Hadoop; big data and data mining; big data and cloud computing; the applications of big data in health care industry; the applications of big data analytics in tourism and hospitality industry; and the challenges and implications of big data in the digital age.

Overview of Big Data

Big data refers to the explosion of digital data created by people, machines, sensors, tools, and other technological mechanisms (Schilling & Bozic, 2014). Boyd and Crawford (2012) defined big data as a cultural, technological, and scholarly phenomenon based on the interplay of technology, analysis, and mythology. Faltesek (2013) viewed big data as a brand name for the relationship between society, technology, and politics. Big data is a term applied to data sets whose size is beyond the ability of available tools to organize their acquisition, access, analytics, and application in a reasonable amount of time (Tien, 2013). Regarding massive technology advances, the term big data is broadly applied to include social and commercial environments (Kwon, Lee, & Shin, 2014).

The term of big data is increasingly being used to refer to the challenges and advantages derived from collecting and processing the vast amounts of data (Marx, 2013). Big data is defined as the quantity of data that exceeds the processing capabilities of a given system in terms of time and memory consumption (Minelli, Chambers, & Dhiraj, 2013). Big data is a collection of the large and complex data sets complicated to process using the on-hand database management tools and traditional data processing applications (Fond, Brunel, Leboyer, & Boyer, 2014). Andrejevic (2013) emphasized the socio-cultural efforts to understand the social world through big data.

Big data is one of the most important areas in information technology (IT) (Fanning & Drogt, 2014). The development of IT has enabled an exponential growth on the data that is produced, processed, stored, shared, analyzed, and visualized (López et al., 2015). Big data involves a collection of large data sets whose size significantly challenges the standard database management systems and promotes the application of knowledge extraction techniques (Zikopoulos, Eaton, DeRoos, Deutsch, & Lapis, 2011). Esposti (2014) indicated that big data represents a socio-technical reality characterized by the heterogeneous, changing, and inconsistent elements. Understanding big data as socio-technical phenomena facilitates the shift to the meaningful and sustainable big data (Shin & Choi, 2015). The applications of big data include enterprise management, the Internet of Things, online social networks, collective intelligence, and smart grid.

Big data is related to the analysis of social networks, automated data aggregation and mining, web and mobile analytics, the visualization of large data sets, sentiment analysis, machine learning, natural language processing, and the computer-assisted content analysis of very large data sets (Parks, 2014). Vitolo et al. (2015) indicated that effective visualization is a key element in applications for decision support, whether to show output data processing and simulation results. Big data brings new opportunities for discovering new values, helps practitioners to gain an in-depth understanding of the hidden values, and obtains new challenges (Hsu et al., 2014). There are the four phases of the value chain of big data (i.e., data generation, data acquisition, data storage, and data analysis) (Chen, Mao, & Liu, 2014). Jiang et al. (2014) stated that the big data resource service platform architecture involves three levels (i.e., data resource identification and access, data resources storage and analysis, and network information service platform).

Volume, Velocity, Variety, Veracity, and Variability of Big Data

While the classic definition of big data includes the three dimensions of volume, velocity, and variety, the fourth dimension, veracity, has recently come to the attention of researchers and practitioners (Bendler, Wagner, Brandt, & Neumann, 2014). Volume refers to the magnitude of data (Gandomi & Haider, 2015). It is difficult to estimate how much total data is electronically stored all over the world (Xin, Wang, Qu, & Wang, 2015). Regarding the survey conducted by IBM in 2012, data sets having over one terabyte are considered as big data (Schroeck, Shockley, Smart, Romero-Morales, & Tufano, 2012). One terabyte stores as much data as would fit on 1500 CDs or 220 DVDs, enough to store around 16 million Facebook photographs. Beaver et al. (2010) reported that Facebook processes up to one million photographs per second. One petabyte equals 1024 terabytes. Facebook stores 260 billion photos utilizing the storage space of over 20 petabytes (Gandomi & Haider, 2015).

Variety refers to the structural heterogeneity in the data set (Gandomi & Haider, 2015). Data variety has been one of the most critical features for multimedia big data (Guo, Pan, Lu, Zhou, & Ma, 2015). Technological advances allow firms to utilize various types of structured, semi-structured, and unstructured data. Structured data refers to the tabular data found in spreadsheets or relational databases. Text, images, audio, and video are the examples of unstructured data, which sometimes lack the structural organization required by machines for analysis. Spanning a continuum between fully structured and unstructured data, the format of semi-structured data does not conform to strict standards. Internet users also generate an extremely diverse set of structured and unstructured data (O'Leary, 2013). Extensible Markup Language (XML), a textual language for exchanging data on the Web 2.0, is a typical example of semi-structured data. XML documents contain the user-defined data tags which make them machine-readable (Gandomi & Haider, 2015).

Velocity refers to the rate at which data is generated and the speed at which it should be analyzed and acted upon (Gandomi & Haider, 2015). The proliferation of digital devices (e.g., smartphones and sensors) has led to an unprecedented rate of data creation and is driving a growing requirement for the real-time analytics and evidence-based planning. Conventional retailers are generating the high-frequency data. For example, Wal-Mart processes more than one million transactions per hour. The data emerging from mobile devices and flowing through mobile applications significantly produces the amount of information that can be utilized to generate the real-time offers for everyday customers. This data provides sound information about customers (e.g., geospatial location, demographics, and past buying patterns) which can be analyzed in real time to create customer value.

IBM coined the term veracity regarding the application of big data, representing the unreliability inherent in the major sources of data (Gandomi & Haider, 2015). For example, customer sentiments in social media are uncertain, since they entail human judgment. Customer sentiments contain valuable information. The need to deal with the imprecise and uncertain data is another concern of big data, which is addressed using tools and analytics developed for the effective management and mining of uncertain data. Mining the potential value hidden behind big data has been a popular research topic around the world (Yang & Fong, 2015). Variability refers to the variation in the data flow rates. Often, big data velocity is not consistent and has periodic peaks and troughs (Gandomi & Haider, 2015).

Privacy and Security of Big Data Applications

Although big data technology has the potential to provide powerful competitive advantages, governments and companies are struggling to establish effective governance and privacy in connection with big data initiatives (Shin & Choi, 2015). Existing concerns with big data, such as the invasion of privacy, imperfect security, and limited interoperability are rarely examined compared to other technology concerns. Big data infrastructure effectively supports the data life cycle and explores the benefits of data storage and aggregation during an indefinite period (Shin & Choi, 2015).

Big data infrastructure must ensure data security and data ownership protection (Agrawal, Das, & Abbadi, 2011). Processing big data requires powerful computations and the possibility to enforce the big data-related policy such that the data can be processed on the trusted systems (Bollier & Firestone, 2010). Zhang et al. (2014) stated that data privacy is one of the most concerned issues because the privacy-sensitive data sets require computation resources provisioned by public cloud computing services. As big data applications are introduced, interoperability standards for big data are required to cope with the challenges including clear provenance of data, reliable researcher standards for the exchange of data between multiple domains, enabling data combination and analysis, and security measures to facilitate research while protecting sensitive data (Kitchin, 2014).

Data anonymization is an effective way for data privacy preservation (Fung, Wang, Chen, & Yu, 2010). Data anonymization refers to the hiding identity and sensitive data for owners of data records (Zhang et al., 2014). Sub-tree anonymization scheme is broadly adopted to anonymize data sets for privacy preservation, producing a good tradeoff between data utility and distortion. There are two ways to accomplish sub-tree anonymization (i.e., top-down specialization and bottom-up generalization) (Zhang et al., 2014). Data sets in big data applications on cloud computing have become large that it is a big challenge for existing sub-tree anonymization algorithms to anonymize such data sets in a scalable manner, due to their lack of parallelization capability (Zhang et al., 2014).

Big Data and Multimedia Utilization

Huge volumes of multimedia (e.g., images, audios, videos, and text documents) are being generated and consumed on a daily basis (Guo et al., 2015). Multimedia has become a pattern of big data which gives the users valuable information (e.g., event occurrence, networks computing, purchase recommendation, and workflow control) (Wang, Liu, Zhang, & Zhang, 2014). Therefore, multimedia content retrieval from big data environment encourages a tremendous amount of research. In the past decades, multimedia retrieval is mainly founded on text-based approaches, which are only based on the text contents surrounding multimedia in certain host files (Guo et al., 2015). Although keywords are utilized to retrieve various types of multimedia documents, this method is not intrinsically supported.

Multimedia retrieval is recognized to achieve an excellent performance because of the noise (Yang et al., 2012). Regardless of the fact that users feel more convenient to retrieve multimedia content through text keywords, content-based retrieval has been broadly utilized in commercial search engines, such as Google and Bing Image Search. However, it is considerably difficult to execute heterogeneous retrieval based on multimedia content (Zhou, Ting, Liu, & Yin, 2012). For example, given a video and audio documents for the same artist, the content-based approaches have no ability to identify the artist or extract other similar features from the binary data of two documents regarding the difference in data formats. In many cases, content-based approach may ignore users' retrieval intent (Guo et al., 2015).

Regarding multimedia applications, da Silva et al. (2011) explained methods for Content-Based Image Retrieval (CBIR) systems based on relevance feedback according to two active learning paradigms (i.e., greedy and planned perspectives). Concerning greedy perspective, the system returns the most relevant images for a query at each iteration. Regarding planned perspective, the most informative images are returned during a few iterations and the most relevant ones are only presented afterwards. CBIR techniques can alleviate the huge manual effort that is put into describing and indexing of digital copies of historical photographs (Song et al., 2015).

Video databases contain huge amounts of data in high dimensions, and clever methods to describe and search these databases are needed (Song et al., 2015). Almeida et al. (2012) presented the method for summarizing video content based on exploiting visual features extracted from the video stream without decoding. Other works report visual content analysis in huge data applications, such as video sharing in social networks and intelligent surveillance systems (Fernandes, Maldague, Batista, & Barcelos, 2011). Multimedia applications representing video events practically include criminal investigation systems (Wu & Wang, 2010), video surveillance (Liu, Li, & Delp, 2009), intrusion detection system (Zhang, Zulkernine, & Haque, 2008), video resources browsing and indexing system (Yu, Pedrinaci, Dietze, & Domingue, 2012), and sports events detection (Xu et al., 2008).

Concept of MapReduce

Big data is the next frontier for innovation, competition, and productivity, and many solutions continue to appear, partly supported by the considerable enthusiasm around the MapReduce paradigm for large-scale data analysis (Dobre & Xhafa, 2014). The volume, velocity, and variety of generated data require special techniques and technologies for data analysis (Shah, Rabhi, & Ray, 2015). MapReduce is a popular data-parallel programming model encompassed with the recent advances in computing technology and has been widely exploited for the large-scale data analysis (Jiang, Chen, Qiao, Weng, & Li, 2015). MapReduce has been integrated with cloud computing to provide powerful computation capability for applications (Dean & Ghemawat, 2010).

MapReduce is a well-known framework for programming commodity computer clusters to perform large-scale data processing algorithm (Song et al., 2015). MapReduce organizes the processing in two major operations (i.e., Map process and Reduce process). A Map process is responsible for dividing the original data set and processing each group of information. A Reduce process collects the results provided in the previous step and combines those results including new treatment if necessary. A Reduce process that divides the original data set can have a strong effect when dealing with imbalanced data sets as the data-related intrinsic characteristic effect is expanded.

The Map stage processes the input set and produces an intermediate set of key/value pairs. The key/value pairs are then grouped to be processed by the Reduce stage, which generates another set of pairs. The Map and Reduce stages can be as simple or complex as required, also composing chains of computations (Vitolo et al., 2015). Regarding MapReduce, the small sample size (Wasikowski & Chen, 2010) is practically generated when the original data set is distributed. The data set-based shift problem (Moreno-Torres, Raeder, Aláiz-Rodríguez, Chawla, & Herrera, 2012) may be encouraged in the process. The addition of these problems reinforce the necessity of properly dealing with imbalanced data sets, not only for the original imbalance that is present in the data, but also for the problems that arise when the data-related partitions are created (López et al., 2015).

Song et al. (2015) indicated that in recent years, facing information explosion, industry and academia have adopted distributed file system and MapReduce programming model to address new challenges the big data has brought. MapReduce programming paradigm has been widely applied to solve the large-scale problems. Intensive studies of MapReduce scheduling have been executed to improve MapReduce system performance (Li, Wei, Fu, & Luo, 2014).

Apache has developed an open source implementation of MapReduce called Hadoop, successfully applied to a wide variety of computational problems. Examples of Hadoop include commercial applications (e.g., Facebook and eBay) and scientific research, such as Geographical Information Systems (Chen, Wang, & Shang, 2008) and cell structure analysis (Zhang, de Sterck, Aboulnaga, Djambazian, & Sladek, 2010). The MapReduce approach has been popular in computing large scale data since Google implemented its platform on Google Distributed File Systems (GFS) followed by Amazon Web Service (AWS) providing the Apache Hadoop platform in inexpensive computing nodes (Woo, 2013).

Concept of Hadoop

Hadoop, an open-source MapReduce implementation, is able to handle the large data sets in a reliable, efficient, and scalable manner. Hadoop is a Java-based programming framework that supports the processing of large data sets in a distributed computing environment. Based on Hadoop, many cloud computing-related data warehouses, such as Hive, HBase (Leonardi et al., 2014), and HadoopDB, are developed and widely applied in various fields.

The Apache Hadoop is one of the most recognized MapReduce implementations (Dean & Ghemawat, 2008), and has been used by scientists as the base of their own research work (Tatebe, Hiraga, & Soda, 2010). Cogset is a generic and efficient engine for the reliable storage and parallel processing of distributed data sets (Valvåg, Johansen, & Kvalnes, 2013). Cogset supports a number of high-level programming interfaces, including a MapReduce interface compatible with Hadoop (Valvåg et al., 2013).

G-Hadoop is a MapReduce implementation targeting on a distributed system with multiple clusters, such as the grid infrastructures (Kolodziej & Xhafa, 2012; Ranjan, Harwood, & Buyya, 2012; Wang, Chen, & Huang, 2011), cloud computing (Ranjan, Mitra, & Georgakopoulos, 2013; Wang, Chen, Hu, Ma, & Wang, 2013; Wang, Kunze, Tao, & Laszewski, 2011), and distributed virtual machines (Wang, Chen, Zhao, & Tao, 2012). In order to share data across multiple domains, G-Hadoop replaces Hadoop's native distributed file system with the Gfarm grid file system (Tatebe et al., 2010).

Big Data and Data Mining

Data is inherently uncertain in most applications (He, Wang, Zhuang, Shang, & Shi, 2015). This data comes from a wide range of sources, such as sensors, digital pictures, videos, purchase transactions, and social media posts (Madden, 2012). The data growth in the last years has increased the interest in effectively acquiring knowledge to analyze and predict future trends (López et al., 2015). Analyzing and extracting knowledge from the large-scale data sets is a very challenging task in modern organizations (Triguero, Peralta, Bacardit, García, & Herrera, 2015). Vitolo et al. (2015) indicated that interpolating available data in space and time is necessary before the data can be fed into models or other algorithms for scenario analysis, hypothesis testing, and prediction.

The analysis and knowledge extraction process from big data become the very difficult tasks for most of the classical and advanced data mining and machine learning tools (Woniak, Graña, & Corchado, 2014). This problem occurs when the number of instances of one class (positive or minority class) is substantially smaller than the number of instances that belong to other classes (negative or majority classes) (López et al., 2015). The importance of this problem resides on its prevalence in the numerous real-world applications, such as telecommunications, finance, and medical diagnosis. In this situation, the interest of the learning is focused toward the minority class as it is the class that needs to be correctly identified in these problems (López, Fernández, García, Palade, & Herrera, 2013). Big data is also affected by this uneven class distribution (López et al., 2015).

Numerous solutions have been proposed to deal with the imbalanced data sets (López, Fernández, Moreno-Torres, & Herrera, 2012). These solutions are typically organized in two groups (i.e., data-level solutions and algorithm-level solutions). Data-level solutions (Chawla, Bowyer, Hall, & Kegelmeyer, 2002) practically modify the original training set to obtain a balanced class distribution that can be used with any classifier. Algorithm-level solutions alter the operations of an algorithm so that the minority class instances have more relevance and are correctly classified. Cost-sensitive solutions (Elkan, 2001) integrate both approaches as they are emphasized in reducing the misclassification costs.

With an increasing amount of scientific and industrial data sets, mining the useful information from big data is growing for business intelligence (Qian, Lv, Yue, Liu, & Jing, 2015). Data mining is the computational procedure of pioneering schemes in the large data sets regarding methods at the integration of artificial intelligence, machine learning, statistics, and database systems (Kasemsap, 2015a). The classical data mining algorithms become more challenging from both data and computational perspectives (Han, Liew, Hemert, & Atkinson, 2011).

The advancements in data storage and data mining technologies allow for the preservation of increasing amounts of data described by a change in the nature of data held by organizations (Cumbley & Church, 2013). Data reduction techniques (Pyle, 1999) emerged as the algorithms that aim to simplify and clean the raw data, enabling data mining algorithms to be applied in a more accurate way by removing redundant data. Data cleansing ensures the integrity of the database, and is intended to remove the incomplete and erroneous data (Mathew et al., 2015).

From the perspective of the attributes space, the most well-known data reduction processes are feature selection and feature extraction (Liu & Motoda, 2007). The perspectives of removing redundant data can be categorized into instance selection (García, Derrac, Cano, & Herrera, 2012) and instance generation (Triguero, Derrac, García, & Herrera, 2012). These data mining-related techniques should facilitate data mining algorithms to address big data problems. However, these methods are affected by the increase in the size and complexity of data sets and they are unable to provide a preprocessed data set in a reasonable time (Triguero et al., 2015).

Big Data and Cloud Computing

Cloud computing and big data provide the significant impacts on current IT industry and research communities (Wang, Zhan, Shi, & Liang, 2012). Cloud computing is one of the most significant shifts in modern information and communication technology (ICT) and service for enterprise applications and has become a powerful architecture to perform the large-scale and complex computing (Hashem et al., 2015). The advantages of cloud computing include virtualized resources, parallel processing, security, and data service integration with scalable data storage (Hashem et al., 2015).

Cloud computing can not only minimize the cost and restriction for automation and computerization by individuals and enterprises but can also provide reduced infrastructure maintenance cost, efficient management, and user access (Chih-Wei, Chih-Ming, Chih-Hung, & Chao-Tung, 2013). Cloud computing includes network access to storage, processing power, development platforms, and software (Kasemsap, 2015b). In cloud computing-based supply chain, logistics process is handled using cloud computing services in which data-related shipping schedule, shipping notice, receiving notice, and payment information are stored and shared through cloud computing applications (Kasemsap, 2015c).

Addressing big data is a challenging and time-demanding task that requires a large computational infrastructure to ensure successful data processing and analysis (Hashem et al., 2015). Big data attracts much attention in a wide variety of areas (e.g., manufacturing, health care, finance, and business) because they have acquired a lot of raw data (Triguero et al., 2015). With the availability of cloud computing platforms, these areas can take various advantages from these massive data sets by extracting valuable information. The rate at which new data are generated is staggering (Kaisler, Armour, Espinosa, & Money, 2013). A major challenge for researchers and practitioners is that the growth rate of data exceeds their ability to design the appropriate cloud computing platforms for data analysis and to update the intensive workloads (Hashem et al., 2015).

Some of the first adopters of big data in cloud computing are users that deployed Hadoop clusters in highly scalable and elastic computing environments provided by vendors, such as IBM, Microsoft Azure, and Amazon AWS (Chang et al., 2013). Virtualization is one of the base technologies applicable to the implementation of cloud computing. The basis for many platform attributes required to access, store, analyze, and manage the distributed computing components in a big data environment is achieved through virtualization. Virtualization is a process of sharing resource in order to increase resource utilization, efficiency, and scalability (Hashem et al., 2015).

Big data provides users the ability to utilize the commodity computing to process the distributed queries across multiple data sets and to return data sets in a timely manner. Big data utilizes distributed storage technology based on cloud computing rather than local storage attached to a computer. Big data evaluation is driven by the fast-growing cloud computing applications using virtualized technologies. Cloud computing can provide the useful facilities for the computation and processing of big data. Cloud computing is correlated with a new pattern for the provision of computing infrastructure and big data processing method for all types of resources available in the cloud computing through data analysis (Hashem et al., 2015).

Regarding big data, data analysts must make sense of large data sets, with more records (Liu, Jiang, & Heer, 2013). Capable and reliable connections to a data repository allow users to rely on a cloud computing to hold and share applications and the data created through their utilization. Cloud computing infrastructure can serve as an effective platform to address the data storage required to perform big data analysis (Hashem et al., 2015). Cloud computing reduces the need for computing power on user devices, lowers costs, and simplifies the operational design (Shin & Choi, 2015).

Zhang et al. (2013) explained that cloud computing provides powerful and economical infrastructural resources for cloud computing users to manage the increasing data sets in big data applications. Several cloud-based technologies have to cope with the new environment because dealing with big data for concurrent processing has become increasingly complicated (Ji, Li, Qiu, Awada, & Li, 2012). MapReduce is a good example of big data processing in a cloud computing environment; it allows for the processing of large amounts of data sets stored in parallel in the cluster (Dean & Ghemawat, 2008).

Applications of Big Data in Health Care Industry

Along with the development and application of the Internet in the field of health care, individual health records, clinical data of diagnosis and treatment, and genomic data have been accumulated dramatically, which generates big data in medical field for clinical research and assessment (Zhang & Zhang, 2014). Many notions have captured the imagination of health care practitioners as much as the advent of big data and the advanced analytical methods and technologies used to interpret it (Szlezák, Evers, Wang, & Pérez, 2014).

There is a great deal of enthusiasm about the prospects for big data practically utilized in health care systems around the world (Keen, Calinescu, Paige, & Rooksby, 2013). In order to draw the meaning from the increasing quantity of health care data, it must be dealt with from a big data perspective, using technologies capable of efficiently processing the massive amounts of data. Observational health care data (e.g., electronic health records and administrative claims databases) provides the longitudinal clinical information at the individual level (McCormick, Ferrell, Karr, & Ryan, 2014).

The introduction of big data in the health care domain has presented opportunities to engage in big data analytics of very large sets containing both structured and unstructured data (Kuiler, 2014). Big data analysis (e.g., Hadoop technique) can be utilized to construct early prediction and intervention models as well as clinical decision-making model for specialist and special disease clinics (Fang, Fan, & Chen, 2014).

Applications of Big Data Analytics in Tourism and Hospitality Industry

The hotel industry is highly competitive in that hotel firms offer essentially homogeneous products and services, which drive the requirement of hotels to distinguish themselves among their competitors through the utilization of big data analytics (Xiang, Schwartz, Gerdes, & Uysal, 2015). Social media and consumer-generated content on the Internet continue to grow and impact the hospitality industry (Browning, So, & Sparks, 2013). The tremendous growth of various data-generating sources has encouraged the development of new approaches to understanding the social and economic perspectives in a variety of disciplines (George, Haas, & Pentland, 2014). Big data analytics emphasizes the capacity to collect and analyze data with an unprecedented breadth, depth, and scale to solve the real-life problems (Mayer-Schönberger & Cukier, 2013).

Big data analytics can be recognized as a new research paradigm, rather than a regular method, that may utilize a diverse set of analytical tools to make inferences about reality applying large data. Although big data analytics does not preclude hypothesis testing, it is often applied to explore modern patterns from the data. Big data analytics aims to generate new insights that can beneficially complement traditional statistics, surveys, and archival data sources that remain largely static (Xiang et al., 2015). While it is broadly accepted as a new approach to knowledge creation, there has been recently voice of concerns about the potential difficulty of spurious correlations, toward calling for theory-based approaches to big data analytics (Boyd & Crawford, 2012).

Big data is generated through many sources including Internet traffic (e.g., clickstreams), mobile transactions, user-generated content, and social media as well as purposefully captured content through sensor networks, business transactions, and other operational domains, such as bioinformatics, health care, and finance (George et al., 2014). Social media technology can facilitate the improved organizational productivity by enhancing the communication and collaboration of employees which aids knowledge transfer and consequently makes organizations more effective (Kasemsap, 2014). With the advent of Web 2.0, IT and knowledge management applications effectively improve the strategic tools for providing the direct link between customers and tourism organizations, thus encouraging the communication channels in global tourism (Kasemsap, 2016a).

Big data analytics can be utilized to understand customers, competitors, market characteristics, products, business environment, impact of technologies, and strategic stakeholders, such as alliance and suppliers. Many cases have been cited to illustrate the applications of big data analytics to discover and solve business problems (Mayer-Schönberger & Cukier, 2013). Big data analytics opens the door to numerous opportunities to develop new knowledge to reshape the understanding of the hospitality industry and to support decision making in tourism and hospitality industry (Xiang et al., 2015). Mining social media and consumer-generated content has attracted much attention for their business value as public and community data (George et al., 2014).

In tourism and hospitality industry, online consumer reviews can be used to predict the hotel product quality (Finch, 1999) and hotel-related stock market volatility (Schumaker & Chen, 2009). Ghose and Ipeirotis (2011) utilized text content and reviewer characteristics to estimate the helpfulness and economic effect of online hotel product reviews. In tourism and hospitality industry, there is a growing interest in utilizing user-generated data to gain the obvious insights into research problems that have not been understood by conventional methods (Yang, Pan, & Song, 2014).

Challenges and Implications of Big Data in the Digital Age

In the global knowledge economy, data becomes the important asset for decision making in various operations (Qin, 2014). Data is the major input to the production of public policy and management research (Pirog, 2014). The application of big data has become the topic for discussion in many executive-level meetings (Schultz, 2014). Big data is very beneficial in bringing new knowledge in modern business (Bantouna et al., 2014). Big data helps firms gain competitive advantage (Worster, Weirich, & Andera, 2014). Big data significantly transforms health care, science, engineering, finance, and business (Hashem et al., 2015).

Large data sets are often from various sources (Variety) yet unstructured, such as social media, sensors, scientific applications, surveillance, video and image archives, Internet texts and documents, Internet search indexing, medical records, business transactions and weblogs; and are of large size (Volume) with the quick movement of data (Velocity) (Xu, Liu, Mei, Hu, & Chen, 2015). Big data has to be of high value (Value). Various technologies are discussed to support the management of big data, such as the massively parallel processing databases (Yuan et al., 2013), scalable storage systems, cloud computing platforms, and MapReduce. Distributed systems are a classical research discipline investigating various distributed computing technologies and applications, such as cloud computing (Yan et al., 2013) and MapReduce (Dan et al., 2013).

Big data transforms the nature of social inquiry and improve the world economy by increasing the productivity of companies and enhancing the functioning of public sector (Skoric, 2014). Big data should be recognized as a new set of practices, in addition to its usual conception as data and analytics technologies (Burns, 2015). Smart devices and online research platforms are changing the landscape of qualitative data collection and analysis (Erwin & Pollari, 2013). Big data-driven approaches can be utilized to test research hypotheses in cross-cultural communication (Park, Baek, & Cha, 2014).

Big data is the foundation on which policy making is based (McNeely & Hahm, 2014). Big data can improve the prediction of several value policy outcomes (Cook, 2014). Big data holds the tremendous potential for public policy analysis (Schintler & Kulkarni, 2014). Big data becomes increasingly important in policy making (Philip, Schuler-Brown, & Way, 2013). The analysis of big data provides public sector-related policymakers with extensive information (Stough & McBride, 2014). There is a need to formulate, evaluate, and implement policies that not only reduce the big data-related risks, but also maximize the benefits of applying big data for policy analysis (Schintler & Kulkarni, 2014). Reliable public sector information serves as a crucial source for big data (Washington, 2014).

The visions of big data utilization tend to be more in line with the original vision of development as the next generation of the ubiquitous computing environment (Shin & Choi, 2015). The visions focus more on increasing the technological capacity by developing new systems or data server components, and less on the applications and social services applied through big data-related infrastructure (Shin, 2014). Big data offers broad accounts based on large data collection (Curran, 2013). There is an increasing interest in the analysis of big data that integrates information from many thousands of persons and various data sources (Kaplan, Chambers, & Glasgow, 2014).

There are many implications for successfully integrating survey data into individual-level models developed by big data (Fanning, 2015). Big data includes a huge and growing amount of less-structured data from enterprise resource planning (ERP) systems, customer relationship management (CRM) programs, social media, and other sources (Fanning & Grant, 2013). The popularity of ERP is attributed to its ability to improve the organizational performance by reducing the time and costs of completing business activities (Kasemsap, 2015d). CRM becomes one of the most important business strategies in the digital age, thus involving organizational capability of managing business interactions with customers in an effective manner (Kasemsap, 2015e). Marketers should be hypothesis-driven with big data, but the scope of ideas is limited by the data that can be collected (Forsyth & Boucher, 2015).

FUTURE RESEARCH DIRECTIONS

The classification of the extensive literature in the domains of big data will provide the potential opportunities for future research. Big data analytics provides modern organizations an opportunity for disruptive change and growth. Organizations can utilize big data analytics in order to leverage their business performance, innovate products, and provide improved customer service. Business intelligence is an emerging technology that helps executives manage complex information in an efficient way (Kasemsap, 2015f). Business analytics is an emerging field that can potentially extend the domain of performance management to provide an improved understanding of business dynamics toward better decision making (Kasemsap, 2015g).

With the advent of Web 2.0 technologies, social media platforms (e.g., Facebook and Twitter) generate huge amounts of data. Big data, Web 2.0 technologies, and social media platforms are certain to remain hot topics for the foreseeable future. Leaders of virtual teams should carry the responsibilities to satisfy their bosses, subordinates, and external customers in a complex environment that is highly dependent on IT perspectives (Kasemsap, 2016b). Exploring the impact of virtual teams on driving big data projects should be further studied. In addition, the relationship among big data, big data analytics, business intelligence, and business analytics will be the beneficial topics for future research directions.

CONCLUSION

This chapter highlighted the overview of big data; the volume, velocity, variety, veracity, and variability of big data; the privacy and security of big data applications; big data and multimedia utilization; the concept of MapReduce; the concept of Hadoop; big data and data mining; big data and cloud computing; the applications of big data in health care industry; the applications of big data analytics in tourism and hospitality industry; and the challenges and implications of big data in the digital age. The data becomes an asset that requires the cost-effective innovations in information processing that enable process automation, enhanced insight, and decision making. Big data platforms and solutions provide the tools, methods, and technologies used to capture, curate, store, and analyze the data to find new correlations, relationships, and trends that were previously unavailable.

Big data is a data management system that can reduce the need for storage facilities for data and lower the computational requirements for various sectors. Big data improves the value of the information at hand to guide future actions that will benefit the company to serve clients better. The utilization of big data becomes the foundation of competition and growth for individual firms, thus enhancing productivity and creating significant value for the world economy by reducing waste and increasing the quality of products and services. Big data becomes a crucial way for many companies to outperform their peers in modern business.

However, sensitivities around privacy and data security are the major obstacle that companies and governments need to overcome if the economic benefits of big data are to be realized. One of the most pressing challenges is a crucial shortage of people with the skills to analyze big data. There are many technological issues that need to be resolved to make use of big data. Legacy systems and incompatible standards often prevent the integration of data and the application of the more sophisticated analytics that create value. Utilizing large digital data sets requires the assembly of a technological stack from storage and computing through analytical and visualization software applications.

Big data can deliver significant value by making information transparent and can be used to develop the next generation of products and services in modern business. Big data can help executives create new growth opportunities and new categories of companies, such as those that aggregate and analyze industry data. Leaders with strong leadership skills across sectors should energetically begin to establish their organizations' big data capabilities toward achieving entrepreneurial success, business growth, and economic development. Applying big data has the potential to increase organizational performance and gain sustainable competitive advantage in the digital age.

REFERENCES

Agrawal, D., Das, S., & Abbadi, A. (2011). *Big data and cloud computing*. Paper presented at the 14th International Conference on Extending Database Technology (EDBT/ICDT 2011), Uppsala, Sweden. doi:10.1145/1951365.1951432

Almeida, J., Leite, N., & Torres, R. (2012). VISON: VIdeo Summarization for ONline applications. *Pattern Recognition Letters*, *33*(4), 397–409. doi:10.1016/j.patrec.2011.08.007

Andrejevic, M. (2013). *Infoglut: How too much information is changing the way we think and know*. New York, NY: Routledge.

Bantouna, A., Poulios, G., Tsagkaris, K., & Demestichas, P. (2014). Network load predictions based on big data and the utilization of self-organizing maps. *Journal of Network and Systems Management*, *22*(2), 150–173. doi:10.1007/s10922-013-9285-1

Beaver, D., Kumar, S., Li, H. C., Sobel, J., & Vajgel, P. (2010). *Finding a needle in haystack: Facebook's photo storage*. Paper presented at the 9th USENIX conference on Operating Systems Design and Implementation (OSDI 2010), Berkeley, CA.

Bendler, J., Wagner, S., Brandt, T., & Neumann, D. (2014). Taming uncertainty in big data. *Business & Information Systems Engineering*, *6*(5), 279–288. doi:10.1007/s12599-014-0342-4

Bollier, D., & Firestone, C. M. (2010). *The promise and peril of big data*. Washington, DC: Aspen Institute.

Boyd, D., & Crawford, K. (2012). Critical questions for big data: Provocations for a cultural, technological, and scholarly phenomenon. *Information Communication and Society*, *15*(5), 662–679. doi:10.1080/1369118X.2012.678878

Browning, V., So, K. K. F., & Sparks, B. (2013). The influence of online reviews on consumers' attributions of service quality and control for service standards in hotels. *Journal of Travel & Tourism Marketing*, *30*(1/2), 23–40. doi:10.1080/10548408.2013.750971

Buck, C., Horbel, C., Kesseler, T., & Christian, C. (2014). Mobile consumer apps: Big data brother is watching you. *Marketing Review St. Gallen*, *31*(1), 26–35. doi:10.1365/s11621-014-0318-2

Burns, R. (2015). Rethinking big data in digital humanitarianism: Practices, epistemologies, and social relations. *GeoJournal*, *80*(4), 477–490. doi:10.1007/s10708-014-9599-x

Chang, L., Ranjan, R., Xuyun, Z., Chi, Y., Georgakopoulos, D., & Jinjun, C. (2013). *Public auditing for big data storage in cloud computing*. Paper presented at the 2013 IEEE 16th International Conference on Computational Science and Engineering (CSE 2013), Sydney, Australia.

Chawla, N. V., Bowyer, K. W., Hall, L. O., & Kegelmeyer, W. P. (2002). SMOTE: Synthetic minority over-sampling technique. *Journal of Artificial Intelligence Research*, *16*, 321–357. doi: 10.1613/jair.953

Chen, M., Mao, S., & Liu, Y. (2014). Big data: A survey. *Mobile Networks and Applications*, *19*(2), 171–209. doi:10.1007/s11036-013-0489-0

Chen, Q., Wang, L., & Shang, Z. (2008). *MRGIS: A MapReduce-enabled high performance workflow system for GIS*. Paper presented at the 2008 IEEE 4th International Conference on eScience (eScience 2008), Indianapolis, IN. doi:10.1109/eScience.2008.169

Chen, Z., Lu, Y., Xiao, N., & Liu, F. (2014). A hybrid memory built by SSD and DRAM to support in-memory big data analytics. *Knowledge and Information Systems*, *41*(2), 335–354. doi:10.1007/s10115-013-0727-6

Chih-Wei, L., Chih-Ming, H., Chih-Hung, C., & Chao-Tung, Y. (2013). *An improvement to data service in cloud computing with content sensitive transaction analysis and adaptation*. Paper presented at the 2013 IEEE 37th Annual Computer Software and Applications Conference Workshops (COMPSACW 2013), Kyoto, Japan.

Cook, T. D. (2014). "Big data" in research on social policy. *Journal of Policy Analysis and Management, 33*(2), 544–547. doi:10.1002/pam.21751

Cumbley, R., & Church, P. (2013). Is big data creepy? *Computer Law & Security Report, 29*(5), 601–609. doi:10.1016/j.clsr.2013.07.007

Curran, J. (2013). Big data or "big ethnographic data"? Positioning big data within the ethnographic space. *Ethnographic Praxis in Industry Conference Proceedings, 2013*(1), 62–73.

da Silva, A., Falcão, A., & Magalhães, L. (2011). Active learning paradigms for CBIR systems based on optimum-path forest classification. *Pattern Recognition, 44*(12), 2971–2978. doi:10.1016/j.patcog.2011.04.026

Dan, C., Zhixin, L., Lizhe, W., Minggang, D., Jingying, C., & Hui, L. (2013). Natural disaster monitoring with wireless sensor networks: A case study of data-intensive applications upon low-cost scalable systems. *Mobile Networks and Applications, 18*(5), 651–663. doi:10.1007/s11036-013-0456-9

Dean, J., & Ghemawat, S. (2008). MapReduce: Simplified data processing on large clusters. *Communications of the ACM, 51*(1), 107–113. doi:10.1145/1327452.1327492

Dean, J., & Ghemawat, S. (2010). MapReduce: A flexible data processing tool. *Communications of the ACM, 53*(1), 72–77. doi:10.1145/1629175.1629198

Debortoli, S., Müller, O., & vom Brocke, J. (2014). Comparing business intelligence and big data skills. *Business & Information Systems Engineering, 6*(5), 289–300. doi:10.1007/s12599-014-0344-2

Dobre, C., & Xhafa, F. (2014). Parallel programming paradigms and frameworks in big data era. *International Journal of Parallel Programming, 42*(5), 710–738. doi:10.1007/s10766-013-0272-7

Elkan, C. (2001). *The foundations of cost-sensitive learning*. Paper presented at the 17th International Joint Conference on Artificial Intelligence (IJCAI 2001), Seattle, WA.

Erwin, K., & Pollari, T. (2013). Small packages for big (qualitative) data. *Ethnographic Praxis in Industry Conference Proceedings, 2013*(1), 44–61.

Esposti, S. (2014). *When big data meets dataveillance: The hidden side of analytics*. Paper presented at the Annual Meeting of the Society for Social Studies of Science (4S), San Diego, CA.

Faltesek, D. (2013). Big argumentation? TripleC: Communication, capitalism & critique. *Journal for a Global Sustainable Information Society, 11*(2), 402–411.

Fang, Z., Fan, X., & Chen, G. (2014). A study on specialist or special disease clinics based on big data. *Frontiers of Medicine, 8*(3), 376–381. doi:10.1007/s11684-014-0356-9 PMID:25186249

Fanning, C. (2015). Research talent in the big data age. *Research World, 2015*(50), 40–41.

Fanning, K., & Drogt, E. (2014). Big data: New opportunities for M&A. *Journal of Corporate Accounting & Finance, 25*(2), 27–34. doi:10.1002/jcaf.21919

Fanning, K., & Grant, R. (2013). Big data: Implications for financial managers. *Journal of Corporate Accounting & Finance, 24*(5), 23–30. doi:10.1002/jcaf.21872

Fernandes, H., Maldague, X., Batista, M., & Barcelos, C. A. Z. (2011). *Suspicious event recognition using infrared imagery*. Paper presented at the 2011 IEEE International Conference on Systems, Man, and Cybernetics (SMC 2011), Anchorage, AK. doi:10.1109/ICSMC.2011.6084001

Finch, B. J. (1999). Internet discussions as a source for consumer product customer involvement and quality information: An exploratory study. *Journal of Operations Management*, *17*(5), 535–556. doi:10.1016/S0272-6963(99)00005-4

Fond, G., Brunel, L., Leboyer, M., & Boyer, L. (2014). Do the treasures of "big data" combined with behavioural intervention therapies contain the key to the mystery of large psychiatric issues? *Acta Psychiatrica Scandinavica*, *130*(5), 406–407. PMID:25131263

Forsyth, J., & Boucher, L. (2015). Why big data is not enough. *Research World*, *2015*(50), 26–27.

Fung, B. C. M., Wang, K., Chen, R., & Yu, P. S. (2010). Privacy-preserving data publishing: A survey on recent developments. *ACM Computing Surveys*, *42*(4), 14:1–14:53.

Gandomi, A., & Haider, M. (2015). Beyond the hype: Big data concepts, methods, and analytics. *International Journal of Information Management*, *35*(2), 137–144. doi:10.1016/j.ijinfomgt.2014.10.007

García, S., Derrac, J., Cano, J., & Herrera, F. (2012). Prototype selection for nearest neighbor classification: Taxonomy and empirical study. *IEEE Transactions on Pattern Analysis and Machine Intelligence*, *34*(3), 417–435. doi:10.1109/TPAMI.2011.142 PMID:21768651

George, G., Haas, M. R., & Pentland, A. (2014). Big data and management. *Academy of Management Journal*, *57*(2), 321–326. doi:10.5465/amj.2014.4002

Ghose, A., & Ipeirotis, P. G. (2011). Estimating the helpfulness and economic impact of product reviews: Mining text and reviewer characteristics. *IEEE Transactions on Knowledge and Data Engineering*, *23*(10), 1498–1512. doi:10.1109/TKDE.2010.188

Guo, H., Wang, L., Chen, F., & Liang, D. (2014). Scientific big data and Digital Earth. *Chinese Science Bulletin*, *59*(35), 5066–5073. doi:10.1007/s11434-014-0645-3

Guo, K., Pan, W., Lu, M., Zhou, X., & Ma, J. (2015). An effective and economical architecture for semantic-based heterogeneous multimedia big data retrieval. *Journal of Systems and Software*, *102*, 207–216. doi:10.1016/j.jss.2014.09.016

Han, L. X., Liew, C. S., Hemert, J. V., & Atkinson, M. (2011). A generic parallel processing model for facilitating data mining and integration. *Parallel Computing*, *37*(3), 157–171. doi:10.1016/j.parco.2011.02.006

Hashem, I. A. T., Yaqoob, I., Anuar, N. B., Mokhtar, S., Gani, A., & Khan, S. U. (2015). The rise of "big data" on cloud computing: Review and open research issues. *Information Systems*, *47*, 98–115. doi:10.1016/j.is.2014.07.006

He, Q., Wang, H., Zhuang, F., Shang, T., & Shi, Z. (2015). Parallel sampling from big data with uncertainty distribution. *Fuzzy Sets and Systems*, *258*, 117–133. doi:10.1016/j.fss.2014.01.016

Honavar, V. G. (2014). The promise and potential of big data: A case for discovery informatics. *Review of Policy Research, 31*(4), 326–330. doi:10.1111/ropr.12080

Hsu, C., Zeng, B., & Zhang, M. (2014). A novel group key transfer for big data security. *Applied Mathematics and Computation, 249*, 436–443. doi:10.1016/j.amc.2014.10.051

Jeong, Y. S., & Shin, S. S. (2015). An efficient authentication scheme to protect user privacy in seamless big data services. *Wireless Personal Communications, 86*(1), 7–19. doi:10.1007/s11277-015-2990-1

Ji, C., Li, Y., Qiu, W., Awada, U., & Li, K. (2012). *Big data processing in cloud computing environments.* Paper presented at the 2012 IEEE 12th International Symposium on Pervasive Systems, Algorithms and Networks (ISPAN 2012), San Marcos, TX. doi:10.1109/I-SPAN.2012.9

Jiang, C., Ding, Z., Wang, J., & Yan, C. (2014). Big data resource service platform for the Internet financial industry. *Chinese Science Bulletin, 59*(35), 5051–5058. doi:10.1007/s11434-014-0570-5

Jiang, H., Chen, Y., Qiao, Z., Weng, T. H., & Li, K. C. (2015). Scaling up MapReduce-based big data processing on multi-GPU systems. *Cluster Computing, 18*(1), 369–383. doi:10.1007/s10586-014-0400-1

Kaisler, S., Armour, F., Espinosa, J. A., & Money, W. (2013). *Big data: Issues and challenges moving forward.* Paper presented at the 2013 46th Hawaii International Conference on System Sciences (HICSS 2013), Wailea, HI. doi:10.1109/HICSS.2013.645

Kaplan, R. M., Chambers, D. A., & Glasgow, R. E. (2014). Big data and large sample size: A cautionary note on the potential for bias. *Clinical and Translational Science, 7*(4), 342–346. doi:10.1111/cts.12178 PMID:25043853

Kasemsap, K. (2014). The role of social networking in global business environments. In P. Smith & T. Cockburn (Eds.), Impact of emerging digital technologies on leadership in global business (pp. 183–201). Hershey, PA: IGI Global. doi:10.4018/978-1-4666-6134-9.ch010

Kasemsap, K. (2015a). The role of data mining for business intelligence in knowledge management. In A. Azevedo & M. Santos (Eds.), *Integration of data mining in business intelligence systems* (pp. 12–33). Hershey, PA: IGI Global. doi:10.4018/978-1-4666-6477-7.ch002

Kasemsap, K. (2015b). The role of cloud computing adoption in global business. In V. Chang, R. Walters, & G. Wills (Eds.), *Delivery and adoption of cloud computing services in contemporary organizations* (pp. 26–55). Hershey, PA: IGI Global. doi:10.4018/978-1-4666-8210-8.ch002

Kasemsap, K. (2015c). The role of cloud computing in global supply chain. In N. Rao (Ed.), *Enterprise management strategies in the era of cloud computing* (pp. 192–219). Hershey, PA: IGI Global. doi:10.4018/978-1-4666-8339-6.ch009

Kasemsap, K. (2015d). Implementing enterprise resource planning. In M. Khosrow-Pour (Ed.), *Encyclopedia of information science and technology* (3rd ed.; pp. 798–807). Hershey, PA: IGI Global. doi:10.4018/978-1-4666-5888-2.ch076

Kasemsap, K. (2015e). The role of customer relationship management in the global business environments. In T. Tsiakis (Ed.), *Trends and innovations in marketing information systems* (pp. 130–156). Hershey, PA: IGI Global. doi:10.4018/978-1-4666-8459-1.ch007

Kasemsap, K. (2015f). Implementing business intelligence in contemporary organizations. In A. Haider (Ed.), Business technologies in contemporary organizations: Adoption, assimilation, and institutionalization (pp. 177–192). Hershey, PA: IGI Global. doi:10.4018/978-1-4666-6623-8.ch008

Kasemsap, K. (2015g). The role of business analytics in performance management. In M. Tavana & K. Puranam (Eds.), *Handbook of research on organizational transformations through big data analytics* (pp. 126–145). Hershey, PA: IGI Global. doi:10.4018/978-1-4666-7272-7.ch010

Kasemsap, K. (2016a). The roles of information technology and knowledge management in global tourism. In A. Nedelea, M. Korstanje, & B. George (Eds.), *Strategic tools and methods for promoting hospitality and tourism services* (pp. 109–138). Hershey, PA: IGI Global. doi:10.4018/978-1-4666-9761-4.ch006

Kasemsap, K. (2016b). Examining the roles of virtual team and information technology in global business. In C. Graham (Ed.), *Strategic management and leadership for systems development in virtual spaces* (pp. 1–21). Hershey, PA: IGI Global. doi:10.4018/978-1-4666-9688-4.ch001

Keen, J., Calinescu, R., Paige, R., & Rooksby, J. (2013). Big data + politics = open data: The case of health care data in England. *Policy & Internet*, *5*(2), 228–243. doi:10.1002/1944-2866.POI330

Kitchin, R. (2014). *The data revolution: Big data, open data, data infrastructures and their consequences*. London, United Kingdom: Sage Publications.

Kolodziej, J., & Xhafa, F. (2012). Integration of task abortion and security requirements in GA-based meta-heuristics for independent batch Grid scheduling. *Computers & Mathematics with Applications (Oxford, England)*, *63*(2), 350–364. doi:10.1016/j.camwa.2011.07.038

Kshetri, N. (2014). Big data's impact on privacy, security and consumer welfare. *Telecommunications Policy*, *38*(11), 1134–1145. doi:10.1016/j.telpol.2014.10.002

Kuiler, E. W. (2014). From big data to knowledge: An ontological approach to big data analytics. *Review of Policy Research*, *31*(4), 311–318. doi:10.1111/ropr.12077

Kwon, O., Lee, N., & Shin, B. (2014). Data quality management, data usage experience and acquisition intention of big data analytics. *International Journal of Information Management*, *34*(3), 387–394. doi:10.1016/j.ijinfomgt.2014.02.002

Leonardi, L., Orlando, S., Raffaeta, A., Roncato, A., Silvestri, C., Andrienko, G., & Andrienko, N. (2014). A general framework for trajectory data warehousing and visual OLAP. *GeoInformatica*, *18*(2), 273–312. doi:10.1007/s10707-013-0181-3

Li, C., Chen, J., Jin, C., Zhang, R., & Zhou, A. (2014). MR-tree: An efficient index for MapReduce. *International Journal of Communication Systems*, *27*(6), 828–838. doi:10.1002/dac.2619

Li, H., Wei, X., Fu, Q., & Luo, Y. (2014). MapReduce delay scheduling with deadline constraint. *Concurrency and Computation*, *26*(3), 766–778. doi:10.1002/cpe.3050

Liu, H., & Motoda, H. (2007). *Computational methods of feature selection*. Boca Raton, FL: Chapman and Hall/CRC Press.

Liu, L., Li, Z., & Delp, E. (2009). Efficient and low-complexity surveillance video compression using backward-channel aware Wyner-Ziv video coding. *IEEE Transactions on Circuits and Systems for Video Technology*, *19*(4), 452–465.

Liu, Z., Jiang, B., & Heer, J. (2013). *imMens*: Real-time visual querying of big data. *Computer Graphics Forum*, *32*(3pt4), 421–430. doi:10.1111/cgf.12129

López, V., del Río, S., Benítez, J. M., & Herrera, F. (2015). Cost-sensitive linguistic fuzzy rule based classification systems under the MapReduce framework for imbalanced big data. *Fuzzy Sets and Systems*, *258*, 5–38. doi:10.1016/j.fss.2014.01.015

López, V., Fernández, A., García, S., Palade, V., & Herrera, F. (2013). An insight into classification with imbalanced data: Empirical results and current trends on using data intrinsic characteristics. *Information Sciences*, *250*, 113–141. doi:10.1016/j.ins.2013.07.007

López, V., Fernández, A., Moreno-Torres, J. G., & Herrera, F. (2012). Analysis of preprocessing vs. cost-sensitive learning for imbalanced classification. Open problems on intrinsic data characteristics. *Expert Systems with Applications*, *39*(7), 6585–6608. doi:10.1016/j.eswa.2011.12.043

Madden, S. (2012). From databases to big data. *IEEE Internet Computing*, *16*(3), 4–6. doi:10.1109/MIC.2012.50

Marx, V. (2013). The big challenges of big data. *Nature*, *498*(7453), 255–260. doi:10.1038/498255a PMID:23765498

Mathew, P. A., Dunn, L. N., Sohn, M. D., Mercado, A., Custudio, C., & Walter, T. (2015). Big-data for building energy performance: Lessons from assembling a very large national database of building energy use. *Applied Energy*, *140*, 85–93. doi:10.1016/j.apenergy.2014.11.042

Mayer-Schönberger, V., & Cukier, K. (2013). *Big data: A revolution that will transform how we live, work, and think.* New York, NY: Houghton Mifflin Harcourt.

McCormick, T. H., Ferrell, R., Karr, A. F., & Ryan, P. B. (2014). Big data, big results: Knowledge discovery in output from large-scale analytics. *Statistical Analysis and Data Mining: The ASA Data Science Journal*, *7*(5), 404–412. doi:10.1002/sam.11237

McNeely, C. L., & Hahm, J. O. (2014). The big (data) bang: Policy, prospects, and challenges. *Review of Policy Research*, *31*(4), 304–310. doi:10.1111/ropr.12082

Minelli, M., Chambers, M., & Dhiraj, A. (2013). *Big data, big analytics: Emerging business intelligence and analytic trends for today's businesses*. Hoboken, NJ: John Wiley & Sons. doi:10.1002/9781118562260

Moreno-Torres, J. G., Raeder, T., Aláiz-Rodríguez, R., Chawla, N. V., & Herrera, F. (2012). A unifying view on dataset shift in classification. *Pattern Recognition*, *45*(1), 521–530. doi:10.1016/j.patcog.2011.06.019

O'Leary, D. E. (2013). Artificial intelligence and big data. *IEEE Intelligent Systems*, *28*(2), 96–99. doi:10.1109/MIS.2013.39 PMID:25505373

Park, J., Baek, Y. M., & Cha, M. (2014). Cross-cultural comparison of nonverbal cues in emoticons on Twitter: Evidence from big data analysis. *Journal of Communication*, *64*(2), 333–354. doi:10.1111/jcom.12086

Park, J., Kim, H., Jeong, Y. S., & Lee, E. (2014). Two-phase grouping-based resource management for big data processing in mobile cloud computing. *International Journal of Communication Systems*, *27*(6), 839–851. doi:10.1002/dac.2627

Park, S. T., Kim, Y. R., Jeong, S. P., Hong, C. I., & Kang, T. G. (2016). A case study on effective technique of distributed data storage for big data processing in the wireless Internet environment. *Wireless Personal Communications*, *86*(1), 239–253. doi:10.1007/s11277-015-2794-3

Parks, M. R. (2014). Big data in communication research: Its contents and discontents. *Journal of Communication*, *64*(2), 355–360. doi:10.1111/jcom.12090

Philip, T. M., Schuler-Brown, S., & Way, W. (2013). A framework for learning about big data with mobile technologies for democratic participation: Possibilities, limitations, and unanticipated obstacles. *Technology. Knowledge and Learning*, *18*(3), 103–120. doi:10.1007/s10758-013-9202-4

Pirog, M. A. (2014). Data will drive innovation in public policy and management research in the next decade. *Journal of Policy Analysis and Management*, *33*(2), 537–543. doi:10.1002/pam.21752

Pyle, D. (1999). *Data preparation for data mining*. San Francisco, CA: Morgan Kaufmann Publishers.

Qian, J., Lv, P., Yue, X., Liu, C., & Jing, Z. (2015). Hierarchical attribute reduction algorithms for big data using MapReduce. *Knowledge-Based Systems*, *73*, 18–31. doi:10.1016/j.knosys.2014.09.001

Qin, S. J. (2014). Process data analytics in the era of big data. *AIChE Journal. American Institute of Chemical Engineers*, *60*(9), 3092–3100. doi:10.1002/aic.14523

Ranjan, R., Harwood, A., & Buyya, R. (2012). Coordinated load management in peer-to-peer coupled federated grid systems. *The Journal of Supercomputing*, *61*(2), 292–316. doi:10.1007/s11227-010-0426-y

Ranjan, R., Mitra, K., & Georgakopoulos, D. (2013). MediaWise cloud content orchestrator. *Journal of Internet Services and Applications*, *4*(1), 1–14.

Schilling, P. L., & Bozic, K. L. (2014). The big to do about "big data". *Clinical Orthopaedics and Related Research*, *472*(11), 3270–3272. doi:10.1007/s11999-014-3887-0 PMID:25141846

Schintler, L. A., & Kulkarni, R. (2014). Big data for policy analysis: The good, the bad, and the ugly. *Review of Policy Research*, *31*(4), 343–348. doi:10.1111/ropr.12079

Schroeck, M., Shockley, R., Smart, J., Romero-Morales, D., & Tufano, P. (2012). *Analytics: The real-world use of big data. How innovative enterprises extract value from uncertain data*. Retrieved from http://www-03.ibm.com/systems/hu/resources/the real word use of big data.pdf

Schultz, J. R. (2014). Big data are, after all, just data. *Performance Improvement*, *53*(5), 20–25. doi:10.1002/pfi.21411

Schumaker, R. P., & Chen, H. (2009). Textual analysis of stock market prediction using breaking financial news: The AZFin text system. *ACM Transactions on Information Systems*, *27*(2), 1–19. doi:10.1145/1462198.1462204

Shah, T., Rabhi, F., & Ray, P. (2015). Investigating an ontology-based approach for big data analysis of inter-dependent medical and oral health conditions. *Cluster Computing*, *18*(1), 351–367. doi:10.1007/s10586-014-0406-8

Shin, D. (2014). A socio-technical framework for internet-of-things design: A human-centered design for the Internet of Things. *Telematics and Informatics*, *31*(4), 519–531. doi:10.1016/j.tele.2014.02.003

Shin, D. H., & Choi, M. J. (2015). Ecological views of big data: Perspectives and issues. *Telematics and Informatics*, *32*(2), 311–320. doi:10.1016/j.tele.2014.09.006

Skoric, M. M. (2014). The implications of big data for developing and transitional economies: Extending the triple helix? *Scientometrics*, *99*(1), 175–186. doi:10.1007/s11192-013-1106-5

Song, J., Guo, C., Wang, Z., Zhang, Y., Yu, G., & Pierson, J. M. (2015). HaoLap: A Hadoop based OLAP system for big data. *Journal of Systems and Software*, *102*, 167–181. doi:10.1016/j.jss.2014.09.024

Stough, R., & McBride, D. (2014). Big data and U.S. public policy. *Review of Policy Research*, *31*(4), 339–342. doi:10.1111/ropr.12083

Szlezák, N., Evers, M., Wang, J., & Pérez, L. (2014). The role of big data and advanced analytics in drug discovery, development, and commercialization. *Clinical Pharmacology and Therapeutics*, *95*(5), 492–495. doi:10.1038/clpt.2014.29 PMID:24642713

Tatebe, O., Hiraga, K., & Soda, N. (2010). Gfarm grid file system. *New Generation Computing*, *28*(3), 257–275. doi:10.1007/s00354-009-0089-5

Tien, J. M. (2013). Big data: Unleashing information. *Journal of Systems Science and Systems Engineering*, *22*(2), 127–151. doi:10.1007/s11518-013-5219-4

Tinati, R., Halford, S., Carr, L., & Pope, C. (2014). Big data: Methodological challenges and approaches for sociological analysis. *Sociology*, *48*(4), 663–681. doi:10.1177/0038038513511561

Triguero, I., Derrac, J., García, S., & Herrera, F. (2012). A taxonomy and experimental study on prototype generation for nearest neighbor classification. *IEEE Transactions on Systems, Man and Cybernetics. Part C, Applications and Reviews*, *42*(1), 86–100. doi:10.1109/TSMCC.2010.2103939

Triguero, I., Peralta, D., Bacardit, J., García, S., & Herrera, F. (2015). MRPR: A MapReduce solution for prototype reduction in big data classification. *Neurocomputing*, *150*, 331–345. doi: 10.1016/j.neucom.2014.04.078

Valvåg, S. V., Johansen, D., & Kvalnes, Å. (2013). Cogset: A high performance MapReduce engine. *Concurrency and Computation*, *25*(1), 2–23. doi:10.1002/cpe.2827

Vitolo, C., Elkhatib, Y., Reusser, D., Macleod, C. J. A., & Buytaert, W. (2015). Web technologies for environmental big data. *Environmental Modelling & Software*, *63*, 185–198. doi:10.1016/j.envsoft.2014.10.007

Wang, J., Liu, Z., Zhang, S., & Zhang, X. (2014). Defending collaborative false data injection attacks in wireless sensor networks. *Information Sciences*, *254*, 39–53. doi:10.1016/j.ins.2013.08.019

Wang, L., Chen, D., Hu, Y., Ma, Y., & Wang, J. (2013). Towards enabling cyberinfrastructure as a service in clouds. *Computers & Electrical Engineering*, *39*(1), 3–14. doi:10.1016/j.compeleceng.2012.05.001

Wang, L., Chen, D., & Huang, F. (2011). Virtual workflow system for distributed collaborative scientific applications on Grids. *Computers & Electrical Engineering*, *37*(3), 300–310. doi:10.1016/j.compeleceng.2011.01.004

Wang, L., Chen, D., Zhao, J., & Tao, J. (2012). Resource management of distributed virtual machines. *International Journal of Ad Hoc and Ubiquitous Computing*, *10*(2), 96–111. doi:10.1504/IJAHUC.2012.048261

Wang, L., Kunze, M., Tao, J., & Laszewski, G. (2011). Towards building a cloud for scientific applications. *Advances in Engineering Software*, *42*(9), 714–722. doi:10.1016/j.advengsoft.2011.05.007

Wang, L., Zhan, J., Shi, W., & Liang, Y. (2012). In cloud, can scientific communities benefit from the economies of scale? *IEEE Transactions on Parallel and Distributed Systems*, *23*(2), 296–303. doi:10.1109/TPDS.2011.144

Washington, A. L. (2014). Government information policy in the era of big data. *Review of Policy Research*, *31*(4), 319–325. doi:10.1111/ropr.12081

Wasikowski, M., & Chen, X. W. (2010). Combating the small sample class imbalance problem using feature selection. *IEEE Transactions on Knowledge and Data Engineering*, *22*(10), 1388–1400. doi:10.1109/TKDE.2009.187

White, P., & Breckenridge, R. S. (2014). Trade-offs, limitations, and promises of big data in social science research. *Review of Policy Research*, *31*(4), 331–338. doi:10.1111/ropr.12078

Wigan, M., & Clarke, R. (2013). Big data's big unintended consequences. *IEEE Computer*, *46*(6), 46–53. doi:10.1109/MC.2013.195

Woniak, M., Graña, M., & Corchado, E. (2014). A survey of multiple classifier systems as hybrid systems. *Information Fusion*, *16*, 3–17. doi:10.1016/j.inffus.2013.04.006

Woo, J. (2013). Market basket analysis algorithms with MapReduce. *Wiley Interdisciplinary Reviews: Data Mining and Knowledge Discovery*, *3*(6), 445–452. doi: 10.1002/widm.1107

Worster, A., Weirich, T. R., & Andera, F. (2014). Big data: Gaining a competitive edge. *Journal of Corporate Accounting & Finance*, *25*(5), 35–39. doi:10.1002/jcaf.21970

Wu, L., & Wang, Y. (2010). *The process of criminal investigation based on grey hazy set*. Paper presented at the 2010 IEEE International Conference on Systems, Man, and Cybernetics (SMC 2010), Istanbul, Turkey.

Xiang, Z., Schwartz, Z., Gerdes, J. H. Jr, & Uysal, M. (2015). What can big data and text analytics tell us about hotel guest experience and satisfaction? *International Journal of Hospitality Management*, *44*, 120–130. doi:10.1016/j.ijhm.2014.10.013

Xin, J., Wang, Z., Qu, L., & Wang, G. (2015). Elastic extreme learning machine for big data classification. *Neurocomputing*, *149*, 464–471. doi:10.1016/j.neucom.2013.09.075

Xu, C., Zhang, Y., Zhu, G., Rui, Y., Lu, H., & Huang, Q. (2008). Using webcast text for semantic event detection in broadcast sports video. *IEEE Transactions on Multimedia*, *10*(7), 1342–1355. doi:10.1109/TMM.2008.2004912

Xu, Z., Liu, Y., Mei, L., Hu, C., & Chen, L. (2015). Semantic based representing and organizing surveillance big data using video structural description technology. *Journal of Systems and Software*, *102*, 217–225. doi:10.1016/j.jss.2014.07.024

Yan, M., Lizhe, W., Dingsheng, L., Tao, Y., Peng, L., & Wanfeng, Z. (2013). Distributed data structure templates for data-intensive remote sensing applications. *Concurrency and Computation*, *25*(12), 1784–1797. doi:10.1002/cpe.2965

Yang, H., & Fong, S. (2015). Countering the concept-drift problems in big data by an incrementally optimized stream mining model. *Journal of Systems and Software*, *102*, 158–166. doi:10.1016/j.jss.2014.07.010

Yang, Y., Nie, F., Xu, D., Luo, J., Zhuang, Y., & Pan, Y. (2012). A multimedia retrieval architecture based on semi-supervised ranking and relevance feedback. *IEEE Transactions on Pattern Analysis and Machine Intelligence*, *34*(4), 723–742. doi:10.1109/TPAMI.2011.170 PMID:21844624

Yang, Y., Pan, B., & Song, H. (2014). Predicting hotel demand using destination marketing organization's web traffic data. *Journal of Travel Research*, *53*(4), 433–447. doi:10.1177/0047287513500391

Yu, H., Pedrinaci, C., Dietze, S., & Domingue, J. (2012). Using linked data to annotate and search educational video resources for supporting distance learning. *IEEE Transactions on Learning Technologies*, *5*(2), 130–142. doi:10.1109/TLT.2012.1

Yuan, D., Yang, Y., Liu, X., Li, W., Cui, L., Xu, M., & Chen, J. (2013). A highly practical approach towards achieving minimum datasets storage cost in the cloud. *IEEE Transactions on Parallel and Distributed Systems*, *24*(6), 1234–1244. doi:10.1109/TPDS.2013.20

Zhang, C., de Sterck, H., Aboulnaga, A., Djambazian, H., & Sladek, R. (2010). *Case study of scientific data processing on a cloud using Hadoop*. Paper presented at the 24th annual High Performance Computing Symposium (HPCS 2010), Toronto, Canada. doi:10.1007/978-3-642-12659-8_29

Zhang, J., & Zhang, B. (2014). Clinical research of traditional Chinese medicine in big data era. *Frontiers of Medicine*, *8*(3), 321–327. doi:10.1007/s11684-014-0370-y PMID:25217972

Zhang, J., Zulkernine, M., & Haque, A. (2008). Random-forests-based network intrusion detection systems. *IEEE Transactions on Systems, Man and Cybernetics. Part C, Applications and Reviews*, *38*(5), 649–659. doi:10.1109/TSMCC.2008.923876

Zhang, X., Liu, C., Nepal, S., Yang, C., Dou, W., & Chen, J. (2013). SaC-FRAPP: A scalable and cost effective framework for privacy preservation over big data on cloud. *Concurrency and Computation*, *25*(18), 2561–2576. doi:10.1002/cpe.3083

Zhang, X., Liu, C., Nepal, S., Yang, C., Dou, W., & Chen, J. (2014). A hybrid approach for scalable sub-tree anonymization over big data using MapReduce on cloud. *Journal of Computer and System Sciences*, *80*(5), 1008–1020. doi:10.1016/j.jcss.2014.02.007

Zhou, G. T., Ting, K. M., Liu, F. T., & Yin, Y. (2012). Relevance feature mapping for content-based multimedia information retrieval. *Pattern Recognition*, *45*(4), 1707–1720. doi:10.1016/j.patcog.2011.09.016

Zikopoulos, P., Eaton, C., DeRoos, D., Deutsch, T., & Lapis, G. (2011). *Understanding big data: Analytics for enterprise class Hadoop and streaming data*. New York, NY: McGraw–Hill.

ADDITIONAL READING

Ainley, J., Gould, R., & Pratt, D. (2015). Learning to reason from samples: Commentary from the perspectives of task design and the emergence of "big data". *Educational Studies in Mathematics*, *88*(3), 405–412. doi:10.1007/s10649-015-9592-4

Baines, D. (2013). Big data: Not just a lot more data. *Prescriber*, *24*(13/16), 7–8. doi:10.1002/psb.1081

Birney, E. (2012). The making of ENCODE: Lessons for big-data projects. *Nature*, *489*(7414), 49–51. doi:10.1038/489049a PMID:22955613

Camacho, J. (2014). Visualizing big data with compressed score plots: Approach and research challenges. *Chemometrics and Intelligent Laboratory Systems*, *135*, 110–125. doi:10.1016/j.chemolab.2014.04.011

Cannon, D. M., Godwin, J. H., & Goldberg, S. R. (2013). The big data revolution, and American turnaround. *Journal of Corporate Accounting & Finance*, *24*(6), 67–69. doi:10.1002/jcaf.21894

Cui, X., Zhu, P., Yang, X., Li, K., & Ji, C. (2014). Optimized big data K-means clustering using MapReduce. *The Journal of Supercomputing*, *70*(3), 1249–1259. doi:10.1007/s11227-014-1225-7

del Río, S., López, V., Benítez, J. M., & Herrera, F. (2014). On the use of MapReduce for imbalanced big data using Random Forest. *Information Sciences*, *285*, 112–137. doi:10.1016/j.ins.2014.03.043

Dubé, L., Labban, A., Moubarac, J. C., Heslop, G., Ma, Y., & Paquet, C. (2014). A nutrition/health mindset on commercial big data and drivers of food demand in modern and traditional systems. *Annals of the New York Academy of Sciences*, *1331*(1), 278–295. doi:10.1111/nyas.12595 PMID:25514866

Fan, W., & Huai, J. P. (2014). Querying big data: Bridging theory and practice. *Journal of Computer Science and Technology*, *29*(5), 849–869. doi:10.1007/s11390-014-1473-2

Fuchs, M., Höpken, W., & Lexhagen, M. (2014). Big data analytics for knowledge generation in tourism destinations: A case from Sweden. *Journal of Destination Marketing & Management*, *3*(4), 198–209. doi:10.1016/j.jdmm.2014.08.002

Harford, T. (2014). Big data: A big mistake? *Significance*, *11*(5), 14–19. doi:10.1111/j.1740-9713.2014.00778.x

Heeg, R. (2015). Who does what in big data and advanced analytics? *Research World, 2015*(50), 34–35.

Hoerl, R. W., Snee, R. D., & de Veaux, R. D. (2014). Applying statistical thinking to "big data" problems. *Wiley Interdisciplinary Reviews: Computational Statistics*, *6*(4), 222–232. doi:10.1002/wics.1306

Kambatla, K., Kollias, G., Kumar, V., & Grama, A. (2014). Trends in big data analytics. *Journal of Parallel and Distributed Computing*, *74*(7), 2561–2573. doi:10.1016/j.jpdc.2014.01.003

Kitchin, R. (2014). The real-time city? Big data and smart urbanism. *GeoJournal*, *79*(1), 1–14. doi:10.1007/s10708-013-9516-8

Kuhn, M., & Johnson, K. (2014). Who's afraid of the big black box?: Statisticians' vital role in big data and predictive modelling. *Significance*, *11*(3), 35–37. doi:10.1111/j.1740-9713.2014.00753.x

Li, G., Zuo, X., & Liu, B. (2014). Scientific computation of big data in real-world clinical research. *Frontiers of Medicine*, *8*(3), 310–315. doi:10.1007/s11684-014-0358-7 PMID:25190349

Liu, L. (2013). Computing infrastructure for big data processing. *Frontiers of Computer Science*, *7*(2), 165–170. doi:10.1007/s11704-013-3900-x

Mitsyn, S. V., & Ososkov, G. A. (2015). Watershed on vector quantization for clustering of big data. *Physics of Particles and Nuclei Letters*, *12*(1), 170–172. doi:10.1134/S1547477115010173

Portmess, L., & Tower, S. (2015). Data barns, ambient intelligence and cloud computing: The tacit epistemology and linguistic representation of big data. *Ethics and Information Technology*, *17*(1), 1–9. doi:10.1007/s10676-014-9357-2

Saey, T. H. (2015). Big data, big challenges: As researchers begin analyzing massive datasets, opportunities for chaos and errors multiply. *Science News*, *187*(3), 22–27. doi:10.1002/scin.2015.187003022

Schultz, T. (2013). Turning healthcare challenges into big data opportunities: A use-case review across the pharmaceutical development lifecycle. *Bulletin of the American Society for Information Science and Technology*, *39*(5), 34–40. doi:10.1002/bult.2013.1720390508

Shen, Y., & Zhang, Y. (2014). Transmission protocol for secure big data in two-hop wireless networks with cooperative jamming. *Information Sciences*, *281*, 201–210. doi:10.1016/j.ins.2014.05.037

Spiess, J., T'Joens, Y., Dragnea, R., Spencer, P., & Philippart, L. (2014). Using big data to improve customer experience and business performance. *Bell Labs Technical Journal*, *18*(4), 3–17. doi:10.1002/bltj.21642

Taylor, L., Cowls, J., Schroeder, R., & Meyer, E. T. (2014). Big data and positive change in the developing world. *Policy & Internet*, *6*(4), 418–444. doi:10.1002/1944-2866.POI378

Yan, D., Yin, X. S., Lian, C., Zhong, X., Zhou, X., & Wu, G. S. (2015). Using memory in the right way to accelerate big data processing. *Journal of Computer Science and Technology*, *30*(1), 30–41. doi:10.1007/s11390-015-1502-9

KEY TERMS AND DEFINITIONS

Anonymization: A process that removes the identity information from a record.

Big Data: The very large sets of data that are produced by people using the Internet, and that can only be stored, understood, and utilized with the help of special tools and methods.

Cloud Computing: The practice of storing the regularly used computer data on multiple servers that can be accessed through the Internet.

Data Mining: The practice of searching through large amounts of computerized data to find useful patterns or trends.

Data Set: An amount of information stored as a file on a computer.

Digital Age: The present time, when most information is in a digital form, especially when compared to the time when computers were not used.

Information Technology: The technology involving the development, maintenance, and use of computer systems, software, and networks for the processing and distribution of data.

MapReduce: A programming model from Google for processing the huge data sets on the large clusters of servers.

Chapter 9
Legal Responses to the Commodification of Personal Data in the Era of Big Data:
The Paradigm Shift from Data Protection towards Data Ownership

Emile Douilhet
Bournemouth University, UK

Argyro P. Karanasiou
Bournemouth University, UK

ABSTRACT

Big Data is a relatively recent phenomenon, but has already shown its potential to drastically alter the relationship between businesses, individuals, and governments. Many organisations now control vast amounts of raw data, and those industry players with the resources to mine that data to create new information have a significant advantage in the big data market. The aim of this chapter is to identify the legal grounds for the ownership of big data: who legally owns the petabytes and exabytes of information created daily? Does this belong to the users, the data analysts, or to the data brokers and various infomediaries? The chapter presents a succinct overview of the legal ownership of big data by examining the key players in control of the information at each stage of processing of big data. It then moves on to describe the current legislative framework with regard to data protection and concludes in additional techno-legal solutions offered to complement the law of big data in this respect.

INTRODUCTION

Big Data is a relatively recent phenomenon, but has already shown its potential to drastically alter the relationship between businesses, individuals, and governments. The issues surrounding privacy of the online users (Mayer-Shoenberger, Cukier 2013) and the overall ethical challenges involved (Schroeder, 2014) make big data a topical issue, especially in the aftermath of the Snowden revelations. Many organi-

DOI: 10.4018/978-1-5225-0182-4.ch009

sations now control vast amounts of raw data, and those industry players with the resources to mine that data to create new information have a significant advantage in the big data market. The use of predictive analytics in processing information tracked across different platforms to identify trends in the behaviour of individuals further adds value to big data (Fotopoulou, 2014) and makes it an important asset for any commercial entity. This rapid commodification of personal data has given rise to a new approach with regard to its legal protection in the era of big data: a shift from the traditional privacy protection regime to a wider protection under property law is considered by scholars as an appropriate legal response to the phenomenon of monetisation of personal data, once seen through the lens of big data (Victor, 2013).

The aim of this chapter is to identify the legal grounds for the ownership of big data: who legally owns the petabytes and exabytes of information created daily? Does this belong to the users, the data analysts, or to the data brokers and various infomediaries? The chapter presents a succinct overview of the legal ownership of big data by examining the key players in control of the information at each stage of the processing of big data. It then moves on to describe the current legislative framework with regard to data protection and concludes in additional techno-legal solutions offered to complement the law of big data in this respect, with a particular focus on the European context[1].

BACKGROUND

The transition from the traditional economic model of neoliberal markets in the post-industrial era to "informational capitalism" (Cohen 2016), based on a data-driven economy has challenged conventional legal thinking. Often referred to as the oil of the 21st century, data has become a valuable asset for the key stakeholders offering services in the digital era. At the same time, the law has been struggling to cope with this overbroad scope and definition of "data", as it does not purely address the user's privacy, being able to reveal one's identity but it can also be valorized and thus imply property entitlements for user generated data. The following section explores how data can be legally assessed during various stages of processing: in doing so, it is intended to demonstrate how big data appears to be an area not overly addressed by the current regulative framework, which focusses mostly on data protection and appears to bear little attention to how data can gain monetary value and thus allow for property based claims.

MAIN FOCUS OF THE ARTICLE

Issues, Controversies, Problems: The Four Stages in the Big Data Processing Cycle and Property Law

There are four main stages in the processing cycle of big data from its raw form to its use in predictive analytics:

1. Collection
2. Processing
3. Mining, and
4. Usage.

In the collection stage, raw data is collected through a number of means – either in a direct and voluntary manner by individuals themselves, or indirectly, inferred from the analysis of other data (Al-Khouri, 2012). In the processing stage, data is aggregated in databases and is formatted to be ready for analysis, either by a corporation or by a third party (a "data processor"). It should be noted that at this point the information is transformed from its original crude form at the collection stage and becomes part of one or more large datasets, put together by one or more separate corporations. Then, in the data mining stage, all gathered and processed data is analysed to create useful information. This new information created is essentially independent of the individual bits of information provided at the collection stage. Although it is the direct outcome of the analysis of segments of data from individual users, at this stage it also becomes the product of an analysis performed by entities completely separate from the data subjects, i.e. the users. Finally, in the usage stage, value is extracted from the information, through predicting analytics, data profiling, and any other number of methods able to exploit information for profit making.

Before however one is able to determine whether there are any legal grounds for data ownership in any of these stages, a preliminary question must be answered first: do property rights apply to data? The idea of propertisation of data, namely the protection of data under property or copyright law has been discussed extensively since the 1970s (Fromholz, 2000). A major difficulty in addressing data as property is its intangible nature added to the fact that it can be replicated many times without concrete evidence that its value is lost. On the other hand, copyright law reviewed in general within a digital environment increasingly shaped by big data, is greatly challenged: works are used 'in bulk' for purposes other than making their content available to the public, such as text mining and content mining (Borghi & Karapapa, 2013). Personal data in that sense –although treated as a tradable commodity online- has not yet received explicit protection under copyright law regime, falling mostly within the protective scope of privacy law. Moreover, the European approach to privacy maintains a narrow conceptual approach, regarding this as a human right, which cannot be traded away (Prins, 2004).

As such, there is no explicit legal right of ownership for individual pieces of information. Were we to apply the legal concept of property to big data in any of the three stages mentioned above, we would need to carefully consider the main legal features of the concept of property in general:

- *Usus* (the right to use),
- *Abusus* (to right to encumber or transfer) and
- *Fructus* (the right to enjoy the right) (Segal and Whinston, 2010).

In the absence of a formal right to ownership of big data, parties enjoying those rights should demonstrate these elements of ownership. Given the large amounts invested by the big data controllers, it would appear that the data collected and aggregated by corporations is under their ownership – they hold it in their databases, they process and aggregate it (*usus*), and they extract value from its analysis (*fructus*) and from selling it to other parties (*abusus*).

Nevertheless, data has a unique feature that complicates matters: the information is related to a person, gaining thereby an added aspect of privacy. Under the right to privacy, individuals enjoy a certain level of protection of their personal data, namely data able to identify them or to reveal private information about them without their consent. In this respect, the individual's right to data protection overrides the property right and economic interests of the data processors (Google Spain and Google Inc v Agencia Espanole de Proteccion de Datos of Mario Costeja, C 131-12, hereafter referred to as a the "Google Spain" case).

One of the most robust legislative frameworks dealing with data protection is the EU Data Protection Directive 95/46 (Levin & Nicholson, 2005). This provides us with a coherent legal regime, unlike the

US data privacy law, which is at large scattered (Gaff, Smedinghoff & Sor, 2012). For this reason, the focus here is mostly on the EU data protection laws. The main three distinctions used in the EU Data Protection Directive are "data subject", "controller", and "data processor". A data subject is an "identified or identifiable natural person [...] an identifiable person is one who can be identified, directly or indirectly, in particular by reference to an identification number or to one or more factors specific to his physical, physiological, mental, economic, cultural or social identity.", while a "controller" means "the natural or legal person, public authority, agency or any other body which alone or jointly with others determines the purposes and means of the processing of personal data." Finally, a processor is "a natural or legal person, public authority, agency or any other body which processes personal data on behalf of the controller". It should be noted that the Directive uses words like "controller" and "processor" and avoids the appellation of "owner". Yet, although in none of the above definitions is the term ownership explicitly expressed, many provisions seem to suggest a property-based approach to data.

The Data Protection Directive establishes a number of rights for individuals relating to their data – such as the fact that collecting an individual's data requires their prior unambiguous consent (Article 7), that individuals should have access to their data (Article 12), or that they should be able to object to the processing of their data if they have compelling legitimate grounds to do so (Article 14). The Directive also notably includes restrictions on what the data's controller can do with the data, including restrictions on the transfer of that data (Article 25). Drafted in 1995, the Data Protection Directive is currently undergoing reform after the proposal of the General Data Protection Regulation (GDPR) in 2012. The GDPR increases the rights that individuals hold over their data, as well as the restrictions of data controllers (Article 29 Working Party, 2014). In particular, the restriction of what constitutes "consent" to the very high standard of "explicit consent" reinforces the idea that individuals have a property based right: the fact that ultimate control lies with the individual's consent is a clear indication of the data subject considered as data "owner". At the same time though, data can be processed without consent for a "legitimate interest pursued by a controller" (Article 6(1) (f) GDPR). Even though this provision is itself mitigated by the fact that "it shall not override the fundamental rights and interests of the data subject", the fact that the individual does not necessarily have a final say in what happens to their data tempers their power over the data.

Finally, an element of ownership can be found in the ability of the data subject to have an enforceable claim with regard to the online indexing of his personal data. The "right to be forgotten", which is gaining traction in the European context and has been enshrined in the recent Google Spain case, gives data subjects the ability to request that their data, held by data controllers, be de-listed from Google's search results. The right to be forgotten, as defined in the GDPR, is broadly defined (Rosen, 2012) and is important because of the fact that the data subject seems to have retained some rights over his data, even after willingly parting with it. This suggests a property-based approach to data.

SOLUTIONS AND RECOMMENDATIONS

Data Rights and Database Rights: How is Ownership Delineated?

The data protection provisions in the Data Protection Directive and the upcoming General Data Protection Regulation have clear indications that individuals are granted certain rights over their data that extend beyond the traditional framework of privacy. Thus, as it was earlier demonstrated, data controllers demonstrate various elements of data ownership while processing big data; at the same time, under the right to be forgotten, it seems that at every stage, the data subject retains control over data being able to request erasure. This poses a legal conundrum: Can one be considered to own something in its entirety if at the same time someone else is further granted a right to command them erasure of indexed data?

Although puzzling, it seems that the issues becomes less complicated if one takes into account that a distinction needs to be drawn between segments of personal data and databases built on such data. So far, the chapter has explored the former; turning to explore now the latter, it appears that indeed there are strong indications in European law for specific provisions for a right to data ownership: the "database right".

The 1996 Database Right Directive 96/9 created a "sui generis" intellectual property right on data, the "database right" (Rendie, 2011), namely "the right to prevent extraction and/or reutilization of the whole or of a substantial part, evaluated qualitatively and/or quantitatively, of the contents of that database." Unlike other intellectual property rights, a database right does not require an original or technical achievement as a prerequisite for affording copyright protection. In fact, a person can have a database right provided that he a substantial investment is made in obtaining, verifying, or presenting data in the database (Reichman & Samuelson, 1997).

In this sense, database rights are automatically granted, and do not require to be registered or applied for. As such, the data constituting a database is not itself owned *per se* – it is rather the database in its entirety, having required time and effort to establish, that is protected. As a result, database rights enshrine in law the current practice of data controllers, granting them thus significant rights over the data they accumulate. Even though personal data is still protected under data protection regulation for the individual, the aggregation, processing and analysis of large amounts of data from a database, appear to have a separate existence separate. Outside the protective remit of privacy, databases are not protected as parts of the individual's identity and can thus be legally owned when one has a "substantial involvement" in it.

As a rule of thumb, EU Courts generally accept that database rights can be legally owned, unlike their components, namely the segments of personal data compiled for a database. The first main guidance for the database right came in 2004 - 8 years after the adoption of the Directive - from four judgments of the European Court of Justice (Aplin, 2005):

- *British Horseracing Board Ltd v William Hill Organization Ltd C-203/02 Judgment of the Court* (Grand Chamber 2004);
- *Fixtures Marketing Ltd v Organismos Prognostikon Agonon Podosfairou (OPAP) C-444/02 Judgment of the Court* (Grand Chamber 2004);
- *Fixtures Marketing Ltd v Svenska Spel AB C-338/02 Judgment of the Court* (Grand Chamber 2004);
- *Fixtures Marketing Ltd v OY Veikkaus Ab C-46/02 Judgment of the Court* (Grand Chamber 2004).

Most importantly, the database right in all these cases emphasise on the importance of organisation and assemblage of data, not on the original creation of the data in a database. Investment in the creation of data does not trigger a database right, assemblage and presentation do. That said, it is worth noting that the CJEU has been recently shifting away from the idea of database rights towards interpreting ToS as contractual obligations that have the potential to outline property over data. One such example is the

Ryanair v PR Aviation, where is was held that the use of data could be restricted by contract (through the online Terms of Use). This development however could be a double edged sword for the consumer, who is at most cases in a restricted bargaining position.

It could be argued that a form of database right also exists in the US (Xu, 2002): In a landmark US Supreme Court case, *Feist* (*Feist Publications, Inc. v. Rural Telephone Service Co., Inc., 499 U.S. 340, 1991*) copyright protection was extended to databases if there is originality in the "selection, coordination, or arrangement of contents for a database". Several cases since have built on this decision, and some state laws also provide from some protection for databases. The protection is however narrow (Gervais, 2007) because of the originality requirement, in contrast to the wider EU provision, which puts the focus on the investment in the database and the arrangement of data.

FUTURE CHALLENGES POSED BY WEARABLE TECH

Harvesting the Fruits of Self-Tracked Data and Controlling Mechanisms

So far it has been contended that although there is no explicit property right in data per se, there seems to be leeway for a property right to apply as far as databases are concerned. The rise of wearable tech, namely devices with sensors measuring the user's daily activities and habits has now posed a new legal challenge: how is legal ownership determined when a dataset is created and curated by the user himself? The growing tendency to self –track and quantify has taken off since its start in 2008 when two former Wired magazine editors, Gary Wolf and Kevin Kelly, co-founded the "Quantified Self" digital tracking group. The term is now used to describe the mainstream phenomenon of adults collecting data as means of recording and analyzing their lifestyle (Haddadi & Brown, 2014). It is estimated that 60% of US adults are currently tracking their weight, diet and exercise routine (Swan, 2014), actively collecting and analyzing their data in the context of their individual experiences (Nafus & Sherman, 2014). Although there is still a corporation acting as a data controller by providing tools for data analysis and storage on their servers, the user can also extract value from this data; this blurs the boundaries of the legal ownership of these commonly created datasets. This issue poses further legal questions, once online health repositories are considered: Microsoft Health Vault and Dossia are two examples of companies offering patients the chance to voluntarily store, collect and share health information with health providers and family members or other users (Steinbrook 2008).

Tim Berners Lee at the 2014 IP Expo Europe stressed the importance of data subjects owning their data instead of the corporations for the purposes of creating "rich" data, namely big data that if merged can be profitable for both the user and the corporations. Although the law has not yet offered a concrete answer to the issue of ownership of such "quantified self" datasets (Purtova, 2011) co-created by the users and the corporations, there is a growing tendency to allow the user for more control and ownership rights over his data with techno-legal solutions and alternative market models (Novotny & Spiekermann, 2013).

Personal Data Vaults (PDS) are currently one of the main technical solutions put forth in order to allow the user to gain control of his data back from the various corporations acting as info-mediaries in the big data market. The idea is to a privacy enhanced architecture enabling the user to access, control and trace their data once shared online (Mun et al, 2010). In this vein, there are many suggestions employing technical means for the user to reclaim control over his data: Once such example is the MIT Open PDS app, which allows the user to see third-party requests for his data and make informed decisions (de Montjoye at al, 2014). An alternative means of user-controlled data comes from Cozy cloud, a French company that provides users with open sourced private clouds to store their personal data. Other examples include a rising number of start-ups, such as "Personal", "Reputation.com" and "Datacoup", whose aim is to help the user monetize and control own data. That said the law is still admittedly lagging behind in terms of providing user with more control over his data (Crawford, Miltner, Gray 2014; Boyd, Crawford, 2012).

Many countries have embraced user-controlled data as a promising economy boosting strategy: The Midata project, announced in 2011 in the UK, is a multi-stakeholder approach to boost consumer empowerment by giving "consumers increasing access to their personal data in a portable, electronic format" enabling them to "use this data to gain insights into their own behaviour, make more informed choices about products and services, and manage their lives more efficiently" (Department for Business & Innovation Skills, 2011). Similarly in the US, the Federal trade Commission (FTC) in its report entitled "Data Brokers: A Call for Transparency and Accountability" issued in May 2014, calls for tighter regulation of the data brokers, namely large companies trading the user's data without the user's knowledge or consent.

CONCLUSION

At present, data controllers have the most control over data under the database right protection and are thus the primary beneficiaries of the value extracted from big data. At the same time, there seems to be a slight shift towards empowering the user to control and perhaps "own" his data, although legally this is has not yet fully been established. Since 2012, when the European Commission first suggested vital changes to the legal framework on data protection in the EU, the issue of user generated data as one's own property has been frequently discussed, yet there is no legal provision supporting such claims.

In December 2015, the trilogue discussions between the European Commission, the Parliament and the Council were concluded and a final text for the GDPR was agreed, which is expected to come into force in the first half of 2018 and will have immediate effect. Although there is no direct reference to data as property (or even an entitlement to digital personhood, which might imply a certain level of control over one's data), the provisions included with regard to transnational data flows, indicate how the issue of trans-border data flows will be heavily discussed in the years to come. The GDPR's expanded territorial reach, offering protection to EU consumers against any data controller/processor targeting them, irrespective of where the latter is based combined with the obligation to implement technical and organizational measures to notify the controller of data breaches are both new additions to the Data Protection Directive that suggest a more nuanced approach towards personal data. Further to this, data portability and interoperable standards, although currently encouraged and not mandated, still present the user with the potential to re-use his own data across a number of platforms for personal purposes.

A right to own one's data is still far from being explicitly mentioned in the final text of the GDPR. It remains yet to be seen, how this nascent area of data prophetization will be further shaped by the CJEU rulings, especially in the light of the EU Digital Single Market.

REFERENCES

Al-Kouri, A. (2012). Data Ownership, Who Owns my Data? *International Journal of Management & Information, 2*(1).

Aplin, T. (2005). *The ECJ Elucidates the Database Right*. London: Intellectual Property Quarterly.

Article 29 Working Party. (2014). *Opinion 06/2014on the notion of legitimate interests of the data controller under Article 7 of Directive 95/46/EC, 9 April 2014,* 844/14/EN WP 217.

Borghi, M., & Karapapa, S. (2013). *Copyright & Mass Digitisation*. Oxford, UK: Oxford University Press.

Boyd, D., & Crawford, K. (2012). Critical Questions for Big Data: Provocations for a Cultural, Technological and Scholarly Phenomenon. *Information Communication and Society, 15*(5), 662–679. doi: 10.1080/1369118X.2012.678878

Cohen, J. (2016). The Regulatory State in the Informational Age. *Theoretical Inquiries in Law, 17*(2).

Crawford, K., Miltner, K., & Gray, M. (2014). Critiquing Big Data: Politics, Ethics, Epistemology. *International Journal of Communication, 8*, 1663.

de Monjoye, Y.-A., Shmueli, E., Wang, S. S., & Pentland, A. S. (2014). Open PDS: Protecting the Privacy of Metadata through SafeAnswers. *PLoS ONE, 10*, 1371.

Department for Business & Innovation Skills. (2011). *The Midata Vision of Consumer Empowerment*. Retrieved from https://www.gov.uk/government/news/the-midata-vision-of-consumer-empowerment

Fotopoulou, A. (2014). *Tracking Biodata: Sharing and Ownership*. Report on Research Placement funded by the RCUK Digital Economy NEMODE Network.

Fromholz, J. (2000). The European Union Data Privacy Directive. *Berk. Tech. LJ, 15*, 461.

Gaff, B. M., Smedinghoff, T. J., & Sor, S. (2012). Privacy and Data Security. *Computer*, (3), 8–10.

Gervais, D. J. (2007). The *Protection of Databases Kent L. Rev., 82*, 1109.

Haddadi, H., & Brown, I. (2014). *Quantified Self and the Privacy Challenge*. Technology Law Futures.

Levin, A., & Nicholson, M. J. (2005). Privacy Law in the United States, the EU and Canada: The Allure of the Middle Ground. *U of Ottawa Law & Technology Journal, 2*(2), 362.

Mayer-Schoenberger, V., & Cukier, K. (2013). *Big Data: A Revolution That Will Transform How We Live, Work and Think*. J Murray.

Mun, M., Hao, S., Mishra, N., Shilton, K., Burke, J., & Govindan, R. et al. (2010). *Personal Data Vaults: A Locus of Control for Personal Data Streams*. ACM CoNext.

Nafus, D., & Sherman, J. (2014). This One Does Not Go Up to 11: The Quantified Self Movement as an Alternative Big Data Practice. *International Journal of Communication, 8*, 1784–1794.

Novotny, A., & Spiekermann, S. (2013). Personal Information Markets AND Privacy: A New Model to Solve the Controversy.*11th International Conference on Wirtschaftsinformatik*, Leipzig, Germany.

Prins, J. E. (2004). The propertization of personal data and identities. *Electronic Journal of Comparative Law, 8*(3).

Purtova, N. (2011). *Property Rights in Personal Data: A European Perspective*. Kluwer.

Reichman, J., & Samuelson, P. (1997). Intellectual Property Rights in Data. *Vand. L. Rev., 50*.

Rendie, A. (2011). *Aggregation: Demystifying Database Rights*. Taylor Wessing.

Rosen, J. (2012). The Right to be Forgotten. *Stanford Law Review*, *64*, 88.

Schroeder, R. (2014). Big Data: Towards a More Scientific Social Science and Humanities. In M. Graham & W. H. Dutton (Eds.), *Society and the Internet: How Networks of Information are Changing our Lives*. Oxford, UK: Oxford University Press.

Segal, I., & Whinston, M. (2012). Property Rights: Handbook of Organizational Economics. Princeton University Press.

Steinbrook, R. (2008). Personally Controlled Online Health Data – The Next Big Thing In Medical Care?' (2008). *The New England Journal of Medicine*, *358*, 16.

Swan, M. (2013). *The Quantified Self: Fundamental Disruption in Big Data Science and Biological Discovery* (Vol. 1). Big Data.

Van Alstyne, M., Brynjolfsson, E., & Madnick, S. (1995). Why Not One Big Database? Principles for Data Ownership. *Decision Support Systems*, *15*(4), 267–284.

Victor, J. M. (2013). The EU General Data Protection Regulation: Toward a Property Regime for Protecting Data Privacy. *The Yale Law Journal*, 513.

Wu, X. (2002)... *EC Data Base Directive. Berkeley Tech. LJ*, *17*, 571.

KEY TERMS AND DEFINITIONS

Infomediaries: Various entities that aggregate and link information on subjects or groups of subjects on behalf of commercial organizations and their potential customers.

Privacy by Design: A policy approach, which suggests a privacy friendly design as a techno-legal means of enforcing data protection legislation.

Privacy Enhancing Technologies: Technologies (both hardware and software) designed to protect the privacy of users in the online context.

Propertisation of Data: The tendency among legal scholars towards developing a theory that aims at conceptualizing data as property, bound by property and ownership rights.

Quantified Self: The use of self-collected personal data, mostly using biosensors built in wearable technologies, to improve one's health and well-being.

ENDNOTE

[1] A detailed version of this chapter has been presented at the 2016 IEEE International Conference on Cloud Engineering Workshops (IC2EW 2016). The authors are grateful to all reviewers for the comments and feedback provided. Any errors or omissions remain the sole responsibility of the authors.

Chapter 10
Big Data and Business Decision Making

Marta Vidal
Complutense University of Madrid, Spain

Javier Vidal-García
University of Valladolid, Spain

Rafael Hernandez Barros
Complutense University of Madrid, Spain

ABSTRACT

The generalization of the big data and new techniques associated with the processing and analysis of large databases is revolutionizing both the scientific work as the management of companies. Applications such as personalized recommendations for Amazon have been a very significant improvement in the purchase experience for consumers. In this work we analyze the possibilities of big data to improve the services offered by companies and the customer experience and increase the efficiency of these companies. The work also examines some aspects associated with the use of big data such as the issues of data privacy and compliance with the regulations on the use of the information.

1. INTRODUCTION

This work tries to give a vision necessarily partial, given speed of change and the extension of the topic, on the possibilities offered by the techniques of big data in the field of business decision making. Certainly big data is not a new field, banks, shops, etc. have long used large amounts of data, for example, for studies of segmentation of their customers. Scientists have been using massive amounts of data for long time. In fact the information that is generated in the social networks or the internet is not the main source of the enormous accumulation of data that occurs every day. Scientific applications such as radio telescopes, the DNA sequencers or particle accelerators generate much more information. For example the LHC (Large Hadron Collider) of CERN produces a petabyte of data every second from sensors that

DOI: 10.4018/978-1-5225-0182-4.ch010

capture all the emissions produced by the collision of particles. From a technological point of view the problem is not the data but that the speed at which we can store the information as it does not progress at the same pace as the information that is generated.

The contributions of the internet (search tool and its application to translators, predictions etc.) and expansion of social networks has had a great impact on what we might call the big data social (analysis of feelings, textual analysis, etc.). But in fact, most of the data that is generated on the planet is produced by the interaction of machines (for example sensors) with other machines. At the moment there is great excitement about the almost unlimited possibilities of big data to improve the productivity and the welfare of the people. In this perspective it is very frequent that in business meetings appear allusions to big data. But the description of the current situation has been characterized by an ironic form by Dan Ariely: big data is like adolescent sex, all talk about it, nobody really knows how to do so, everyone thinks that all the others are doing and, therefore, all over the world ensures that they also do.

2. BACKGROUND

At present many lines of research in computational sciences and many new businesses refers to the use of big data. The definition of big data is complex because many of the techniques that accompany these massive databases were known by other names such as data mining. By big data normally means the construction, organization and use of enormous amounts of data to extract relationships or create new forms of value in markets, organizations, public services, etc. This definition should be qualified to understand better the importance of the big data since the domain of these techniques is not only related to the size of the databases that use. In the first place when you think of big data is thought to have an enormous volume of information.

Secondly an application of big data involves the aggregation of information from various sources, which make it particularly important to the process of management and merging of data. The data can come from sensors, GPS of millions of phones, clicks, logs of servers, emails, etc. Therefore it is not a question of numeric data arranged in a standard fashion (for example in tables). The data is very heterogeneous and can include images, texts, sounds, etc. Companies also, by the own heterogeneity of the data, usually prevent data stored in fixed structures such as the classical relational database. The management of the data is done using NoSQL systems (not only SQL) as opposed to the traditional language of SQL queries. This tool is essential when companies work with many gigabytes of data or millions of observations with heterogeneous formats and whose structure may change in time and need to be easily scalable. Some of the tools used to manipulate big data are becoming the industry standard as Hadoop, MapReduce, Pig, None, OpenRefine, Hive, HBase, Mahout, ZooKeeper or Impala. The vast majority of these tools have as objective to allow the parallel processing necessary when working with huge databases.

Thirdly the information used usually has a very heterogeneous level of signal-noise ratio, although there is much more noise than in typical applications that use administrative data, surveys or internal information systems of business organizations (Grossman & Siegel (2014)). Fourthly the objective of the techniques of big data in general is not to discover causalities but produce predictive models. By contrast with the fundamental vision that is explained in the courses of traditional statistics and econometrics, in big data only matters correlations while the causality is irrelevant. Finally, the use and analysis of information tends to occur at a very high speed (Kruschwitz (2011).

Mayer-Schönberger and Cukier (2014) describe big data as a change of mentality that assumed in the first place the ability to analyze massive amounts of data in place of resort to samples, the acceptance of the dirt or inaccuracy of the data of the real world as something inseparable instead of seeking the accuracy in the data, and the growing with regard to the correlation in place of the continuous search for elusive causality.

Therefore a project of big data uses principles of informatics, mathematics and statistics developed in three stages. The first phase is the process of capture and manipulation of data. The huge amount of information that is to manipulate involves the use of parallel processes, specific programs for the reduction of dimension (for example MapReduce) and managers NoSQL. The second phase involves the analysis of the data to find useful predictive relations. In this phase it is used statistical techniques and "machine learning". The difference between both fields is diffuse. Breiman (2001) notes that while statistics imposes a model (regression, logistics, etc.) to try to capture the nature of the relationship between an input and an output, in "machine learning" the goal is to find a function that can predict an outcome from a few inputs without required model on the nature of this relationship. In a third stage, as important as the previous, display techniques are used to present the results and communicate them to end users.

An important aspect of big data is the reuse of this data. With big data the value of the data changes depending on your use (primary or potential use in the future). With this perspective, the design that the changes have on the business value of your data and press companies to change their business models and thinking on how to use the data they have at their disposal in the most efficient way possible. In the past the data generated by a business was a collateral result of the management of the business (McAfee, Brynjolfsson, Davenport, Patil, & Barton (2012)). Data is increasingly considered valuable by itself and its attainment and storage becomes an important part of the business model.

3. BIG DATA APPLICATIONS TO THE ECONOMY

The applications of big data to the field of the economics are increasingly abundant although the deployment of this methodology in the economy is recent. It is increasingly common to find methodologies that make estimates in real time of the evolution of the prices or the cost of goods (Varian (2014)). The Billion Prices Project of MIT employs millions of prices of shops in internet in dozens of countries to obtain a price index online that is updated in real time. This technology uses the stability or changes of the components between tags of language HTML used to build web pages to determine the changes in the prices of products in time (Butler (2008)). A program can, using these principles, identify the relevant information on a product and its price. The URL of the page where these products are indexed can be used to sort the products by category. For example, Cavallo (2012) uses hundreds of thousands of prices of products on the internet to compare the evolution of the official inflation and the obtained from catches of price information from online stores. Cavallo (2012) shows that while in Brazil, Chile, Colombia and Venezuela the evolution of the official inflation and the obtained from prices online follow similar patterns, in Argentina the differences is very significant. On average inflation in Argentina, between 2007 and 2011, as defined by the online price index was 20.14% compared to the official inflation that was only 8.38%. This implies a cumulative difference of 65% by March 2011.

Choi and Varian (2012) used Google Trends to improve the predictive ability of models on economic indicators obtained with very high frequency. The idea is to complement the information of the past of a series with the searches present in some categories. For example, the Department of Labor of the United

States announces each Thursday the number of people who have requested unemployment benefits. Adding to a model AR(1) of historical data the information on searches for words in categories such as jobs, welfare, unemployment, improving a 6% the predictive capacity in general, and the changes of cycle in particular. Using the same system for the index of consumer confidence is achieved an improvement of 9.3% in the predictive capacity.

The use of aggregate information on credit cards and TPV is another important source of economic research at present. In a series of articles that has proved to be very influential, Mian and Sufi (2009) have used the information about credit cards to perform economic analysis on the causes of the real estate bubble and the financial crisis. Mian, Rao and Sufi (2013) analyze the elasticity of consumption with respect to the housing wealth. The calculation of consumption at county level is performed using the purchases made by credit card or debit intermediaries by MasterCard. An important advantage of these data for their study is that spending on consumption is classified with the NAICS codes that provide each trade where spending is performed. Mian and Sufi (2009) used all the mortgages individualized produced between 1990 and 2007 (available for any citizen thanks to the Home Mortgage Disclosure Act) and the data on credit between 1991 and 2007 by type of credit that provides Analytical Services, a data provider from group Equifax. Adding by the information on debt counties, defaults and mortgage loans (granting or denial among other variables), Mian and Sufi (2009) show that in the counties where there was the greatest credit restrictions before the start of the real estate bubble is where the credit increased with the start of the expansion of real estate and where housing prices grew more. They also show that at the beginning of the crisis in those same counties is where prices fell more intensively and foreclosures increased more.

In a very recent example, Jimenez et al. (2014) use information about 24 million individual loans to analyze the impact of monetary policy in the assumption of risk from financial institutions.

How Big Data Creates Value

It is important to understand that the big data, or at least the massive data generation, is not an option, is simply a reality that we face as a result of the use of computing devices and digital networks (Edelman (2015)).

However, there are two ways to confront this deluge of data: see it as a problem or as an opportunity to create value. Its complexity makes it quite understandable that when it began to catch a glimpse of the potential of this trend was considered a problem, but the technology is demonstrating not only to be able to handle it but also that the opportunities associated are enormous.

The aim of the big data is to understand the keys of the activity to which we dedicate ourselves through analytical process. Either define patterns of patients of a disease or improve a distribution strategy, the results are clearly the point that most interests, but to create value through the big data it is necessary to understand the whole process.

The expectations around big data are enormous and its scope can have social benefits in addition to the economic: the improved logistics techniques by the analysis of the big data will generate optimized distribution strategies, with what the impact on the environment of the carriage of containers will be less.

The administrations of the countries of the third world and the so-called developing countries could use the analysis of the information to improve the conditions of life of its inhabitants. Charitable organizations and large institutions like the UN could carry out actions much more successful.

Big data promises a new world in which the organizations will find ways to work more productively, more sustainable and more profitable, but to do so it will be necessary also to seek new forms of organization for priority to be given to the use of the information.

4. THE BUSINESS OF BIG DATA

According to a study carried out by McKinsey Global Institute, the benefits derived from big data will be different for companies depending on the sector to which they belong (Biesdorf, Court, & Willmott (2013)). However, the main brakes to its implementation are related to the resistance that managers of companies have to adopt measures to manage the data on a large scale. The signature refers to this resistance as the barriers to use of the big data.

The sectors of information and electronic and computer products are best positioned to generate value from big data. Companies have access to a large amount of useful data and the implementation of the innovation is a fundamental element of its market.

Administrations and the financial sectors have a great potential to leverage the big data because they have a transactional level and participation of users very high. However the resistance to use analytical big data is a particularly important factor in this sector, since a large part of the information they generate and manage is very sensitive.

There is a group of sectors that reflects a low level of growth in productivity (construction, education, arts and entertainment, etc.). McKinsey blames the strong systemic barriers they face these sectors. If they were eliminated, the big data would have the potential to improve the productivity also in these sectors.

In regard to the rest of the sectors, there is a very clear difference between those that move in international markets, that are accustomed to the increases in productivity, and those that do so in local markets, whose growth of productivity is very low. However the majority of these sectors, regardless of the nature of their trade, might notice improvements relevant in the said growth if demolish the barriers that prevent them from using the big data in their favor.

Examples of possible benefits of big data in some sectors:

- **Financial Services:** Data obtained from the mobile phones may allow a deep understanding of the habits of spending and saving in different sectors and regions. The Digital Payment histories allow users to generate a credit history, generating the possibility that users become candidates for loans and other services of financial credit.
- **Health:** The data collected through the mobile devices, captured by the professionals of the sector, submitted by individuals or analyzed in the form of exhaust data (large amounts of data before being processed), can be a useful tool for understanding trends in health of the population or curb the epidemic outbreaks. When harvested in a context of individual health records, this data do not only improve continuity in the care of the patients, but that can be used to create huge databases for the treatments and results can be compared efficiently and inexpensively.
- **Agriculture:** Mobile payments of agricultural products, purchases and subsidies can help governments to improve their predictions on trends in production of products and their incentives. This knowledge may be used to ensure the adequacy of the storage of crops, reduce waste and the de-

terioration of products and to provide better information on the types of financial aid that farmers need. The pattern of behavior of the use of the mobile phone can help governments and NGOS to identify areas at risk. Early detection can help prevent families to abandon their lands and the decrease in agricultural production.

5. IMPLEMENTATION OF BIG DATA FOR BUSINESS ENVIRONMENT

The term big data refers to the tendency of advancing technologies have opened the door to a new approach to understanding and decision making, which is used to describe huge amounts of data that would take too long to load on a relational database for further analysis. Therefore, big data will apply to any information that cannot be processed through traditional methods.

A database is a collection of interrelated data. When speaking of relational database theory reference to the relational data model work of IBM researcher Edgar Codd in 1970 and enjoys a strong mathematical base is made. The relational model is characterized by stating that all information must be contained in tables, and relationships between data must be explicitly represented in the same way. What is achieved with this model is always working on interrelated tables. Avoiding duplication of records and ensuring referential integrity. The big drawback is the time it takes to handle large amounts of data, but thanks to big data this is accomplished. On the other hand what users get when working with databases is to combine different types of data and a formalized manner.

Therefore the advantages of a relational database could be defined as:

- **Referential Integrity** (without duplicity ...).
- **Standardization** (standard SQL arise ...).
- **Sets Roles** (permissions entries tables).

However there are also disadvantages of using relational databases:

- **Limited Amount of Data Management.**
- **Read Only of Structured Languages.**
- **Aimed at Meeting Objectives Old Applications**.

These three disadvantages are resolved by resolve big data, because its structure is able to store and process large amounts of data and three possible types of data (structured, semi-structured and unstructured), its architecture is also oriented to current programs.

Once the importance of big data is known mainly thanks to the improvement that meant about relational models, we will explain the possible implementation of big data for business environment, however this potential implementation not necessarily have to apply to all organizations because each company competes in a different business environment.

Here are the most important situations where big data can be implemented:

- **Change Management**:
  - Search for new business opportunities through improved segmentation and cross-selling (improved strategy).

- By applying analytical and predictive modeling data customer accounts and transaction history, the solution allows agents to carry out a segmentation based on the likelihood that the customer contracted services or complementary products or services from more value (improved segmentation).
- By analyzing consumption of services and products, the company can optimize cross-selling strategies, refine marketing messages and provide specific offers. Clients can more accurately predict which products are most appropriate for each customer (improved strategy).
- Provide the right mix of services and products improving the effectiveness and efficiency of the sales force of the company, while more personalized treatment helps agents to forge closer ties with customers, which improves loyalty (improved strategy).
- Operational improvements: Increased capacity of business visibility through more detailed reports.

- **Analysis of Web Browsing Habits and Online Consumption**:
  - Social Network Analysis: Determine the social circles of customers from phone interactions and social networks online generates a complete view of customers, identifying their role in their circles and degree of influence.
  - Viral marketing (marketing that exploits social networks ...): Detects most influential clients, social roles ... to maximize the dissemination of products and services (better knowledge of customers and the market in social networks).
  - Analysis of data navigation: Analyzes Web browsing and online habits of consumption: extract valuable new customer prospects. It identifies the user (location, terminal status, access services), sites and word searches, visited urls, browsing time, etc. are monitored (Better knowledge of the customer).
  - Dashboard in real time, the information is always available without waiting for updating the data (real time information).
- **Anticipating Problems**:
  - A predictive analysis system and data matching allows us to anticipate possible problems that may arise in the future, such as a prediction of disaster risk that would adjust the pricing and provisioning funds for possible payments (utility to view accuracy of the data to inaccurate data).
- **Process Improvement**:
  - It allows simplifying current processes and business control (cost reduction).
  - Safety Analysis. Proactive analytics allows reducing risks and losses against fraud (cost reduction).
  - It can detect complex patterns of fraud in real time analyzing historical data, the pattern of use of geolocation information, analysis of transactions and suspicious transactions (cost reduction).
- **Support Decision Making Through Automatic Algorithms**:
  - Sophisticated analytics to analyze all reports and data, help decision-making, reducing risks and discover information that previously could be hidden, yet important (aid to decision-making).
- **Cost Reduction.**
- **Reduction Times.**
- **Development of New Products.**

- **Optimized and Personalized Offers.**
- **Take Smarter Decisions with Previous Business Intelligence Systems.**
- **Intelligent Security Filters in e-Business.**

All these applications can be grouped into a main objective: To obtain more information and knowledge from customers of the company, including the company itself and the competition to gain a competitive advantage over competitors offering customers what they want or even to create a need that customers do not have yet.

When referring to obtain more information and knowledge does not refer to a lot of data, but we must differentiate between data-information-knowledge.

- **Data**: It is a primary element of information alone are irrelevant to the decision. The clearest way to see this is with an example. A phone number or a name of a person, are data, without purpose or usefulness are useless.
- **Information:** It can be defined as a set of processed data and that has relevance or purpose and therefore are useful for people who use it for decision-making.
- **Knowledge**: It is a mixture of experience, values, information and know-how to apply for connoisseurs of this decision.

Where big data really comes into play is in the process of finding information which can be transformed into knowledge among these large amounts of data collected by organizations and not on how the data are collected. The optimistic vision of a perfect big data is one in which companies would be able to obtain data from any source, leverage that data and get the information that would become useful knowledge for the organization allowing incorporate all the previously mentioned advantages.

6. TOOLS FOR IMPLEMENTATION OF BIG DATA

In this section we describe the main tools and technology used for implementing big data:

- **Data Warehouse:** Is an evolution of systems relational databases, it is a process, not a product. In 1988, IBM researchers Barry Devlin and Paul Murphy invented the term Warehouse information, although considered the father of the Data Warehouse is William Harvey Inmon.

The Data Warehouse were created in the decade of the 90s and are a set of data that organizations use to support decision making and which at the same time be consulted by the technologies of Data Mining.

The definition of William Harvey Inmon says: "A collection of data used to support decision making, organized by subject, integrated, non-volatile and in which the concept of time varies over traditional systems".

- **Data Mining:** Is a tool to extract knowledge from the data we have stored to treat them and turn them into useful and objective information that will help the employer make the right decisions. The definition of data mining given by (Fayad et al 1996), "is a non-trivial process valid, novel identification, potentially useful and understandable understandable patterns that are hidden in the data," mining data is defined as no light extraction, previously unknown and potentially useful data from implicit information. In today's information society, data mining is a key to effectively analyze and exploit them for the objectives of any organization form tool.

- **Cloud Computing:** It is a young technology like big data technology that gives us the ability to offer services via the internet. This new technology aims to have all our files and information on the internet without worrying about having enough capacity to store said information. Cloud computing takes force when the provision of hardware becomes a problem because the hardware has besides the monetary costs have space, scalability is where cloud computing is a great alternative.
- **Business Intelligence:** It can be considered a business tool with the ability to transform data into information and then that information into knowledge. From a more theoretical perspective it could be defined as the set of methodologies, applications, and technologies that aim to obtain, debug and modify data from transactional systems for the exploitation of such information by the company making it useful knowledge. In other words what is achieved with business intelligence is to obtain a competitive advantage for organizations to obtain information and helping decision making of senior management.
- **Big Data Analystics:** It is a new business tool which will allow to examine large data repositories big data, in order to assist in decision making discovering hidden patterns, unknown correlations, predictions and other useful information and allow competitive advantage for companies or organizations that possess.

The main objective of big data analytics is to help in making business decisions by allowing analyze large volumes of data from transactional databases and other data sources that can be untapped by business intelligence (BI). These other data sources may include web server logs and data on the internet, reports social media activities, detailed records of mobile phone calls, the information captured by the sensors, email, tweets, etc. Big data analytics should not be associated exclusively to large volumes of data and large data analysis with unstructured data and also take into account databases with structured data like relational databases.

Big data anlytics also collects data from sources of unstructured or semi-structured data. Related technologies to big data analytics include NoSQL databases, Hadoop and MapReduce. These technologies form the core of the platform open source software that supports processing of large volumes of data across clustered systems.

7. BIG DATA FOCUSED ON CLIENTS

The majority of companies identified their objectives as being focused on the customer as the highest priority for them. Companies are committed to improving the customer experience and with a better understanding of the preferences and the behavior of the same. Understanding the consumer of today, much more skilled than previous ones, is also identified as a high level priority.

Companies consider that big data provides the ability to understand and better predict the behavior of the customers and, in so doing, improve their experience. Transactions, multichannel interactions, social networking, syndicated data through sources such as loyalty cards and other information related to the customers have increased the ability of companies to create a complete picture of the preferences and demands of customers: an objective of the departments of marketing, sales and customer service for decades.

Through this deep understanding, companies of all kinds are finding new ways to interact with their current and future clients. This principle is applicable to the retail trade, but also to telecommunications, health, government, banking and finance and the sector of consumer products, where end users and citizens are involved in interactions business-to-business (B2B) between partners and suppliers.

In fact, big data can be a two-way road between clients and companies: for example, the electric Ford Focus produces huge amounts of data while it is being conducted and when it is parked. While it is in motion the driver receives constantly updated information about the acceleration, braking, the charging of the battery and the location of the vehicle. This is useful for the driver, but this same data also arrive to Ford engineers, who receive information about the driving habits of clients, including how, when and where loaded their cars. And while the vehicle is stopped continues sending data about pressure of the tires and the battery system to the nearest smart phone.

Big data allows obtaining a more complete picture of the preferences and demands of clients; through this deep understanding companies of all kinds are finding new ways to interact with their present and future clients.

This scenario focused on the client derives multiple advantages because big data makes possible new and valuable forms of collaboration (Barney (1991)). Drivers receive useful information every second while the engineers in Detroit gather the information concerning the behavior at the wheel with the purpose of extracting knowledge about customers and develop enhancements to the products. And utilities and other external suppliers analyze millions of kilometers of driving data to decide where to locate new charging stations and how to protect the fragile service networks of the overloads.

Companies around the world are able to provide a better service to its clients and to improve operations thanks to big data. Companies such as:

Mcleod Russel India Limited have completely eliminated the downtime of the systems in the tea trade thanks to a more accurate monitoring of the crops, the production and marketing of up to 100 million kilos of tea every year.

Premier Healthcare Alliance resorted to functions of exchange of data and analytical advanced to improve patient outcomes and at the same time reduce their spending on 2,850 million dollars.

Santam improved the customer experience when deploying the predictive analysis with the objective of reducing the fraud (Barker, D'Amato, & Sheridon (2008); Hoffmann & Birnbrich (2012).

In addition to the objectives focus on the client, other functional goals are also dealt with through the first applications of big data. Operational optimization, for example, was one of the objectives cited by 18% of respondents, but consists mainly in pilot projects. Other applications of big data that are frequently mentioned include the financial management/risks, employee collaboration and enabling new business models.

8. APPLICATION EXAMPLES OF BIG DATA

The analysis of data to establish new business models or define commercial strategies will be one of the greatest opportunities for businesses and industries in the coming years, and increasingly more sectors are realizing. Traveling with big data can become a whole experience in delivering new services or products, but this opportunity will depend on the ability of firms and economic sectors to adapt to one of the most important assets today: the management of the information (Butler (2013); (Lazer, Kennedy, King, & Vespignani (2014)).

At this time, there are several practices of use of big data both in giants of the web such as Google, Facebook or Linkedin as in more traditional companies. See below for brief examples of economic sectors or companies where big data is beginning to be used:

- **Public Sector**: Intelligence services, defense and protection (communications control, surveillance, interception of telephone networks, accumulation of all kinds of data); protection of the fishing fleet; surveillance, safety and signalling and projects of smart cities, locations by GPS, fraud detection, control of public budgets, protection of public infrastructure, protection against abuse, etc (Chen, Chiang, & Storey (2012)).
- **Health**: Remote monitoring of patients, location of emergencies and storage of medical histories, x-rays, scanners and all kinds of tests centrally, elaboration of statistics about incidences of certain diseases by specific areas, rapprochement of the home-based care, clinical research: drug studies, clinical trials, human genome, etc.
- **Retail-Mass Consumption**: The practices of exploitation of big data are the core of business from many years ago, more important than transactional applications: Control of the manufacturing chain, analysis of ticket, custom marketing and RFID (Radio Frequency Identification) in commercial centers.
- **Telecommunications**: Control of the network, sale of localization services, advertising services associated with the pattern of calls or downloaded applications, getting rich consumer profiles and exploitation of RFID to segment and customize offers, analysis of abandonment, risk and fraud in customers, satisfaction and loyalty of clients, analysis of CDR (Call Data Record) or call log), etc (see Lambrecht & Tucker (2013)).
- **Utilities**: Interpretation of smart meters in all homes, control of the communications network, piping, underground network and signage projects of tranches of maintenance.
- **The Tourism Sector**: One of the last areas in jump on the bandwagon of big data has been the tourism. According to a report prepared by the company Amadeus, the integration of technology of data analysis in this sector will constitute a revolution that could define the guidelines to be followed to overcome the future challenges of the tourism sector. The study highlights some of the most innovative practices and interesting, within the technology big data, which are being carried out in the sector to establish commercial strategies and stimulate a sector punished by the current economic situation.

A good example of a tourism company that gets competitive advantages from the use of big data is British Airways. The objective of this airline is to understand their customers better than any other through its program "Know me", which analyzes data from tens of millions of points of contact for the customer. The company recognizes and reward the loyalty of its customers, monitors all type of inconvenience, and provides clients with custom offerings. Another example of it is the central reservations online Kayak uses technology big data to predict the price that will have the flights in a period of between 7 and 10 days, with the aim of offering the best offer of flights at competitive prices for the habitual users of this platform.

Another example of the use of technologies big data is the case of airlines such as Air France-KLM that uses technology from Hadoop as the basis of the management system of the company's revenues at corporate level. The advantages of big data in decision-making and in the ability to anticipate the preferences and habits of consumption of customers are keys to establish more diversified services and establish better relations with clients, thanks to the application of new strategies in the management of clients, benefits and internal operations (McGuire, Manyika, & Chui (2012)). A challenge in a sector which is so sensitive to external factors such as tourism.

In any case, the jump in the travel industry and tourism to the big data should overcome challenges and short-term obstacles such as fragmentation of data across multiple systems, the potential friction by the coexistence of management architectures of big data and traditional architecture and the limited supply of specialized professionals with scientific profile data for the management and analysis of information.

Among the services offered by big data in the tourist sector are price optimization, generation of personalized offers and the analysis of feelings.

- **Financial Markets**: As experts from BNY Mellon state: "World economic growth will probably be faster. In exchange, the resulting implications for the global capital markets are enormous. Construction of infrastructures, international capital flows, the change of currency, the diversification of assets, the thematic selection, product innovation and, perhaps most important, economic and financial policies will depend on the results of the new methods of Big Data".

The implications of this revolution can also transform the current manner of interpreting the financial markets. "Several of the dozens of interpretations of the monthly rate of employment in the United States are probably unnecessary" thanks to the big data, according to BNY Mellon.

On the other hand, the publication of macro data (GDP, inflation, PMIs), "may become more accurate and less surprising". But BNY Mellon goes even further: "The big data will rebuild the asset management industry", since that will utilize new approaches to the information available in "search, analysis, distribution, trading and risk management". Its experts believe that the new tools will abandon definitively the aphorisms and equity will examine with even more detail both the fundamental components of the companies and the credit as the thematic differentiation.

They also consider that a faster and more efficient processing will increase the difficulty of managers to generate alpha; in a market where the main determinants of the volatility will be only irrational movements or unwanted geopolitical events, believe that it will become increasingly common passive management track indexing or ETF "to the detriment of the thematic differentiation" (Nickerson & Rogers (2014)).

Among applications of big data in the financial sector include the services of trademark protection, protection against risks and fraud, personalized services to customers, search for patterns of use of financial products, marketing custom, creation of location-based services, etc.

9. CASES OF SUCCESSFUL IMPLEMENTATION OF BIG DATA

- **Vestas Wind Systems**: Danish wind turbine manufacturer uses the analysis of the data, among which include temperature, precipitation, wind speed, the humidity and the atmospheric pressure, to determine the optimum location of a wind turbine. Thanks to the use of a solution of big data in a supercomputer, and of a modeling solution designed to take advantage of the information from a broad set of data including both structured and unstructured data, now the company can help clients to optimize the location of the wind turbine, and as a result their performance.

- **Automercados Plaza's**: A family chain of food stores in Venezuela, they realized that it had more than 6 terabytes of information about products and customers stored in different databases and systems. By integrating the information throughout the company, the chain of stores has seen how their income increased by approximately 30% and its annual profitability increased by 7 million dollars. For example, the company has avoided losses in approximately 35% of their products now that can schedule price reductions to sell perishable products before they are wasted.
- **Netflix**: Following the decisions of Netflix to go through a review of the behavior and the taste of their customers. Netflix is a service to watch movies and series in streaming. What clients may not know is that the series House of Cards (in its North American version) is a production of the own Netflix, which spent 100 million dollars. Such amount is without doubt a risky investment. Why Netflix decided to produce its own series, if for less money could have bought the rights of other series of proven success? Simply because the company knew that the series would be a success. And how do they know? Thanks to the big data. Netflix analyzes how many viewers have seen a complete series, at what day and time see an episode, from what devices, when stop or accelerate the playback, and up to what they do when they reach the credit titles, to see if the viewer wants to see another episode when ends or closes the application. There is more data: Netflix calls on its customers who appreciate their interest in different genres or films that have seen. The algorithm of recommendation is suggested after titles adapted to their tastes. And it seems that it is quite successful, since 75% of what users see originates in the recommendations. The processing of all this information was essential to Netflix to take one of the most important strategic decisions in its history: compete with channels such as HBO or AMC to get the rights for the US of the English series House of Cards.
- **Smart Cities**: Big data for cities in the twenty-first century. The key points in the discussion on the uses of big data for cities: predictive analytics, the management of complexity, security and networks (cameras, sensors), administration of the overall performance of a city, ways to optimize the existing infrastructure, the mines of census data, display methods of urban space and the called city cloud, which allows companies to create competitive advantages for a city (Purcell (2013).

The development and use of GIS (Geographic Information System) is one of the strong points. The objective is to maximize the potential of GIS for designing communities to live in, taking into account that in the most densely populated countries in the world the limited amount of land forces to allocate the ground and use of resources with minimum margins of error.

Singapore is using 3D technology to guide the people who work in urban planning to make simulations that will appreciate in advance the potential impacts of the buildings and do more detailed studies on urban developments (More information in FutureGov Asia). Examples of the use of these systems in large data are also offered in cities as Lyon, where the municipal government has partnered with IBM to create a platform that helps responsible operators for the traffic to predict congestion and act to reduce it (changing time programming of lights, for example).

In Boston, the Office of New Urban Mechanical has a program called “Adopt a hydrant” (Water) through which they have located more than 13 thousand hydrants throughout the city and invite the population to take one or more. In the United States, Seattle has started, with Microsoft and Accenture, a pilot project to reduce the use of electrical energy by a 25% through a program that collects and analyzes data on equipment and operation of buildings in the center of the city, in order to establish what work properly, what does not and how to change them for a efficient saving.

10. RECOMMENDATIONS

The conclusions from the analysis carried out by IBM “Big Data @ Work Study” has provided new knowledge about how companies promote their initiatives of big data in each phase (Shroeck & Shockley (2012)). Driven by the need to overcome the business challenges, and in view of the technologies in development and the changing nature of the data, firms are beginning to look more closely at the potential benefits of big data. To get more value out of big data the IMB analysis provides a wide range of recommendations to companies as they progress in the implementation of big data:

- **Focus on the Customer**: It is essential that companies focus their initiatives of big data in areas which can provide the maximum value to the business. For many sectors, this will mean begin with a client analytics that provide a better service to them as a result of truly understand their needs and be able to anticipate their future behaviors.
- **Develop a Project of Big Data for the Entire Company**: A project embraces the vision, the strategy and the requirements of big data within a company and is essential to harmonize the needs of business users with the road map for the implementation of it. This creates a common understanding of how the company intends to use big data to improve their business goals. An effective project defines the scope of big data within the company to identify the key business challenges to which it will apply, the requirements of the business process that define how to use these data in bulk and architecture that includes the data, tools and hardware necessary to achieve it.
- **Start with the Existing Data to Achieve Results in the Short Term**: To be able to achieve results in the short term, at the same time that it creates the momentum and experience to support the program of big data, it is essential that companies adopt a pragmatic approach. The most logical place and profitable to start to find these new knowledge is within the company. Most of the organizations want to do this to take advantage of the information stored in existing repositories, while expanding its data warehouse in order to manage volumes and varieties of larger data.
- **Develop Analytics**: Companies will have to invest in purchasing both, tools and skills. As part of this process is expected to emerge new roles and models of career paths for individuals with the necessary balance of analytical skills, functional and IT. Focus on the professional development and the progress of the trajectory of the analysts, who are already familiar with the challenges and unique business processes of the company, should be a priority for business managers. At the same time universities and individuals themselves, regardless of their training or specialty, have the obligation to develop strong analytical skills.
- **Create Business on Quantifiable Results:** To develop a strategy of big data comprehensive and viable, as well as the subsequent roadmap requires a strong business case, which should be

quantifiable. It is therefore important to have the involvement and support of one or more business managers throughout the process. Equally important to achieve long-term success is a business collaboration that should be constant through time and solid. Many companies base their business cases in the following advantages that can be derived from big data:

- **More Intelligent Decisions:** Take advantage of new sources of data to improve the quality of decision-making.
- **Faster Decisions:** Allow a capture and analysis of data in real time to support decision-making at the point of impact, for example when a customer is browsing through the web site or on the phone with a customer service representative.
- **Decisions that Make a Difference:** Focus initiatives of big data in areas that provide a true differentiation.

11. CONCLUSION

The use of big data is transforming the management of many entrepreneurial activities. The possibilities that open are enormous both to reduce prices and improve the quality of the services that clients receive as well as to reduce the costs of companies (Lambrecht & Skiera (2006)). The availability of vast databases is also revolutionizing economic research both in methodologies as well as in specific techniques. The traditional approaches of regression lines or logistics, cluster analysis, selective analysis or prediction using time series are complemented with ideas of machine learning to work with huge databases. The growth of big data as a sector of activity linked to the business is generating a great demand for mathematicians, statistical computing and professional with knowledge of economics.

The big data is called to transform the industry, trade and public services. Businesses of all sizes, educational and research institutions, non-profit organizations and public administrations will find, some already do, in the tools of big data, competitive advantages, strategies to improve productivity and solutions to complex problems.

But to achieve this, organizations need to adapt to a model in which the use of the information and the management of data is placed in the center of the strategy. This model requires changes in the structure of the organization and in the hierarchical relationships to break down the barriers.

Organizations have developed over the years a model that considered the information a double-edged sword that had to protect competition, other markets, other departments and employees, and colleagues. If the information was valuable in the previous model, big data form part of the assets of the organizations in the current, and must as such be of use in favor of the company objectives.

The use of the avalanche of data that is currently generated creates important issues related to privacy, data protection and the fulfillment of some regulations (see Heffetz & Ligett (2014)). It is important to take into account these considerations before companies begin a project of big data. Companies will also have to analyze, as with any other investment, the cost-benefit ratio of the project as well as having a computer expert who is able to extract knowledge from data and is attentive to the update of the processes, as well as understand the changes in the determinants that affect the objectives of the project. The Errors of Google Flu Trend should serve as a reminder to find a balance between the search for factors with predictive ability and the analysis of the reasons for which these factors have that influence avoiding convert the analysis of data in a huge big black box.

REFERENCES

Barker, K. J., D'Amato, J., & Sheridon, P. (2008). Credit card fraud: Awareness and prevention. *Journal of Financial Crime*, *15*(4), 398–410. doi:10.1108/13590790810907236

Barney, J. (1991). Firm resources and sustained competitive advantage. *Journal of Management*, *17*(1), 99–120. doi:10.1177/014920639101700108

Breiman, L. (2001). Statistical modeling: The two cultures. *Statistical Science*, *16*(3), 199–231. doi:10.1214/ss/1009213726

Butler, D. (2013). When Google got the flu wrong. *Nature*, *494*(7436), 155–156. doi:10.1038/494155a PMID:23407515

Cavallo, A. (2012). Online and official price indexes: Measuring Argentina's inflation. *Journal of Monetary Economics*, *60*(2), 152–165. doi:10.1016/j.jmoneco.2012.10.002

Chen, H., Chiang, R. H., & Storey, V. C. (2012). Business intelligence and analytics: From big data to big impact. *Management Information Systems Quarterly*, *36*, 1165–1188.

Choi, H., & Varian, H. (2012). Predicting the present with Google Trends. *Economic Inquiry*, *88*, 2–9.

Edelman, B. (2015, April). How to launch your digital platform. *Harvard Business Review*.

Grossman, R. L., & Siegel, K. (2014). Organizational models for big data and analytics. *Journal of Organization Design*, *3*(1), 20–25. doi:10.7146/jod.9799

Heffetz, O., & Ligett, K. (2014). Privacy and data-based research. *The Journal of Economic Perspectives*, *28*(2), 75–98. doi:10.1257/jep.28.2.75

Hoffmann, A., & Birnbrich, C. (2012). The impact of fraud prevention on bank-customer relationships. *International Journal of Bank Marketing*, *30*(5), 390–407. doi:10.1108/02652321211247435

Jiménez, G. S., Ongena, S., Peydro, J. L., & Saurina, J. (2014). Hazardous times for monetary policy: What do 23 million loans say about the impact of monetary policy on credit risk-taking. *Econometrica*, *82*, 463–505. doi:10.3982/ECTA10104

Kruschwitz, N. (2011). First look: The second annual new intelligent enterprise survey. *MIT Sloan Management Review*, *52*, 87–89.

Lambrecht, A., & Skiera, B. (2006). Paying too much and being happy about it: Existence, causes, and consequences of tariff-choice biases. *JMR, Journal of Marketing Research*, *43*(2), 212–223. doi:10.1509/jmkr.43.2.212

Lambrecht, A., & Tucker, C. (2013). When does retargeting work? Information specificity in online advertising. *JMR, Journal of Marketing Research*, *50*(5), 561–576. doi:10.1509/jmr.11.0503

Lazer, D., Kennedy, R., King, G., & Vespignani, A. (2014). The parable of Google Flu: Traps in big dataAnalysis. *Science*, *343*(6176), 1203–1205. doi:10.1126/science.1248506 PMID:24626916

Mayer-Schunberger, V., & Cukier, K. (2014). *Big data: A revolution that will transform how we live, work, and think*. Houghton Mifflin Harcourt.

McAfee, A., Brynjolfsson, E., Davenport, T. H., Patil, D., & Barton, D. (2012). Big data. The management revolution. *Harvard Business Review*, *90*, 61–67. PMID:23074865

McGuire, T., Manyika, J., & Chui, M. (2012). Why big data is the new competitive advantage. *Ivey Business Journal*, *76*, 1–4.

Mian, A., Rao, K., & Sufi, A. (2013). Household balance sheets, consumption and economic slump. *The Quarterly Journal of Economics*, *128*(4), 1687–1726. doi:10.1093/qje/qjt020

Mian, A., & Sufi, A. (2009). The consequences of mortgage credit expansion: Evidence from the U.S. mortgage default crisis. *The Quarterly Journal of Economics*, *124*(4), 1449–1496. doi:10.1162/qjec.2009.124.4.1449

Nickerson, D., & Rogers, T. (2014). Political campaigns and "big data". *The Journal of Economic Perspectives*, *28*(2), 51–74. doi:10.1257/jep.28.2.51

Purcell, B. M. (2013). *Big data using cloud computing*. Holy Family University working paper.

Varian, H. (2014). "Big data": New tricks for econometrics. *The Journal of Economic Perspectives*, *28*(2), 3–28. doi:10.1257/jep.28.2.3

ADDITIONAL READING

Biesdorf, S., Court, D., & Willmott, P. (2013). Big data: What's your plan. *The McKinsey Quarterly*, *2*, 40–51.

Butler, D. (2008). Web data predict flu. *NATNews*, *456*, 287–288. PMID:19020578

Shroeck, M., & Shockley, R. (2012). Analytics: The real-world use of big data. IBM Institute of Business Value in collaboration with Said Business School, University of Oxford.

KEY TERMS AND DEFINITIONS

Big Data: Large volume of data that inundates a business on a day-to-day basis.

Business Decision Making: Decision making is an essential aspect of business success.

Data Management: Development and execution of policies and procedures to manage the information of a company in an effective manner.

Financial Institutions: An institution that provides financial services to potential clients.

Financial Services: Economic services provided by the finance industry.

Information Technology: It is the use of any computers, storage, networking and other processes to create, store and exchange electronic data.

Online Security: Computer security related to the internet involving browsing and network security. It is designed to establish measures to use against attacks through internet.

Online Trading: Individual investors buy and sell stocks over an electronic network through a brokerage company.

Chapter 11

Using Big Data to Improve the Educational Infrastructure and Learning Paradigm

Areej Fatemah Meghji
Mehran University of Engineering and Technology, Pakistan

Naeem A. Mahoto
Mehran University of Engineering and Technology, Pakistan

ABSTRACT

In higher education, the demand for improved information in relation to educational and learning outcomes is greater than ever before. Leveraging technology, new models of education have emerged that are not only improving modes of lecture delivery and information retention, but also generating huge amounts of data. This data is potentially a gold mine that needs to be explored to uncover patterns associated with student behavior and how information is processed, retained and used by the students. This chapter proposes a generic model that uses the techniques of educational data mining to explore and analyze Big Data being generated by the education sector. This chapter also examines the various questions that can be answered using educational data mining methods and how the discovered patterns can be used to enrich the learning experience of a student as well as help teachers make pedagogical decisions.

INTRODUCTION

Big Data has been used in fields ranging from business, consumer marketing and banking to fraud detection, social network analysis, health care and climate science. Today, there is one other field generating huge volumes of data (Baker & Inventado, 2014b). The introduction of advanced modern day technology in classrooms is reshaping the modes of learning and the sector of education is generating massive amounts of data using varied sources including, surveys, assessments, feedback, online software and metric based learning tools (Siemens & Baker, 2012).

DOI: 10.4018/978-1-5225-0182-4.ch011

The emerging Big Data from the education industry has the potential to produce equally striking results as the other fields benefitting from the methodologies used in Big Data. It is also the key to reshaping the educational and learning paradigm. There is an ever growing need for a generic model that incorporates the various forms of data being generated by educational institutes and in turn generates intelligence that can be used by these institutes to enhance learning and teaching infrastructures.

This chapter begins by reviewing evolution in the modes of education in the past decade and new formats of education being endorsed in educational institutes. A further analysis on the introduction of technology in the sector of education, the addition of advanced metrics and analytics to the learning systems and the kinds of data that are being gathered using these metrics has also been provided.

The main focus of this chapter is the exploration of patterns and features associated with student learning that are emerging from Big Data being produced by the education sector (Baker & Inventado, 2014b; Romero & Ventura, 2007). The approaches of Educational Data Mining (EDM) including prediction, regression, classification, latent knowledge estimation, causal mining, associative rule mining and network analysis have been discussed to provide an overview of how big data in education can be mined for intelligence that can help discover how learning takes place, predict learning patterns and understand student behavior.

BACKGROUND

Education shapes nations; for many years the traditional method of educating students has been by providing them instructions. These instructions have been delivered to a vast number of students in a classroom. The focus of the education system has always been on the teacher; who has almost always used lecture delivery as the focal method of conveying these instructions (Mazur, 2009; Romero, & Ventura, 2007). The teachers or instructors would keep themselves updated in their disciplines through seminars, workshops, trainings and other professional and academic development programs.

Learning has always been the sole responsibility or the burden of the student, and its measurement has not been given a high priority. This has been the archaic model of transferring information from the teacher to the student since centuries and in many parts of the world this traditional mode of education has changed very little over the course of time. In its true spirit this mode of learning may be referred to as teacher centric.

The authors John Tagg and Robert Barr in their article, "From Teaching to Learning: A New Paradigm for Undergraduate Education.", emphasize that the archaic model of education has imprisoned our faculty and scholars. The faculty follows the guidelines of the system instead of having the freedom to create a system that promotes learning. Grading systems perfectly disregard the academic potential of individual students (Barr & Tagg, 1995). The courses are designed keeping an average student in mind without efforts been taken to enhance the abilities of the below average students or help the outstanding students reach their full potential. Educational institutes today focus more on picking talent instead of devising mechanisms to develop talent.

According to Bransford et al. (1999), feedback loops are fundamental to learning. A student attempts to solve a task given by a teacher and seeing this attempt the teacher uncovers how well the student has grasped the concepts delivered in class. The teacher not only discovers what the student has understood, but more importantly, what the student has not. This understanding helps the teacher revise or modify the instructions, eventually improving the understanding of the student. It is important to keep in mind however, that no two students are alike. Every student comes from a different academic background and learns and forgets concepts at his or her own rate. Similarly each student has a different skill set, intellect, method of studying and attention span.

The system discussed above has been tried and tested and works quite well in a small setting, but once the number of students in a class increases, this system loses its effectiveness. Also, educational institutes provide a generalized syllabus and the teachers due to the lack of time and resources cater to the needs of the average and above average students and sadly, the 'leave no man behind' strategy, is not practiced. A subject is taught in a class overflowing with students and when some student has difficulty in coping with the material being taught, the only option to improve in the subject to opt for side courses or seek tuitions. Should a student fail to learn the subject, the student is held back. The system and methodology do not change, the teaching methods remain the same and the cycle is repeated without any provisions being made to improve the methodology that can significantly enhance learning. This mode of education also leads to what educators call the "Achievement Gap", the space between the top bright students and those at the bottom (Langham, 2009).

The dawn of the 21st century has reshaped and changed many familiar things. People prefer reading books on electronic devices, news is not confined to the newspapers; information of events happening thousands of miles away spread across the globe in mere seconds, social media keep users engaged from minutes to hours in a day, research on latest topics is shared online and people from all over the globe participate in learning new technologies through these forums. With information on so many topics being available readily the sanctity and the relation a teacher has with his student in a classroom, has also undergone a transformation. To be a good teacher, in this day and age, the teacher needs to be more than just a subject or domain expert. Educational Institutes need to be designed in a way that equips them with the latest mechanisms to keep the students engaged by providing them a healthy learning environment (Prensky, 2008).

A huge emphasis has been paid in the last decade on improving the system of education. After all, the youth today is living, probably, in the most intensely stimulating era in the history of this planet. They are being overwhelmed with information from every corner: internet, smartphones, tablets and television channels. A stronger focus is being paid on what the students are learning and how well the students are able to truly, in the long term, understand the concepts been delivered in the classrooms. Curriculums have been designed and redesigned to match the progress of the changing times. The structure of the classrooms has also evolved providing a learning centered environment. A modern classroom today is equipped with digital displays, tablets, wireless internet, multimedia displays, and sound systems (Windham, 2005).

The years that followed the article by Tagg and Barr saw demand for improved information in relation to student outcomes in higher education. This lead to the development of Total Quality Management or Quality Enhancement Cells, Outcome Based Learning Models, Management by Objectives and Knowledge Cells. Educational institutes conducted comprehensive and detailed surveys providing valuable data in the form of feedback to the teachers on how the students perceived the courses being taught (Barrie, Ginns & Prosser, 2005; Ma, Liu, Wong, Yu & Lee, 2000).

Although feedback and surveys aided the closure of the achievement gap, it was soon realized that to truly foster an environment of learning, educators would require the use of modern day technology in the system of education. A considerable emphasis was thus given on improving the education standard and to induce learning as the central component through the introduction of educational and learning analytics and the use of various Educational Data Mining approaches.

The model proposed in this chapter recognizes the importance of a student centric educational framework. It leverages modern day technology to capture data being generated by the education sector to induce learning at the heart of the educational infrastructure.

EMERGING CHANGES IN EDUCATIONAL INFRASTRUCTURE AND LEARNING PARADIGM

The phrase "The medium is the Message" was coined by Marshall McLuhan. He influenced a change in how technology is perceived and how technology could be used to shape the learning paradigm. According to McLuhan (1994), the right use of technology can greatly influence knowledge retention and understanding.

A Shift in the Education Paradigm

Those days are a memory where in order to find out or learn something people used to turn to libraries and text books. Information on latest trends and research is no longer filtered through the teacher before reaching the students. Use of the electronic medium has transformed how learning takes place. The 21st century has given way to a new age of interactive and keen learners and the availability of vast online resources today takes learning to a completely new level. Students today expect immediate, exact and abundant information regarding their queries and subjects.

Technology Enters Classrooms

Classrooms today comprise of technology used to deliver several forms of media such as text, audio, images and videos. Numerous classrooms are equipped with the latest information and communication technologies. Laptops, tablets, smartphones are forms of interactive technology, actively being used to boost the learning experience as well as provide a rich platform for collaborative learning (Greenfield & Calvert, 2004). The use of technology benefits both the teacher as well as the student; it has been shown to be effective in increasing the knowledge of a student when compared to normal classroom instructions (Kulik & Kulik, 1991). Teachers have the opportunity, now more than ever, to use numerous online tools and resources to not only transform lecture delivery, but also to ensure enhanced learning. Lessons can be designed using various strategies that make learning much more effective for the students. Multimedia presentations, tutorials and hand-on exercises keep the students engaged. This helps them learn advanced topics in a comfortable environment and at the same time, students can showcase their learning in several ways, for example, through interactive presentations or animations. With the addition of modern day technology in the class online assessments, computerized tests, quizzes and surveys are also widely being implemented in the education sector greatly moving educational institutes towards meeting outcome based targets. The subsequent section presents some learning trends that have emerged due to the increased use of technology in the framework of education.

Modern Day Learning Trends

The embrace of technology in educational institutes has given rise to new formats of education that ensure the students have a more active role in the learning process. Some popular and useful trends discussed in this chapter include:

1. Blended Learning
2. E-Learning
3. Distance Learning

Blended Learning

Blended Learning is also referred to as 'Hybrid', 'Technology Oriented' or 'Mixed' Learning. Blended Learning takes the use of technology in learning much further than the presence of computers and multimedia aid in the classrooms. According to Bailey et al. (2013), using this approach learning occurs not only in the class, but using modern day technology the teachers can now utilize different mediums to provide learning material to their students outside the classroom. As depicted in Figure 1, lectures can be prerecorded, instructional videos and podcasts can be prepared, study materials are then sent through digital channels such as blogs and emails, etc., and learning occurs in part at the educational institute and in part outside the class.

One trend that has quickly become popular and is considered an off-shoot of blended learning is the *Flipped classroom*. The idea behind a flipped classroom, as shown in Figure 2, is quite simple; essentially you flip between classwork and homework (Mazur & Hilborn, 1997). A teacher can publish an instructional video comprising of the lecture and the students can view that video at home. Each student can utilize this system to learn at his or her own pace and the available class time provides students the time and attention they need to maximize learning This approach towards learning gives each student in the class the opportunity to express his or her opinion on a topic and bring forward ideas in class that are then shared and discussed increasing and fostering better and in-depth understanding and clarification of concepts (Hamdan, McKnight, McKnight & Arfstrom, 2013).

Figure 1. The Blended Learning approach

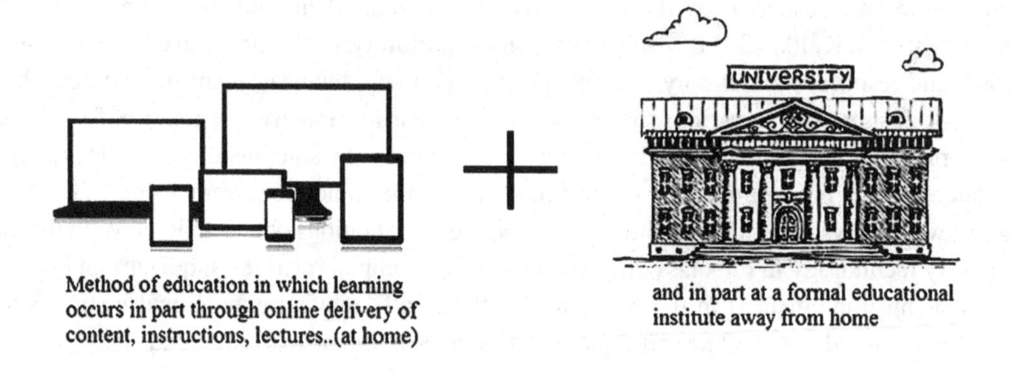

Figure 2. The traditional v/s the flipped classroom

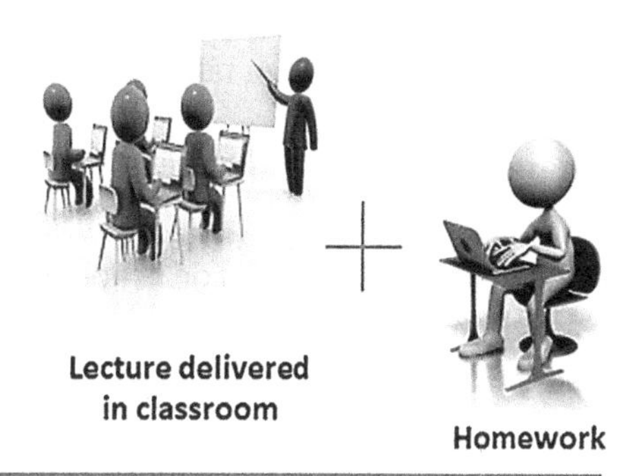

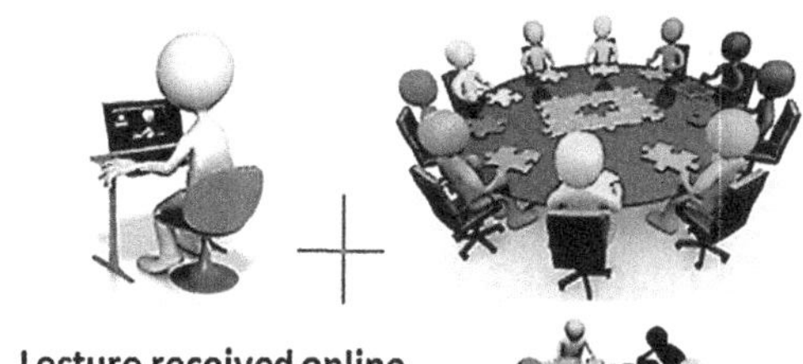

The findings publishes in the "American Journal of Physics" Volume 69, Issue 9 revealed that students who were exposed to flipped classrooms did considerably better than the students who were taught using traditional in-class lectures (Crouch & Mazur, 2001).

E-Learning

E-Learning provides provisions through which the learning process and education, partially or completely, can leave the confinements of a classroom and enter the home of the students (Bailey, Ellis, Schneider & Vander, 2013). Put simply, e-learning encompasses use of electronic media such as computers, tablets or mobile phone supported with Information and Communication Technologies (ICT) to educate learners. E-learning has rapidly evolved from use of computers in classrooms to display multimedia presentations with audio and visual aids to online lecture delivery, podcasts, simulations and videos that can be streamed any time of the day.

E-Learning is discrete in nature; students can register for a course and follow the course on-line until the course ends according to the provided schedule. The need for a physical presence onsite or in a classroom can be eliminated in this form of learning. Interaction between the students and teacher always occurs in some form or the other but not face to face ("E-Learning, Concepts", 2014). For instance, interaction between students can occur through discussion blogs and similarly discussion between the teacher and student can occur utilizing the electronic mediums available. Lectures can be pre-recorded or delivered live; in the latter case, students may interact with the instructor in real time. Evaluation occurs based on student assignment submissions, participation in discussions and test scores. This form of E-Learning is also called Online or Virtual Learning. E-Learning that is specifically developed for tablets or mobile devices is referred to as Mobile-Learning. (El-Hussein & Cronje, 2010). This form of learning focuses on the mobility of the learners and can take place anywhere at any time.

Distance Learning

E-Learning that is not bound by time and does not require a strict schedule that learners need to follow is often referred to as Distance Learning. Thus, distance education is basically e-learning that takes place completely outside the confinements of a classroom. The instructors and the learners are separated by distance/ geography and time. Physical onsite presence is not needed throughout the duration of the course (Moore, Deane & Galyen, 2011). Massive Online Open Courses (MOOC) is a popular approach in distance learning. MOOC targets interactive participation on a large and dispersed scale by providing access to all participants using the web and ICT.

TECHNOLOGY – A SOURCE FOR GENERATING BIG DATA

In the digital age, technology has a great impact on everything one does. It is evident from consumer experiences over the web that numerous algorithms are being developed to exploit data generated by users to dedicatedly analyze choices and monitor user behavior and thus adapt accordingly. These algorithms not only shape what is done in the moment, but also steer users towards what they do next. This can readily be observed when using Netflix (Kruse & Pongsajapan, 2012). Consider an example of selecting a movie using Netflix. Members may browse the categories provided and view the selection of movies or they may search for a movies based on its title, actor or director. When they finish watching the movie, the users are asked to rate how well they enjoyed the movie. The more the user uses the system, the better the system recommends what movies the user would enjoy watching by simply learning user preferences.

Similarly, when using amazon or instagram, the suggestions made by the system are made based on the previous usage history of the user. With the implementation of the educational models discussed above, technology can be leveraged to obtain significant amounts of student data; as with technology being adopted in the classrooms, students today leave a digital trail just as a user does while using Netflix. This digital trail provides a unique opportunity to create profound and stronger feedback loops.

As discussed earlier, knowledge management cells are actively collecting more and more data that helps understand not only what the students in a class are learning or where they are having difficulty, but also adapting practices to understand how to better teach the students. Traditionally some data comprising of assessment results, assignment scores, descriptive student data, feedback regarding subjects and surveys from the students and teachers was stored and mined for the generation of intelligence which was reinforced in the education sector to improve learning. This information was collected by the cells at the end of each term or semester and compiled to view the class as a whole. The goal of this analysis was to improve teaching mechanisms and although it provides a good opportunity to improve subjects and teaching, this mode of data analysis did not support individual growth nor fully support the *leave no man behind strategy.*

Presently, knowledge management cells are leveraging modern technology in the framework of education to collect detailed data of each student. Technology today has the capability to log and monitor every movement made by the student in a web based, online, intelligent tutoring or learning management system; with the added potential to be more exquisite in the level of detail it records. Teachers prepare their instructional materials, videos, notes, quizzes, assessments, surveys etc., and metrics are being added to these resources. The data captured and stored by these systems is not only Big Data, it is a potential gold mine (Beck et al., 2004).

Big Data in Education

Educational institutes, primarily, generate two forms of student data; descriptive and behavioral. Descriptive data includes fields like gender, age, marital status, address of a student, grades, geographic profile, academic profile, financial status, if the student is a local or international student, belongs to a minority group etc. Behavioral data includes information regarding the subjects the student is enrolled in, assessment marks of the subject, attendance record, details of how the student is progressing in the studies obtained through teacher surveys etc.

Apart from these two forms of data, using technology, educational institutes are now attaining a better understanding of student mindsets through attitudinal data. Attitudinal data provides insights into the thinking and attitude of students by extracting data from social media, feedback forms or student surveys. Another form of data, emerging through the use of metrics in web based, intelligent tutoring and simulation based learning software, is interactional data. This data comprises of email correspondence, participation or lack of participation in online discussions, frequency of inactivity in logging into a university web account, web click streams etc. As discussed in the white paper by Eduventures (2013), with more and more data being collected through online sources, attitudinal and interactional data is increasing day by day. The types of data being generated by the education sector have been broadly summarized in Figure 3.

The collected attitudinal and interaction data is not only detailed, it is also enormous. Consider that a student is given an assignment to watch an instructional video and then to solve certain tasks. The

Figure 3. Data generated by the education sector

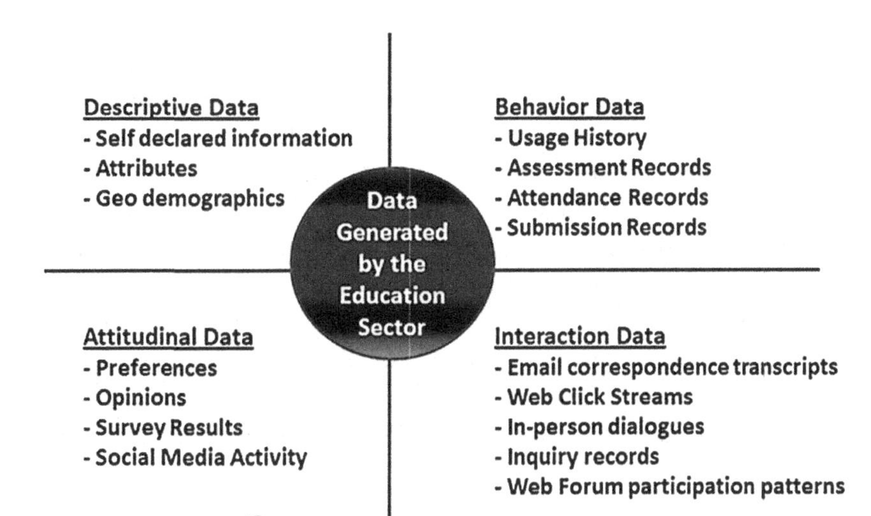

metrics added to the learning content store data including the time each student takes to watch the video, the number of times the video is played back, the sections of the video replayed the most, the parts of the video that are skipped, the frequency with which these sections are skipped, if the video is an extension of a topic covered in some other video, which students paused and reviewed the previous video etc.

Similarly technology is helping collect online assessment/survey data including the time each student takes in answering a question, record of the sources used, the questions skipped, the amount of back study done, the questions the student took the most time to answer, the major concepts that were clear based on the assessment and which instructions work best on the student etc. Data through online forms of interaction, social media and blogs, is also being actively collected through technology.

The NSF-funded Pittsburg Science and Learning Center, also referred as the 'DataShop' or 'LearnLab' lead by John Stanpor, has data from thousands of hours of student learning that can be downloaded for research and study purposes. This datashop has proved to be a key resource in serving as a repository for securing and storing data as well as providing the tools needed for its analysis.

Dietz-Uhler and Hurn (2013) review data commonly being collected by knowledge management cells using learning system. The increased accumulated student data holds the secrets to understanding student learning patterns and according to Corbett (2001), using the digital trail of students, lectures and exercises can be fashioned that maximize individual learning. There is thus an ever growing need to analyze this data for the extraction of meaningful patterns that can lead to the creation of an adaptive and student centric learning framework.

EXPLORING BIG DATA IN EDUCATION

Several methods can be employed for exploring Big Data in Education. These methods are commonly referred to as Educational Data Mining (Romero, Ventura, Pechenizkiy & Baker, 2010) or they may be called Learning Analytics (LA). The goal of these methods is to explore the massive data that is available on students and how they learn (Prabha & Shanavas, 2014).

Educational Data Mining

EDM aims to make new discoveries on how to improve the learning process for each individual student. It is the use of different analytical techniques for understanding of relations, patterns, structures and even casual pathways that can exist in large datasets that are hard to analyze (Romero & Ventura, 2013). Early attempts at EDM involved mining of website log and trace data but, with technological advancement, today a huge variety of data (big data) is available for mining from traditional, web based, simulation based, intelligent tutoring, learning and gaming systems. EDM works to design adaptive/intelligent learning systems by understanding how individual students learn within the system (Baker, 2014a, 2014b) and the creation of assessment frameworks that target each student to meet his or her full potential.

Learning data of the students as mentioned in the Big Data in Education section is collected and models are made to classify data or to find relationships between various sets of data. The goal of EDM is to transform unstructured student data, into meaningful intelligence that can be used to make better pedagogical decisions.

A unique feature of Educational Data (ED) is that it is hierarchical. Data at different levels correlates and helps in predicting an overall pattern. Data from levels starting from the keystroke or mouse movements, to the answer, duration of student interaction or session as well as data at the student level, class level, teacher to the school level are all nested and inside one another (Baker, 2011; Romero & Ventura, 2013). Other features of ED may include time, underlying context or sequence. Time is a very important feature which may include parameters such as time taken to learn or duration of a training session. Context is important for the explanation of results and to predict which models work under different circumstances. Sequence defines how concepts are interrelated; they define the ordering of topics as often these concepts build on one another. Techniques for hierarchical modeling and mining of data have greatly shaped the mining of ED.

Thus, among other things, EDM is often employed to help, i) sequence topics in the most effective way for individual students, ii) uncover patterns that aid development of individual skills and enhancement of knowledge, iii) discover new patterns of student behavior, iv) find student actions associated with better learning, v) predict student success, vi) uncover student actions that indicate learning progress, satisfaction, frustration and engagement levels, vii) develop concept maps and viii) discover pedagogical strategies that lead to effective learning.

A MODEL FOR USING BIG DATA IN EDUCATION

As the data gathered by knowledge management cells, through technology, increases, it becomes harder to manage and analyze this unstructured data. A generic model that uses the Big Data to improve educational infrastructure and learning paradigm is presented in Figure 4.

Data is collected ideally from a wide range of sources, as identified in Figure 4, using surveys (student, teacher, employer and alumni), self-assessment modules, metrics from online learning system and social media.

Self-assessment surveys help provide great insights into how each individual student perceives the course being taught and the suggestions, in their own words, on what parameters can aid and improve their learning. The feedback obtained from alumni and employers helps ascertain the gap between academia and the industry and help the discovery of patterns associated with successful outcomes. Massive data collected from intelligent tutoring and learning software provides detailed information on each and every action the student takes.

A unique feature of this model is the use of as many sources of data as possible to obtain a complete understanding of student background, behavior, attitude, social interaction and latent skills. The collected data is archived and fed to a knowledge/adaptation engine. One or multiple methods of EDM, discussed in the subsequent section, are employed by the knowledge engine to extract meaningful insights about student learning behavior. The use of varied EDM methods allows the model to flexibly handle the various forms of data emerging through an educational institute.

The predictions, patterns and structures thus discovered are, in essence, intelligence needed to enhance the system of education and learning. This intelligence is stored in a knowledge base and provided to the educational institute to utilize the discoveries to make better decisions, improve course structure, develop superior assessments, incorporate industry practices and provide teachers with the necessary information needed to promote learning.

Figure 4. A generic model for using big data in education

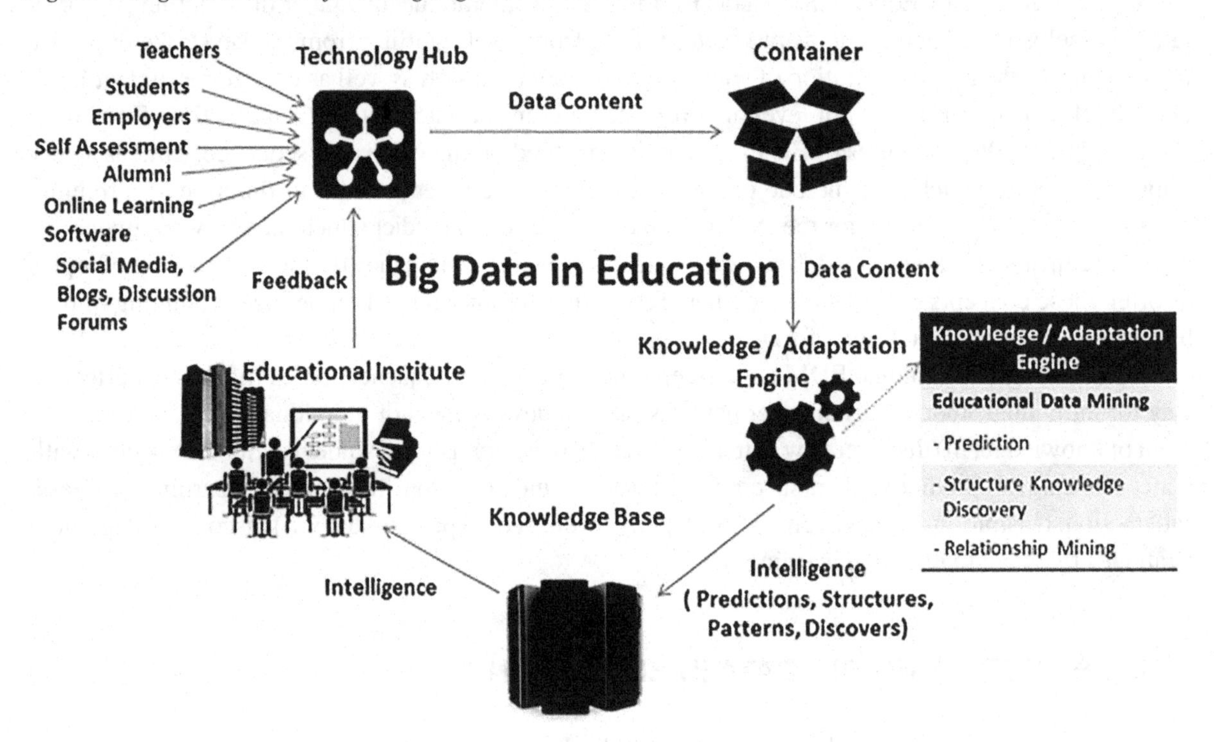

As new approaches of adaptive learning are applied in the framework of education, the stored patterns in the knowledge base help discover how learning of a student evolves. They also help map similar patterns and apply successfully tested patterns on new students exhibiting recognized behavior. Apart from this, intelligence storage helps understand how effective the overall system has been, what practices work and the reasons why certain changes show promise, limited promise or no promise. This approach opens doors to better understanding of student behavior for future analysis and creation of better learning systems.

As the educational institute implements adaptive learning, further data is generated for analysis. This data is thus collected from the institutes; creating a loop of constant improvement in the framework of learning.

EDUCATIONAL DATA MINING METHODS

There are several types of EDM methods. A subset of the popular classes of EDM methods provided by Baker, Gowda and Corbett (2011) is listed below:

- Predication
    - Regression
    - Classification
    - Latent Knowledge Estimation

- Relationship Mining
    - Correlation Mining
    - Casual Data Mining
    - Associative Rule Mining
- Structure Knowledge Discovery
    - Network Analysis

These EDM classes and some methods in these classes have been described in this section.

Prediction

Prediction is the basic class of EDM methods in which models are developed that can infer an aspect of the data in regards to some combination of other aspects of the data (Baker, 2011; 2014b). This approach strives to extract information from data and in turn use that information to predict patterns and trends existing in that data (Baker, 2010). The data/features (variables) that need to be inferred are termed labels or predicted variables and the features (variables) used to predict the label are termed predictor variables. Labels, in prediction, represent a trusted ground truth regarding the predicted variable value and can emerge from varied sources such as test and exam scores (Feng & Heffernan, 2007), instructor or field observations (Baker, Corbett & Koedinger, 2004) or even video coding (D'mello et al., 2008).

Prediction has great scope in EDM. Prediction can be used to connect student data to effective actions by establishing reliable conclusions about present conditions, as well as scenarios that may occur in the future. Prediction allows educational institutes to exploit patterns found in student data to identify improvement opportunities before the need arises for serious actions. Decisions can be guided proactively and thus produce better outcomes. Several algorithms, including Naïve Bayes, KNN, MLP, C4.5, Logistic Regression and Support Vector Machines are used for prediction.

Research was conducted by Smith, Lange, and Huston (2012), on a sample size of 539 students enrolled in online courses in Rio Salado College. Student data was collected from RioLearn, a proprietary learning management system. A model was created that used parameters of login frequency, pace in the subject, site visits and assignments grades, to predict course outcomes and likelihood of success in completing the course through the Naïve Bayes classification technique. To ensure the accuracy of the model, cross validation using the random sub-sampling method was performed. This study demonstrates how prediction can be used to strengthen linkages between teachers and students in a dynamic, online environment

Using prediction methods an educational institute can not only determine what the student is likely to score in an upcoming (Feng & Heffernan, 2007), but also predict various aspects of student behavior. Falakmasir and Jafar (2010), researching on a sample of 824 students, found that active participation in discussion forums influenced the final grade of the students in online synchronous virtual classrooms. Similarly based on the performance of a student using a software tool, it can be predicted whether the student possesses the expertise to solve the current set of problems (Baker, Gowda & Corbett, 2011). It can also be used to discover and thus allow grouping students that are hint-driven, uncover frequent misconceptions regarding a lesson, point out student lacking high motivation and to determine actions that may be taken to decrease failure rates.

Questions Prediction can answer:

- Which students will achieve academic excellence?
- Which students need supportive interventions?
- How effective are the interventions?
- Which student is at the risk of performing poorly?
- Which student is misusing the system?
- Which student will fail in the subject?

Some common prediction models are discussed below:

Regression

Prediction relies greatly on the use of regression models. Using these models the data/labels that need to be predicted represent a numerical value. Regression works by creating a mathematical equation as a model that is used to represent these labels and the interaction these labels have with the predictor variables. Using regression several numerical entities may be predicted, such as:

- The *time* a student takes in answering a question.
- What the student is going to *score* in an exam or test.
- How *long* is the attention span of the student.
- How many *times* has online help or extra assistance been provided to the student.

Thus in the examples provided above the system will predict the time in seconds, the marks scored out of 10, 50 or 100, the attention span in minutes and the number of times hints or assistance has been provided to the student. Popular regressors in the field of EDM include regression trees and linear regression.

Hijazi & Naqvi (2006) used linear regression analysis on a sample of 300 students to determine that academic performance of a student was significantly related with hours spent studying, education level of student's mother, family income and student attitude towards class attendance.

Classification

Classification is a type of prediction which attempts to classify objects into distinct categories based on their other known characteristics (Hamalainen & Vinni, 2010). Classification is an essential part of education and is used to classify students based on their knowledge, behavior, enthusiasm, self-efficacy and learning drive. The answers classification algorithms attempt to find represent distinct categories and not numerical values like regression. The answer may be binary, thus belong to one of two categories such a Yes/No or Right/Wrong; or the answer can belong to one of several categories provided.

Binary classification is used to answer questions such as:

- Will the student be able to solve the given task? (Yes / No)
- Will the student fail the class? (Yes / No)

- Will the student need assistance? (Yes / No)
- Is the student gaming the system? (Yes / No)

Other forms of classification may answer questions where one category needs to be chosen as an answer, such as:

- The student will perform the best in subjA, SubjB, SubjC, SubjD or SubjE?
- The student needs most help in subjA, SubjB, SubjC, SubjD or SubjE?
- The student associates best with StudentA, StudentB or StudentC?
- The student is at the following level of understanding; Level1, Level2 or Level3?

Exploring data from an intelligent tutoring system, classification has been used to predict student behavior in terms of boredom, level of concentration, frustration, unease and happiness (Baker, 2010) and the affective states of flow, confusion, frustration and boredom of students (D'Mello, 2008). Similarly, working on data from an intelligent tutoring system, Baker, Corbett & Koedinger (2004) used classifiers to build a model using the forward selection algorithm on a set of latent response models. Classifiers were used on data obtained from 70 students to find the students that were gaming the system.

Learning Online Network with Computer-Assisted Personalized Approach (LON-CAPA), is a learning system implemented in Michigan State University. Manaei-Bidgoli et al. (2003) collected data of 227 student in order to predict final grades using time spent exploring a problem, number of attempts in solving the task, reading material used and several other features. This data was collected from two databases of LON-CAPA; the first database was used to collect data regarding quizzes, reading material and exams, while the second database was used to collect data of each individual student. Several classifiers were used in this study including Pazen window, multilayer perceptron, 1-nearest neighbor, Quadratic Bayesian classifier, k-nearest neighbor and decision tree.

Decision trees, a prominent classification method, have been extensively used in the education industry. Decisions trees are equipped to handle both numeric (quantitative), as well as categorical features. These methods have been embedded mainly in tutoring systems and are being used to drive adaptive behavior (Walonoski & Heffernan, 2006), build detectors for student joy, distress and concentration (Conati & Maclaren,, 2009), predict difference in student learning and infer slipping or low self-efficacy (Mcquiggan, Mott & Lester,2008).

Latent Knowledge Estimation

Knowledge has always been a key component of any learning system. Since knowledge plays such an important role in any academic infrastructure, it is important to know the steps that can be taken for its measurement. At this point, some people might even wonder why take any steps to measure student knowledge at all? Well, as stated earlier, the ultimate aim of education is to enhance student knowledge. How can any institute enhance student knowledge if the institute cannot even measure it? Once the institute is able to measure the current knowledge level of a student, considerable steps can be taken to enhance it further.

While regression and classification models helped predict if a student would correctly answer a question or not, these models did not provide information whether the student actually had the latent skills needed to answer the question correctly. Measurement of student knowledge provides extremely useful information (Feng & Heffernan, 2007).

Latent knowledge estimation is a method that attempts to estimate the knowledge a student possesses with respect to a specific skill, topic or subject. The measurement takes place based on a student's performance; performance is monitored over a period of time to ensure accuracy and a record of how correct the student has been in understanding a concept or a skill is tabulated based on test results, surveys and online interaction with automated software. Latent knowledge estimation can be helpful in devising lessons to maximize learning efficiency as well as make instructive decisions such as evaluating when a student is ready to advance in a curriculum (Corbett & Anderson, 1995).

Several algorithms are used for latent knowledge estimation. Bayes Nets is a popular algorithm for complex knowledge structures (Shute, 1995), Bayesian Knowledge Tracing has been used in scenarios where each problem is basically associated with a single skill set (Corbett & Anderson, 1995) whereas, Performance factor assessment has shown promise in cases where multiple skills are relevant to a problem (Pavlik et al., 2009).

Relationship Mining

Relationship Mining attempts to uncover relationships between variables in some dataset that contains a large number of variables (Baker, 2014a). This is done to find which variables are strongly associated with other variables or which features are dependent on each other (Scheuer & McLaren, 2011).

The practical use of this approach can be to find misconceptions that co-occur or to link educational content with student types in order to build suggestions for future educational content targeting specific student types. It can also be helpful in mining sequential behavior of students, for instance students asking for assistance after they are stuck in solving a given task (Baker, 2004, 2014a).

The most prominent feature of relationship mining is discovering associations between the course delivery structure and the performance of the student. This approach is being used actively to discover strategies that lead to better and more effective learning.

Some techniques of relationship mining are discussed here briefly.

Correlation Mining

Correlation mining focuses on finding linear correlations between variables. These correlations may be positive or negative. Thus using this approach one may attempt to find how the various set of variables in the dataset correlate to a variable of interest in the dataset or how each of the variables in the dataset correlates to each other.

In an educational setting this approach has been used to investigate the relationships between hint driven behavior and student attitudes (Arroyo & Woolf, 2005), to monitor if students game the systems as well to design intelligent tutoring systems (Baker, 2004, 2010).

Causal Mining

Causal mining focuses on finding the cause of things or in other terms causal relationships. An attempt is made to uncover if the occurrence of one event causes some other event to occur. Causal mining focuses on patterns of covariance between labels and other variables in the dataset. Rai and Beck (2011) have studied how gender and attitudes influence behavior in tutoring systems and Eberhardt and Scheines (2006) have researched the effects of interventions and hints provided to students after they make errors.

Association Rule Mining

Association Rule Mining (ARM) aims to uncover associations that naturally occur in a data set. These associations are given the form of if-then rules and can be used to find patterns of co-occurrence (Merceron & Yacef, 2010; Agrawal, Imielinski & Swami, 1993).

In ARM if a set of variables with a specific value is found, then the associated variables will generally also have a specific value.

As an example consider:

If a student is confused *Then* the student will ask for help.
Or another rule may take the form,
If a student is bored *Then* the student will go off task in the next 60 seconds.

Association rule mining has been used in e-learning systems for recommending suggestions during online learning and to provide hints and shortcuts (Zaiane, 2002), providing feedback to teachers based on emerging student patterns (Romero, Ventura & Bra, 2004), generating learning content (Lu, 2004) and discovering errors that students often make together (Merceron & Yacef, 2004).

Structure Knowledge Discovery

In Structure discovery attempts are made to uncover patterns of data that emerge naturally without prior knowledge of what should or can be discovered. These patterns can be used to divide datasets into various categories. Structure discovery is immensely good at handling and analyzing data as varied as content posted online in forums and cognitive dialogues (Vellido, Castro & Nebot, 2010; Trivedi, 2011).

Since these algorithms find patterns that emerge naturally they cannot be trained to predict specific labels and thus unlike the methods used in prediction, the algorithms or methods used in structure discovery do not have specific label or predicted variable.

Network Analysis

Network analysis (NA) comprises of analyzing relationships across a connections spread out over a network. Social networks are increasingly being analyzed using this approach. These connections that may be analyzed by network analyses can include the connections between

- Students in a classroom.
- Students in a task group or assignment group.
- Students collaborating during a term or thesis project.

The people, in case of EDM teachers or students, making up the network are seen as nodes or vertices. Figure 5 depicts a network of 5 nodes each node representing one of the Student A, B, C, D and E respectively. Each node has a connection with some other node thus forming a network. The connection

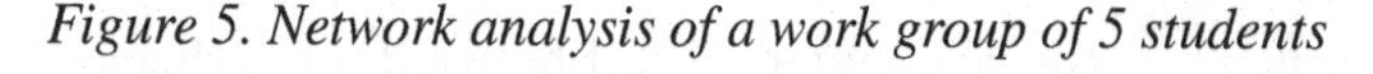

Figure 5. Network analysis of a work group of 5 students

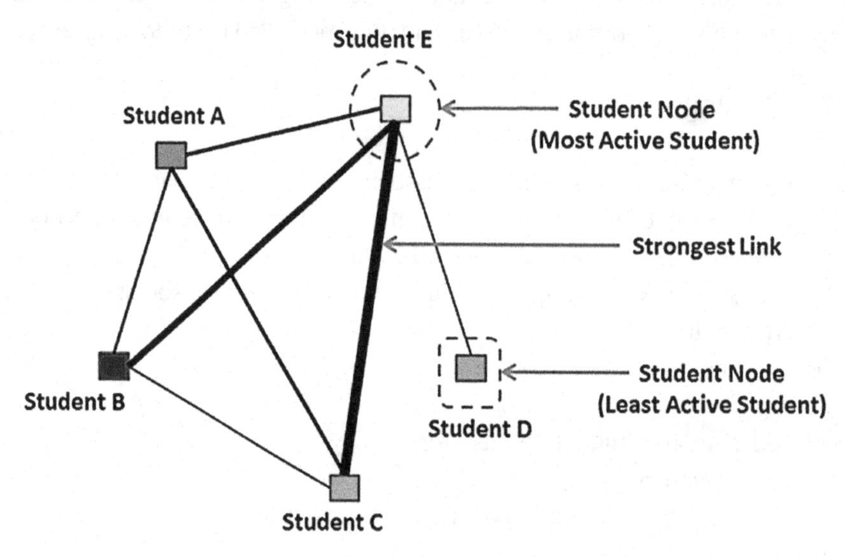

between the nodes is referred to as a link. Each link between the nodes may have a different identity as well as a different strength. The links between the nodes may represent correspondence between the students such as email correspondence, communication over discussion forums, class blogs or social media. The strength of the link can be the frequency of the correspondence.

The network in Figure 5 shows variance in the strength the links across the network. Student E has strong connections with almost all the other students in the network. Also, the strongest link is between student E and student C. this network presents quite a clear description of how these students work in the group and based on this network it can quite easily be seen that Student E is the most collaborative student in the group and has made good ties with all the other members. Student D is least collaborative and has a single very weak connection in the group.

These patterns can be monitored with time to uncover how students work in teams. NA reveals information on student groups that work best together, the students that are team players, the students that take initiative, the students that collaborate the most as well as who collaborate the least etc. This information can be used to group students more effectively and in ways that promote and enhance collaboration and learning,

APPLICATIONS AND LIMITATIONS

Exploration of Big Data in education can be leveraged upon to flip the standardized education and learning practices and introduce a problem solving and creative approach to learning. The key application areas of EDM include improving student models, discovering domain models (models of the knowledge structure of the domain), discovering effective pedagogical support based on student success and scientific discovery of learners and learning.

Thus using EDM, analysis of data emerging from the sector of education can help understand student behavior in terms of their attention spans, frustration levels (D'Mello et al., 2008), tendency to go off-task

(Baker, 2007; Walonoski & Heffernan, 2006), game the system (Baker et al., 2004) or even if a student is experiencing poor self-efficacy (McQuiggan et al., 2008). It can also determine the effectiveness of the learning system, instruction modes and course structures for varied sets of students.

EDM methods incorporated in the proposed model help predict student knowledge, future outcomes, constructs that are dependent on one another, how well students will excel in various subjects, factors that cause students to perform poorly, effects of various course delivery structures on student performance, commonly occurring misconceptions and student groups that work best together. An educational institute can use these discoveries to provide personalized learning content to each student, implement more effective course delivery structures, create student workgroups that work most effectively and thus create an environment of education that truly fosters learning.

The limitation of this model and the implementation of data mining approaches in the field of education in general, arise from the extensive use of technology in the format of learning. Availability of data across multiple dimensions, access to data and consistency in the format of data across multiple systems and privacy of the results obtains are some other concerns. Also, as the implementation of EDM methods in the education sector is still an evolving field, there is a lack of sophisticated tools that support intelligence discovery (Baker, 2010). However, as Big Data in education shows a lot of promise, researchers are addressing the limitations highlighted to magnify the potential impact Big Data exploration can have on the education sector.

FUTURE RESEARCH DIRECTIONS

Although the field of EDM is still evolving, the recent contribution of this field to the learning sciences and educational practices significantly suggests that this contribution will not only continue, but also grow.

Early studies in the field of EDM focused on collecting data from traditional data sources such as surveys, institute based grading systems and log data (Merceron & Yacef, 2010), but as seen in this chapter the field of inquiry and data collection has greatly expanded and much of the focus of recent research centers around web based and online learning environments (Smith, Lange, & Huston, 2012; Falakmasir & Jafar, 2010; Romero, Ventura & Bra, 2004; Minaei-Bidgoli, Kashy, Kortemeyer, & Punch, 2003; Zaiane, 2002), intelligent tutoring systems (McQuiggan et al., 2008; Baker, 2007; Walonoski & Heffernan, 2006; Beck et al., 2004, Baker et al., 2004), social learning environments and forum dialogues (Vellido, Castro & Nebot, 2010; Trivedi, 2011) and simulation based environments.

In the years to come additional data sources and unexplored parameters can be seen entering the ongoing research in EDM. Research can also be seen to further expand towards self-paced learning in web based environments. Also, with the growth of this field new methods may emerge through which adaptive learning courses may be provided to students in various other learning environments.

CONCLUSION

Societies prosper when the education level of an average individual is increased; the individual becomes a productive part of society. This chapter explores the shift in education and learning paradigms being witnessed by the world today, the embrace of technology to educate the masses, the learning trends that have evolved with the adoption of advanced technology, the addition of metrics in these learning trends and the generation of priceless data through this technology that has the potential to reshape the way learning takes place.

Using Big Data generated by educational institutes is still an evolving area of research. As the data generated by the educational institutes increases, researchers explore several approaches, existing and new, to uncover patterns that can be utilized to make discoveries to help improve the system of education.

This Big Data may not be as huge as data being generated by other industries but there is certainly a massive volume of data. As discussed in this chapter, using EDM methods, there is great opportunity to truly understand the relationships that exist between student behavior and educational outcomes.

This chapter explores the Big Data generated by the education sector and a generic model is proposed that incorporates the use of EDM methods to unveil insights about student behavior and attitude. Using the suggested model educational institutes can gain several benefits including:

- Establishment of frameworks and tools that maximize learning.
- Devising learning systems and educational platforms that develop individual skills and enhance knowledge.
- Design of syllabi based on current and latest problems and trends.
- Creation of formative assessments as well as adaptive learning models to truly accomplish the '*leave no man behind*' strategy.
- Enhanced opportunities for feedback, reflection and modification.
- Creation of communities dedicated to understanding cognition and learning patterns.
- Study of disengaged behavior exhibited by the students including off task behavior and gaming the system.
- Understanding why some students make careless mistakes while possessing skills needed to correctly answer questions.

REFERENCES

Agrawal, R., Imieliński, T., & Swami, A. (1993). Mining association rules between sets of items in large databases. *SIGMOD Record*, *22*(2), 207–216. doi:10.1145/170036.170072

Arroyo, I., & Woolf, B. P. (2005). Inferring learning and attitudes from Bayesian Network of log file data. In *Proceedings of the 12th International Conference on Artificial Intelligence in Education* (pp. 33-40).

Bailey, J., Ellis, S., Schneider, C., & Vander, T. (2013). *Blended Learning Implementation Guide*. Foundation for Excellence in Education In Association with: Getting Smart DTLN Smart series.

Baker, R., Gowda, S. M., & Corbett, A. T. (2011). Automatically detecting a student's preparation for future learning: Help use is key. In *Proceedings of the 4th international conference on educational data mining*.

Baker, R. S. (2007). Modeling and understanding students' off-task behavior in intelligent tutoring systems. In *Proceedings of the SIGCHI conference on Human factors in computing systems* (pp. 1059-1068). ACM. doi:10.1145/1240624.1240785

Baker, R. S. (2010). Mining data for student models. In *Advances in intelligent tutoring systems* (pp. 323–337). Springer Berlin Heidelberg. doi:10.1007/978-3-642-14363-2_16

Baker, R. S. (2014a). Educational data mining: An advance for intelligent systems in education. *IEEE Intelligent Systems*, *29*(3), 78–82. doi:10.1109/MIS.2014.42

Baker, R. S., Corbett, A. T., & Koedinger, K. R. (2004). Detecting Student Misuse of Intelligent Tutoring Systems. In *Proceedings of the 7th International Conference on Intelligent Tutoring Systems* (pp. 531-540). Springer Berlin Heidelberg. doi:10.1007/978-3-540-30139-4_50

Baker, R. S., & Inventado, P. S. (2014b). Educational data mining and learning analytics. In *Learning Analytics* (pp. 61–75). Springer New York.

Barr, R. B., & Tagg, J. (1995). From teaching to learning—A new paradigm for undergraduate education. *Change: The Magazine of Higher Learning, 27*(6), 12-26.

Barrie, S., Ginns, P., & Prosser, M. (2005). Early impact and outcomes of an institutionally aligned, student focused learning perspective on teaching quality assurance 1. *Assessment & Evaluation in Higher Education*, *30*(6), 641–656. doi:10.1080/02602930500260761

Beck, J., Baker, R., Corbett, A., Kay, J., Litman, D., Mitrovic, T., & Ritter, S. (2004). Workshop on Analyzing Student-Tutor Interaction Logs to Improve Educational Outcomes. In *Intelligent Tutoring Systems* (pp. 909-909). Springer Berlin Heidelberg.

Bransford, J. D., Brown, A. L., & Cocking, R. R. (1999). *How people learn: brain, mind, experience, and school.* Washington, DC: National Academy Press.

Conati, C., & Maclaren, H. (2009). Empirically building and evaluating a probabilistic model of user affect. *User Modeling and User-Adapted Interaction*, *19*(3), 267–303. doi:10.1007/s11257-009-9062-8

Corbett, A. (2001). Cognitive computer tutors: Solving the two-sigma problem. In *User Modeling 2001* (pp. 137–147). Springer Berlin Heidelberg. doi:10.1007/3-540-44566-8_14

Corbett, A., & Anderson, J. (1995). Knowledge traching: Modeling the acquisition of procedural knowledge. *User Modeling and User-Adapted Interaction*, *4*(4), 253–278. doi:10.1007/BF01099821

Crouch, C. H., & Mazur, E. (2001). Peer instruction: Ten years of experience and results. *American Journal of Physics*, *69*(9), 970–977. doi:10.1119/1.1374249

D'mello, S. K., Craig, S. D., Witherspoon, A., Mcdaniel, B., & Graesser, A. (2008). Automatic detection of learner's affect from conversational cues. *User Modeling and User-Adapted Interaction*, *18*(1-2), 45–80. doi:10.1007/s11257-007-9037-6

Dietz-Uhler, B., & Hurn, J. E. (2013). Using learning analytics to predict (and improve) student success: A faculty perspective. *Journal of Interactive Online Learning*, *12*(1), 17–26.

E-LEARNING, Concepts, Trends, Applications. (2014). San Francisco, CA: Epignosis LLC.

Eberhardt, F., & Scheines, R. (2007). Interventions and causal inference. *Philosophy of Science*, *74*(5), 981–995. doi:10.1086/525638

Eduventures, Inc. (2013). *Predictive Analysis in Higher Education, Data Driven Decision Making for the Student Life Cycle*. Boston: Eduventures, Inc. Retrieved from http://www.eduventures.com/wp-content/uploads/2013/02/Eduventures_Predictive_Analytics_White_Paper1.pdf

El-Hussein, M. O. M., & Cronje, J. C. (2010). Defining Mobile Learning in the Higher Education Landscape. *Journal of Educational Technology & Society*, *13*(3), 12–21.

Falakmasir, M. H., & Habibi, J. (2010). *Using Educational Data Mining Methods to Study the Impact of Virtual Classroom in E-Learning*. Pittsburgh, PA: EDM.

Feng, M., & Heffernan, N. T. (2007). Towards live informing and automatic analyzing of student learning: Reporting in assessment system. *Journal of Interactive Learning Research*, *18*(2), 207.

Greenfield, P. M., & Calvert, S. L. (2004). Electronic media and human development: The legacy of Rodney R. Cocking. *Journal of Applied Developmental Psychology*, *25*(6), 627–631. doi:10.1016/j.appdev.2004.09.001

Hamalainen, W., & Vinni, M. (2010). Classifiers for educational data mining. In Handbook of Educational Data Mining. Chapman & Hall / CRC Press.

Hamdan, N., McKnight, P. E., McKnight, K., & Arfstrom, K. M. (2013). *A review of Flipped Learning. Flipped Learning Network*. Pearson.

Hijazi, S. T., & Naqvi, R. S. M. M. (2006). Factors affecting student's performance: A Case of Private Colleges. *Bangladesh e- Journal of Sociology (Melbourne, Vic.)*, *3*(1).

Kruse, A., & Pongsajapan, R. (2012). Student-centered learning analytics. *CNDLS Thought Papers*, 1-9.

Kulik, C. L. C., & Kulik, J. A. (1991). Effectiveness of computer-based instruction: An updated analysis. *Computers in Human Behavior*, *7*(1), 75–94. doi:10.1016/0747-5632(91)90030-5

Langham, B. A. (2009). The achievement gap: What early childhood educators need to know. *Texas Child Care Quarterly*. Retrieved from https://www.collabforchildren.org/sites/default/files/downloads/achievegap09.pdf

Lu, J. (2004). Personalized e-learning material recommender system. In *International conference on information technology for application* (pp. 374-379).

Ma, Y., Liu, B., Wong, C. K., Yu, P. S., & Lee, S. M. (2000, August). Targeting the right students using data mining. In *Proceedings of the sixth ACM SIGKDD international conference on Knowledge discovery and data mining* (pp. 457-464). ACM. doi:10.1145/347090.347184

Manaei-Bidgoli, B., Kashy, D. A., Kortmeyer, G., & Punch, W. (2003). Predicting student performance: An application of data mining methods with an educational web-based system (LON-CAPA). In *ASEE/IEEE Frontiers in Education Conference*. IEEE.

Mazur, E., (2009). Farewell, lecture. *Science*, *323*(5910), 50-51

Mazur, E., & Hilborn, R. C. (1997). Peer Instruction: A User's Manual. Physics Today, 50(4), 65.

McLuhan, M. (1994). *Understanding media: The extensions of man*. MIT Press.

Mcquiggan, S. W., Mott, B. W., & Lester, J. C. (2008). Modeling self-efficacy in intelligent tutoring systems: An inductive approach. *User Modeling and User-Adapted Interaction*, *18*(1-2), 81–123. doi:10.1007/s11257-007-9040-y

Merceron, A., & Yacef, K. (2010). Measuring correlation of strong symmetric association rules in educational data. In Handbook of Educational Data Mining. Boca Raton, FL: CRC Press. doi:10.1201/b10274-20

Moore, J. L., Dickson-Deane, C., & Galyen, K. (2011). e-Learning, online learning, and distance learning environments: Are they the same? *The Internet and Higher Education*, *14*(2), 129–135. doi:10.1016/j.iheduc.2010.10.001

Pavlik, P. I. Jr, Cen, H., & Koedinger, K. R. (2009). Performance Factors Analysis--A New Alternative to Knowledge Tracing. In *Proceedings of the 14th international conference on artificial intelligence in education*.

Prabha, S. L., & Shanavas, D. A. M. (2014). Educational data mining applications. *Operations Research and Applications: An International Journal*, *1*(1).

Prensky, M. (2008). The role of technology in teaching and the classroom. *Educational Technology*. Retrieved from http://www.marcprensky.com/writing/Prensky-Thc_Role_of_Technology-ET-11-12-08.pdf

Rai, D., & Beck, J. (2011). *Exploring user data from a game-like math tutor: a case study in causal modeling*. EDM.

Romero, C., & Ventura, S. (2007). Educational data mining: A survey from 1995 to 2005. *Expert Systems with Applications*, *33*(1), 135–146. doi:10.1016/j.eswa.2006.04.005

Romero, C., & Ventura, S. (2013). Data mining in education. *Wiley Interdisciplinary Reviews: Data Mining and Knowledge Discovery*, *3*(1), 12–27.

Romero, C., Ventura, S., & Bra, P. D. (2004). Knowledge discovery with genetic programming for pro viding feedback to courseware author. *User Modeling and User-Adapted Interaction: The Journal of Personalization Research*, *14*(5), 425–464. doi:10.1007/s11257-004-7961-2

Romero, C., Ventura, S., Pechenizkiy, M., & Baker, R. S. J. d. (Eds.). (2010). *Handbook of Educational Data Mining*. CRC Press. doi:10.1201/b10274

Scheuer, O., & McLaren, B. M. (2011). Educational data mining. In *The Encyclopedia of the Sciences of Learning*. New York, NY: Springer.

Shute, V. J. (1995). SMART: Student modeling approach for responsive tutoring. *User Modeling and User-Adapted Interaction*, *5*(1), 1–44. doi:10.1007/BF01101800

Siemens, G., & Baker, R. S. (2012). Learning analytics and educational data mining: towards communication and collaboration. In *Proceedings of the 2nd international conference on learning analytics and knowledge* (pp. 252-254). ACM. doi:10.1145/2330601.2330661

Smith, V. C., Lange, A., & Huston, D. R. (2012). Predictive modeling to forecast student outcomes and drive effective interventions in online community college courses. *Journal of Asynchronous Learning Networks*, *16*(3), 51–61.

Trivedi, S., Pardos, Z. A., Sarkozy, G. N., & Heffernan, N. T. (2011). *Spectral Clustering in Educational Data Mining*. EDM.

Vellido, A., Castro, F., & Nebot, A. (2010). *Clustering educational data. In Handbook of Educational Data Mining* (pp. 75–92). Chapman and Hall/CRC Press. doi:10.1201/b10274-8

Vellido, A., Castro, F., & Nebot, A. (2011). *Clustering Educational Data. Handbook of Educational Data Mining*. Boca Raton, FL: Chapman and Hall/CRC Press.

Walonoski, J. A., & Heffernan, N. T. (2006). Detection and analysis of off-task gaming behavior in intelligent tutoring systems. In *International Conference on Intelligent Tutoring Systems*, (pp. 382-391). Springer Berlin Heidelberg. doi:10.1007/11774303_38

Windham, C. (2005). The student's perspective. In Educating the Next Generation. Educause.

Zaïane, O. R. (2002). Building a recommender agent for e-learning systems. In *Computers in Education: Proceedings. International Conference on* (pp. 55-59). IEEE. doi:10.1109/CIE.2002.1185862

ADDITIONAL READING

Ayesha, S., Mustafa, T., Sattar, A. R., & Khan, M. I. (2010). Data mining model for higher education system. *Europen Journal of Scientific Research, 43*(1), 24–29.

Baker, R. S. J. d. (2013). *Learning, Schooling, and Data Analytics. Handbook on Innovations in Learning for States, Districts, and Schools* (pp. 179–190). Philadelphia, PA: Center on Innovations in Learning.

Baradwaj, B. K., & Pal, S. (2012). Mining educational data to analyze students' performance. *IJACSA*, 2(6).

Kabakchieva, D. (2013). Predicting student performance by using data mining methods for classification. *Cybernetics and information technologies, 13*(1), 61-72.

Tair, M. M. A., & El-Halees, A. M. (2012). Mining educational data to improve students' performance: A case study. *International Journal of Information, 2*(2).

KEY TERMS AND DEFINITIONS

Association Rule Mining: Mining of associations occurring naturally between variables in large datasets. These associations are represented using if-then structures.

Causal Mining: Causal mining attempts to uncover the cause of certain actions or outcomes. It aims to explore if the occurrence of some action may influence the occurrence of some other action(s).

Educational Data Mining: Set of data mining methods aimed at exploring student data made available through online resources to discover patterns of student learning behavior.

Prediction: An approach that is used to discover some unknown feature or attribute in a dataset by using the known features and attributes in the dataset.

Structure Discovery: An approach that aims to discover patterns and structures in datasets without prior knowledge of what patterns may be discovered.

Chapter 12
Vehicle to Cloud:
Big Data for Environmental Sustainability, Energy, and Traffic Management

Alper Ozpinar
Istanbul Commerce University, Turkey

Serhan Yarkan
Istanbul Commerce University, Turkey

ABSTRACT

The population of humanity has become more than seven billion. Daily used devices, machines, and equipment, are also increasing quicker than the human population. The number of mobile devices in use like phones, tablets and IoT devices already passed the two billion barrier and even more than one billion as vehicles are also on the roads. Combining these two will make the one of the biggest Big Data Environment about the daily life of human beings after the use of internet and social applications. For the newly manufactured vehicles, internet operated entertainment and information Systems are becoming a standard equipment delivering such an information to the manufacturers but most of the current vehicles do not have a system like that. This chapter explains the combined version of IoT and vehicles to create a V2C vehicle to cloud system that will create the big data for environmental sustainability, energy and traffic management by different technical and political views and aspects.

INTRODUCTION

Starting from the early days of civilization to nowadays, one of the irrefutable facts about the humanity is the endless technology development and research beyond the imagination of his ancestors. Behavioral issues for most of the civilizations took place in early days behavioral can be explained by Maslow's hierarchy of needs, which focuses on describing the stages of growth in humans starting from bottom including the physiological needs, safety needs, love and belonging needs, esteem as well as self-actualization and self-transcendence (Maslow, 1943). However, the world gets more and more sophisticated, complex and

DOI: 10.4018/978-1-5225-0182-4.ch012

complicated; therefore, majority of the earlier assumptions and theories themselves should continuously evolve to change or reshape in light of the technological improvements and innovations. Contemporary modern daily life enforces people to use digital devices such as computers, personal digital assistants, cell phones as well as online services and infotainment systems which heavily rely on Internet. In this regard, hierarchy of needs could easily be extended in such a way that digital products and services are also included. It is critical to keep in mind that both number and capabilities of these digital products and services increase dramatically in the last two decades in parallel to the escalating demands. In order to meet the requirements, Microsoft, AMD, Intel and IBM has already passed the five billion barrier in the microprocessor transistor counts in the device and making a huge scatter from the Moore's Law of the doubling of transistors per square inch on integrated circuits. (Schaller, 1997; Moore, 1998). This implies that the future of the humanity will also reshape and adapt itself to the contemporary conditions while more devices and sensors becoming online. In parallel with these, one should bear in mind that more computational power will be available for artificial intelligence and self-aware systems. It is obvious that these next generation systems should be tuned to optimize for sustainable a future.

Sustainability is based on a simple way of thinking about the idea of everything that humanity needs for survival and well-being depends, either directly or indirectly, on the natural surrounding conditions. The ability to keep something around for this aim creates and maintains the conditions under which humans and nature can exist in productive harmony allowing a continuous satisfaction of the items. Main concern areas of sustainability starts with the E3 concept of energy, economy, environment and as well as enriching with commercial, social, financial, agricultural, educational, health related issues of present and future.

Among all these issues, energy is the key controllable crucial one that controls, limits and connects most of them. A clean, free and unlimited energy may result in environmental and economical sustainability and the rest will also improve and adapt accordingly. However, in reality of nowadays harsh conditions, energy is mostly produced from limited fossil fuels which also generate high emissions and leads to global warming and climate change. There are many regulating bodies and institutions around the globe concerning these problems. International Energy Agency (IEA) is one of them which aims to promote energy security to physical disruptions in oil supply and looking for ensure reliable, affordable and clean energy for the world. IEA periodically publish several general annual reports as well as key subjects with detailed focus reports on energy policies and perspectives and future projections. Those reports provide a common and detailed information to the energy related issues. According to IEA reports since the first Conference of the Parties (COP) in 1995, greenhouse-gas (GHG) emissions have risen by more than one-quarter and the atmospheric concentration of these gases has increased steadily to 435 parts per million carbon-dioxide equivalent (ppm CO_2-equivalent) in 2012. According to the International Panel on Climate Change (IPCC), humanity and all the countries have to take fully committed and urgent action otherwise climate change will have severe and irreversible impacts across the world. The international commitment to keep the increase in long-term average temperatures to below two degrees Celsius (2 °C), relative to pre-industrial levels, will require substantial and sustained reductions in global emissions. In order to reach this level and attain the goals, energy sector, operating rules, conditions, policies and procedures of operating need to be changed since two-thirds of all made by people and greenhouse-gas formed by energy production. The World Data Center for Greenhouse Gases (WDCGG) provides data for The Carbon Dioxide Information Analysis Center (CDIA) in USA which works on climate-change data and is a very good source for finding statistical and deep information about the subject. In order to collect information for measuring greenhouse (GHG) and ozone depleting gases and aerosols in clean air environments special air pollution stations are required where air is unaffected by regional pollution sources like nearby cities or industry areas that would contaminate the air quality. Cape Grim, on Tasmania's west coast, is one of these stations operated by The Commonwealth Scientific and Industrial Research Organization (CSIRO) of Australia and Figure 1 shows the pollution statistics of the station.

It is assumed to be the energy sector which can achieve a peak in GHG emissions by the year 2020, with almost the same level of economic growth and development. There are three main scenarios widely

Figure 1. Emission statistics from Cape Grim stations, Source: (CSIRO, 2015)

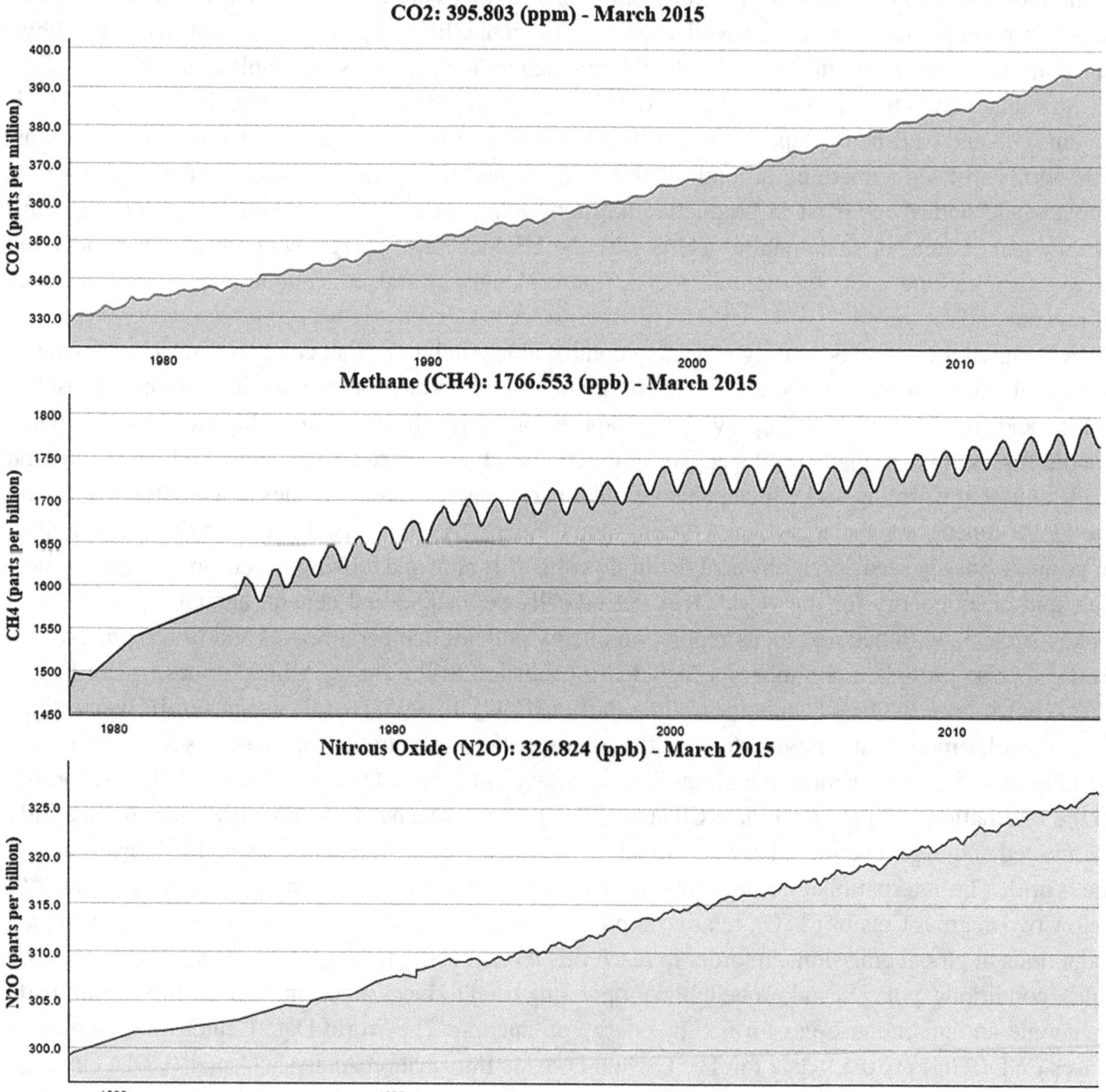

CO2: 395.803 (ppm) - March 2015

CO2 (parts per million)

Methane (CH4): 1766.553 (ppb) - March 2015

CH4 (parts per billion)

Nitrous Oxide (N2O): 326.824 (ppb) - March 2015

N2O (parts per billion)

accepted in order to control the worldwide warming and climate change. Kyoto Rules of conduct and Copenhagen Climate Change Conference studies and their results are becoming outdated and replaced with new policies and situations. Those scenarios have a common goal but they differ from their ideas about the change for the better sustainability and application of government policies. These scenarios are the "Intended Nationally Determined Contributions (INDC) Scenario", the "Bridge Scenario" and the "450 Scenario". The common sense in those scenarios is to keep the increase in long-term average temperatures to below two degrees Celsius (2 °C) or similar to limit emission below 450ppm CO_2 equivalent as explained before.

As can be seen from Figure 2, pushing the critical limits will result in global warming which causes catastrophic outcomes like the increasing sea level rise and storm damage, loss of coastal wetlands, increasing malnutrition, diarrheal, cardio-respiratory and infectious diseases, increasing mortality from heatwaves, droughts, floods, decreasing water availability and increasing drought in mid-to low latitudes, small glaciers disappear, threatening water supplies, localized negative impacts on small land holders, subsistence farmers, fishers, increasing risk of dangerous feedbacks and abrupt shifts in the climate system and many more (Birol, 2008; Parry, 2007).

According to the studies global warming is caused by the emission of greenhouse gases released to the atmosphere from different sources related with human civilization. The ingredients of totally emitted GHG formed by 72% by carbon dioxide (CO_2), 18% by methane and 9% by nitrous oxide (NOx). Carbon dioxide related emissions therefore are the most important cause of global warming.

CO_2 is inevitably created by burning fossil fuels e.g. oil, natural gas, diesel, organic-diesel, petrol, organic-petrol, and ethanol. Figure 3 shows the CO_2 emissions by sector. Electricity production, transportation and industry are the top key sources. These are the world average numbers, in some countries the portion of transportation is even higher like U.S greenhouse gas emissions from transportation accounted for about 27% of total U.S. greenhouse gas emissions and greenhouse gas emissions from transportation have increased by about 16% since 1990.

As a result of the above mentioned facts an optimization methodology, any improvements for the technology related with the consumption and generated emission related with transportation should be established. Green transportation concept is an important part of such an idea. Next generation transportation systems, vehicles, engines are required to obtain high performances and efficiencies with reduced fuel consumption and carbon emission.

Since like all the mechanical systems, vehicle maintenance status along with some other critical error/malfunction preventing and identifying data should steadily be checked, watched, monitored, tracked, and stored for further research possibilities. It is known that vehicles that are poorly maintained and tuned or even not maintained in an appropriate manner on regular basis lead to fall down below the factory standards, low operating performance or more emissions produced.

Vehicle telematics and information along with some other conveniences such as entertaining information systems, location-based services and applications are expected to improve safety, availability, and reliability of next generation transportation systems. From this point of view, intelligent/smart transport systems (ITS) seems to be a promising candidate solution which includes all of the previously-mentioned topics as well as vehicle-to-vehicle (V2V), vehicle-to-infrastructure (V2I), and vehicle-to-cloud (V2C) opportunities which will be explained in the following section.

Therefore, in this chapter, an idea-based model that links vehicle telematics to the cloud along with V2V communications facility is proposed and an early model based on IEEE 802.11x protocol suite is

Figure 2. The role on energy in climate policy, Source: (Birol, 2008)

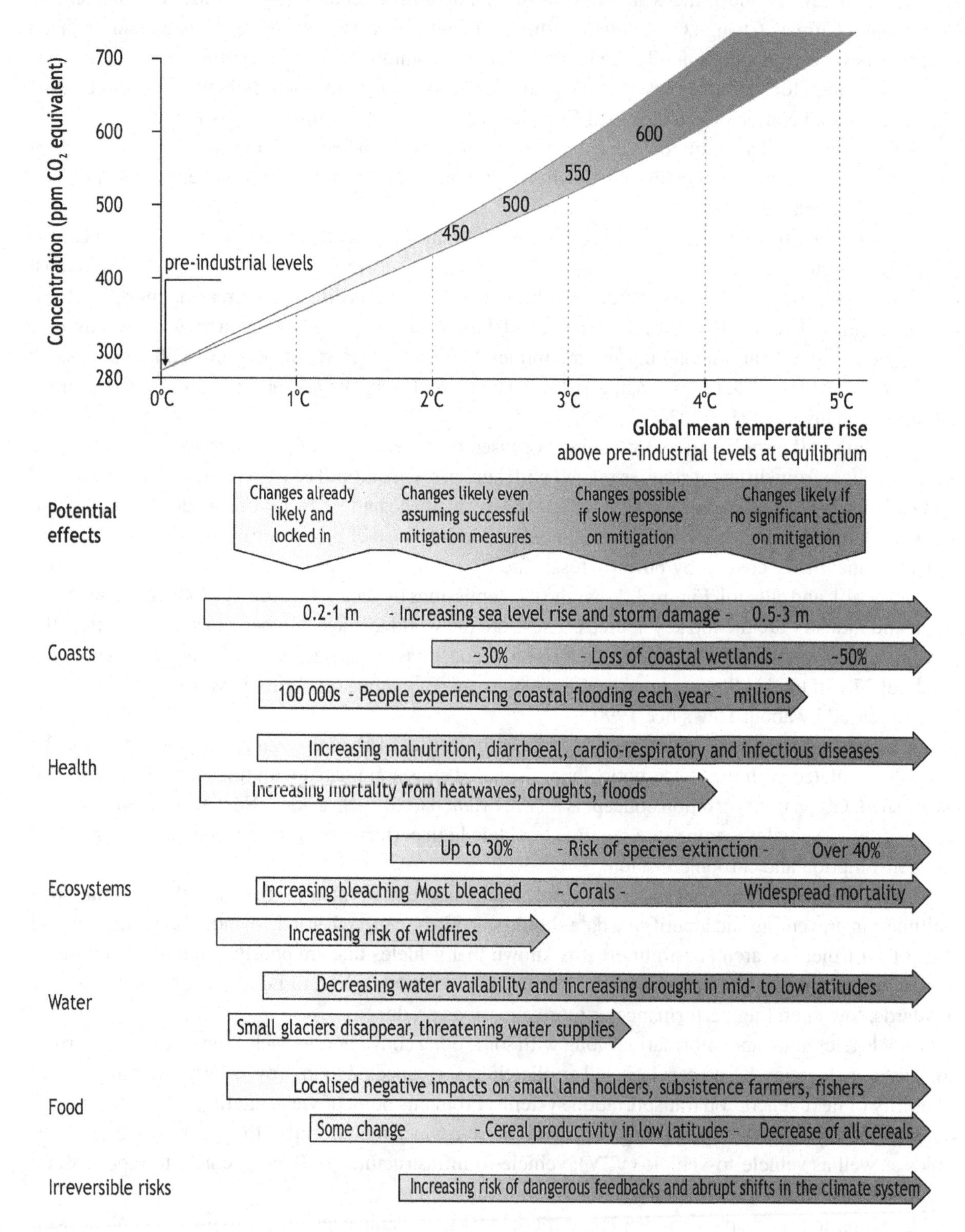

Figure 3. World CO_2 Emission by sector, Source: (IEA, 2014)

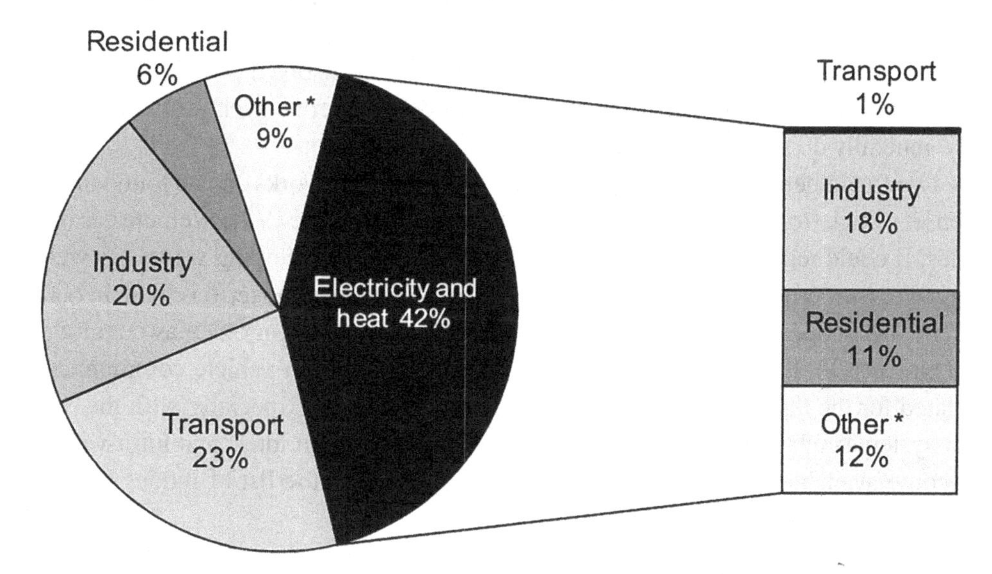

provided with mobile data collection and measurement options. Also in the proposed model and solution, the mobile data are collected and transferred from one location to another, which could possibly employ computers to store these data and maintain them. It is important to note that the proposed model paves the way for big data leading to further research opportunities for car manufacturers, policy makers, and the individual researchers.

WIRELESS COMMUNICATIONS FOR VEHICULAR NETWORKS

The term "vehicular networks" covers a vast variety of network topologies, structures, formations, technologies including diverse communications infrastructures. Among those, wireless communications and related technologies along with infrastructures have a special place since vehicular networks require strong mobility support. In order to better understand why and how wireless communications lie in the heart of vehicular networks technologies, several important characteristics of vehicular networks should be studied.

Broadly speaking, vehicular networks consist of multiple nodes (possibly mobile) which are connected to each other via direct or indirect (relay) links. It is obvious that such a broad definition raises important questions regarding the differences between mobile networks, mobile ad-hoc networks (MANETs), and vehicular networks, all of which exhibit significant similarities. Mobile networks generally necessitate almost a ubiquitous communications infrastructure as in cellular mobile networks, whereas vehicular networks do not require the presence of such an infrastructure. On the other hand, MANETs do not require a ubiquitous infrastructure; however, their limitations, constraints, and mobility patterns are quite different from those of vehicular networks. For instance, a mobile node in a MANET is generally assumed to move in a stochastic direction with a relatively low-speed, whereas nodes of a vehicular network are assumed to move generally in a quasi-deterministic or completely deterministic direction with a very high speed as compared to that in a MANET. Furthermore, battery is a critical constraint for MANETs, whereas it is not a critical constraint for vehicular networks. In vehicular networks, some communications signals such as emergency messages and/beacons are vital; therefore, any problems with their authenticity, delay, and integrity cannot be tolerated, since unsolved problems lead to hazardous and even life-and-death situations. In contrast, MANETs could tolerate such problems to some extent because they generally do not operate in life-threatening environments.

There are two fundamental modes of operations for vehicular networks can be found in the literature in general sense: vehicle-to-vehicle (V2V) and vehicle-to-infrastructure (V2I). Vehicle has many aspects in both modes. It could represent a node that is transmitting and/or receiving signals as well as a relay carrying messages over other nodes present in the network. Of course, the term vehicle in both V2V and V2I gains a broader scope with the emerging technologies and paradigms such as cognitive radio and Internet of Things (IoT). From this perspective, inter-vehicle and intra-vehicle communications could be contemplated for the term "vehicle" in V2V and V2I topologies. Especially with the emergence of infotainment systems embedded in vehicles, new dimensions for both inter- and intra-vehicle communications become available; therefore, they should be appended to the list of modes of operations for vehicular networks.

Intelligent Transportation Systems

Intelligent transportation systems (ITS) are dealing with the ecosystem of humans, machines, devices vehicles, sensors, loop detector, video surveillance systems, roadside radars, speed cameras interacting with each other by using information technology with physical and digital communication infrastructure While connecting the continents, countries, and cities the transportation systems are crowded large-scale systems heterogeneously distributed by means of location, time, and population. Since transportation systems are highly uncertain, dynamic, and nonlinear type of systems, they require a special attention to manage, track, and control. Contemporary examples of ITS include flexible and dynamic pricing like congestion pricing, road enforcements for special vehicle types, law enforcement like variable speed limits, emergency lane usage detection, red light violation, parking zones breaching, road weather information and signaling and so on.

Common Model as Vehicle-to-X (V2X) Model

Within the core of all transportations systems, there exist a vehicle that is in the center of all the progress. If there are more than one vehicle, in that case multi-vehicle system can be considered or in general it can be defined as traffic. But once again all of the vehicles can arrange themselves assuming that they are in the center of the system. So the rest of the system details can be indicated with a variable notation X. As explained in the future sections of this chapter, in cloud computing the abbreviation of EaaS or sometimes XaaS refers to any information technology can be eumployed within a service based architecture in general sense "Everything as a Service".

A similar analogy can be applied for the vehicle and traffic systems. In the common model of V2X, vehicles stay in the center of their custom system definition and communicate with the rest of the items or members of the ecosystem within their boundaries. In practice, X will be a vehicle by definition, infrastructure, communication hub, cloud computing connection, pedestrian, bicycler, traffic light, parking lot, intelligent road signs, gates, toll bridges, and so on.

Vehicle-to-Cloud (V2C) Model

As the technological requirements and the technical aspects of the system evolve common definitions of V2V and V2I also have to be expanded with new possible definitions. One of the extension is for the concept of V2I is the extension of the infrastructure network to the cloud computing network for more intelligent applications and decision making processes.

Vehicle-to-Cloud (V2C) Extended with FOG Computing Model and IoT (V2CeF)

Fog Computing is a highly virtualized computation platform that provides the service about computers, storage, and networking as services between end devices network and traditional Cloud Computing Data Centers, typically, but not exclusively located at the edge of the communication network (Bonomi, Milito, Zhu, & Addepalli, 2012). Even with the next generation wireless networks that provide high speed operation and wide coverage, there may exist a network or a hardware related problems within the boundaries such as congestion, packet loss, cascading failures, hardware problems, and some instant delays within the network. A dynamic collaboration is required between the edge devices and the core devices. The scope and dimension of the data processed are narrow in space and time at the fog side (edge), and wide at the core like in cloud computing. So in the hierarchical organizational architecture of the network, computer and storage resources at the edges within the transportation system will improve the overall system capabilities and performance (Bonomi, Milito, Natarajan, & Zhu, 2014). This model is especially important and increases the performance with the applications like storing the details of the vehicle maintenance and millage data, control, measurement and tracking with precise time domain indices. The application and system details of V2CeF will be explained in detail in the following sections.

Technical Details of the Vehicle-to-Cloud (V2C) Model

In the technical background and the architecture of the V2C Ecosystem, the proposed conceptual system model consists of the following technical details and modules:

Main modules will be the Vehicle Computer Interface (VCI), an RF frontend and an IEEE 802.11x suite. The modules except for the RF frontend are considered to have cross-layer capabilities with a robust security support on both PHY and upper layers. In the proposed V2C ecosystem model the key module is the IEEE 802.11x suite since it is responsible for the communication way of vehicle data to the cloud. It is important to keep in mind that cross-layer functionality could both be employed on IEEE 802.11x suite and VCI; therefore, security support could be established both on VCI and IEEE 802.11x suite. From this perspective, the proposed system model provides PHY-layer security on VCI, whereas MAC (and possibly upper) layer security on IEEE 802.11x suite. Main task of VCI is to establish a fast, reliable, and secure short range wireless communications between the vehicle and the IEEE 802.11x suite. Considering the fact that majority of the on-board diagnostics data are fed to VCI without a substantial security support, VCI is believed to remedy these shortcomings.

Furthermore, VCI provides a vast variety of both wireless and wired communications interfaces to IEEE 802.11x suite. As will be discussed subsequently, IEEE 802.11x suite is used as a communications hub for the vehicle; therefore, a versatile VCI is required. IEEE 802.11x suite is the key component of the proposed system model. It enables vehicle data to reach the cloud via VCI; establishes communications between various peripherals and extensions; and more importantly allows the vehicle to enter a V2V network and maintain it.

Furthermore, IEEE 802.11x suite could be modified and tailored to specific requirements, applications, and/or services. In contrast to VCI and IEEE 802.11x suite, RF frontend is the least adaptable and/or flexible component among these three. Its only task is to provide interface between the physical propagation medium and the digital domain. Of course, it is expected RF frontend to support multi-band operations with high performance with a possible MIMO support (Boyaci, Ozpinar, Ozturk, & Yarkan, 2015).

CLOUD COMPUTING AND BIG DATA

Cloud Computing General Concerns

Cloud computing is the popular, fancy keyword for the current status of the evolution with the genotypes of computational power within cloud computing is based on parallel processing, extensive storage and virtualization of computer systems as the system genes which results in the latest phenotypes like massive flexibility, scalability and complex computing. The common idea behind the cloud computing is delivering all suitable types of information technology related products and services via high speed internet as a service based business model namely "X as a Service" (XaaS) or "Everything as a Service" (EaaS) model. The X or E can be replaced by well-known services like software (SaaS), infrastructure (IaaS) and platform (PaaS) as well as lots of unique or extended possibilities like network (NaaS), communication (CaaS), education (EaaS) and so on (Mell & Grance, 2011) . Since the overall book is related with the subject, no more general information will be provided in this section.

Actors in V2C Ecosystem

Actors in the cloud computing clearly defined in NIST Cloud Computing Reference Architecture. (Liu et al., 2011). Table 1 is the extended version of the definitions modified for V2C systems. In normal cloud computing operations like traditional software applications hosted on the cloud or use of email and office applications from the cloud this model is simpler. Most of the time consumer purchases a system from a company and uses any carrier to reach that system without the need of specialized auditors and brokers. However in the case of V2C, the system has numerous parties some of which have a position of conflict of interest like vehicle manufacturers. But for the overall case governments and authorities deal with the whole system. In order to operate the V2C system both cloud auditors and cloud broker bodies have to work in collaboration and transparent to the public. Traceability of the vehicles with different dimensions like location, time, frequency, and identity details requires a high level of privacy concerns and issues. Security control operations therefore involves the management, operational and technical safeguards or countermeasures employed within V2C ecosystem to protect the data (keeping private information private), and availability of the system and its information in different levels to consumers. For security auditing, a cloud auditor can make a test/evaluation of the security controls in the information system to figure out the extent to which the controls are put into use correctly, operating as meant, and producing the desired result with respect to the security needed things for the system. The security

Table 1. Extended V2C and cloud computing actors

NIST Actor	NIST Definition	V2C Operator / System
Cloud Consumer	A person or organization that maintains a business relationship with, and uses service from, Cloud Providers.	Vehicle owners Vehicle manufacturers Policy makers V2C Public Private Authorities
Cloud Provider	A person, organization, or entity responsible for making a service available to interested parties	Government institutions Tech companies (Network, GSM, R&D, ISP vs)
Cloud Auditor	A party that can conduct independent assessment of cloud services, information system operations, performance and security of the cloud implementation.	Related ministry and government institutions Municipalities Police Department Highway Authorities
Cloud Broker	An entity that manages the use, performance and delivery of cloud services, and negotiates relationships between Cloud Providers and Cloud Consumers.	System integrators Value added resellers Installation and vehicle services
Cloud Carrier	An intermediary that provides connectivity and transport of cloud services from Cloud Providers to Cloud Consumers.	GSM operators WiFi and WLAN providers

auditing should also include the checking for truth of the obedience of regulation and security policy. For example, a person who carefully checks V2C records can be given the job of securing and making sure that the correct policies are applied to data keeping, storing, and recording according to clearly defined transparent rules for the legal control.

Scope of Controls between Cloud Provider and Cloud Consumer

The Cloud Provider and Cloud Consumer share the control of resources in V2C ecosystem. Various service models affect an organization's control over the computational resources and thus what can be done in a cloud system (Liu et al., 2011). The following definitions explains the classic software layers and their positions in V2C systems.

The V2C Application Layer

This layer includes IoT embedded, mobile device, desktop, and internet applications targeted at end users or programs. The applications are used by SaaS consumers like the vehicle owners, vehicle manufacturer in order to follow up with the information related to their side like the maintenance schedule, carbon emissions, taxes, consumptions. Most of the V2C ecosystem these application can be implemented on PaaS or IaaS depending on the architecture. FOG systems could reduce the use of IaaS at the consumer level.

The V2C Middleware Layer

This layer provides software building blocks for the developers and devices that enables rapid and integrated developing V2C applications in the cloud. The middleware is used by PaaS consumers, installed/managed/maintained by IaaS consumers or PaaS providers, and hidden from SaaS consumers.

The V2C OS Layer

This layer includes operating system and drivers on the devices, and is hidden from SaaS consumers and PaaS consumers. In classical cloud computing applications consumers can choose the OS to be hosted, however in V2C ecosystem, OS layer requirement and interoperability issues are defined by the regulatory bodies and cloud auditors.

V2C Cloud Service Management

In this section of the chapter, NIST definitions for Cloud Service Management has adapted for V2C ecosystem conditions.

Business Support

Business support deals with the business-related services with the V2C ecosystem and it includes the software applications, call centers to the end used to run the operations. Business support will be provided by different operators and sides depending on the service level. If the V2C system is supported and implemented directly by the government, then energy efficiency, traceability and reduce in emissions will be achieved. Most probably the ecosystem will be controlled and supported by laws, acts and agreements. In that case business support can be directly provided by the government bodies or outsourced to private operators in order to increase the support network.

- **Customer Management:** Manage the end users accounts like vehicle owners and corporate accounts like vehicle manufacturers accounts, open/close/terminate accounts, manage user profiles up a defined security level, manage customer relationships by providing points-of-contact and resolving customer issues and problems with a call center support or online services.
- **Contract Management:** Manage service contracts, setup/negotiate/close/terminate contract between the operators and vehicle owners and possibly the government.
- **Inventory Management:** Set up and manage service catalogs, etc.
- **Accounting and Billing:** Manage customer billing information, send billing statements, process received payments, track invoices if the system will be a payed system. It may be a free of charge service supported or sponsored by the governments, vehicle manufacturer, or service providers.
- **Reporting and Auditing:** Monitor user operations, generate reports mostly performed by the government, limited versions available for service providers and policy makers
- **Pricing and Rating:** Evaluate cloud services and determine prices, handle promotions and pricing rules based on a user's profile may be available for corporate accounts and will be possible if there is more than one integrators available approved by the government or the authorities.

Provisioning and Configuration

- **Rapid Provisioning:** Automatically deploying V2C systems based on the requested service / resources / capabilities for the vehicle owners, road side stations, municipality departments
- **Resource Changing:** Adjusting configuration/resource assignment for repairs, upgrades and joining new nodes into the V2C system, this will be like an ongoing maintenance program for all the devices, sensors, IoT equipment in the field

- **Monitoring and Reporting:** Discovering and monitoring virtual resources, monitoring cloud operations and events and generating performance reports performed by the service providers and not related with the end users of V2C system
- **Metering:** Providing a metering capability at some level of abstraction appropriate to the type of service, however according to the V2C system implementation model vehicle owners mostly pay the same amount of service fee depending on the service type, however for the vehicle manufacturers and the related bodies metering will be performed on the basis of data variance, number of vehicles, time to store the information, dynamic pricing calculations CPU usage or similar.
- **SLA Management:** Encompassing the SLA contract definition for legal issues basically between the sides like the government, manufacturer and the owners

Portability and Interoperability

This topic is completely a technical issue not specifically regarding to the V2C ecosystem and it will be similar to the general applications of cloud computing. However, in the case of multiple service providers and different operators approved to provide the same service for vehicle owners and vehicle manufacturers, this issue provides them flexibility so that they can move their data within the other integrators with low cost and minimal disruption. Another concern is the interoperability between the sides. For example, road side information devices have to be compatible with all car manufacturers common data submission where broadband network connection may not be available due to some reasons.

Communication Issues

Considering the fact that the number of wireless nodes and vehicles will increase more and more in the near future, the amount of data obtained with many types, dimensions and relations will be created, stored, and processed will also increase with the implementation of big data. Of course, successfully dealing with such a huge information flow of different types could only be possible with non- traditional approaches including working together in collaborative work and information processing, big data storage, and virtualization. Therefore, cloud computing computers, super computers and high performance computers that do the computing and optimization as distributed and parallel, should be included into the scenario even maintained by other groups, companies, countries in cloud computing.

Although there are many studies in the literature, it known that an ITS prepared with NGWN is still not complete without big data. Therefore, for the V2C ecosystem model, an idea-based model that links vehicle telematics to the cloud along with V2V communications facility is proposed and an early model based on IEEE 802.11x suite is employed. In the proposed model, the mobile data are transferred to create the big data for further research opportunities for car manufacturers, policy makers and with the concern of security issues.

As required by all ITS applications, NGWN should support cloud computing. There are different ITS applications in the literature where data processing and collecting will improve the service quality and performance. For instance, a smart speed change algorithms adapted to Global Packet Radio System (GPRS) has tested by (Servin, Boriboonsomsin, & Barth, 2006). A sensitivity analysis has performed in (Tielert et al., 2010) providing information like the distance from the traffic light and optimized gear choice provided via a road network improving the performance. In (Morris, Tran, Scora, Trivedi, &

Barth, 2012), average traffic fuel economy, carbon dioxide-monoxide and a few other emissions are guessed using a computer-vision-based methods. On the other hand in (Boriboonsomsin, Barth, Zhu, & Vu, 2012), an energetic/changing roadway network is proposed for eco-routing based on energy/emissions factors available. There are several other studies in the literature which merge several parts of ITS and NGWN. Interested readers could refer to (d'Orey & Ferreira, 2014) for a very described/explained and a more elaborative list of studies in this field of research with a complete and thorough discussion.

Big Data Concerns

There is a tremendous increase in the volume and detail of data captured by different sources, organizations, such as the rise of social media, devices forming the IoT, and multimedia. This provides an overwhelming flow of data in either structured or unstructured format (Hashem et al., 2015). Since the amount of data collected, generated, captured is colossal and requires rapid processing. Considering the fact that the data are mostly unstructured; come from different sources; and are big as compared to traditional database sizes such as ERP, MRP, CRM or sales automation system, it becomes unstable under classical relational database systems or old fashioned hierarchical database systems. These characteristics of the data are coined by the term "Big Data" and require new perspectives and approaches in solving the related problems. Big data receives a significant attention from academicians, engineers, finance and business companies, government institutions, and healthcare industry.

What makes data "big" is investigated from different perspectives in the literature. A technology research company, Gartner, started the definitions by volume, velocity and variety in 2001 not directly naming as big data (Laney, 2001). In the process, other characteristics such as veracity added by IBM scientists. Some other characteristics such as complexity, variability, and value have been appended to the list by various contributors (Assuncao, Calheiros, Bianchi, Netto, & Buyya, 2014).

Those characteristics of big data transform and adapt the big data storage and analysis processes to cloud computing with key technologies like no SQL database systems, map reduce algorithms and Hadoop. Big data provides users the ability to use commodity computing to process distributed queries across multiple datasets and return resultant sets in a timely manner (Andreolini, Colajanni, Pietri, & Tosi, 2015)

Cloud computing provides the underlying engine and service through the use of open source software for reliable, scalable, distributed computing framework namely Apache Hadoop. Hadoop is ready to distribute and operate on the cloud platform by using Hadoop Distributed File System (HDFS) storage. HDFS provides a class of distributed data-processing platforms from large data sources from the cloud and forming the big data in a distributed fault-tolerant database and processed through a programing model for large datasets with a parallel distributed algorithm in a cluster.

Data from Vehicles and Analysis of Big Vehicle Data in V2C Ecosystem

Total number of cars and vehicles has already reached and passed the one billion barrier in the previous years. Assuming the vehicles as mobile sensors for data generators with different aspects is not a new subject. The idea already has started with acquisition of road traffic data and it is a crucial and necessary activity for a traffic management information system as well as creating the big data for different purposes like planning, tracking, modelling (Messelodi et al., 2009). The term floating car data (FCD) refers to the data being collected (continuously) by a fleet of vehicles, nowadays it can be considered as a huge distributed network of sensors providing lots of data without the problem of energy management to the sensors. (Andreolini et al., 2015)

Sensors and VCI data include engine status, fuel consumption, geolocation, shifts and gears, service statistics, motor heat, tire pressure and exhaust greenhouse gas emissions such as carbon dioxide (CO_2), methane (CH_4), nitrous oxide (N_2O) emitted during combustion of fossil fuels. All kind of similar sets of data are planned to be collected in order to see the big picture and big data for the vehicles, traffic and social behaviors.

Analysis of the big vehicle data can be used for different purposes as well as classified by descriptive data analysis, predictive data analysis and prescriptive data analysis. Descriptive analytics from vehicles uses historical vehicle data to identify and set the patterns, trends, statistics and create decision making reports for the future namely modelling past behavior for future. Predictive vehicle data analytics attempts to predict the future by using the past and current data dynamically and serve for short term decisions. Prescriptive data analysis of vehicle data helps decision makers in decisions by determining actions and assessing their impact regarding policies, legal infrastructures, social and political aspects as well as business models, requirements, and constraints for companies.

Main Characteristics of Vehicle Big Data (Multi-V Model) in V2C Ecosystem

Volume

Volume is one of the key characteristics of vehicle big data since there are millions of cars, intelligent devices, sensors on the transportation systems that are active all over the world at any time anywhere. So the volume of the V2C ecosystem data, unremittingly expand each day from all sources around the world roads.

Variety

Variety refers to the different types of data collected via different vehicle models, sensors, and devices. Dimensions are vehicle type, fuel type, brand, origin of the fuel, national marker of the fuel, driving profiles, driver profiles and demographics, geolocations, distance to the road side stations, gear information, taxing information, road crowding ratio, nearest vehicles information and communication. These examples will be improved, classified, segmented and increased depending on the policies, requirements and promises of the governments for the reduction of emissions.

Velocity

Velocity refers to the speed of data transfer depending on the variety of the data in vehicle big data. The flow rate of the data mostly stable and constant during the daytime traffic and operation. However under special conditions depending on the extreme weather conditions, congestions, unexpected traffic jams due to accidents, dynamic tariff management and social events will change the data flow rate to the system.

Value

Value is the most important aspect of vehicle big data; since it can be used to improve human life quality by using the traffic management. Vehicle manufacturers can analyze the data to produce more custom and flexible designs improved for local performance. Policy makers and government use the data for carbon taxes, decreasing the environmental pollutions, reaching the targets for the scenarios.

Veracity

Quality of the data obtained from sensors in vehicle big data. This characteristics mostly depends on the technology of the sensors and their calibration frequencies. There will be plenty of implementation problems in this topic, which include sensor hardware, software, and sensing technology issues. For example in order to monitor the emission from the exhaust systems special sensors are needed in order to monitor continuously since, emission sensor needs to be bypass clean air to clean the hardware and nozzles otherwise they will totally become unusable. Moreover, the quality, the calibration, and the certification of the sensors are some other critical issues.

Complexity

Since the data obtained come from different manufacturers, sensors, and sources normalization and collaboration of data add another dimension of complexity to the problem.

Data Management, Privacy, and Security Issues

Two of the major concerns about the cloud computing are security and privacy (Wei et al., 2014; Kshetri, 2013a). There are also legal aspects of it such as who the owners of data should be if the data are hosted and processed on hardware that is provided by another party as a part of service (Kemp, 2014).

Also the value of the data to be collected from the vehicles is priceless. Combined with customer experience, service and maintenance data, real fuel consumption and economy data are crucial and strategic since there is a huge competition between the vehicle manufacturers. Similar concerns have been addressed already in the literature like gathering medical records (Lin, Dou, Zhou, & Liu, 2011) and storing that medical data (Yang, Li, & Niu, 2015). Driven by these concerns, improvements in the big data architecture focusing on increasing security have already been addressed and solved in the Hadoop architecture (Zhao et al., 2014; Kshetri, 2013b). An improved architecture by using a multi stage hybrid cloud structure will be proposed as a part of future work. It is clear that all parts, modules, and aspects of the system should be contemplated in terms of security and privacy. A direct consequence of such a strategy implies that even the governments who will control the overall of the system should not have a free and unlimited access to all the data in the system and cloud. There are some trade secrets that will not be revealed to the public or government unless declared by the laws and regulations. Similar privacy and the anonymity of the data parts are required to protect all the users of the ecosystem to some extent.

APPLICATIONS IN V2C ECOSYSTEM WITH BIG DATA

The transportation related emission as defined in the earlier sections of the chapter is nearly one third of the emissions related with fossil fuel based energy production. V2C ecosystem keeps track of the vehicle related emissions information combined with improved details data which can be obtained from the vehicle. Extra sensors and modifications will be mounted on the suitable locations depending on the responsibility of the V2C ecosystem member. For example commercial tracks may provide the information about the origin of transported good type, required transportation temperature if it belongs to cold chain distribution and so forth. As can be inferred, there is a direct connection between these applications and the sustainable environment. The main areas for sustainable environment can be listed as follows:

Active 7/24 Emission Control

As mentioned before, emission sensors attached to the exhaust system that track and record the real time emissions of the vehicle on different road conditions, speed, gear, torque, weather conditions, and even the driving patterns of drivers like accelerated driving, forcing the engine to up to the inefficient RPMs. Obviously, optimization depending on the analysis of the big data may yield the optimum transportation pattern for each driver, truck, and good type transported. Using a real-time, improved decision supported system with information panels and possible auto-gearing system, optimum engine performance and low carbon emission can be reached for V2C system as well.

Fuel and Carbon Cost Control

Since the quality and octane levels of the fuels are different for different countries and vary from the origin of the product, refinery and seller station, V2C system keeps track of all the information related and feeds the big data environment. Then, by analyzing the big data possible outcomes could be obtained such as the quality and engine –vehicle driver capability with which type of gasoline, diesel, kerosene, fuel oil, LPG.

Carbon Tax, Carbon Footprint, and Social Cost of Carbon Calculations for International Transportation

In order to reduce the emission, one of the powerful actors is using carbon taxes based on the real time calculation of the carbon footprint affiliated with the trips. These taxes will be used to regulate the usage of fossil fuels, optimize the emissions related especially to international transportation. Since the transport is global; it enables economic growth and job creation as well as it requires strong international cooperation and a side effect of generating emission based on the transportation of goods between countries. The big data analysis stores information about the following transportation mods wherever available:

- Land transportation,
- Sea transportation,
- River transportation,

- Rail transportation,
- Air transportation.

For each mode, the following parameters will be considered with Map Reduce algorithms

- The total weight of the freight;
- Nature of the freight, such as fresh produce, chemicals, etc.
- The distance of the embarking/arrival points to points of origin and destination;
- Restrictions on transportation options, if any;
- Cost per ton, volume, etc.;
- Approximate carbon emission levels;
- Any other appropriate parameter.

V2C ecosystem then optimizes the following variables in order:

- Total time of the freight journey;
- Routes with minimum traffic congestion and avoiding major cities, at least minimizing travel within major city boundaries;
- Minimizing total CO_2 emissions;
- Minimizing the cost of freight movement;
- Minimizing the customs and country boundaries crossings.

Traffic Management

A real time integrated V2I, V2C and V2V system collects and stores the information about the movements of the vehicles. And then the obtained big data can be analyzed with Map Reduce to extract more meaningful data that will be clustered, segmented and can be used in linear programming, dynamic programming, metaheuristic algorithms, machine learning, and artificial intelligence algorithms. For example supervised learning can be used for learning the road and path usage levels depending on the time and the weekday so a dynamic routing with tariffs, retiming of traffic lights can be performed to increase the flow rate of the traffic.

FUTURE RESEARCH DIRECTIONS

V2C Ecosystem and big data analysis will become more important even after the real data collected from the systems since it will create an immense amount of data environment for the researches. The future research of the authors will deal with the security concerns, stable operation, and data mining from the big data for policy makers. Also necessary technology developments as hardware like integrated data collecting sensors into transportation heavy-duty vehicles and an expert software system architecture for tracking and managing the progress have to be improved as a part of IoT devices and sensors.

CONCLUSION

This chapter aims to reach the conclusion that green transportation, sustainable environment, and energy and traffic management aspect of the problem all intersect with reducing the emissions and greenhouse gases. Main sources of greenhouse gases like carbon dioxide (CO_2), methane (CH_4), nitrous oxide (N_2O) emitted during combustion of fossil fuels are due majority to electricity production and transportation and minority percentage to industry, heating, agriculture. In order to tackle the problem, first it should be quantified properly so that a proper strategy is devised accordingly. In this regard, carbon footprint is a new way of describing the direct and indirect effects of all kinds of combustion.

The objectives presented in this chapter can be reached by the theoretical research for legal infrastructure, information and data about all the dimensions of transportation and also technology development both as hardware and software for transportation modeling, planning, supervision, evaluation, tracking, and optimization within the Vehicle to Cloud Ecosystem and big data architecture.

This chapter explains the possible outcomes of V2C ecosystem to reduce the emissions and carbon footprint by creating a roadmap for policy makers and governments by a model of social cost of carbon (SCC), carbon cost, and carbon taxes.

REFERENCES

Andreolini, M., Colajanni, M., Pietri, M., & Tosi, S. (2015). Adaptive, scalable and reliable monitoring of big data on clouds. *Journal of Parallel and Distributed Computing*, (0). doi:10.1016/j.jpdc.2014.08.007

Assuncao, M. D., Calheiros, R. N., Bianchi, S., Netto, M. A. S., & Buyya, R. (2014). Big Data computing and clouds: Trends and future directions. *Journal of Parallel and Distributed Computing*, (0). doi:10.1016/j.jpdc.2014.08.003

Birol, F. (2008). *World Energy Outlook 2008*. Academic Press.

Bonomi, F., Milito, R., Natarajan, P., & Zhu, J. (2014). Fog computing: A platform for internet of things and analytics. In *Big Data and Internet of Things: A Roadmap for Smart Environments* (pp. 169–186). Springer. doi:10.1007/978-3-319-05029-4_7

Bonomi, F., Milito, R., Zhu, J., & Addepalli, S. (2012). Fog computing and its role in the internet of things.*Proceedings of the first edition of the MCC workshop on Mobile cloud computing* (pp. 13-16) ACM. doi:10.1145/2342509.2342513

Boriboonsomsin, K., Barth, M. J., Zhu, W., & Vu, A. (2012). Eco-routing navigation system based on multisource historical and real-time traffic information. *Intelligent Transportation Systems IEEE Transactions on, 13*(4), 1694–1704.

Boyaci, A., Ozpinar, A., Ozturk, E., & Yarkan, S. (2015). EV2C: Extended Vehicle-to-Cloud Model and Conceptual Implementation for Big Data.*IEEE Sixth International Conference on Modeling, Simulation and Applied Optimization (ICMSAO'15)*.

CSIRO. (2015). *Commonwealth Scientific and Industrial Research Organisation*. CSIRO.

d'Orey, P. M., & Ferreira, M. (2014). ITS for sustainable mobility: A survey on applications and impact assessment tools. *Intelligent Transportation Systems. IEEE Transactions on, 15*(2), 477–493.

Hashem, I. A. T., Yaqoob, I., Anuar, N. B., Mokhtar, S., Gani, A., & Ullah Khan, S. (2015). The rise of "big data" on cloud computing: Review and open research issues. *Information Systems, 47*(0), 98–115. doi:10.1016/j.is.2014.07.006

IEA. (2014). *CO_2 Emissions from Fuel Combustion Highlights Organization for Economic Cooperation.* IEA.

Kemp, R. (2014). Legal aspects of managing Big Data. *Computer Law & Security Report, 30*(5), 482–491. doi:10.1016/j.clsr.2014.07.006

Kshetri, N. (2013). Privacy and security issues in cloud computing: The role of institutions and institutional evolution. *Telecommunications Policy, 37*(4-5), 372-386. doi:10.1016/j.telpol.2012.04.011

Laney, D. (2001). *3D data management: Controlling data volume, velocity and variety*. META Group Research Note, 6.

Lin, W., Dou, W., Zhou, Z., & Liu, C. (n.d.). A cloud-based framework for Home-diagnosis service over big medical data. *Journal of Systems and Software*. doi:10.1016/j.jss.2014.05.068

Liu, F., Tong, J., Mao, J., Bohn, R., Messina, J., Badger, L. et al. (2011). *NIST cloud computing reference architecture*. NIST special publication, 500, 292.

Maslow, A. H. (1943). A theory of human motivation. *Psychological Review, 50*(4), 370–396. doi:10.1037/h0054346

Mell, P., & Grance, T. (2011). *The NIST definition of cloud computing*. Retrieved from Computer Security Division, Information Technology Laboratory, National Institute of Standards and Technology Gaithersburg. doi:10.6028/NIST.SP.800-145

Messelodi, S., Modena, C. M., Zanin, M., De Natale, F. G. B., Granelli, F., Betterle, E., & Guarise, A. (2009). Intelligent extended floating car data collection. *Expert Systems with Applications, 36*(3, Part 1), 4213–4227. doi:10.1016/j.eswa.2008.04.008

Moore, G. E. (1998). Cramming more components onto integrated circuits. *Proceedings of the IEEE, 86*(1), 82–85. doi:10.1109/JPROC.1998.658762

Morris, B. T., Tran, C., Scora, G., Trivedi, M. M., & Barth, M. J. (2012). Real-time video-based traffic measurement and visualization system for energy/emissions. *Intelligent Transportation Systems IEEE Transactions on, 13*(4), 1667–1678.

Parry, M. L. (2007). Climate Change 2007: impacts, adaptation and vulnerability: contribution of Working Group II to the fourth assessment report of the Intergovernmental Panel on Climate Change (4th ed.). Cambridge University Press.

Schaller, R. R. (1997). Moore's law: past, present and future. *Spectrum, IEEE, 34*(6), 52-59. Retrieved from IEEE.

Servin, O., Boriboonsomsin, K., & Barth, M. (2006). An energy and emissions impact evaluation of intelligent speed adaptation. *Intelligent Transportation Systems Conference* (pp. 1257-1262) IEEE. doi:10.1109/ITSC.2006.1707395

Tielert, T., Killat, M., Hartenstein, H., Luz, R., Hausberger, S., & Benz, T. (2010). The impact of traffic-light-to-vehicle communication on fuel consumption and emissions. *Internet of Things, 2010*, 1–8.

Wei, L., Zhu, H., Cao, Z., Dong, X., Jia, W., & Chen, Y. (2014). Security and privacy for storage and computation in cloud computing. *Information Sciences, 258*(0), 371–386. doi:10.1016/j.ins.2013.04.028

Yang, J. J., Li, J. Q., & Niu, Y. (2015). A hybrid solution for privacy preserving medical data sharing in the cloud environment. *Future Generation Computer Systems, 43-44*, 74-86. doi:10.1016/j.future.2014.06.004

Zhao, J., Wang, L., Tao, J., Chen, J., Sun, W., Ranjan, R., & Georgakopoulos, D. et al. (2014). A security framework in G-Hadoop for big data computing across distributed Cloud data centres. *Journal of Computer and System Sciences, 80*(5), 994–1007. doi:10.1016/j.jcss.2014.02.006

KEY TERMS AND DEFINITIONS

Cloud Computing: A model for accessing information technology solutions over ubiquitous networks and consuming them as a service and on the basis of pay as you use.

Cyber-Physical Systems: CPS are information networks contained/made up of sensors and other technologies deeply set within/surrounded by and part of physical objects and linked via wired and wireless networks.

Hadoop: An open-source software framework able to analyze and process very large data sets in distributed storages known as Apache Hadoop.

Internet of Things: The network of physical objects or "things" embedded with electronics, software, sensors, and connectivity to enable objects to exchange data with the manufacturer, operator and/or other connected devices based on standards.

Map Reduce: A parallel and distributed programming model for analyzing the big data.

Next Generation Wireless Networks: Future wireless network technologies with faster and wider range like 4G,5G, LTE, 802.11p.

NoSQL Database: A database structure that provides mass storage and querying of data without using relational database structured query languages.

Ubiquitous Computing: computing can happen using all kind of internet connection, operating systems, mobile devices, sensors, microprocessors and IoT.

Vehicle to Cloud: A model of information and data transfer from vehicles to the cloud computing.

Chapter 13
Point Cloud Manager:
Applications of a Middleware for Managing Huge Point Clouds

Omar A. Mures
University of A Coruña, Spain

Emilio J. Padrón
University of A Coruña, Spain

Alberto Jaspe
CRS4, Italy

Juan R. Rabuñal
University of A Coruña, Spain

ABSTRACT

Recent advances in acquisition technologies, such as LIDAR and photogrammetry, have brought back to popularity 3D point clouds in a lot of fields of application of Computer Graphics: Civil Engineering, Architecture, Topography, etc. These acquisition systems are producing an unprecedented amount of geometric data with additional attached information, resulting in huge datasets whose processing and storage requirements exceed usual approaches, presenting new challenges that can be addressed from a Big Data perspective by applying High Performance Computing and Computer Graphics techniques. This chapter presents a series of applications built on top of Point Cloud Manager (PCM), a middleware that provides an abstraction for point clouds with arbitrary attached data and makes it easy to perform out-of-core operations on them on commodity CPUs and GPUs. Hence, different kinds of real world applications are tackled, showing both real-time and offline examples, and render-oriented and computation-related operations as well.

INTRODUCTION

Presently, acquisition technologies such as LIDAR (Laser Imaging Detection and Ranging) (Van Genderen, 2011) have seen an unprecedented amount of advancements in terms of the quality and precision of the acquisition hardware. These devices measure distance by using a laser to illuminate a target and then analyzing the reflected light. This distance information is combined with different data obtained from other techniques such as photogrammetry, radiometry, etc. These measurements are repeated for all surfaces of the target reachable by the laser scanner, resulting in a set of points with information about

DOI: 10.4018/978-1-5225-0182-4.ch013

their position, color, reflectivity, etc. This acquisition procedure leads to high precision georeferenced 3D scans of the real world with an exceptional amount of data, sometimes exceeding billions of points. The processing and visualization of these datasets on commodity systems present several challenges that can be addressed from a Big Data perspective by applying High Performance Computing and Computer Graphics techniques (Yuan, 2012).

In order to manage these huge point clouds and perform operations seamlessly on them, we have developed a middleware we have named Point Cloud Manager (PCM) (Jaspe, 2012) (Mures, 2014a). This software package (Mures, Jaspe, Padrón, & Rabuñal, 2013) comprises a multiplatform library and a set of tools around it that allows the management of massive point clouds with arbitrary attached data on commodity hardware. The library provides an abstraction for an arbitrarily large point cloud stored in secondary memory (HDD, SSD, NFS...), exposing a simple and clear API to get access to the dataset in RAM or VRAM and perform out-of-core operations on CPU or GPU. The two main pillars behind PCM are a multiresolution spatial structure and a hierarchy of software caches as can be seen in Figure 1.

Given the spatial nature of the point clouds datasets, the multiresolution structure used in PCM is strongly inspired in the space subdivision techniques usually applied in 3D computer graphics. This structure is exploited by PCM to provide interactive access to the dataset when needed, for example for visualization, or an iterative computation based on the multiresolution levels, that is, converging towards a solution by traversing the multiresolution structure with a certain threshold.

Figure 1. System overview of PCM

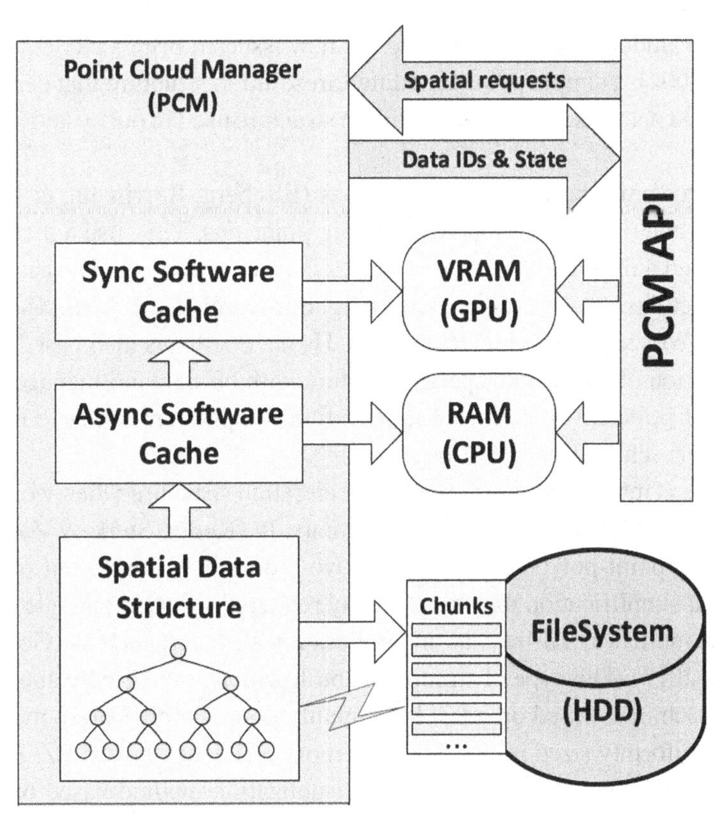

A hierarchy of two software caches is used for the transparent and efficient out-of-core access to the dataset, a synchronous software cache in VRAM to exploit GPGPU capabilities or simply perform advanced point-based rendering, and an asynchronous one in RAM to provide multi-thread support for CPU(s). Thus, chunks of 3D point data are transferred when needed, as a response to the high level API calls.

Hence, from low-level memory management to conversion and visualization of the point clouds, PCM makes out-of-core point cloud operations easier and more efficient for the programmer. The usage of this framework allows us to use datasets with unprecedented precision, since it is not necessary to decimate clouds before processing them. This means that we can perform operations taking advantage of the high precision of the scanners, sometimes even reaching micrometer precision. This can be especially relevant in fields such as civil engineering, topography or architecture, where applications are usually forced to decimate huge point clouds to be able to manage them and apply certain algorithms.

This article shows in a didactic manner the application of the aforementioned techniques to real world case studies.

BACKGROUND AND RELATED WORK

The first point-based rendering techniques appeared long ago (Levoy & Whitted, 1985), when datasets were small and the main research effort was devoted to displaying points with the highest quality possible. As years passed, the acquisition hardware improved greatly, leading to datasets with millions of points, and causing research to shift towards achieving not only the best possible rendering results, but also dealing with huge amounts of point data and the new issues it brings along. An example of this is (Gobbetti & Marton, 2004), a simple point-based multiresolution structure that deals with the problems associated with big point datasets. The multiresolution structure used in our system was strongly inspired by this important work.

Novel approaches for point-based renderers such as (Elseberg, Borrmann, & Nüchter, 2013) focus on memory efficiency and out-of-core rendering of big point sets. They use a memory efficient octree that uses fixed depth and a minimum number of points in its construction. The acceleration structure is employed for frustum culling, ray casting, nearest neighbor search and RANSAC (for plane detection). Another recent work (Wenzel, Rothermel, Fritsch, & Haala, 2014b) is also based on an octree, in this case allowing the creation of a dynamic spatial structure with on-demand management of memory for loading and writing of points. This proposal is tested with a photogrammetric filtering algorithm in (Wenzel, Rothermel, Fritsch, & Haala, 2014a).

Although the octree is maybe the most popular acceleration structure when working with point sets, other spatial structures have also been used over the years. In (Kuder, Šterk, & Žalik, 2013) a quadtree is used to render hybrid point-polygon models. This work does not address out-of-core rendering, but performs a point cloud simplification that is eventually rendered by using triangle meshes and textures. Other approaches use multi-way kd-trees as an acceleration structure such as (Goswami, Erol, Mukhi, Pajarola, & Gobbetti, 2013). This type of structure is built with an out-of-core approach and applying a multiresolution approach. It is based on a fast high quality point simplification method, which leads to a balanced tree with uniformly sized nodes. Since memory efficiency is key, LZO compression is used to minimize the memory footprint and an efficient visualization method based on a rendering budget is used to display the points. This system is also capable of performing occlusion culling and back-face culling, which will aid when dealing with huge datasets.

None of the above approaches propose a general-purpose out-of-core multiresolution middleware like PCM. PCM's out-of-core kd-tree has the main advantage of having dynamic logarithmic depth and a multiresolution approach that will yield benefits when either visualizing the clouds or computing on it. PCM pushes the boundaries of out-of-core point rendering even in low-end hardware, being able to work with really huge datasets (more than 10 K Million points), increasing in an order of magnitude the number of points tested in other approaches. All this exposing an interface oriented to the creation of new out-of-core point cloud algorithms in an almost transparent way for the user/programmer.

MAIN FOCUS OF THE ARTICLE

This article focuses on showcasing how the above mentioned framework can be used to perform arbitrary operations on massive point clouds, showing different real world applications built using PCM, in both real-time and offline, render-oriented and computation-related operations as well. An insightful description about PCM, the design decisions, how the implemented software caches work and the API exposed to the programmers are the objectives of this chapter (Jaspe, Mures, Padrón, & Rabuñal, 2014). How to perform common types of point cloud filtering, processing, visualization and object detection using PCM will be shown. Employing PCM when working with huge point clouds will offer several advantages that will be outlined in the following sections.

Point Cloud Filtering and Processing

The first filter we have chosen is a statistical outlier filter, which is typically used to remove noise or registration errors. Removing these outliers is good to facilitate further calculations, such as normal or radius estimation. This example performs a statistical analysis of each point neighborhood, eliminating those points that meet a certain criteria. Using PCM to implement such a simple filter as this one is quite fast, since we do not have to worry about point cloud formats or implementing an acceleration structure for neighborhood queries. In PCM the clouds are divided in *chunks* that are subsets of points, which make dealing with these datasets easier for the programmer. The use of these artifacts not only helps the programmer, but will allow the writing of pseudocode very similar to the actual implementation of these algorithms using PCM in C++. For this purpose, we will start by computing the mean distance $\overline{D}$ to each point neighbor:

$$\overline{D} = \frac{\sum_j \left\| p_j - p \right\|}{k}, \forall p_j \in \mathcal{N}_k(p)$$

Being $\mathcal{N}_k(p)$ the neighbors of point p. Assuming that the resulting distribution will be Gaussian in nature, it will have a mean and a standard deviation. Points that have a mean distance that does not fall in an interval can be removed with confidence. This interval is given by the mean and standard deviation of all the global distances. The mean is calculated with the following equation:

$$\mu = \frac{\sum_j \overline{D_j}}{N}, \forall \overline{D_j} \in \mathcal{D}_N$$

Being $\mathcal{D}_N$ the mean distances to the neighbors of each point. The next equation is used in the calculation of the standard deviation:

$$\sigma = \sqrt{\frac{\sum_j (\overline{D_j - \mu})^2}{N}}, \overline{D}_j \in \mathcal{D}_N$$

Once these two values are known, we could use the following pseudocode to perform the filtration:

Algorithm 1. The Statistical Outlier Filtering Algorithm Using PCM

```
Initialize distances to 0
for each node of point cloud do
    Request point cloud chunk
    for each point of chunk do
       distances ← K mean distance to neighbors
    end for
    Free point cloud chunk
end for
for each distance of distances do
    sum ← sum + distance
    sumsquared ← sumsquared + distance * distance
end for
mean ← sum / N of points
variance ← (sumsquared - sum * sum / N of points) / (N of points - 1)
stddev ← sqrt(variance)
threshold ← mean + factor * stddev
for each node of point cloud do
    Request point cloud chunk
    for each point of chunk do
       if distance <= threshold then
            Store point
        else
            Discard point
        end if
    end for
    Free point cloud chunk
end for
```

The second filter we have chosen as an example of application is a voxel grid filter. Even though PCM can manage arbitrarily dense point clouds, as multiresolution layers are inherently being applied, we may need to obtain less precise clouds, generating new lightweight datasets from our huge clouds by down sampling them. This can be useful, if the datasets want to be used in other point cloud software that is not able to deal with these vast amounts of points. We have implemented a voxelized grid approach in conjunction with PCM to achieve this. This filter creates a 3D voxel grid from the cloud data, approximating all the points within each voxel by its centroid. This results in a less dense cloud depending on the filter parameters, and also in a more constant density in the point cloud, which is really important for certain visualization applications. PCM makes it easy to obtain an efficient implementation of this kind of filters. The first step to apply this filter is dividing the space in a set of 3D boxes (voxel grid). Once the points $\mathcal{V}_N$ that belong to a voxel are isolated, we can use the following equation to compute the centroid of the voxel:

$$C = \frac{\sum_j p_j}{N}, \forall p_j \in \mathcal{V}_N$$

Being p the position of the corresponding point. In the above equation, we could substitute position for color, normal or any other point attribute; to obtain the rest of the centroid data. The calculated centroid will be the down sampled point corresponding to the voxel in the filtered cloud. The following pseudocode shows how to implement this filter with PCM:

Algorithm 2. The Voxel Grid Filtering Algorithm Using PCM

```
Initialize indexes to 0
minbb ← minimum point coordinate * inverse voxel size
for each node of point cloud do
    Request point cloud chunk
    for each point of chunk docoord ← point coordinate
        indexes ← coord * inverse voxel size - minbb
    end for
    Free point cloud chunk
end for
Sort indexes
total ← number of different values in indexes
for each index of indexes do
    Request point cloud chunk
    Request point
    centroid ← point coordinate
    Free point cloud chunk
    points ← 0
    while index is equal do
        Request point cloud chunk
        Request point
```

```
        centroid ← centroid + point coordinate
        Free point cloud chunk
        points ← points + 1
    end while
    centroid ← centroid / points
    Store centroid
end for
```

Since a point does not possess volume or area, points are not directly useable in normal 3D applications. Because of this, another common necessity when trying to obtain a high quality visualization of a point cloud, is the estimation of the point radius. This is another typical preprocessing step performed in a point cloud. This can be used by the most advanced point-rendering techniques, to obtain a higher quality visualization. This computation could be carried out applying a naive approach, but the massive size of the clouds makes it difficult to perform this computation in a reasonable amount of time. By performing this calculation using PCM, a dramatic reduction in both the computation time and the amount of work needed to implement this operation is achieved. With this example, we also showcase the parallel opportunities when using PCM, as we use a GPU kernel to achieve the desired result. In order to estimate the point radii, its k-nearest neighbors $\mathcal{N}_k(p)$ must be obtained first, this operation can be performed using PCM. Next, a watertight surface is desirable, that is a surface bounding a closed solid; or even better a closed manifold. This should be kept in mind when the point radii are estimated. When the point normal is available, the following equation will be used:

$$r = max_j \quad (p_j - p) - n^T(p_j - p)n \ , \forall p_j \in \mathcal{N}_k(p)$$

Being p_j the neighbor position and n the point normal. If the point normal is not available, we could use the next equation:

$$r = max_j \quad p_j - p \ , \forall p_j \in \mathcal{N}_k(p)$$

Having these two equations in mind, the following algorithm can be used in conjunction with PCM to perform this calculation using a GPU:

Algorithm 3. The Radii Estimation Algorithm Using PCM

```
for each node of point cloud do
    Request point cloud chunk
    for each point of chunk do
        coord ← point coordinate
        Request point cloud neighboring chunks to GPU cache (VBOs)
        for each VBO of VBOs do
            Make VBO available in OpenCL
            Make coord available in OpenCL
```

```
            Launch kernel sorting by distances to neighbors in VBO
            k-neighbors ← read buffer with results
            Radius ← biggest distance to k-neighbors
        end for
    end for
    Set chunk write flag
    Free point cloud chunk
end for
```

Point Cloud Rendering

The first approaches to point rendering like (Zwicker, Pfister, Van Baar, & Gross, 2001) were CPU based, this was clearly not the right approach for real-time point rendering. To increase performance, the massively parallel computing power of GPUs should be taken advantage of. In a similar fashion to how triangle meshes are rendered nowadays, we will offload rendering to the graphics hardware freeing the CPU to perform other tasks. This will provide much higher performance than a CPU based solution.

Obviously, having at one's disposal a visualization tool to manage even the hugest point clouds in real-time is ideal in these areas, so an out-of-core visualizer implementing some of the most advanced point-based rendering techniques has been built using PCM (Mures, 2014). The software caches transparently load the points in VRAM when needed; exploiting again the inherent multiresolution features in PCM, and OpenGL is used to get a quality render with interactive frame rates. This application is also useful as a GUI for applying other operations on the point clouds being managed. The next pseudocode will show how a basic visualizer can be implemented using the software caches available in PCM as can be seen in Figure 2:

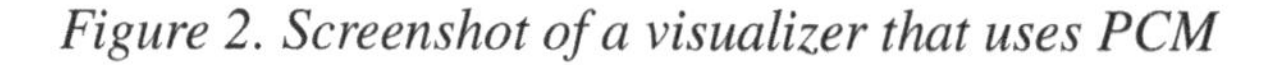
Figure 2. Screenshot of a visualizer that uses PCM

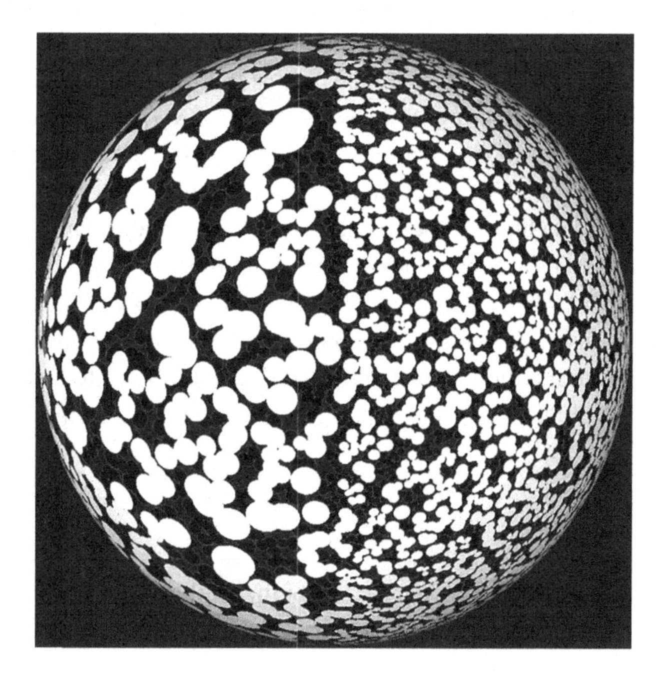

Algorithm 4. The Visualization Algorithm Using PCM

```
while render do
    mvp ← model view projection matrix
    Bind shader program
    for each cloud of point clouds do
        Pass shader arguments
        chunks ← Query multiresolution structure
        list ← Request chunks to GPU cache
        for each node of list do
            for each VBO of node do
                Bind VBO
                Set attribute buffer data
                Enable attribute buffer
                Draw points in VBO
                Disable attribute buffer
            end for
        end for
    end for
    Release shader program
    Swap buffers
end while
```

Architecture and Civil Engineering Applications

Civil engineering, architecture and related areas are nowadays an important target for point cloud applications and models. An example can be found in the building preservation and conservation field; where measuring and testing the correctness of a built structure might be needed. This could be easily achieved by coding a kernel on PCM to estimate the closest point-to-point or point-to-triangle distance, just disposing a 3D model of the structure obtained from the CAD plans and a point cloud dataset of the real structure, obtained from a LIDAR scanner, for example. When the minimum distance exceeds a given threshold there is a high possibility that we have encountered a defect, so these points are marked to alert the user about it. This technique could also be applied in industrial design for CAD based inspection, obtaining a point cloud of a manufactured part and then use a similar process to compare the CAD design with the real part. The out-of-core features in PCM allow us to take advantage of the full precision available in the dataset, avoiding the need to decimate even the biggest point clouds.

In order to achieve the aforementioned objective, it will be necessary to be able to calculate a point-to-point distance. This is easily achieved for points p_1 and p_2 with the following formula:

$$D_p = \left\| p_1 - p_2 \right\|$$

The point-to-triangle distance is a little harder to obtain. In this case, the minimum distance will be computed using the squared-distance function for any point in a triangle t to the point p.

$$D_t(u,v) = \left|t(u,v) - p\right|^2$$

For the following (u,v) values:

$$(u,v) \in S = \{(u,v) : u \in [0,1], v \in [0,1], u + v \le 1\}$$

The goal will be to minimize $D_t(u,v)$ over S. Knowing that D_t is a differentiable function, the minimum will occur either in the boundary of S or where the gradient $\Delta S = (0,0)$ (Eberly, 1999).

Taking all of this into account, PCM can now be used to compute the minimum point-to-point or point-to-triangle distances for two 3D models, a point cloud against a triangle mesh or another point cloud. The CPU version will be showcased since it is easier to understand, but it could also be implemented using a GPU.

Algorithm 5. The Minimum Distances Algorithm Using PCM

```
Initialize distances to 0
for each node of point cloud do
    Request point cloud chunk
    for each point of chunk do
        for each triangle of mesh do
            dist ← point-triangle distance
            if dist < distances then
               distances ← dist
            end if
        end for
    end for
    Free point cloud chunk
end for
```

Another useful application of PCM in the fields of architecture and civil engineering could be object detection in point clouds. By applying a RANSAC-like algorithm on top of PCM we can find planes, cylinders and spheres easily and quickly in massive point clouds. RANdom Sample Consensus is an iterative method to estimate parameters of a mathematical model from a set of observed points which can contain outliers. This is a non-deterministic algorithm, since we are not able to guarantee that it will produce a correct result. The probability of reaching a reasonable result will improve as the number of iterations increases. We showcase how this algorithm can be interactively used to detect the aforementioned primitives in point clouds. This can aid architects in the creation of CAD floor plans from point clouds, civil engineers in the documentation of existing structures, etc. For this purpose we will also demonstrate how to export the estimated primitives in a CAD friendly format. This might seem trivial at first, but since the estimated primitives are of parametric nature and some of them are not bounded, this is not an easy task. It is also useful for interactively removing objects in the point clouds, since we are able to perform primitive estimation in real-time.

To illustrate how this can be achieved using PCM, the use case of estimating a plane in a point cloud in real-time is chosen. The first step, is selecting a subset of points in the dataset, this can be done by the end user or randomly. Next, RANSAC is used to estimate the mathematical parameters of the plane. The basic assumption is that the data contains *inliers*, though it may contain noise and *outliers* (Figure 3). Outliers can appear because of errors or imprecise measurements, extreme values of noise, etc. RANSAC assumes that for a given set of inliers, there should exist a procedure that can estimate the unknown parameters of the plane model that will fit this data.

The essence of the basic RANSAC algorithm can be outlined in the following steps:

Step 1: Select randomly the minimum set of points to compute the model parameters.
Step 2: Solve for the parameters of the model (i.e. with a least squares method).
Step 3: Test how many points in the dataset fit the estimated model with a predefined tolerance ε .
Step 4: If the fraction of inliers over the total number of points is enough, then the mathematical model is re-estimated (since it was only estimated using the initial inliers).
Step 5: Finally, the model is evaluated by estimating the error against the inliers.

This procedure is repeated for a certain number of times, each time obtaining a new model which can be rejected if too few points are classified as inliers or a better model with its corresponding error measure.

Once the parameters of the plane are obtained, since it is infinite, it will need to be bounded. This is achieved calculating its intersection with the axis aligned bounding box (AABB) of the point cloud. This means that a common ray-plane intersection test has to be performed for each edge. The result of this process will be a polyline directly exportable to a CAD format. The point of intersection in the plane can be written as:

$$\hat{n} \cdot x = -p$$

This is called the Hessian normal form of a plane (Figure 4). For the ray, it can be written as:

$$x = x_0 + t\hat{v}$$

Figure 3. Result of RANSAC fitting of a line in a set of points that contain outliers and inliers

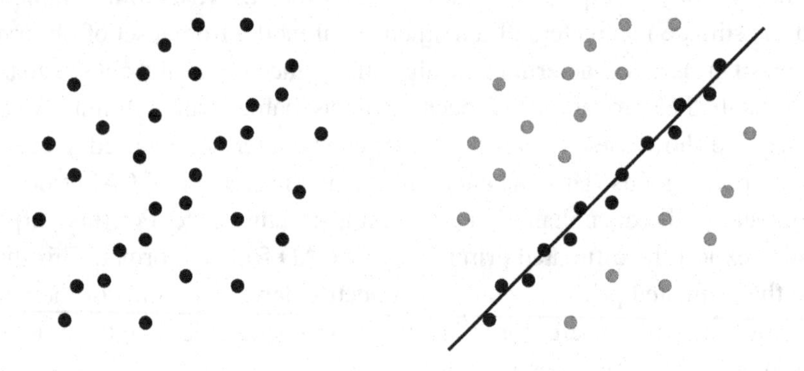

Figure 4. Hessian normal form of a plane

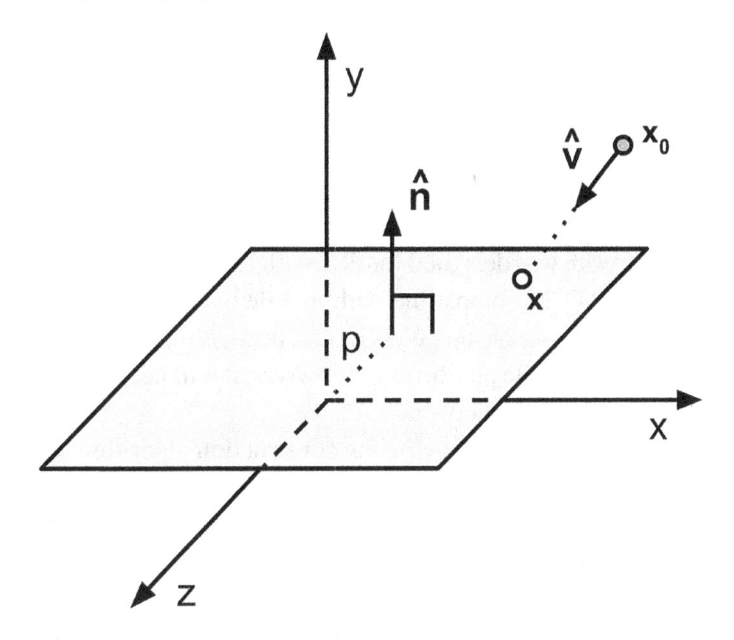

Being x_0 the origin of the ray, $\hat{v}$ the direction and t:

$$t = \frac{-(x_0 \cdot \hat{n} + p)}{\hat{v} \cdot \hat{n}}$$

Once all the intersection points have been calculated, they are tested to check if they fall inside the AABB. After this the vertices of the bounded plane are ready to be exported as a polyline. The pseudo-code necessary to implement this use case in PCM is showcased in the following code block.

Algorithm 6. The Plane Estimation Algorithm Using PCM

```
selectedpoint ← get user selected intersection point
for each node of neighborhood do
    Request point cloud chunk
    for each point of chunk do
        dist ← distance between point and selectedpoint
        if dist <= sampledistance then
            samples ← point
        end if
    end for
    Free point cloud chunk
end for
coefficients ← segment plane from samples
Color plane coefficients in GPU point data
```

```
intpoints ← Compute intersection of the plane with cloud AABB
polyline ← Sort intpoints
Write polyline to CAD compatible file
```

FUTURE RESEARCH DIRECTIONS

The current version of the software was designed for PCs with Linux/GNU, Windows or MacOS. Future research could focus on making PCM compatible with mobile operating systems (Android, iOS, etc.), or even better modern internet browsers using WebGL and decoupling it in a client-server approach. In order to be able to utilize PCM in mobile platforms or browsers, it will need point streaming capabilities, this will mean transferring clouds over a network.

Other future improvements could be improving the construction algorithm of the acceleration structure, so points are distributed in a better manner between levels. Alternative acceleration structures could also be explored, since the multiresolution structure is not the most optimal acceleration system for tasks not related to visualization.

But certainly, one of the most innovative lines of research in point based rendering, is using virtual reality headsets to visualize these datasets. It has incredible possibilities in the fields of architecture and civil engineering, since it provides professionals with new tools to interact with clients or among them with an unprecedented amount of detail and immersion.

CONCLUSION

In this article, several applications of the out-of-core point management framework PCM were shown. It was designed to deal with arbitrary size datasets; simplifying greatly programming tasks that involve point clouds. From point cloud processing to real-time visualization, PCM is of great help and frees the programmer from dealing with problems like point cloud formats, memory management, point cloud manipulation, acceleration structures, etc. Additionally, the library also exploits the full potential of both modern CPUs and GPUs, facilitating the use of parallel processing to reduce the computation time as much as possible.

Furthermore, having a system that is able to manage such a huge amount of data, will let the user take advantage of the full potential of datasets generated by cutting-edge 3D capture devices. These datasets present great opportunities for a wide range of fields, but these new types of 3D models present a great challenge because of the vast amounts of data they generate. Thanks to the techniques explained, researchers or professionals will be able to manage these massive point clouds transparently using the already mentioned framework.

ACKNOWLEDGMENT

This work is financed by the CDTI, Enmacosa and partially supported with FEDER funds. The project in which this work was developed is ToVIAS: Topographic Visualization, Interaction and Analysis System (IDI-20120575). This research has also received funding from the DIVA Marie Curie Action of the People programme of the EU FP7/2007- 2013/ Program under REA grant agreement 290227. This research has also received funding from the DIVA Marie Curie Action of the People programme of the EU FP7/2007-2013/ Program under REA grant agreement 290227.

REFERENCES

Eberly, D. (1999). Distance between point and triangle in 3D. *Magic Software.* Retrieved from http:// www. magic-software. com/Documentation/pt3tri3. pdf

Elseberg, J., Borrmann, D., & Nüchter, A. (2013). One billion points in the cloud–an octree for efficient processing of 3D laser scans. *ISPRS Journal of Photogrammetry and Remote Sensing*, *76*, 76–88. doi:10.1016/j.isprsjprs.2012.10.004

Gobbetti, E., & Marton, F. (2004). Layered point clouds: A simple and efficient multiresolution structure for distributing and rendering gigantic point-sampled models. *Computers & Graphics*, *28*(6), 815–826. doi:10.1016/j.cag.2004.08.010

Goswami, P., Erol, F., Mukhi, R., Pajarola, R., & Gobbetti, E. (2013). An efficient multi-resolution framework for high quality interactive rendering of massive point clouds using multi-way kd-trees. *The Visual Computer*, *29*(1), 69–83. doi:10.1007/s00371-012-0675-2

Jaspe, A., Mures, O. A., Padrón, E. J., & Rabuñal, J. R. (2014). *A Multiresolution System for Managing Massive Point Cloud Data Sets. Technical Report.* University of A Coruña.

Kuder, M., Šterk, M., & Žalik, B. (2013). Point-based rendering optimization with textured meshes for fast LiDAR visualization. *Computers & Geosciences*, *59*(0), 181–190. doi:10.1016/j.cageo.2013.05.012

Levoy, M., & Whitted, T. (1985). *The use of points as a display primitive.* University of North Carolina, Department of Computer Science.

Mures, O. A. (2014). *ToView point cloud visualizer.* Retrieved from https://youtu.be/cyeOUs0PyNw

Van Genderen, J. (2011). Airborne and terrestrial laser scanning. *International Journal of Digital Earth*, *4*(2), 183–184. doi:10.1080/17538947.2011.553487

Wenzel, K., Rothermel, M., Fritsch, D., & Haala, N. (2014a). Filtering of point clouds from photogrammetric surface reconstruction. *International Archives of the Photogrammetry. Remote Sensing and Spatial Information Sciences*, *1*, 615–620.

Wenzel, K., Rothermel, M., Fritsch, D., & Haala, N. (2014b). *An out-of-core octree for massive point cloud processing.* Paper presented at the Iqmulus 1st Workshop On Processing Large Geospatial Data.

Yuan, C. (2012). *High performance computing for massive LiDAR data processing with optimized GPU parallel programming.* The University of Texas at Dallas.

Zwicker, M., Pfister, H., Van Baar, J., & Gross, M. (2001). *Surface splatting.* Paper presented at the Proceedings of the 28th annual conference on Computer graphics and interactive techniques.

KEY TERMS AND DEFINITIONS

GPGPU: General-purpose computing on graphics processing units is the utilization of graphics processing units (GPU), which typically handles computer graphics workloads, to perform computation in applications traditionally handled by the central processing unit (CPU).

LiDAR: Remote sensing technology that measures distance to a target by illuminating it with a laser and analyzing the reflected light.

Multiresolution: A technique that allows you to break an image down into multiple levels (or layers) so that every zoom level has good resolution.

Out-of-Core: Type of algorithm that is designed to process data that is too large to fit into a computer's main memory at one time. These algorithms must be optimized to efficiently fetch and access data stored in slow secondary memory such as hard drives.

Photogrammetry: The science of making measurements from photographs, especially for recovering the exact positions of surface points.

Point Cloud: Set of vertices or points in a three-dimensional coordinate system. These vertices are usually positioned in 3D space and have a set of coordinates (x, y, z). These sets of points normally are representative of the external surface of an object.

Rendering: The process of generating an image or set of images from a 2D or 3D model, by means of computer software.

Chapter 14
Big Data Management in Financial Services

Javier Vidal-García
University of Valladolid, Spain

Marta Vidal
Complutense University of Madrid, Spain

ABSTRACT

Many organizations are beginning to feel frustrated by the limited progress of their companies with the application of new technologies to date. At the same time is convenient to remember that this is something that always happens when new technologies are introduced, companies must accept the challenge of self-assessment and measure the barriers that threaten to prevent them from reaching to get the maximum potential derived from big data and analytics In financial services, there are significant opportunities to obtain benefits by applying technologies and methodologies of big data and analytics. Regulatory pressure has forced many businesses, particularly in banking, to invest in areas such as risk management, compliance and operations. This has accelerated the trend toward enterprise data management.

INTRODUCTION

The combination of an impressive explosion of data and the rapid development of new technologies to store and process this information will transform the way companies manage their business. After an initial period in which big data was considered optional for most companies, their value is widely recognized today. Big data and analytics are becoming part of everyday business.

Organizations around the world have begun to exploit the opportunities that big data offers. However, progress has been very small in terms of value quantification to get to the analysis of structured and unstructured data together, to generate knowledge to support decision-making. The biggest advantage of big data and analytics is the value that is derived from the management of the data and transforming it into useful knowledge, the three challenges that are so often mentioned associated with big data are the following:

DOI: 10.4018/978-1-5225-0182-4.ch014

- **Volume**: Huge amount of data that cannot be handled by traditional management tools databases.
- **Variety**: Data from a wide variety of sources, both internal and external, and with different formats, both structured and unstructured.
- **Speed**: data change and evolve at a rapid rate, and business needs that require analysis and answers almost in real time.

Many companies have not yet developed the appropriate framework to generate this value. The projects, many of them still only proof of concept or pilot, are being developed as separate and individual rather than as part of a comprehensive plan at the level of the entire organization (Biesdorf, Court, & Willmott (2013)). Often, companies are even know what questions they need to raise, what are the business problems that require a response from the realm of big data and analytics (Turner, Shroeck, & Shockley (2013)). Similarly, they are still rare organizations that already have a global view of the barriers to get to maximize the value of their data, and include aspects such as the huge volume of data to manage, lack of capacity and skills in areas as analytics, or legal and regulatory issues type.

BACKGROUND

In financial services (banking and insurance), there are significant opportunities to obtain benefits by applying technologies and methodologies of big data and analytics. With the crisis of the financial sector in 2008, regulatory pressure has forced many businesses, particularly in banking, to invest in areas such as risk management, compliance and operations. This has accelerated the trend toward enterprise data management, which is a good starting point in adopting new and more advanced initiatives exploit them (Kruschwitz (2011)).

From the point of view of the opportunities perceived by the industry, the main application area of the big data and analytics provides advanced customer segmentation. The incorporation of new data sources to traditional segmentation allows obtaining a vision and a complete understanding of companies by the customer, which entails the definition of more value propositions tailored to different profiles of customers. This allows a tighter targeting, and it translates into greater efficiency and performance of commercial activities (Lambrecht & Tucker (2013)).

Customer loyalty is emerging as the second application of these techniques, especially relevant to insurance companies. After a deep crisis in the sector, which has led to heavy loss of confidence by customers, it is important to detect abandonment in advance (especially for high-value customers) and define efficient retention actions has become a priority for companies, in this sense big data and analytics can help improve this area.

A better management of multiple channels, so important in a context in which the new technologies made available to customers a greater number of improved communication channels and high capacity of transaction with businesses, and the definition of strategies of dynamic pricing by customer segment, in a context that is closer to real time, also appear in prominent positions when asked by the main areas of application of big data (McAfee, Brynjolfsson, Davenport, Patil, & Barton (2012)).

With respect to the benefits expected by financial institutions, there is a broad consensus in indicating support in complex processes of decision making as the first differential aspect. How is reviewed previously, the main departure point to denote the adoption of big data and analytics strategy should be identify issues of business that needed a response, this being the way to guarantee success in the generation of value of these initiatives.

The integration of data from internal and external sources to obtain "intelligence" in this combination of sources is for both banks and insurance companies a great advantage to obtain (Barney (1991)).

The combination of big data and analytics enables institutions to tap new sources of data to improve the quality of decision-making, enabling a data analysis and generation of information useful in time more real and providing a true differentiation, which translates into business outcomes, both by the increase of market efficiency and by increase in income.

big data is usually described in terms of volume, variety, speed and accuracy, and many organizations are currently facing each of these measures. Companies do not have the means, technological and human, to manage the huge growth in the volume and the variety of data (structured and unstructured, from internal and external sources). While it is recognized that converting data into information constitutes a major advantage, issues such as the concept of analytics in real time, veracity of the different data sources, or tools and technologies to use are, without doubt, barriers that slow down the implementation of projects of big data (Grossman & Siegel (2014)).

MAIN FOCUS OF THE CHAPTER

Benefit of Big Data for Financial Institutions

Financial institutions, historically expert users of data and analytics, are increasingly dependent on the data and information technology as the basis of an efficient operation, compliance and the growth and future profitability. This dependence of generalized data involves both risks and opportunities.

Beyond financial opportunity, the role of data and information is now integral to the entire company from the back office to marketing and sales, and from management of risks to the expectations of the managers and the regulators, and presents in many opportunities:

- **Efficiency**: It is clear that the balance sheets of the banks are being completely refurbished by the new regulatory initiatives that have followed in the wake of the financial crisis. In some cases, they are pushing return on the assets below the cost of capital. As a result, and with the objective of obtaining sustainable benefits and acceptable levels of organic capital, banks have no alternative but to become more agile, simple and profitable in their operations. As a key element of the processes and efficient workflows, technology has an important role to play.
- **Knowledge**: The domain of the enormous increase in the streaming data and to extract more value from the same is fundamental to the health of the organization and its success. The consequences are ex- tend to through the model of business operation. In customer service and sales, financial services companies are facing real challenges in the management and give meaning to the great amount of information available about the attitudes, behavior and the needs of the customers, their perspectives and objectives. Technologies such as the analysis of data in real time are becoming increasingly important as a basis for effective marketing, cross-selling.

- **Customer Experience**: The technologies of the information and data management are fundamental, such for the maintenance of relations established with clients who are increasingly demanding more continuous access to their financial services providers through mobile platforms. The integration of the different technologies and offer high-quality data are essential elements in creating agile and satisfactory communications with customers. Consumers do not want complexity, delays or in- consistencies. The companies that cannot have the necessary systems with their speed will overtaken by the innovative, new players and new technologies.
- **Risk Management**: The financial crisis and the new rules of broad scope have put to greater emphasis on the need for an efficient management of risks in all contexts: the reputational risk, operational and regulatory frameworks. Now companies are facing the dual challenge of improved risk management sustainable and the submission of evidence of its efficiency to interested parties: regulators, customers, and shareholders. Collect, analyze and present the relevant data is today essential for the creation and maintenance of strong relations with interest groups.
- **Operational Improvement**: The optimization of the day to day operations means maximizing the use of scarce resources and the guarantee that people have the right information to make optimal decisions at the right time. This requires accurate and consistent data, which can serve both to support the operational health of the company and meet internal and external requirements.

The new technologies are the way of the future and if this promise is adequately developed, will be achieved major improvements in the internal efficiency, external competitiveness and, perhaps most important, better relations with the customers. Enterprises that do not adopt these models and technologies will probably be out of business due to the competitive disadvantage (McGuire, Manyika, & Chui (2012)). In times of revolution as these, miss the development that will change the rules of the game will be equivalent to a suicide competitive. What we have seen with the organizations that were neglected with the emergence of the internet and which is likely to see it again with the emergence of a society based on data.

The universal importance of a good management of data and information through the business word places a huge importance to the capacity to collect, add and analyze the data to create a single view of the truth: a single complete information resource and with internal coherence that is able to meet all needs. Whether operations which are customer-facing, systems and internal procedures or external reports, the winners will be those who can collect data in a consistent manner to meet these multiple needs with greater efficiency.

The sources of data should be accurate, complete, traceable and transparent, so that regulators and the business can rely in the source data, and managers can be sure to take the right decisions.

The access and government of the data, which includes the assessment of the value and relevance of the data, has become a fundamental lever. In close relationship is the ability to synthesize data through the operational and financial information, and customers. This capability raises two important issues. The first are the necessary internal negotiations with the owners of the data and of the potential sources of information. The second question, perhaps even more important is the awareness that many areas of finance has not been exploited even data that already have access.

Most of the companies are only partially involved in this exercise and at present the scenario is even more complex by the amount of new data types. The organization must first define what needs and the metric leaders of these measures to manage the business and define its strategy. The company then must understand their own information and portfolio of data to align the application of new methods and technologies for a coordinated global strategy. This approach allows the company to address cross-cutting initiatives, avoiding the silos of information and facilitating the inclusion of new data types in a deliberately and organized that will align and will be compatible with a wider strategy.

Big data is also having an effect on the skills required for the resources of the department of finance, since the financial skill set is evolving. It is expected that the new employees have not only to be fluent with data and the experience with the tools needed to explore such data, but also social skills with the fn to contribute to streamline the organization. This includes a deeper understanding of the operational areas of the Organization. The future leaders of finance must have data-oriented skills, either at the level of strategic or operational. Some of the initiatives that are being pursued with big data currently require exclusively a skill set that is not concentrated in finance. The new profiles must be able to identify new opportunities in a more comprehensive manner within the organization and possess the skills to create consensus between the functions of the data unified collectively in support of strategic opportunities.

The challenge of big data and analytics, therefore, is not about collecting data but rather of the translation of data into knowledge and ideas that will help to build a better society and best companies. The social value of this current is at the same time something without precedent as inevitable.

A new generation is going to organize society in such a way that it is still barely conceivable. If we are able to properly deal with the facet of this more complex evolution, such as the issues of privacy, big data and analytics will not be perceived as a big brother, but as a big value.

The role of the CFO and the CIO will be essential to help define the overall strategy of an organization in this context of rapid development and guide investment decisions on the basis of a clear vision of the risks and benefits.

Main Challenges for Implementation of Big Data

The main barriers identified in the adoption of a strategy of big data in surveyed companies relate primarily to the technological capacities necessary. There is a perception in the industry that it is necessary to perform heavy investments in technology to be able to undertake such initiatives, something difficult to assume if you take into account the current budgetary constraints and the difficulty to estimate and quantify the return and profitability of these investments.

In a discipline so novel, the lack of knowledge and talent is also a serious problem for many companies, a fact that has been manifested in a special way in the insurance entities participating in the survey. It is necessary to count with data from scientists, experts in visualization, business analysts, professionals in the management of data and other specialists as experts in confidential data processing, and the development of these capabilities within the entities is complex in the short term (Varian (2014)).

In addition to these barriers, others such as the lack of a comprehensive approach in place of isolated initiatives and limited within the enterprise, difficulty to build the business case for these projects, the need to conform to the compliance on issues of data processing, and even the lack of knowledge on the part of the companies of what to do with all available data, are aspects that should be considered and resolved when you design and implement strategies for big data and analytics.

From the experience of financial companies, the way to address these challenges passes to follow different activities aimed at the generation of company value:

Companies should decide what is what they want to achieve with the data. Identify the business problems to solve, pose hypotheses and leverage the data and analytical tools to test or discard these hypotheses. It is recommended starting with data already existing in the company, with the aim of accelerating the achievement of results, thus generating confidence and credibility within the organization.

Define modes to measure the results. The success of the initiatives of big data and analytics are ultimately measured by its impact on profitability, through lower costs or, more frequently, by increasing revenues. Organizations should develop measures to quantify the specific impact of the efforts of big data. Decide what metrics are relevant will depend on the initiative implemented, and may include expenditure by the customer or the cost of capital. The development of these metrics will allow efforts to be concentrated on those areas where it generates greater value and allows the generation of results, which can be used in the construction of business cases to support future initiatives.

Generate knowledge from data. Transforming the data in a type of information that the organization can use. There are practical considerations to resolve, such as the storage of large volumes of data, how to check the quality and accuracy of the different sources and types of data, the analytical tools to employ or the assessment of whether the company has the skills and talents needed to perform these analyzes. The development of analytical skills must be carried out gradually and aligned with business priorities.

Prepare for the transformation. All changes and relevant in the organizations must start at the top management. They are the ones to lead the change and identify the internal talent, encouraging that most senior executives and the rest of the organization adopt the best systems, technologies and analytics for the company. To get the value of big data and analytics, it is necessary that all the strategic functions (financial management, technology department, marketing management, strategic management, etc.) work together and aligned, which is in many cases an important transformation that affects the entire organization.

Manage the risks. Minimize and mitigate risk, for example by adopting a more proactive attitude to aspects such as the privacy of the data or the cyber-security, with emphasis on the flexibility and adaptability and responsibility. The changing regulatory environment, ever more demanding, constitutes the most important risk of all.

And finally, it is important to define the plans of action that can be implemented in order to efficiently exploit and maximize the results obtained in these projects, with the identification of its impact on processes, technology and organization.

Smart Data

CAPTURE + STORE + PROCESS + MONETIZE = SMART DATA

The ability to extract valuable business information from massive amounts of data is becoming a competitive advantage in all sectors. To check this you only need to enter at Amazon and perceive as the web knows our tastes and offers us proactively articles that are more relevant to our consumer profile. And no one sells so many books and as profitably as Amazon.

The big data has been democratized because the cost of storage and processing of information has been greatly reduced. But the key is not to invest in technology but to convert the big data in smart data that will allow us to find business opportunities or reduce costs. This is not easy because the data quickly become obsolete and so valuable, that is to interpret trends to predict behavior, is not within the reach of everyone (Nickerson & Rogers (2014)).

If banks are able to acquire this skill to handle big data, this is going to be a game changer because they have more data than any other company in any sector on its own customers and put them in value is part of its defense against the competition with the ultimate goal of maintaining its historical position.

Banks are machines to capture and store valuable data about your customers, as: Any operation, of minimum entity, made by the customers pays a fee and has just recorded in the bank (payments with credit card, direct debit, transfers, payroll charges or income, etc.). And the Bank Regulation (AML, etc.) has favored the large-scale registration of data of its customers.

Banks cannot wait for the future to have these data and achieve this ability of processing (which at the moment is only incipient) because it is not something that is going to be able to buy with money so that we are in a race against time, but financial institutions can be ahead:

- **Relying on Suppliers of these Technologies**: Able to print a greater dynamism to take advantage of the use of structured and unstructured data to make reengineering of the traditional business (for example, credit scoring through crawl on social networks).
- **Encouraging the Collection of Data on the Behavior of their Clients**: For example, taking advantage of those who today are stored but are not used, buying data to external suppliers to enrich the internal information and even favoring the consumer will provide paying or spent money (as when Google creates free tools), which increasingly easier to achieve with a generation that is already accustomed to lose a certain level of privacy.

The future of financial institutions is not going to stand in a network of offices with ATMs or in a physical process but in the ability to give access to the bank utility in the right place at the right time, which will require the domain of the Real Time Analytics. Banks need to have intelligence in the system with respect to the next best offer/action, which requires matching appropriate offers with appropriate clients (Chen, Chiang, & Storey (2012)).

The great improvement in the banking automatic process is not going to be the incorporation of advanced technologies or interfaces, but to anticipate the needs of the customers. Big data is the oil of the twenty-first century.

The traditional intermediaries face the possible deconstruction of your business if they are not able to protect their own place in the value chain of purchase using technology and innovation. For example in a mobile payment the difference is going to give the context of that payment, that is to say that in the time of pay you report of alternative tenders, of your available balance, the form of payment most beneficial, etc.

The new value of the banking system is not to be simply a bank because when your customers what evaluate it will not set in their capital levels, its network of offices, their products or types of interest. In what is going to fix customers is in the capacity that has your bank to facilitate access, without friction, banking services when they need them and how much they can rely on him in the implementation.

Financial institutions must build a relationship with the digital consumer and thus achieve the customer engagement (Edelman, 2015). To achieve this, the customer must perceive the Bank as its customer advocate and this requires the bank to use the customer information to advise and to anticipate the needs of your lifestyle by providing access in the right place and at the right time to the best financial products.

The customer already has no tolerance to the small letter or communication confusing or misleading.

Client Advocacy → Client Advocacy → Increase in consumption of products of your brand +30%

In recent years, the customer has been felt more abandoned than ever, just at a time when required customization and reach this requires a change of technology and in the mentality of financial institutions.

This sense of abandonment would explain that the group of unbanked (clients that do not feel identified with the banking system) has grown, contrary to what it seems logical. And the group of people that feel highly identified has a high educational level and with purchasing power.

In recent years, it has frequent to listen presidents of banks to say that the best assets of the bank are its professionals. That is no longer going to remain so, the best asset is going to be the data of its customers and the craft human work is going to be replaced by algorithms so that now it is more convenient to invest in technology that in human resources. Even the management is not going to be largely intuition and will become large amounts of data.

The future is going to require a higher efficiency and operational excellence and banks will have to focus on their main fortresses having to establish partnerships for everything else. That is a philosophy of achieving more by doing less.

The client is a growing feeling that is unique and that does not belong to any segment and needs to perceive that the bank will treat him this way. Clients are a moving target and financial institutions should offer him value-added services and executables at the time. There are two aspects to consider in order to classify clients (Lambrecht & Skiera (2006)): The segmentation of the customers for their purchasing power is becoming less useful and is becoming increasingly useful the segmentation by their behavior (way of interacting with the bank, etc.).

However, it must be understood that it is not even good enough the segmentation of clients by their behavior because segment customers is a technique to simplify the messages when we do not have all the data from clients. Today this is no longer the case and there is a lot of data to customize offers to specific customers. The products are going to go in two opposite directions:

1. Products with no differentiation and super massive, pure commodity.
2. Highly customized products to the customer concerned.

The technology of today allows response to this approach that brings value to the customer and leads to the consolidation of a client-bank relationship.

Storage and Processing

One of the characteristics of the big data is that their volume beyond the capacities of any computer, by very powerful it may be. Problems arise for both storage and processing and later service. The only way to give answer is therefore split the problem so that you can take advantage of the power of multiple machines in whole, grouped in a cluster. This is the common feature of all the technologies big data (Mayer-Schönberger & Cukier, 2014, p. 6).

Google was one of the first companies that had to deal with a problem associated with a data volume excessive: how to perform a search of information that would lead to search among all the internet pages. By its size, the problem required new strategies. On the way, Google developed its own paradigm for the storage and processing of data: MapReduce. In 2004 the paradigm was made public in a famous article científco. Finally Doug Cutting created an open source version of MapReduce call Hadoop (subsequently has contributed in a significant way Yahoo!), which is without any doubt the key technology behind the big data.

Hadoop is a distributed system that runs on a collection of machines. Allows the storage of massive data through its distributed file system, which leverages the individual capacity of storage for each machine of a joint way. But it is not enough to store them. Also it has to be able to process such a large amount of information. To do this, Hadoop implements the distributed programming paradigm MapReduce, which processes the information, exploiting the processing capacity of each individual machine.

Hadoop is flexible, fault tolerant and scale horizontally, including more machines, more storage capacity and processing. It works on basic hardware and even heterogeneous. The processing of information is carried out by batch: Each lot receives files as input, processes the information and generates files as output. That is to say, Hadoop is not real-time.

However, Hadoop is tremendously powerful. It is the main responsible of the new and counter-intuitive rule of big data: reprocess it everything is more efficiently to update a single state with the information that is new.

Hadoop is the key tool for storing and processing large amounts of data. However, it does not solve the question of how we are to serve as the data once already processed. Hadoop nor is a real-time technology.

These tasks have been commonly performed by relational databases. But the big data leaves these databases back. The restrictions imposed by the relational model and the SQL does not work well in a distributed environment. As a result of this, there have emerged new systems of databases that relax the requirements of the relational model in order to scale. Or support a subset of operations SQL, or restricted are simple key/value stores. This is the reason why they have come to be called NoSQL: do not support SQL. Some examples of these databases are Mongo-DB, Redis, Cassandra, HBase or Amazon DynamoDB.

There are many different NoSQL databases, each with a different quality that makes it more appropriate for a problem that for another. But all of them have emerged from the need to have databases as to handle the flood of data that represents the big data.

Both Hadoop as the databases NoSQL work on groups of multiple machines, and depending on the load of each system will be necessary provision more or less hardware. At these levels, when you begin to speak of use ten, a hundred, or a thousand machines, the provision of hardware can be converted into a problem: first, it is a costly and difficult task, second, is very little hose: Makes lack a clear plan well in advance and responds very badly to demand peaks and valleys.

This is the reason for the utility of cloud computing services such as Amazon Web Services or Rackspace Cloud. Through them is very simple provisioning hardware, with a click of the mouse can be ordered, set up and start as many machines as necessary. Once that will be of utility, we shut them and thus dispense with the cost. These services make use of virtualization to be able to offer such flexibility.

Another advantage is that the cost of managing systems decreases, since part of these tasks is handled by cloud services.

In conclusion, cloud computing is the third element, which together with Hadoop and databases NoSQL allows you to extract added value of big data.

The Risks of Big Data

Certainly the techniques based on big data have a huge potential for improving the provision of financial services and the satisfaction of the customers. However, used indiscriminately and without the right objectives, may represent a danger. This section discusses some of these potential problems.

In the first place, if it is true that big data provides very useful tools in an environment of greater uncertainty, regulation and lack of consumer confidence in the financial sector, it is not less true that the transformation of a draft big data in a program of success is not guaranteed. These projects are at risk and if is not oriented properly, using evidence to indicate that this activity can be successful, can be converted into expensive exercises that are lost in a sea of data. It is evident that the accumulation of information has diminishing returns and to analyze data with redundant information cannot help to solve any problem. The data do not in themselves provide a competitive advantage to not be that the analysis is appropriate so it is very important to have a professional team of analytics that can remove appropriate conclusions from the data. It is also useful to make a cost-benefit study or an estimate of the ROI of a project of big data before moving from a pilot to overall implementation.

This task is not as simple as it might seem. And this is the second point. The existence of large amounts of data cannot make us forget the foundations of science statistics, the influence of the measurement errors or the caution against the use of spurious correlations. In addition to the technical knowledge you need to be willing to continuously analyze the predictive ability of the models and make adjustments as the system loses explanatory power. The experience of Google trends in the prediction of the expansion of the flu provides a signal of alert (Butler (2008)). The GFT (Global Flu Trends) worked dramatically in 2009 being able to predict the expansion of the flu with enough accuracy to a highly disaggregated level while the Center for Disease Control (CDC) took weeks to provide the same information. The procedure of the GFT is based mainly on the implementation of thousands of models to the Google search for related terms, at least theoretically, with concern for the flu. Several recent articles ((Butler (2013); Lazer, Kennedy, King, & Vespignani (2014)) show that the predictions of GFT were not as precise as from 2012 and in 2013 the estimate of Google was double the estimate of the CDC. A model that combines Google Flu trends, delays of the estimate of the CDC, delays in the error of GTF and seasonal variables per week has a much higher predictive power.

The third issue has to do with privacy in the use of the data (Hoffmann & Birnbrich (2012)). The cases of anonymous medical reports of officials of Massachusetts, the award of Netflix or the publication of a database of AOL searches have revealed that in many cases you can get re-identify individuals (Heffetz & Ligett (2014)). The speed with which new data are generated and special situations with the same implies that the data protection laws always be behind the reality. The issue is not simply the protection of the data but also the use of patterns from the analysis of the data you can generate situations questionable from the point of view of privacy, if a model can predict the likelihood of pregnancy of the client of a shopping center.

The new clauses of consent in interactions with internet service providers try to avoid these problems. However, since the right is speaks of the fallacy of the consent because the client gives their consent in the vast majority of cases without reading the conditions (Barker, D'Amato, & Sheridon (2008)). In addition the consent must be linked not only to the data but also to their use for a particular purpose for which the data were collected. However in big data the concept of reusing the data is a fundamental element: data that have been collected with a goal to time can find other use completely different to the original objective. Finally there is the question of the value of the data of the user. This is a controversial issue because if it is true that users access to the use of your data without receiving any direct compensation, in most of the things the efficiency gains achieved by the procedures of big data have an impact on the prices paid by the customers. The case of automobile insurance is a clear example.

In fourth place is the possibility that errors in the capture, merger or clean data generate negative consequences for citizens from the application of techniques of big data to specific problems. An example is the industry of generation of credit scores from big data captured in internet (Purcell (2013)). The National Consumer Law Center (2014) analyzed the available information by several agencies of the generation of credit scores from data on the internet. In the previous section is commented that the objective of the use of big data for the analysis of the credit quality of consumers is to overcome the problems that have families on which enterprises have traditionally made scoring of individuals (Equifax, TransUnion or Experian) have no information. The National Consumer Law Center (2014) has selected five companies of big data and obtained the reports on 15 volunteers for the study. The reports received had plenty of errors, inordinate estimates (double the real wage of applicant), incorrect address, multitude of missing information (including accounts in social networks, etc.) Certainly the data of the traditional business of generation of credit score of consumers are also very improvable. A study of 2013 of the Federal Trade Commission of the United States pointed out that 20 per cent of the credit reports from these companies contain errors and a 5 per cent of these errors resulted in a reduction of the credit score that prevented the customers get a credit or entailed pay a higher rate. The problem of the agencies that are based on big data is that customers have no way of knowing how it has calculated its credit score. There is no way to independently confirm the predictive ability of the algorithm used. In this way the consumer can end up being adversely affected by a credit score calculated on the basis of erroneous data although, unlike in the case of traditional agencies, it is more difficult to estimate whether this has affected their capacity to get credit.

The poor quality of some data used not only can have negative effects on the clients but also may violate any regulation. For example in the United States The Fair Credit Reporting Act (FCRA) requires that the rating agencies of consumers produce reports truthful and adjusted to protect the reputation and privacy of consumers. In addition consumers have the right to receive the free credit report if because of the same a consumer has been denied a request for credit (even if it is a credit card or a loyalty card of a trade). The use of big data can produce violations of the Equal Credit Oportunity Act (AUS) in the United States even if the predictive model does not include racial characteristics of individuals since many other variables are correlated with these and could lead to a breach implicit AUS. Many companies for the sale of data include since some time ago in the contracts a limitation of liability on the grounds that their data do not constitute a report on a consumer or can be used for establishing the eligibility of individuals for loans or insurance or for jobs or promotions. In any case the FTC indicates that if the reports are used for the granting of credits or the selection of staff then, with independence of the limitation of liability clause, you must respect the regulation.

The location of the applicants of credit (e.g. the postal code where is located the IP from where it updates a Facebook page or Twitter), or the credit quality of customers in establishments where the complainant of credit has recently purchased can also affect the credit score and again, its legality under certain regulations could be questioned.

Finally the scoring methods that use data primarily of internet in addition to use variables with a lot of noise and little signal is facing the possibility of manipulation. If the scoring depends on the friends you have on Facebook is not difficult to think of ways to increase the score simulating friends.

CONCLUSION

Big data generated ample opportunities to develop new business models and improve the performance of financial institutions, but also requires the redesign and upgrading of various aspects of the design of the organization.

As a minimum, the creation of an analytical capacity requires financial institutions to develop skills to create new analytical models based on big data, as well as skills for the use of these models in the execution of their day-to-day transactions. Obviously this requires not only an advanced IT infrastructure, but also an organizational culture and government to support different initiatives. However, to begin to exploit the benefits of big data is not strictly necessary to carry out such profound changes immediately. Organizations can develop their analytical capacity incrementally involving key personnel in the processes that support their effectiveness and analytical intelligence. These efforts can generate market results quickly, starting the transition of the company toward the goal of successfully implementing a strategy based on big data.

Big data and analytics have an enormous potential to change the business. The rapid technological advances and their availability are making it possible to process and analyze huge volumes of data multi-structured, who come from various sources (both internal and external) and that change at a high speed.

Although only a small percentage of companies in the financial sector have developed big data, it is time to begin to eliminate the barriers to the development of these initiatives, undertaking a profound process of training and transformation that must occur in a coordinated manner, from the corporate strategy and customers and with the ongoing support of the technology.

Companies in the financial sector should lead this revolution: continuously generating and acquiring new information already have rules for the treatment of data and the risk management and have the technological capabilities required to exploit big data and analytics and gain competitive advantage.

It is necessary for the companies to assume that this process of transformation should be addressed globally, although gradually, as companies should prioritize the needs of business and develop the relevant capacities, and should cover all areas of the business, and not just some of them. Only in this way can ensure the success of big data and analytics and the utilization of all the advantages and differentiation that can bring to businesses.

Big data is ready for take off. Those companies that are not able to resolve the strategic aspects, technological and risk associated and define a global approach, will be left behind.

REFERENCES

Barker, K. J., D'Amato, J., & Sheridon, P. (2008). Credit card fraud: Awareness and prevention. *Journal of Financial Crime*, *15*(4), 398–410. doi:10.1108/13590790810907236

Barney, J. (1991). Firm resources and sustained competitive advantage. *Journal of Management*, *17*(1), 99–120. doi:10.1177/014920639101700108

Butler, D. (2013). When Google got the flu wrong. *Nature*, *494*(7436), 155–156. doi:10.1038/494155a PMID:23407515

Chen, H., Chiang, R. H., & Storey, V. C. (2012). Business intelligence and analytics: From big data to big impact. *Management Information Systems Quarterly*, *36*, 1165–1188.

Edelman, B. (2015, April). How to launch your digital platform. *Harvard Business Review*.

Grossman, R. L., & Siegel, K. (2014). Organizational models for big data and analytics. *Journal of Organization Design*, *3*(1), 20–25. doi:10.7146/jod.9799

Heffetz, O., & Ligett, K. (2014). Privacy and data-based research. *The Journal of Economic Perspectives, 28*(2), 75–98. doi:10.1257/jep.28.2.75

Hoffmann, A., & Birnbrich, C. (2012). The impact of fraud prevention on bank-customer relationships. *International Journal of Bank Marketing, 30*(5), 390–407. doi:10.1108/02652321211247435

Kruschwitz, N. (2011). First look: The second annual new intelligent enterprise survey. *MIT Sloan Management Review, 52*, 87–89.

Lambrecht, A., & Skiera, B. (2006). Paying too much and being happy about it: Existence, causes, and consequences of tariff-choice biases. *JMR, Journal of Marketing Research, 43*(2), 212–223. doi:10.1509/jmkr.43.2.212

Lambrecht, A., & Tucker, C. (2013). When does retargeting work? Information specificity in online advertising. *JMR, Journal of Marketing Research, 50*(5), 561–576. doi:10.1509/jmr.11.0503

Lazer, D., Kennedy, R., King, G., & Vespignani, A. (2014). The parable of Google Flu: Traps in "big data". *Analytical Sciences, 343*(6176), 1203–1205. doi:10.1126/science.1248506 PMID:24626916

Mayer-Schunberger, V., & Cukier, K. (2014). *Big data: A revolution that will transform how we live, work, and think*. Houghton Mifflin Harcourt.

McAfee, A., Brynjolfsson, E., Davenport, T. H., Patil, D., & Barton, D. (2012). Big data. The management revolution. *Harvard Business Review, 90*, 61–67. PMID:23074865

McGuire, T., Manyika, J., & Chui, M. (2012). Why big data is the new competitive advantage. *Ivey Business Journal, 76*, 1–4.

Nickerson, D., & Rogers, T. (2014). Political campaigns and "big data". *The Journal of Economic Perspectives, 28*(2), 51–74. doi:10.1257/jep.28.2.51

Purcell, B. M. (2013). *Big data using cloud computing*. Holy Family University working paper.

Varian, H. (2014). "Big data": New tricks for econometrics. *The Journal of Economic Perspectives, 28*(2), 3–28. doi:10.1257/jep.28.2.3

ADDITIONAL READING

Biesdorf, S., Court, D., & Willmott, P. (2013). Big data: What's your plan. *The McKinsey Quarterly, 2*, 40–51.

Butler, D. (2008). Web data predict flu. *NATNews, 456*, 287–288. PMID:19020578

National Consumer Law Center (2014). Bid data: a big disappointment for scoring consumer credit risk.

Turner, D., Shroeck, M., & Shockley, R. (2013). Analytics: The real-world use of big data in financial services. IBM Institute of Business Value in collaboration with Said Business School, University of Oxford.

KEY TERMS AND DEFINITIONS

Data Management: Development and execution of policies and procedures to manage the information of a company in an effective manner.

E-Banking: The performance of banking business through the internet. It is also known as "internet banking" or "Online banking".

Electronic Commerce: A business model that enables to conduct business over the internet.

Financial Institutions: An institution that provides financial services to potential clients.

Financial Services: Economic services provided by the finance industry.

Information Technology: It is the use of any computers, storage, networking and other processes to create, store and exchange electronic data.

Online Security: Computer security related to the internet involving browsing and network security. It is designed to establish measures to use against attacks through internet.

Online Trading: Individual investors buy and sell stocks over an electronic network through a brokerage company.

Chapter 15
Recommender System in the Context of Big Data:
Implementing SVD-Based Recommender System using Apache Hadoop and Spark

Khadija Ateya Almohsen
Ahlia University, Bahrain

Huda Kadhim Al-Jobori
Ahlia University, Bahrain

ABSTRACT

The increasing usage of e-commerce website has led to the emergence of Recommender System (RS) with the aim of personalizing the web content for each user. One of the successful techniques of RSs is Collaborative Filtering (CF) which makes recommendations for users based on what other like-mind users had preferred. However, as the world enter Big Data era, CF has faced some challenges such as: scalability, sparsity and cold start. Thus, new approaches that overcome the existing problems have been studied such as Singular Value Decomposition (SVD). This chapter surveys the literature of RSs, reviews the current state of RSs with the main concerns surrounding them due to Big Data, investigates thoroughly SVD and provides an implementation to it using Apache Hadoop and Spark. This is intended to validate the applicability of, existing contributions to the field of, SVD-based RSs as well as validated the effectiveness of Hadoop and spark in developing large-scale systems. The results proved the scalability of SVD-based RS and its applicability to Big Data.

INTRODUCTION

Advances in technology, the wide spread of its usage and the connectivity of everything to the Internet have led the world to experience unusual rate of generating and storing data; resulting in what is being called Big Data phenomenon. As a consequence of this emerging fluid of data, normal tasks and activities become challenges. For instance, browsing the web and searching for interesting information or products

DOI: 10.4018/978-1-5225-0182-4.ch015

is a routine and common task. However, the massive amount of data on the web is expanding the noise there making it harder and more time consuming to choose the interesting pieces of information from all this noise (Villa, 2012; Schelter & Owen, 2012).

Likewise, the currently available systems, technologies and tools show their limitation in processing and managing this massive amount of data. This leads to the invention of new technologies, such as Map Reduce of Google, Hadoop of Yahoo! And Spark from University of California, Berkely. These technologies are just like the telescopes which allow us to comprehend the universe (Schönberger & Cukier, 2013). With this in mind, existing systems have been adapted to meet Big Data by using the newly invented tools and technologies. One of these systems is recommender system and it is the one under study in this chapter.

Recommender systems have been implemented long time ago by several Internet giants; like Amazon.com, Facebook and Google. These systems suggest new items that might be of interest to the user by analyzing user's profiles, their activities on the websites as well as their purchase history; if applicable. However, Big Data increases the cognitive load on the user, posing more challenges on recommender systems as it should provide many recommendations of high quality by analyzing huge data of customers and products. In another word, high quality, scalability and performance become concerns. (Berkeley School: Lecture12 -Analyzing Big Data with Twitter: Recommender Systems, 2012; Chiky, et al, 2012; Thangavel, et al, 2013). This encourages more research work on recommendation algorithms and the use of new tools and frameworks like Appache Hadoop and Spark, i.e. Big Data tools, in the development of scalable systems as well as preventing the computational cost from going up while processing vast amount of data (Schelter & Owen, 2012; Zhao & Shang, 2010).

This chapter provides a comprehensive and self-contained description of this research area. Such a work will constitute a milestone for studies on Big Data; since it will provide review of key references which will be useful in the search for research topics dealing with Big Data. To achieve such goal, this chapter will review the literature on Big Data and recommendation engines. In addition, survey the promising approaches of recommender systems that are expected to perform well while handling Big Data; such as Singular Value Decomposition. Furthermore, assess the applicability and viability of Big Data technologies (i.e. Apache Hadoop and Spark) to the field of recommendation system as well as develop a scalable recommender system that can handle large volume of data.

BACKGROUND

Recommender System Overview

Recommender system's (RS) main mission is to find the taste of a person and automatically suggests, new, relevant content for him/her. These suggestions aid to decision-making; for example: which item to buy, which music to listen to, or which news to read. This is achieved by finding patterns in people opinions, even though their opinions vary. These patterns are useful in predicting what a user might like or dislike. For illustration, people like something which is similar to what they liked before, or they like what others of similar taste and opinion seem to like (Owen et al., 2012; Ricci et al., 2011).

Most of recommender systems aim to provide a personalize websites by suggesting different items to different users. However, there are some recommendations which are non-personalized such as: Top ten selections of movies in a magazine or a web site. Such recommendations are much easier than personalized one (Ricci et al., 2011)

In the case of personalized recommendations, the system comes up with a ranked list of most relevant items. This is achieved by analyzing the user preference that is usually expressed explicitly- in terms of rating- or expressed implicitly through user action and activities in the website; for example: by considering the navigation to a specific product page. After obtaining the ranked list of recommendation, the user can view the recommendations and have the choice of accepting or rejecting them. In addition, the user may have the option of providing a feedback on them (Ricci et al., 2011).

Recommender System's Problem Formulation

Suppose that a Big Data set records the preferences of big number of users; denoted by m; for some or all of n items. The preference record usually takes the form of tuple (userID, itemID, rating); where rating takes a value on a numerical scale (for example from 1-5) and that expresses how much the user holding userID likes the item with itemID.

Let R be a user–item matrix of size $m \times n$, where m is the number of users and n is number of items. This matrix represents the preference records such that each one of the m rows represents the preferences of onc user to the available n items. In another word, the value of a particular cell R_{ij} either holds the rating given by user i to item j or null if the user did not rate the item yet, as shown in Figure 1. In most of the cases, this matrix is sparse because each user does not normally rate all the items in the data set.

The mission of a RS is to predict the missing ratings; i.e. predict how a user would rate an item in the future. This aids the recommender system in recommending items that are predicted to receive high rating by the user (Melville & Sindhwani, 2010).

Recommender System Approaches

The commonly used approach of recommender system is collaborative filtering. It makes recommendation based on the existing relationship between users and items (i.e. who bought which item? Who viewed which item? Who liked which item?). This approach is relying on the following assumptions:

Figure 1. User-item matrix

	$item_1$	$item_2$	$item_3$	...	$item_n$
$user_1$		5	2		1
$user_2$	3				
$user_3$	1		3		
. . .					
$user_{m-1}$	5		4		2
$user_m$		4			3

1. People may have similar taste and preferences.
2. People interest and preferences are stable.
3. We can rely on past preferences to predict their new choices.

The two common variations of collaborative filtering approach are:

1. **User-based collaborative filtering** (which is also called nearest-neighbor collaborative filtering):

It examines the entire data set of users and items to generate recommendations by identifying users that have similar interests to the target one and then recommends items that have been bought by others and not the target user. This proceeds by constructing user-item matrix, computing some statistical metrics on it to measure the similarity between different rows and finding the nearest neighbors. These neighbors are supposed to have similar interest with the target user. This will be followed by combining the neighbors' preferences and finding the top N items that have been rated highly by neighbors and not by the target user. These N items will form the top N recommendations. (Thangavel, *et al*, 2013).

Despite the fact that this approach has been adapted widely, it suffers from scalability problem which was not considered a big issue few decades ago when the number of users and items was relatively small. However, as the data set size increases in big data era, computing the similarity between users is increasing exponentially because of the need for comparing each user with all the other users. Moreover, as the users interact with more items and change their preferences, the similarity needs to be recomputed; i.e. similarity pre-computation becomes useless. This is degrading the performance of RSs and that is why it is being considered as a big problem today. Furthermore, having a sparse user-item matrix, which is usually the case because users interact with relatively small set of items, also adds to the difficulty of computing user's similarity since the number of common items is relatively small if not zero (Thangavel, et al, 2013; Walunj & Sadafale, 2013b; Owen et al., 2012; Lee & Chang, 2013).

2. Item-based collaborative filtering:

It examines the set of items rated by the target user and finds other items similar to them (which are called neighbors), by considering other users' preferences. With the hope of finding neighbors, each item will be represented by a vector of the ratings given by the different users, and then, the similarity of two items will be measured by computing the similarity between their vectors. These neighbors will form the recommendations and will be ranked after predicting the preference of the target user for each one of them. The prediction $P_{u,i}$ of the target user to one of the neighbors, item i, is given by:

$$P_{u,i} = \frac{\sum_{i=1}^{N} Sim(i,j) \times R_{u,j}}{\sum_{i=1}^{N} Sim(i,j)}$$

Where N is the number of neighbors, $Sim(i,j)$ is the similarity between the item j and its neighbor i, $R_{u,j}$ is the rating given by user u to item j. (Lee & Chang, 2013; Gong, et al, 2009).

However, measuring the similarities between items takes long time and consumes lots of computer resources. This is the main pitfall of this method. Anyhow, changes in items are not as frequent as changes in users and, thus, such computations can be pre-calculated in an offline mode. Another strength of this algorithm is that it is not affected by having a sparse user-item matrix. This is because with large number of user, there will be enough number of ratings for each item which enable measuring the similarity between the different items and getting significant statistics. (Thangavel, et al, 2013; Walunj & Sadafale, 2013b; Lee & Chang, 2013).

Generally speaking, CF whether it is an item-based or a user based approach, has a well-known strength in which it is not domain specific, and thus, does not rely on the items' properties and attributes. That is why it is applicable to different domains: movie recommendation, book recommendation, flowers, food and others. However, CF suffers from the following problems:

1. **Scalability**: RSs are being fed with massive amount of data which should be processed rapidly. However, CF algorithms computation time grows up with the continuous increase in the number of users and items (Lee & Chang, 2013).
2. **Data Sparsity**: In an e-commerce website, users usually rate small fraction of all the available items resulting in sparse data set. This degrades the accuracy of the RS because it complicates the process of finding similarities between users as the number of common items becomes relatively small (Lee & Chang, 2013).
3. **Cold-Start Problems**: This problem emerged as a consequence of data sparsity problem; where new users cannot get personalized recommendation unless they rate a sufficient number of items. Likewise, new items cannot be recommended before getting reasonable number or ratings (Kabore, 2012).
4. **Synonymy:** Different products have different names in the data set even if they are similar to each other. In this case, a standard CF RS will treat them differently and will not infer the hidden association between them. For illustration, "cartoon film" and "cartoon movie" are two phrases refereeing to the same item. However, ordinary implementations of CF algorithms had treated them differently! (Sarwar et al, 2000).
5. **Grey Sheep**: It addresses users whose opinions do not match with any other group of users. Consequently, CF cannot serve grey sheep since it mainly relies on the similarity between users' previous preferences (Walunj & Sadafale, 2013a).

The aforementioned, standard, implementation of item-based and user-based CF are following memory-based approach in which the entire data set is kept in memory while processing it and searching for similarities between users or items in order to make recommendation. The other approach of implementing CF algorithm is called model based approach in which the data set is used in an offline mode to generate a model by utilizing some data mining, machine learning or statistical techniques. This model could be used later on to predict the ratings for unseen items without the need of processing the entire data set again and again. Examples of this approach are: decision trees, clustering methods and matrix factorization models (Pagare & Patil, 2013).

Point often overlooked is that model-based approach generates predictions with lower accuracy when compared with memory based approach. However, it has better scalability. Thus, many researchers are investing their effort in studying and enhancing model-based CF algorithms. One of these algorithms is Singular value decomposition (SVD) based recommenders and it is the one under study in this chapter.

Singular Value Decomposition Recommender System:

SVD is one of the famous matrix factorization techniques that decompose a matrix R of size $m \times n$ and rank $= r$ into three matrices U, S and Vas follows:

$$R = U.S.V^T$$

where:

U: an orthonormal matrix of size $m \times r$ holding left singular vectors of R in its columns; i.e. its r columns hold eigenvectors of the r nonzero eigenvalues of RR^T.
S: a diagonal matrix of size $r \times r$holding the singular values of R in its diagonal entries in decreasing order; i.e. $s_1 \geq s_2 \geq s_3 \geq \ldots\ldots \geq s_r$. These r values are the nonnegative square roots of eigenvalues of RR^T.
V: an orthonormal matrix of size $n \times r$ holding the right singular vectors of R in its columns; i.e. its r columns hold eigenvectors of the r nonzero eigenvalues of R^TR .

Furthermore, S could be reduced by taking the largest k singular values only and thus obtain S_k of size $k \times k$. Accordingly, U and V could be reduced by retaining the first k singular vectors and discarding the rest. In another word, U_k is generated by eliminating the last r-k column of U and, similarly, V_k is generated by eliminating the last r-k column of V. This will yield U_k of size $m \times k$ and V_k of size $n \times k$. As a consequence, $R_k = U_k . S_k . V^T_k$ and $R_k \approx R$, where R_k is the closest rank k approximation to R (Lee & Chang, 2013; Sarwar et al., 2000; Berry, et al, 1995).

Applying SVD on Recommender System

This approach assumes that the relationship between users and items as well as the similarity between users / items could be induced by some hidden lower dimensional structure in the data. For illustration, the ratings given by a specific user to a particular movie, assuming that items are movies, depends on some implicit factors like the preference of that user across different movie genres. As a matter of fact, it treats users and items as unknown feature vectors to be learnt by applying SVD to user–item matrix and breaking it down into three smaller matrices: U, V and S (Melville & Sindhwani, 2010).

With this in mind, applying SVD to RSs proceeds as follow:

Construct user-item matrix R of size $m \times n$ from the input data set; which is usually a sparse matrix. Unfortunately, this sparsity degrades the accuracy of the predictions computed by SVD. That is why it is common in the literature to impute the sparse R before computing its SVD. There are several imputation techniques and here are the most common one (Ghazanfar & Bennett, 2012):

1. **Impute by Zero (ByZero):** which fills all the missing entries by zero. However, this leads to predicting ratings close to zeros because of the abundance of zeros in the imputed matrix.
2. **Impute by Item Average (ItemAvgRating):** which fills the missing values in each column by the average rating of the corresponding item.
3. **Impute by User Average (UserAvgRating):** which fills the missing values in each row by the average rating of the corresponding user.

4. **Impute by the mean of ItemAvgRating and UserAvgRating (Mean_ ItemAvgRating&UserAvgRating):** which fills each missing value by the average of its corresponding item's average rating and its corresponding user's average rating.

As a result, a dense matrix R_{filled} is obtained and this could be interpreted as overcoming the sparsity problem associated with RSs. Furthermore, R_{filled} is normalized by subtracting the average rating of each user from its corresponding row resulting in R_{norm}. The last step is useful in offsetting the difference in rating scale between the different users (Vozalis & Margaritis, 2006).

At this point, SVD could be applied to R_{norm} to compute U_k (this holds users' features), S_k (holds the strength of the hidden features) and V_k (holds items' features) such that their inner product will give the closest rank-k approximation to R_{norm}. This lower-rank approximation of user-item matrix is better than the original one since SVD eliminate the noise in the user-item relationship by discarding the small singular values from S (Sarwar *et. al.*, 2000).

Henceforth, the preference of user i to item j could be predicted by the dot product of their corresponding features vectors; *i.e.*, compute the dot product of the ith row of $(U_k.S_k)$ and jth column of V^T_k and add back the user average rating that was subtracted while normalizing R_{filled}. This could be expressed as:

$$P_{ij} = \bar{r}_i + \left(U_k.S_k\right)_{i,\_} .V^T_{\_,j}$$

Where p_{ij} is the predicted rating for user i and item j, $\bar{r}_i$ is the user average rating, $V^T_{\_,j}$ is the jth column of V^T and $(U_k.S_k)$ is the ith row of the matrix resulting from multiplying U_k and S_k.

In point of fact, the dot product of two vectors measures the cosine similarity between them. Thus, the above formula could be interpreted as finding the similarity between user i and item j vectors and then adding the user average rating to predict the missing rating $p_{ij.}$

EXPERIMENTS AND EVALUATIONS

Experimental Environment

All the experiments, behind this chapter, were implemented using Scala programming language on Eclipse, running on MacBook Pro with X 10.9.3 OS, 2.4 GHz Intel Core i5 processor and 8 GB of RAM. This machine served as a single node cluster for Apache hadoop 2.4.0 which was configured in pseudo-distributed mode. Moreover, Apache spark v. 1.0.2 was used as it provides fast distributed computations.

Data Set

The data set used in this work is the 1M MovieLens set which contains 1million ratings provided by more than 6000 users to around 3900 movies in the form of tuple (userID, MovieID, rating, timestamp). Ratings take integer values in the interval [1, 5] indicating how much the user likes the movie.

The aforementioned data set was divided into training set and test set based on different ratios (i.e. training ratios). Furthermore, the training set was used to fill the user-item matrix R of size 6040×3900;

which will be used to compute SVD, come-up with U, S and V matrices as well as predict ratings for unrated items. On the other hand, the test set was used to evaluate the accuracy of the predicted ratings.

Evaluation Metric

Different empirical evaluation metrics are there to assess the quality of the estimated predictions. The most common metrics are the statistical one such as Mean Absolute Error (MAE) and Root Mean Square Error (RMSE). In this chapter, MAE is used.

The evaluation process of this work started by dividing the data set into two disjoint sets; one for training and the second for testing the system. The predicted ratings will be compared with the actual ratings in the test set by measuring MAE which will compute the average of the absolute difference between each predicted value and its corresponding actual rating (Sarwar *et al.*, 2000), *i.e.*

$$MAE = \frac{\sum_{I=1}^{N} \left| p_{i,j} - r_{i,j} \right|}{N}$$

Where N is the size of the test set, $p_{i,j}$ is the predicted rating for user i and $r_{i,j}$ is the actual ratings for user u. A smaller value of MAE refers to a higher prediction accuracy and thus better recommendations.

Choosing the Number of Dimensions

Reducing the dimensions of the original matrix R is useful because it aids in eliminating the noise and focusing on the important information. With this in mind, an appropriate value of k should be selected such that it can filter out the noise but not leads to the loose of important information. In another word, the value of k should be large enough to ensure capturing the essential structure of matrix R but small enough to filter out noise and avoid overfitting (Sarwar *et al.*, 2000; Berry, Dumais, & O'Brien, 1995). The best value of k will be experimentally determined by trying different values.

Experiments and Results

Our work started by loading 1M MovieLens data set into HDFS, where part of it, *i.e.* the training set, was used to fill the user-item matrix R. After that, R underwent two preprocessing operations: imputation and normalization. The imputation was done by Mean_ItemAvgRating&UserAvgRating, i.e. mean of item average rating and user average rating, after experimentally proving its superiority over other imputation techniques (refer to Experiment 2). Furthermore, the normalization step subtracted the average rating of each user from its corresponding row resulting in R_{norm}.

This was followed by using Apache Spark to compute SVD and come up with: U_k, V_k, and S_k. This is equivalent to extracting both user's and items' features from R. For that purpose, k was set to 20 after the results of experiment 1.

In order to compute a missing rating for one user, its corresponding row of ($U.S$) was multiplied by V^T column that corresponds to the target item and then denormalized by adding the user average rating.

Experiment 1: Determining the Appropriate Number of Dimensions

The work was executed several times with different values of k, ranging from 10 to 300, and different training ratio denoted as x. The results are presented in table 1 by demonstrating the value of MAE obtained for each pair of (k, x) after imputing the rating matrix by the mean of user average rating and item average rating .

As a result, 20 is found to be a good value of k and thus it is fixed in the other experiments.

Experiment 2: Determining the Best Imputation Technique

Four techniques of imputation (i.e. impute ByZero, impute by ItemAvgRating, impute byUserAvgRating and impute by Mean_ItemAvgRating&UserAvgRating) were tested against multiple values of k. The results presented in table 2 shows the superiority of imputing by Mean_ItemAvgRating&UserAvgRating as it gives the lower values of MAE. Thus, it will be used in the other experiment.

Experiment 3: Evaluating the Accuracy of SVD on different training ratio

The work was executed several times with different training ratios ranging from 35% to 95%, with k =20 and k = 100. Note that the user-item matrix R was imputed by Mean_ItemAvgRating&UserAvgRating before computing its SVD. This experiment intended to study the real effect of the number of dimensions k on the prediction quality. Its results are presented in table 3.

Table 1. MAE Measured for different training ratios and different values of k

	Training Ratio		
k	**x= 40%**	**x= 60%**	**x= 80%**
10	0.752063387	0.740626631	0.729999025
20	0.751235952	0.737954414	0.724461829
30	0.751605786	0.738107001	0.723582636
40	0.752364535	0.738714968	0.723803209
50	0.753327523	0.739710017	0.725192112
60	0.754025958	0.740751258	0.726154802
70	0.754724263	0.741471676	0.727282644
80	0.755378978	0.742729653	0.728420107
90	0.755930363	0.743485881	0.729623117
100	0.756510921	0.744293948	0.730338578
150	0.759248743	0.748479721	0.735940524
200	0.761302063	0.752022533	0.740869085
250	0.762834111	0.754352648	0.744583552
300	0.764142161	0.756565002	0.747871699

Table 2. MAE for Different Imputation Techniques and Different Values of k

	Imputation Technique			
k	ByZero	UserAvgRating	ItemAvgRating	Mean_ UserAvgRating&ItemAvgRating
10	1.287082589	0.763900832	0.738045498	0.729999025
20	1.340593039	0.758800163	0.732242767	0.724461829
30	1.351316283	0.758681267	0.731619885	0.723582636
40	1.342134276	0.760268678	0.731981172	0.723803209
50	1.331709429	0.762213489	0.733055102	0.725192112
60	1.317791963	0.764543289	0.733818382	0.726154802
70	1.303016117	0.766207466	0.734838138	0.727282644
80	1.288611141	0.768863197	0.736044939	0.728420107
90	1.274236198	0.770501176	0.737138793	0.735940524
100	1.261225796	0.772165966	0.738514469	0.730338578
150	1.198043117	0.780474068	0.744252067	0.735940524

Table 3. MAE for different training ratios with k=20 and k=100

	k	
Training Ratio x	k=20	k=100
0.35	0.7549804	0.759679233
0.4	0.751235952	0.756510921
0.45	0.747814989	0.753365509
0.5	0.744018997	0.749880733
0.55	0.741011898	0.747432557
0.6	0.737954414	0.744293948
0.65	0.734098595	0.740644033
0.7	0.731331182	0.737610654
0.75	0.727741033	0.734113758
0.8	0.724461829	0.730338578
0.85	0.721460479	0.727461993
0.9	0.72096045	0.726117655
0.95	0.733633592	0.740065812

The figure compares the MAE values of different training ratio for two values of *k*. It is obvious that MAE takes less values for *k=20* than those of *k = 100*; but not significant. This is validating what has been stated repeatedly in the literature; that a larger value of *k* does not necessarily gives better predictions despite the fact that it gives a closer approximation to the original matrix.

DISCUSSION

The main computational advantage of running these experiments, which implement SVD-based recommender system, using Hadoop, Spark and Scala is its easy parallelization. This proves the powerfulness of these frameworks/APIs in implementing large-scale systems with parallelized operations in distributed mode.

The results are comparable with the results of other works, discussed previously in the literature review, such as the one conducted by Sarwar and his colleagues, by Gong and Dai as well as by Zhou and his colleagues; that were carried on significantly smaller data set (i.e. 100 K MovieLense Data Set). This proves that SVD approach is not only effective for, ordinary, small data but even for Big Data sets.

Indeed, this work resulted in better predictions when compared with Sarwar *et. al.* work although it has been carried on much bigger data set. To put it differently, the best predictions obtained by Sarwar *et. al.* on 100K MovieLense data set were using training data set of 80% and $k \in [20, 100]$ as they get MAE ranging from 0.748 to 0.732 (Sarwar, *et al*, 2000). However, the MAE obtained by our implementation, for the same values of k, the same training ratio and 1M MovieLense data set, were ranging between 0.7230 and 0.723.

While looking for the best value of k, 20 was found as the favorable one since it gave a small value of MAE when checking it over different training ratios. This is reasonable when comparing it with previous works which found $k = 14$ (Sarwar, *et al*, 2000; Sarwar *et. al.*, 2002) or $k = 15$ (Gong, Ye & Dai, 2009) for smaller data set. Notable, increasing the volume of the data set to 1 million ratings did not, dramatically, increase the value of k which validates other researchers' opinions, reported in some research papers, in which a small number of dimensions usually give pretty good results with good approximation to the original matrix R. This is simply because a small value of k is sufficient to capture the important features of users and items and thus make good predictions. However, increasing the value of k might simply represent adding more noise to the data which does not add value to the process of making predictions.

Furthermore, trying different imputation techniques and tracking their MAE showed the importance of pre-processing steps and its effect on the prediction accuracy. As per our experiments, Mean_ItemAvgRating&UserAvgRating outperformed other imputation techniques since it gave lower MAE.

Moreover, repeating the experiments multiple times with different values of k and different values of training ratio x; revealed the sensitivity of the prediction quality to the sparsity of the data set since MAE values decrease as the training ratios increase and the sparsity decrease. Added to that, it revealed the significant effect of the value of k on the prediction quality, as well as the effectiveness of SVD in dealing with cold-start cases.

FUTURE RESEARCH DIRECTIONS

The work presented in this chapter is just the starting point in exploring the current state of recommender system in Big Data Era. One might extend the work by deploying the system on multi-node cluster in order to be able to assess its scalability, performance and accuracy in a distributed mode. Another future direction could be to implement a hybrid approach of SVD that combines stochastic version of SVD proposed by Lee and Chang (Lee & Chang, 2013), incremental version of SVD proposed by Sarwar, B. et al. (Sarwar, B. et al., 2002) and Expectation Maximization technique presented by Kurucz et al. (Kurucz et al., 2007). This will be an iterative process that applies a stochastic version of SVD, repeatedly, to a matrix and use the outcome of one iteration to impute the input of the next iteration. Stochastic SVD could be done in an incremental manner such that the advent of a new user will not imply re-computing the decomposition of user-item matrix; but the new user will be projected to the existing SVD model.

CONCLUSION

As recommender systems proved their powerfulness in personalizing the web content for each user, more research efforts have been devoted to improving it and evaluate its different algorithms. The commonly adapted approach is collaborative filtering that mines the interaction records between users and items to infer user's taste and thus recommends items that match his taste. Surprisingly, CF techniques have started facing some challenges with the dawn of Big Data era. This new phenomenon is inflaming the data volume to be processed by RS and thus raises some concerns about the sparseness of the available data, scalability of RSs as well as the quality of the predictions. As a consequence, new approaches of CF have been proposed and studied such as Singular value decomposition. In addition, various Big Data frameworks and APIs (such as Hadoop, Mahout and Spark) have been released and tried in building large-scale recommender systems.

This chapter contributes to the state of the art of recommender systems as it provides an implementation of a large scale SVD-based recommender system using both Apache Hadoop and Spark. This came as a result of an intensive study to the literature as well as conducting several experiments using Scala programming language on top of apache Hadoop and Spark. The study involved several topics which are: Big Data phenomenon, the different techniques and approaches of recommender systems together with their pros and cons, the challenges posed by big data on recommender systems and CF in particular, the applicability of SVD for recommender systems as well as its effectiveness in solving the aforementioned challenges. The experiments were conducted to determine the optimal values of two essential parameters that affect SVD-based RS which are: the imputation technique to be used in filling the user-item matrix before processing it and the number of dimensions to be retained after decomposing the matrix. The results showed that the best imputation technique is using the average of both item average rating and user average rating and that the optimal number of dimensions is k=20 as it gave the lowest MAE.

This work solved the scalability problem by utilizing Hadoop and its valuable features. In addition, it showed that pretty good quality could be achieved by choosing a robust imputation technique (as a preprocessing step) before applying SVD to the user-item matrix. Moreover, it asserted that Apache Spark comes with attractive merits which enable easy integration with Hadoop and easy development of parallelizable code.

This drew a conclusion that a careful implementation of a scalable SVD-based collaborative filtering recommender system is effective when choosing the right parameters and the appropriate frameworks and APIs.

REFERENCES

Berkeley School. (2012). *Lecture 12 -Analyzing Big Data with Twitter: Recommender Systems*. Retrieved February 10, 2014, from http://www.youtube.com/watch?v=NSscbT7JwxY

Berry, M. W., Dumais, S. T., & O'Brien, G. W. (1995). Using linear algebra for intelligent information retrieval. *SIAM Review*, *37*(4), 573–595. doi:10.1137/1037127

Bizer, C., Boncz, P., Brodie, M. L., & Erling, O. (2011). The Meaningful Use of Big Data: Four Perspectives - Four Challenges. *SIGMOD*, *4*(4), 56 – 60. Retrieved from http://www.sigmod.org/publications/sigmod-record/1112/pdfs/10.report.bizer.pdf

Baker, K. (2013). *Singular Value Decomposition Tutorial*. Retrieved December 26, 2014, from http://www.ling.ohio-state.edu/~kbaker/pubs/Singular_Value_Decomposition_Tutorial.pdf

Bloor Research. (2012). *Big Data Analytics with Hadoop and Sybase IQ*. London: Bloor.

Buros, W. M. (2013). *Understanding Systems and Architecture for Big Data*. IBM Research Report. Retrieved December 23, 2014 from http://cnf-labs.org/pdf/research-report-ibm.html#

Casey, E. (2014). *Scalable Collaborative Filtering Recommendation Algorithms on Apache Spark*. (Unpublished Senior Thesis). Claremont Mckenna College, USA.

Chen, J., Chen, Y., Du, X., Li, C., Lu, J., Zhao, S., & Zhou, X. (2013). Big Data Challenge: A data management perspective. *Frontiers of Computer Science*, *7*(2), 157-164. Retrieved from http://iir.ruc.edu.cn/~jchchen/FCSBigData.pdf

Chiky, R., Ghisloti, R., & Aoul, Z. K. (2012). Development of a distributed recommender system using the Hadoop Framework. In *Proceedings of EGC 2012* (pp. 495 – 500).

Cloudera & Teradata. (2011). *Hadoop and the Data Warehouse: When to Use Which*. Cloudera, Inc. and Teradata Corporation.

Databricks. (2014). *Intro to Apache Spark*. Retrieved October 24, 2014, from http://stanford.edu/~rezab/sparkclass/slides/itas_workshop.pdf

Dittrich, J., & Ruiz, J. A. Q. (2012). Efficient Big Data Processing in Hadoop MapReduce. In *Proceedings of VLDB Endowment* (pp. 2014-2015). VLDB Endowment. doi:10.14778/2367502.2367562

Fayyad, U. M. (2012). Big Data Everywhere, and No SQL in sight. *SIGKDD Explorations*, *14*(2), 1–2. Retrieved from http://www.sigkdd.org/sites/default/files/issues/14-2-2012-12/V14-02-01-editorial.pdf

Ghazanfar, M. A., & Bennett, A. P. (2012). The advantage of Careful imputation source in sparse data-environment of recommender systems: generating improved SVD-based recommendations. *Informatica, 37*, 61-92. Retrieved from http://citeseerx.ist.psu.edu/viewdoc/download?doi=10.1.1.368.2112&rep=rep1&type=pdf

Gong, S., Ye, H., & Dai, Y. (2009.) Combining Singular Value Decomposition and Item-based Recommender in Collaborative Filtering.*Second International Workshop on Knowledge discovery and data mining*, (pp. 769-722). doi:10.1109/WKDD.2009.132

Gower, S. (2014). *Netflix prize and SVD*. Retrieved December 20, 2014, from http://buzzard.ups.edu/courses/2014spring/420projects/math420-UPS-spring-2014-gower-netflix-SVD.pdf

Hortonworks. (2012). *Apache Hadoop: The Big Data Refinery*. Hortonworks.

Kabore, S. C. (2012). *Design and implementation of a recommender system as a module for Liferay portal.* (Unpublished master dissertation). University Polytechnic of Catalunya (UPC), Spain.

Kluver, D., & Konstan, J. A. (2014). Evaluating Recommender Behavior for New Users. *RecSys, 14*, 121–128.

Lee, C. R., & Chang, Y. F. (2013). Enhancing Accuracy and Performance of Collaborative Filtering Algorithm by Stochastic SDV and Its MapReduce Implementation. *2013 IEEE 27th International Symposium on Parallel & Distributed Processing Workshops and PhD Forum*, (pp. 1869-1878).

Melville, M., & Sindhwani, V. (2010). Recommender Systems. In *Encyclopedia of Machine Learning* (pp. 829-838). http://vikas.sindhwani.org/recommender.pdf

Odersky, M., Spoon, L., & Venner, B. (2008). *A Scalable Language*. Retrieved December 15, 2014, from http://www.artima.com/scalazine/articles/scalable-language.html

Owen, S. (2012). *Mahout in Action*. New York: Manning Publications.

Pagare, R., & Patil, S. A. (2013). Study of Collaborative Filtering Recommendation Algorithm – Scalability Issue. *International Journal of Computers and Applications, 67*(25), 10–15. doi:10.5120/11742-7305

Papagelis, M., Rousidis, L., Plexousakis, D., & Theoharppoulous, E. (2005). Incremental Collaborative Filtering for Highly-Scalable Recommendation Algorithms. In M. Said Hacid, N. V. Murray, Z. W. Ras, & S. Tsumoto (Eds.), *Foundations of Intelligent System*. New York: Springer Berlin Heidelberg.

ParAccel Inc. (2012). *Hadoop's Limitations for Big Data Analytics*. ParAccel; doi:10.1007/11425274_57

Quora. (2011). *LinkedIn Recommendations: How does LinkedIn's recommendation system work?* Retrieved April 28, 2014, from http://www.quora.com/LinkedIn-Recommendations/How-does-LinkedIns-recommendation-system-work

Ricci, F., Rokach, L., & Shapira, B. (2011). Introduction to Recommender Systems Handbook. In F. Ricci et al. (Eds.), *Recommender Systems Handbook*. New York: Springer. doi:10.1007/978-0-387-85820-3_1

Sarwar, B. (2000). Application of Dimensionality Reduction in Recommender System -- A Case Study. *ACM WebKDD 2000 (Web-mining for Ecommerce Workshop)*. Retrieved from http://files.grouplens.org/papers/webKDD00.pdf

Sarwar, B. (2001). Item-based Collaborative Filtering Recommendation Algorithms. In *Proceedings of the 10th International Conference on World Wide Web* (pp. 285-295). New York: ACM.

Sarwar, B. (2002). Incremental Singular Value Decomposition Algorithms for Highly Scalable Recommender Systems. In *Proceedings of Fifth International Conference on Computer and Information Science* (pp. 27- 28).

Schelter, S., & Owen, S. (2012). Collaborative Filtering with Apache Mahout. RecSysChallenge. Dublin: ACM. Retrieved from http://ssc.io/pdf/cf-mahout.pdf

Schönberger, V. M., & Cukier, K. (2013). *Big Data: A revolution that will transform how we live, work, and think*. New York: Houghton Mifflin Harcourt.

Soft Layer. (2014). *Big Data Hosting*. Retrieved December 30, 2013, from: http://www.softlayer.com/solutions/big-data/

Spark Summit. (2014). *Spark Summit 2014*. Retrieved October 16, 2014, from: http://spark-summit.org/2014

Spark 1.2.0. (2014). *Spark Programming Guide*. Retrieved October 24, 2014, from: http://spark.apache.org/docs/latest/programming-guide.html

Thangavel, S. K., Thampi, N. S. & I, J. C. (2013). Performance Analysis of Various Recommendation Algorithm Using Apache Hadoop and Mahout. *International Journal of Scientific and Engineering Research, 4*(12), 279-287. Retrieved from http://www.ijser.org/researchpaper%5CPerformance-Analysis-of-Various-Recommendation-Algorithms.pdf

TutorialsPoint. (2014). *Scala Tutorial*. Retrieved December 22, 2014, from: http://www.tutorialspoint.com/scala/scala_pdf_version.htm

Ullman, J. D. (2012). *Designing Good MapReduce Algorithms*. Retrieved May 5, 2014, from: http://xrds.acm.org/article.cfm?aid=2331053

Villa, A. (2012). *Transfering Big Data Across the Globe*. University of New Hampshire Durham.

Vozalis, M. G., & Margaritis, K. G. (2006). Applying SVD on generalized Item-based filtering. *International Journal of Computer Science & Application, 3*(3), 27-51. Retrieved from http://www.tmrfindia.org/ijcsa/v3i34.pdf

Walunj, S. & Sadafale, K. (2013a). Price based Recommendation System. *International Journal of Research in Computer Engineering and Information Technology, 1*(1).

Walunj, S., & Sadafale, K. (2013b). An Online Recommendation System for E-commerce Based on Apache Mahout Framework. In *Proceedings of the 2013 annual conference on Computers and people research* (pp. 153-158). New York: ACM. doi:10.1145/2487294.2487328

Ward, J. S., & Barker, A. (2013). *Unified By Data: A Survey of Big Data Definitions*. Retrieved December 15, 2014, from: http://arxiv.org/pdf/1309.5821v1.pdf

White, T. (2011). *Hadoop: The definitive Guide*. O'Reilly Media.

Zhao, Z. D., & Shang, M. S. (2010). User-based Collaborative-Filtering Recommendation Algorithms on Hadoop. In *Proceedings of Third International Conference on Knowledge Discovery and Data Mining* (pp. 478-481). IEEE.

Zikopoulous, P. C. (2012). *Understanding Big Data: Analytics for Enterprise Class; Hadoop and Streaming Data*. New York: McGraw Hill.

Zhou, X., He, J., Huang, G., & Zhang, Y. (2012). A personalized recommendation algorithm based on approximating the singular value decomposition (ApproSVD). *2012 IEEE/WIC/ACM International Conferences on Web Intelligence and Intelligent Agent Technology*. IEEE.

KEY TERMS AND DEFINITIONS

Apache Hadoop: An open source framework that provides a distributed data storage and computation utilizing commodity servers.

Apache Spark: An open source framework supporting in-memory data analysis and distributed programming that has been built on top of Apache Hadoop to facilitate distributed computation.

Column-Orthonormal Matrix: A matrix where all its vectors length is 1 and the dot of any two of them is zero since they are orthogonal.

Matrix-Rank: The number of rows that are linearly independent.

Matrix-Transpose: A matrix resulting from swapping row-vectors with column vectors.

Recommender System: An automated system that suggests relevant, not seen yet, items to the user.

Scala: A programming language that facilitate the development of scalable systems.

Singular Value Decomposition: Breaking down a matrix into three, smaller matrices, U, S and V in which their product yields back the original matrix.

Related References

To continue our tradition of advancing knowledge management and discovery research, we have compiled a list of recommended IGI Global readings. These references will provide additional information and guidance to further enrich your knowledge and assist you with your own research and future publications.

Abril, R. M. (2011). The quality attribution in data, information and knowledge. In D. Schwartz & D. Te'eni (Eds.), *Encyclopedia of knowledge management* (2nd ed., pp. 1343–1354). Hershey, PA: Information Science Reference; doi:10.4018/978-1-59904-931-1.ch129

Abufardeh, S. (2013). KM and global software engineering (GSE). In S. Saeed & I. Alsmadi (Eds.), *Knowledge-based processes in software development* (pp. 12–34). Hershey, PA: Information Science Reference; doi:10.4018/978-1-4666-4229-4.ch002

Aggestam, L., Backlund, P., & Persson, A. (2010). Supporting knowledge evaluation to increase quality in electronic knowledge repositories.[IJKM]. *International Journal of Knowledge Management, 6*(1), 23–43. doi:10.4018/jkm.2010103002

Aggestam, L., Backlund, P., & Persson, A. (2012). Supporting knowledge evaluation to increase quality in electronic knowledge repositories. In M. Jennex (Ed.), *Conceptual models and outcomes of advancing knowledge management: New technologies* (pp. 24–44). Hershey, PA: Information Science Reference; doi:10.4018/978-1-4666-0035-5.ch002

Aiken, P., Gillenson, M., Zhang, X., & Rafner, D. (2011). Data management and data administration: Assessing 25 years of practice.[JDM]. *Journal of Database Management, 22*(3), 24–45. doi:10.4018/jdm.2011070102

Akabawi, S., & Hodeeb, H. (2013). Implementing business intelligence in the dynamic beverages sales and distribution environment. In M. Khosrow-Pour (Ed.), *Cases on performance measurement and productivity improvement: Technology integration and maturity* (pp. 194–221). Hershey, PA: Business Science Reference; doi:10.4018/978-1-4666-2618-8.ch010

Al-Busaidi, K. A. (2011). A social and technical investigation of knowledge utilization from a repository knowledge management system. In M. Al-Shammari (Ed.), *Knowledge management in emerging economies: Social, organizational and cultural implementation* (pp. 122–139). Hershey, PA: Information Science Reference; doi:10.4018/978-1-61692-886-5.ch007

Al-Busaidi, K. A. (2012). The impact of supporting organizational knowledge management through a corporate portal on employees and business processes. In M. Jennex (Ed.), *Conceptual models and outcomes of advancing knowledge management: New technologies* (pp. 208–229). Hershey, PA: Information Science Reference; doi:10.4018/978-1-4666-0035-5.ch011

Alaraifi, A., Molla, A., & Deng, H. (2013). An empirical analysis of antecedents to the assimilation of sensor information systems in data centers.[IJITSA]. *International Journal of Information Technologies and Systems Approach*, *6*(1), 57–77. doi:10.4018/jitsa.2013010104

Alguezaui, S., & Filieri, R. (2010). Social capital: Knowledge and technological innovation. In P. López Sáez, G. Castro, J. Navas López, & M. Delgado Verde (Eds.), *Intellectual capital and technological innovation: Knowledge-based theory and practice* (pp. 271–296). Hershey, PA: Information Science Reference; doi:10.4018/978-1-61520-875-3.ch013

Alhashem, A., & Shaqrah, A. A. (2012). Exploring the relationship between organizational memory and business innovation.[IJKBO]. *International Journal of Knowledge-Based Organizations*, *2*(3), 32–46. doi:10.4018/ijkbo.2012070102

Allan, M. B., Korolis, A. A., & Griffith, T. L. (2011). Reaching for the moon: Expanding transactive memory's reach with wikis and tagging. In M. Jennex (Ed.), *Global aspects and cultural perspectives on knowledge management: Emerging dimensions* (pp. 144–156). Hershey, PA: Information Science Reference; doi:10.4018/978-1-60960-555-1.ch010

Alsmadi, I., & Alda, S. (2013). Knowledge management and semantic web services. In S. Saeed & I. Alsmadi (Eds.), *Knowledge-based processes in software development* (pp. 35–48). Hershey, PA: Information Science Reference; doi:10.4018/978-1-4666-4229-4.ch003

Alstete, J. W., & Meyer, J. P. (2011). Expanding the model of competitive business strategy for knowledge-based organizations.[IJKBO]. *International Journal of Knowledge-Based Organizations*, *1*(4), 16–31. doi:10.4018/ijkbo.2011100102

Alstete, J. W., & Meyer, J. P. (2013). Expanding the model of competitive business strategy for knowledge-based organizations. In J. Wang (Ed.), *Intelligence methods and systems advancements for knowledge-based business* (pp. 132–148). Hershey, PA: Information Science Reference; doi:10.4018/978-1-4666-1873-2.ch008

Alves da Silva, N. S., Alvarez, I. M., & Rogerson, S. (2011). Glocality, diversity and ethics of distributed knowledge in higher education. In G. Morais da Costa (Ed.), *Ethical issues and social dilemmas in knowledge management: Organizational innovation* (pp. 131–159). Hershey, PA: Information Science Reference; doi:10.4018/978-1-61520-873-9.ch009

Anantatmula, V. S., & Kanungo, S. (2011). Strategies for successful implementation of KM in a university setting. In M. Jennex & S. Smolnik (Eds.), *Strategies for knowledge management success: Exploring organizational efficacy* (pp. 262–276). Hershey, PA: Information Science Reference; doi:10.4018/978-1-60566-709-6.ch014

Andreu, R., & Sieber, S. (2011). External and internal knowledge in organizations. In D. Schwartz & D. Te'eni (Eds.), *Encyclopedia of knowledge management* (2nd ed., pp. 298–307). Hershey, PA: Information Science Reference; doi:10.4018/978-1-59904-931-1.ch029

Andriessen, D. (2011). Metaphor use in knowledge management. In D. Schwartz & D. Te'eni (Eds.), *Encyclopedia of knowledge management* (2nd ed., pp. 1118–1124). Hershey, PA: Information Science Reference; doi:10.4018/978-1-59904-931-1.ch107

Angelopoulos, S., Kitsios, F., & Moustakis, V. (2012). Transformation of management in the public sector: Exploring the strategic frameworks of e-government. In T. Papadopoulos & P. Kanellis (Eds.), *Public sector reform using information technologies: Transforming policy into practice* (pp. 44–58). Hershey, PA: Information Science Reference; doi:10.4018/978-1-60960-839-2.ch003

Anselma, L., Bottrighi, A., Molino, G., Montani, S., Terenziani, P., & Torchio, M. (2013). Supporting knowledge-based decision making in the medical context: The GLARE approach. In J. Wang (Ed.), *Intelligence methods and systems advancements for knowledge-based business* (pp. 24–42). Hershey, PA: Information Science Reference; doi:10.4018/978-1-4666-1873-2.ch002

Arh, T., Dimovski, V., & Blažic, B. J. (2011). ICT and web 2.0 technologies as a determinant of business performance. In M. Al-Mutairi & L. Mohammed (Eds.), *Cases on ICT utilization, practice and solutions: Tools for managing day-to-day issues* (pp. 59–77). Hershey, PA: Information Science Reference; doi:10.4018/978-1-60960-015-0.ch005

Ariely, G. (2011). Operational knowledge management in the military. In D. Schwartz & D. Te'eni (Eds.), *Encyclopedia of knowledge management* (2nd ed., pp. 1250–1260). Hershey, PA: Information Science Reference; doi:10.4018/978-1-59904-931-1.ch119

Assefa, T., Garfield, M., & Meshesha, M. (2014). Enabling factors for knowledge sharing among employees in the workplace. In Y. Al-Bastaki & A. Shajera (Eds.), *Building a competitive public sector with knowledge management strategy* (pp. 246–271). Hershey, PA: Business Science Reference; doi:10.4018/978-1-4666-4434-2.ch011

Assudani, R. H. (2011). Negotiating knowledge gaps in dispersed knowledge work. [IJKBO]. *International Journal of Knowledge-Based Organizations*, *1*(3), 1–21. doi:10.4018/ijkbo.2011070101

Assudani, R. H. (2013). Negotiating knowledge gaps in dispersed knowledge work. In J. Wang (Ed.), *Intelligence methods and systems advancements for knowledge-based business* (pp. 75–96). Hershey, PA: Information Science Reference; doi:10.4018/978-1-4666-1873-2.ch005

Atkins, R. (2011). Supply chain knowledge integration in emerging economies. In M. Al-Shammari (Ed.), *Knowledge management in emerging economies: Social, organizational and cultural implementation* (pp. 104–121). Hershey, PA: Information Science Reference; doi:10.4018/978-1-61692-886-5.ch006

Aung, Z., & Nyunt, K. K. (2014). Constructive knowledge management model and information retrieval methods for software engineering. In *Software design and development: Concepts, methodologies, tools, and applications* (pp. 253–269). Hershey, PA: Information Science Reference; doi:10.4018/978-1-4666-4301-7.ch014

Aziz, M. W., Mohamad, R., & Jawawi, D. N. (2013). Ontology-based service description, discovery, and matching in distributed embedded real-time systems. In M. Nazir Ahmad, R. Colomb, & M. Abdullah (Eds.), *Ontology-based applications for enterprise systems and knowledge management* (pp. 178–190). Hershey, PA: Information Science Reference; doi:10.4018/978-1-4666-1993-7.ch010

Badia, A. (2011). Knowledge management and intelligence work: A promising combination. In D. Schwartz & D. Te'eni (Eds.), *Encyclopedia of knowledge management* (2nd ed., pp. 612–623). Hershey, PA: Information Science Reference; doi:10.4018/978-1-59904-931-1.ch059

Badr, K. B., & Ahmad, M. N. (2013). Managing lessons learned: A comparative study of lessons learned systems. In M. Nazir Ahmad, R. Colomb, & M. Abdullah (Eds.), *Ontology-based applications for enterprise systems and knowledge management* (pp. 224–245). Hershey, PA: Information Science Reference; doi:10.4018/978-1-4666-1993-7.ch013

Bakshi, K. (2014). Technologies for big data. In W. Hu & N. Kaabouch (Eds.), *Big data management, technologies, and applications* (pp. 1–22). Hershey, PA: Information Science Reference; doi:10.4018/978-1-4666-4699-5.ch001

Ballou, D. P., Belardo, S., & Pazer, H. L. (2012). A project staffing model to enhance the effectiveness of knowledge transfer in the requirements planning phase for multi-project environments. In M. Jennex (Ed.), *Conceptual models and outcomes of advancing knowledge management: New technologies* (pp. 77–98). Hershey, PA: Information Science Reference; doi:10.4018/978-1-4666-0035-5.ch005

Baporikar, N. (2011). Knowledge management and entrepreneurship cases in India. In M. Al-Shammari (Ed.), *Knowledge management in emerging economies: Social, organizational and cultural implementation* (pp. 325–346). Hershey, PA: Information Science Reference; doi:10.4018/978-1-61692-886-5.ch020

Baporikar, N. (2014). Knowledge management initiatives in Indian public sector. In Y. Al-Bastaki & A. Shajera (Eds.), *Building a competitive public sector with knowledge management strategy* (pp. 53–89). Hershey, PA: Business Science Reference; doi:10.4018/978-1-4666-4434-2.ch002

Baporikar, N. (2014). Organizational barriers and facilitators in embedding knowledge strategy. In M. Chilton & J. Bloodgood (Eds.), *Knowledge management and competitive advantage: Issues and potential solutions* (pp. 149–173). Hershey, PA: Information Science Reference; doi:10.4018/978-1-4666-4679-7.ch009

Barioni, M. C., Kaster, D. D., Razente, H. L., Traina, A. J., & Júnior, C. T. (2011). Querying multimedia data by similarity in relational DBMS. In L. Yan & Z. Ma (Eds.), *Advanced database query systems: Techniques, applications and technologies* (pp. 323–359). Hershey, PA: Information Science Reference; doi:10.4018/978-1-60960-475-2.ch014

Baroni de Carvalho, R., & Tavares Ferreira, M. A. (2011). Knowledge management software. In D. Schwartz & D. Te'eni (Eds.), *Encyclopedia of knowledge management* (2nd ed., pp. 738–749). Hershey, PA: Information Science Reference; doi:10.4018/978-1-59904-931-1.ch072

Barroso, A. C., Ricciardi, R. I., & Junior, J. A. (2012). Web 2.0 and project management: Reviewing the change path and discussing a few cases. In I. Boughzala & A. Dudezert (Eds.), *Knowledge management 2.0: Organizational models and enterprise strategies* (pp. 164–189). Hershey, PA: Information Science Reference; doi:10.4018/978-1-61350-195-5.ch009

Baskaran, V., Naguib, R., Guergachi, A., Bali, R., & Arochen, H. (2011). Does knowledge management really work? A case study in the breast cancer screening domain. In A. Eardley & L. Uden (Eds.), *Innovative knowledge management: Concepts for organizational creativity and collaborative design* (pp. 177–189). Hershey, PA: Information Science Reference; doi:10.4018/978-1-60566-701-0.ch010

Bebensee, T., Helms, R., & Spruit, M. (2012). Exploring the impact of web 2.0 on knowledge management. In I. Boughzala & A. Dudezert (Eds.), *Knowledge management 2.0: Organizational models and enterprise strategies* (pp. 17–43). Hershey, PA: Information Science Reference; doi:10.4018/978-1-61350-195-5.ch002

Becerra-Fernandez, I., & Sabherwal, R. (2011). The role of information and communication technologies in knowledge management: A classification of knowledge management systems. In D. Schwartz & D. Te'eni (Eds.), *Encyclopedia of knowledge management* (2nd ed., pp. 1410–1418). Hershey, PA: Information Science Reference; doi:10.4018/978-1-59904-931-1.ch134

Benbya, H. (2013). Valuing knowledge-based initiatives: What we know and what we don't know. In M. Jennex (Ed.), *Dynamic models for knowledge-driven organizations* (pp. 1–15). Hershey, PA: Business Science Reference; doi:10.4018/978-1-4666-2485-6.ch001

Berends, H., van der Bij, H., & Weggeman, M. (2011). Knowledge integration. In D. Schwartz & D. Te'eni (Eds.), *Encyclopedia of knowledge management* (2nd ed., pp. 581–590). Hershey, PA: Information Science Reference; doi:10.4018/978-1-59904-931-1.ch056

Berger, H., & Beynon-Davies, P. (2011). Knowledge-based diffusion in practice: A case study experience. In A. Eardley & L. Uden (Eds.), *Innovative knowledge management: Concepts for organizational creativity and collaborative design* (pp. 40–55). Hershey, PA: Information Science Reference; doi:10.4018/978-1-60566-701-0.ch003

Berio, G., Di Leva, A., Harzallah, M., & Sacco, G. M. (2012). Competence management over social networks through dynamic taxonomies. In I. Boughzala & A. Dudezert (Eds.), *Knowledge management 2.0: Organizational models and enterprise strategies* (pp. 103–120). Hershey, PA: Information Science Reference; doi:10.4018/978-1-61350-195-5.ch006

Bhatt, S., Chaudhary, S., & Bhise, M. (2013). Migration of data between cloud and non-cloud datastores. In A. Ionita, M. Litoiu, & G. Lewis (Eds.), *Migrating legacy applications: Challenges in service oriented architecture and cloud computing environments* (pp. 206–225). Hershey, PA: Information Science Reference; doi:10.4018/978-1-4666-2488-7.ch009

Bloodgood, J. M., Chilton, M. A., & Bloodgood, T. C. (2014). The effect of knowledge transfer motivation, receiver capability, and motivation on organizational performance. In M. Chilton & J. Bloodgood (Eds.), *Knowledge management and competitive advantage: Issues and potential solutions* (pp. 232–242). Hershey, PA: Information Science Reference; doi:10.4018/978-1-4666-4679-7.ch013

Boersma, K., & Kingma, S. (2011). Organizational learning facilitation with intranet (2.0): A socio-cultural approach. In D. Schwartz & D. Te'eni (Eds.), *Encyclopedia of knowledge management* (2nd ed., pp. 1280–1289). Hershey, PA: Information Science Reference; doi:10.4018/978-1-59904-931-1.ch122

Bond, P. L. (2010). Toward a living systems framework for unifying technology and knowledge management, organizational, cultural and economic change. In D. Harorimana (Ed.), *Cultural implications of knowledge sharing, management and transfer: Identifying competitive advantage* (pp. 108–132). Hershey, PA: Information Science Reference; doi:10.4018/978-1-60566-790-4.ch006

Bordogna, G., Bucci, F., Carrara, P., Pepe, M., & Rampini, A. (2011). Flexible querying of imperfect temporal metadata in spatial data infrastructures. In L. Yan & Z. Ma (Eds.), *Advanced database query systems: Techniques, applications and technologies* (pp. 140–159). Hershey, PA: Information Science Reference; doi:10.4018/978-1-60960-475-2.ch006

Boughzala, I. (2012). Collaboration 2.0 through the new organization (2.0) transformation. In I. Boughzala & A. Dudezert (Eds.), *Knowledge management 2.0: Organizational models and enterprise strategies* (pp. 1–16). Hershey, PA: Information Science Reference; doi:10.4018/978-1-61350-195-5.ch001

Bratianu, C. (2011). A new perspective of the intellectual capital dynamics in organizations. In B. Vallejo-Alonso, A. Rodriguez-Castellanos, & G. Arregui-Ayastuy (Eds.), *Identifying, measuring, and valuing knowledge-based intangible assets: New perspectives* (pp. 1–21). Hershey, PA: Business Science Reference; doi:10.4018/978-1-60960-054-9.ch001

Bratianu, C. (2011). Universities as knowledge-intensive learning organizations. In A. Eardley & L. Uden (Eds.), *Innovative knowledge management: Concepts for organizational creativity and collaborative design* (pp. 1–17). Hershey, PA: Information Science Reference; doi:10.4018/978-1-60566-701-0.ch001

Breu, K., Ward, J., & Murray, P. (2000). Success factors in leveraging the corporate information and knowledge resource through intranets. In Y. Malhotra (Ed.), *Knowledge management and virtual organizations* (pp. 306–320). Hershey, PA: Idea Group Publishing; doi:10.4018/978-1-930708-65-5.ch016

Briones-Peñalver, A., & Poças-Rascão, J. (2014). Information technologies (ICT), network organizations, and information systems for business cooperation: A focus on organization and strategic knowledge management. In G. Jamil, A. Malheiro, & F. Ribeiro (Eds.), *Rethinking the conceptual base for new practical applications in information value and quality* (pp. 324–348). Hershey, PA: Information Science Reference; doi:10.4018/978-1-4666-4562-2.ch015

Brock, J. K., & Zhou, Y. J. (2011). MNE knowledge management across borders and ICT. In D. Schwartz & D. Te'eni (Eds.), *Encyclopedia of knowledge management* (2nd ed., pp. 1136–1148). Hershey, PA: Information Science Reference; doi:10.4018/978-1-59904-931-1.ch109

Brunet-Thornton, R., & Bureš, V. (2011). Meeting Czech knowledge management challenges head-on: KM-Be.At-It. In M. Al-Shammari (Ed.), *Knowledge management in emerging economies: Social, organizational and cultural implementation* (pp. 20–46). Hershey, PA: Information Science Reference; doi:10.4018/978-1-61692-886-5.ch002

Bucher, T., & Dinter, B. (2012). Situational method engineering to support process-oriented information logistics: Identification of development situations.[JDM]. *Journal of Database Management*, *23*(1), 31–48. doi:10.4018/jdm.2012010102

Burstein, F., & Linger, H. (2011). Task-based knowledge management approach. In D. Schwartz & D. Te'eni (Eds.), *Encyclopedia of knowledge management* (2nd ed., pp. 1479–1489). Hershey, PA: Information Science Reference; doi:10.4018/978-1-59904-931-1.ch141

Butler, T. (2011). Anti-foundational knowledge management. In D. Schwartz & D. Te'eni (Eds.), *Encyclopedia of knowledge management* (2nd ed., pp. 1–11). Hershey, PA: Information Science Reference; doi:10.4018/978-1-59904-931-1.ch001

Butler, T., & Murphy, C. (2011). Work and knowledge. In D. Schwartz & D. Te'eni (Eds.), *Encyclopedia of knowledge management* (2nd ed., pp. 1556–1566). Hershey, PA: Information Science Reference; doi:10.4018/978-1-59904-931-1.ch148

Cabrilo, S., & Grubic-Nesic, L. (2013). The role of creativity, innovation, and invention in knowledge management. In S. Buckley & M. Jakovljevic (Eds.), *Knowledge management innovations for interdisciplinary education: Organizational applications* (pp. 207–232). Hershey, PA: Information Science Reference; doi:10.4018/978-1-4666-1969-2.ch011

Cabrita, M. D., Machado, V. C., & Grilo, A. (2010). Intellectual capital: How knowledge creates value. In E. O'Brien, S. Clifford, & M. Southern (Eds.), *Knowledge management for process, organizational and marketing innovation: Tools and methods* (pp. 237–252). Hershey, PA: Information Science Reference; doi:10.4018/978-1-61520-829-6.ch015

Cagliero, L., & Fiori, A. (2013). Knowledge discovery from online communities. In *Data mining: Concepts, methodologies, tools, and applications* (pp. 1230–1252). Hershey, PA: Information Science Reference; doi:10.4018/978-1-4666-2455-9.ch063

Camisón-Zornoza, C., & Boronat-Navarro, M. (2010). Linking exploration and exploitation capabilities with the process of knowledge development and with organizational facilitators. In M. Russ (Ed.), *Knowledge management strategies for business development* (pp. 159–179). Hershey, PA: Business Science Reference; doi:10.4018/978-1-60566-348-7.ch008

Carneiro, A. (2010). Change knowledge management: Transforming a ghost community into a real asset. In E. O'Brien, S. Clifford, & M. Southern (Eds.), *Knowledge management for process, organizational and marketing innovation: Tools and methods* (pp. 120–132). Hershey, PA: Information Science Reference; doi:10.4018/978-1-61520-829-6.ch007

Carrillo, F. J. (2010). Knowledge-based value generation. In K. Metaxiotis, F. Carrillo, & T. Yigitcanlar (Eds.), *Knowledge-based development for cities and societies: Integrated multi-level approaches* (pp. 1–16). Hershey, PA: Information Science Reference; doi:10.4018/978-1-61520-721-3.ch001

Cartelli, A. (2012). Frameworks for the benchmarking of digital and knowledge management best practice in SME and organizations. In A. Cartelli (Ed.), *Current trends and future practices for digital literacy and competence* (pp. 166–175). Hershey, PA: Information Science Reference; doi:10.4018/978-1-4666-0903-7.ch015

Castellano, G., Fanelli, A. M., & Torsello, M. A. (2010). Soft computing techniques in content-based multimedia information retrieval. In K. Anbumani & R. Nedunchezhian (Eds.), *Soft computing applications for database technologies: Techniques and issues* (pp. 170–192). Hershey, PA: Information Science Reference; doi:10.4018/978-1-60566-814-7.ch010

Chalkiti, K., & Carson, D. (2010). Knowledge cultures, competitive advantage and staff turnover in hospitality in Australia's northern territory. In D. Harorimana (Ed.), *Cultural implications of knowledge sharing, management and transfer: Identifying competitive advantage* (pp. 203–229). Hershey, PA: Information Science Reference; doi:10.4018/978-1-60566-790-4.ch010

Chang, W., & Li, S. (2011). Deploying knowledge management in R&D workspaces. In A. Eardley & L. Uden (Eds.), *Innovative knowledge management: Concepts for organizational creativity and collaborative design* (pp. 56–76). Hershey, PA: Information Science Reference; doi:10.4018/978-1-60566-701-0.ch004

Chawla, D., & Joshi, H. (2013). Impact of knowledge management dimensions on learning organization: Comparison across business excellence awarded and non-awarded indian organizations. In M. Jennex (Ed.), *Dynamic models for knowledge-driven organizations* (pp. 145–162). Hershey, PA: Business Science Reference; doi:10.4018/978-1-4666-2485-6.ch008

Chen, E. (2012). Web 2.0 social networking technologies and strategies for knowledge management. In I. Boughzala & A. Dudezert (Eds.), *Knowledge management 2.0: Organizational models and enterprise strategies* (pp. 84–102). Hershey, PA: Information Science Reference; doi:10.4018/978-1-61350-195-5.ch005

Chihara, K., & Nakamori, Y. (2013). Clarification of abilities and qualities of knowledge coordinators: The case of regional revitalization projects. In G. Yang (Ed.), *Multidisciplinary studies in knowledge and systems science* (pp. 1–17). Hershey, PA: Information Science Reference; doi:10.4018/978-1-4666-3998-0.ch001

Christidis, K., Papailiou, N., Apostolou, D., & Mentzas, G. (2011). Semantic interfaces for personal and social knowledge work.[IJKBO]. *International Journal of Knowledge-Based Organizations, 1*(1), 61–77. doi:10.4018/ijkbo.2011010104

Christidis, K., Papailiou, N., Apostolou, D., & Mentzas, G. (2013). Semantic interfaces for personal and social knowledge work. In J. Wang (Ed.), *Intelligence methods and systems advancements for knowledge-based business* (pp. 213–230). Hershey, PA: Information Science Reference; doi:10.4018/978-1-4666-1873-2.ch012

Chua, C. E., Storey, V. C., & Chiang, R. H. (2012). Knowledge representation: A conceptual modeling approach.[JDM]. *Journal of Database Management, 23*(1), 1–30. doi:10.4018/jdm.2012010101

Clinton, M. S., Merritt, K. L., & Murray, S. R. (2011). Facilitating knowledge transfer and the achievement of competitive advantage with corporate universities: An exploratory model based on media richness and type of knowledge to be transferred. In M. Jennex (Ed.), *Global aspects and cultural perspectives on knowledge management: Emerging dimensions* (pp. 329–345). Hershey, PA: Information Science Reference; doi:10.4018/978-1-60960-555-1.ch020

Colomb, R. M. (2013). Representation of action is a primary requirement in ontologies for interoperating information systems. In M. Nazir Ahmad, R. Colomb, & M. Abdullah (Eds.), *Ontology-based applications for enterprise systems and knowledge management* (pp. 68–76). Hershey, PA: Information Science Reference; doi:10.4018/978-1-4666-1993-7.ch004

Colucci, S., Di Noia, T., Di Sciascio, E., Donini, F. M., & Mongiello, M. (2011). Description logic-based resource retrieval. In D. Schwartz & D. Te'eni (Eds.), *Encyclopedia of knowledge management* (2nd ed., pp. 185–197). Hershey, PA: Information Science Reference; doi:10.4018/978-1-59904-931-1.ch018

Connell, N. A. (2011). Organisational storytelling. In D. Schwartz & D. Te'eni (Eds.), *Encyclopedia of knowledge management* (2nd ed., pp. 1261–1269). Hershey, PA: Information Science Reference; doi:10.4018/978-1-59904-931-1.ch120

Cooper, L. P., & Rober, M. B. (2012). Moving wikis behind the firewall: Intrapedias and work-wikis. In I. Boughzala & A. Dudezert (Eds.), *Knowledge Management 2.0: Organizational Models and Enterprise Strategies* (pp. 44–63). Hershey, PA: Information Science Reference; doi:10.4018/978-1-61350-195-5.ch003

Corallo, A., De Maggio, M., & Margherita, A. (2011). Knowledge democracy as the new mantra in product innovation: A framework of processes and competencies. In A. Eardley & L. Uden (Eds.), *Innovative knowledge management: Concepts for organizational creativity and collaborative design* (pp. 141–156). Hershey, PA: Information Science Reference; doi:10.4018/978-1-60566-701-0.ch008

Costa, G. (2011). Knowledge worker fair compensation: Ethical issues and social dilemmas. In G. Morais da Costa (Ed.), *Ethical issues and social dilemmas in knowledge management: Organizational innovation* (pp. 215–231). Hershey, PA: Information Science Reference; doi:10.4018/978-1-61520-873-9.ch013

Costello, R. (2014). Evaluating e-learning from an end user perspective. In M. Pańkowska (Ed.), *Frameworks of IT prosumption for business development* (pp. 259–283). Hershey, PA: Business Science Reference; doi:10.4018/978-1-4666-4313-0.ch017

Crasso, M., Zunino, A., & Campo, M. (2013). A survey of approaches to web service discovery in service-oriented architectures. In K. Siau (Ed.), *Innovations in database design, web applications, and information systems management* (pp. 107–138). Hershey, PA: Information Science Reference; doi:10.4018/978-1-4666-2044-5.ch005

Croasdell, D., & Wang, Y. K. (2011). Virtue-nets. In D. Schwartz & D. Te'eni (Eds.), *Encyclopedia of knowledge management* (2nd ed., pp. 1545–1555). Hershey, PA: Information Science Reference; doi:10.4018/978-1-59904-931-1.ch147

Cucchiara, S., Ligorio, M. B., & Fujita, N. (2014). Understanding online discourse strategies for knowledge building through social network analysis. In H. Lim & F. Sudweeks (Eds.), *Innovative methods and technologies for electronic discourse analysis* (pp. 42–62). Hershey, PA: Information Science Reference; doi:10.4018/978-1-4666-4426-7.ch003

Cudanov, M., & Kirchner, K. (2011). Knowledge management in high-growth companies: A case study in Serbia. In M. Al-Shammari (Ed.), *Knowledge management in emerging economies: Social, organizational and cultural implementation* (pp. 227–248). Hershey, PA: Information Science Reference; doi:10.4018/978-1-61692-886-5.ch014

Cuel, R., Bouquet, P., & Bonifacio, M. (2011). Distributed knowledge management. In D. Schwartz & D. Te'eni (Eds.), *Encyclopedia of knowledge management* (2nd ed., pp. 198–208). Hershey, PA: Information Science Reference; doi:10.4018/978-1-59904-931-1.ch019

Daidj, N. (2012). The evolution of KM practices: The case of the Renault-Nissan international strategic alliance. In I. Boughzala & A. Dudezert (Eds.), *Knowledge management 2.0: Organizational models and enterprise strategies* (pp. 190–213). Hershey, PA: Information Science Reference; doi:10.4018/978-1-61350-195-5.ch010

Daniel, B. K., Zapata-Rivera, J., & McCalla, G. I. (2010). A Bayesian belief network methodology for modeling social systems in virtual communities: Opportunities for database technologies. In K. Anbumani & R. Nedunchezhian (Eds.), *Soft computing applications for database technologies: Techniques and issues* (pp. 125–152). Hershey, PA: Information Science Reference; doi:10.4018/978-1-60566-814-7.ch008

Darchen, S., & Tremblay, D. (2010). Attracting and retaining knowledge workers: The impact of quality of place in the case of Montreal. In K. Metaxiotis, F. Carrillo, & T. Yigitcanlar (Eds.), *Knowledge-based development for cities and societies: Integrated multi-level approaches* (pp. 42–58). Hershey, PA: Information Science Reference; doi:10.4018/978-1-61520-721-3.ch003

Davenport, D. L., & Hosapple, C. W. (2011). Knowledge organizations. In D. Schwartz & D. Te'eni (Eds.), *Encyclopedia of knowledge management* (2nd ed., pp. 822–832). Hershey, PA: Information Science Reference; doi:10.4018/978-1-59904-931-1.ch079

Davenport, D. L., & Hosapple, C. W. (2011). Social capital knowledge. In D. Schwartz & D. Te'eni (Eds.), *Encyclopedia of knowledge management* (2nd ed., pp. 1448–1459). Hershey, PA: Information Science Reference; doi:10.4018/978-1-59904-931-1.ch138

De Maggio, M., Del Vecchio, P., Elia, G., & Grippa, F. (2011). An ICT-based network of competence centres for developing intellectual capital in the Mediterranean area. In A. Al Ajeeli & Y. Al-Bastaki (Eds.), *Handbook of research on e-services in the public sector: E-government strategies and advancements* (pp. 164–181). Hershey, PA: Information Science Reference; doi:10.4018/978-1-61520-789-3.ch014

Dehuri, S., Patra, M. R., Misra, B., & Jagadev, A. (2013). Intelligent techniques in recommendation systems: Contextual advancements and new methods (pp. 1-350). doi:10.4018/978-1-4666-2542-6

Delbaere, M., Di Zhang, D., Bruning, E. R., & Sivaramakrishnan, S. (2014). Knowledge management and the roles it plays in achieving superior performance. In M. Chilton & J. Bloodgood (Eds.), *Knowledge management and competitive advantage: Issues and potential solutions* (pp. 90–108). Hershey, PA: Information Science Reference; doi:10.4018/978-1-4666-4679-7.ch006

Delgado-Verde, M., & Cruz-González, J. (2010). An intellectual capital-based view of technological innovation. In P. López Sáez, G. Castro, J. Navas López, & M. Delgado Verde (Eds.), *Intellectual capital and technological innovation: Knowledge-based theory and practice* (pp. 166–193). Hershey, PA: Information Science Reference; doi:10.4018/978-1-61520-875-3.ch008

Deltour, F., Plé, L., & Roussel, C. S. (2012). Knowledge sharing in the age of web 2.0: A social capital perspective. In I. Boughzala & A. Dudezert (Eds.), *Knowledge management 2.0: Organizational models and enterprise strategies* (pp. 122–141). Hershey, PA: Information Science Reference; doi:10.4018/978-1-61350-195-5.ch007

Derballa, V., & Pousttchi, K. (2011). Mobile technology for knowledge management. In D. Schwartz & D. Te'eni (Eds.), *Encyclopedia of knowledge management* (2nd ed., pp. 1158–1166). Hershey, PA: Information Science Reference; doi:10.4018/978-1-59904-931-1.ch111

Dieng-Kuntz, R. (2011). Corporate semantic webs. In D. Schwartz & D. Te'eni (Eds.), *Encyclopedia of knowledge management* (2nd ed., pp. 131–149). Hershey, PA: Information Science Reference; doi:10.4018/978-1-59904-931-1.ch014

Diosteanu, A., Stellato, A., & Turbati, A. (2012). SODA: A service oriented data acquisition framework. In M. Pazienza & A. Stellato (Eds.), *Semi-automatic ontology development: Processes and resources* (pp. 48–77). Hershey, PA: Information Science Reference; doi:10.4018/978-1-4666-0188-8.ch003

Donate-Manzanares, M. J., Guadamillas-Gómez, F., & Sánchez de Pablo, J. D. (2010). Strategic alliances and knowledge management strategies: A case study. In M. Russ (Ed.), *Knowledge management strategies for business development* (pp. 240–260). Hershey, PA: Business Science Reference; doi:10.4018/978-1-60566-348-7.ch011

Donnet, T., Keast, R., & Pickernell, D. (2010). Up the junction? Exploiting knowledge-based development through supply chain and SME cluster interactions. In K. Metaxiotis, F. Carrillo, & T. Yigitcanlar (Eds.), *Knowledge-based development for cities and societies: Integrated multi-level approaches* (pp. 179–195). Hershey, PA: Information Science Reference; doi:10.4018/978-1-61520-721-3.ch011

Douglas, I. (2011). Organizational needs analysis and knowledge management. In D. Schwartz & D. Te'eni (Eds.), *Encyclopedia of knowledge management* (2nd ed., pp. 1290–1297). Hershey, PA: Information Science Reference; doi:10.4018/978-1-59904-931-1.ch123

Edvardsson, I. R., & Oskarsson, G. K. (2013). Outsourcing in knowledge-based service firms. In J. Wang (Ed.), *Intelligence methods and systems advancements for knowledge-based business* (pp. 97–113). Hershey, PA: Information Science Reference; doi:10.4018/978-1-4666-1873-2.ch006

Elenurm, T. (2013). Knowledge management and innovative learning. In S. Buckley & M. Jakovljevic (Eds.), *Knowledge management innovations for interdisciplinary education: Organizational applications* (pp. 108–131). Hershey, PA: Information Science Reference; doi:10.4018/978-1-4666-1969-2.ch006

Eppler, M. J., & Burkhard, R. A. (2011). Knowledge visualization. In D. Schwartz & D. Te'eni (Eds.), *Encyclopedia of knowledge management* (2nd ed., pp. 987–999). Hershey, PA: Information Science Reference; doi:10.4018/978-1-59904-931-1.ch094

Ergazakis, K., Metaxiotis, K., & Ergazakis, E. (2011). Exploring paths towards knowledge cities developments: A research agenda. In D. Schwartz & D. Te'eni (Eds.), *Encyclopedia of knowledge management* (2nd ed., pp. 288–297). Hershey, PA: Information Science Reference; doi:10.4018/978-1-59904-931-1.ch028

Eri, Z. D., Abdullah, R., Jabar, M. A., Murad, M. A., & Talib, A. M. (2013). Ontology-based virtual communities model for the knowledge management system environment: Ontology design. In M. Nazir Ahmad, R. Colomb, & M. Abdullah (Eds.), *Ontology-based applications for enterprise systems and knowledge management* (pp. 343–360). Hershey, PA: Information Science Reference; doi:10.4018/978-1-4666-1993-7.ch019

Erickson, G. S. (2014). Government as a partner in knowledge management: Lessons from the US freedom of information act. In Y. Al-Bastaki & A. Shajera (Eds.), *Building a competitive public sector with knowledge management strategy* (pp. 90–103). Hershey, PA: Business Science Reference; doi:10.4018/978-1-4666-4434-2.ch003

Erickson, G. S., & Rothberg, H. N. (2011). Assessing knowledge management needs: A strategic approach to developing knowledge.[IJKM]. *International Journal of Knowledge Management*, *7*(3), 1–10. doi:10.4018/jkm.2011070101

Erickson, G. S., & Rothberg, H. N. (2011). Assessing knowledge management needs: A strategic approach to developing knowledge.[IJKM]. *International Journal of Knowledge Management*, *7*(3), 1–10. doi:10.4018/jkm.2011070101

Erickson, G. S., & Rothberg, H. N. (2011). Protecting knowledge assets. In D. Schwartz & D. Te'eni (Eds.), *Encyclopedia of knowledge management* (2nd ed., pp. 1336–1342). Hershey, PA: Information Science Reference; doi:10.4018/978-1-59904-931-1.ch128

Erickson, G. S., & Rothberg, H. N. (2013). Assessing knowledge management needs: A strategic approach to developing knowledge. In M. Jennex (Ed.), *Dynamic models for knowledge-driven organizations* (pp. 180–189). Hershey, PA: Business Science Reference; doi:10.4018/978-1-4666-2485-6.ch010

Evermann, J., & Wand, Y. (2011). Ontology based object-oriented domain modeling: Representing behavior. In K. Siau (Ed.), *Theoretical and practical advances in information systems development: Emerging trends and approaches* (pp. 37–60). Hershey, PA: Information Science Reference; doi:10.4018/978-1-60960-521-6.ch003

Fadel, K. J., Durcikova, A., & Cha, H. S. (2011). An experiment of information elaboration in mediated knowledge transfer. In M. Jennex (Ed.), *Global aspects and cultural perspectives on knowledge management: Emerging dimensions* (pp. 311–328). Hershey, PA: Information Science Reference; doi:10.4018/978-1-60960-555-1.ch019

Fazel-Zarandi, M., Fox, M. S., & Yu, E. (2013). Ontologies in expertise finding systems: Modeling, analysis, and design. In M. Nazir Ahmad, R. Colomb, & M. Abdullah (Eds.), *Ontology-based applications for enterprise systems and knowledge management* (pp. 158–177). Hershey, PA: Information Science Reference; doi:10.4018/978-1-4666-1993-7.ch009

Ferri, F., & Grifoni, P. (2011). Sketching in knowledge creation and management. In D. Schwartz & D. Te'eni (Eds.), *Encyclopedia of knowledge management* (2nd ed., pp. 1438–1447). Hershey, PA: Information Science Reference; doi:10.4018/978-1-59904-931-1.ch137

Filho, C. G., Baroni de Carvalho, R., & Jamil, G. L. (2011). Market knowledge management, innovation and product performance: Survey in medium and large Brazilian industrial firms. In M. Jennex & S. Smolnik (Eds.), *Strategies for knowledge management success: Exploring organizational efficacy* (pp. 32–50). Hershey, PA: Information Science Reference; doi:10.4018/978-1-60566-709-6.ch003

Fink, D., & Disterer, G. (2011). Knowledge management in professional service firms. In D. Schwartz & D. Te'eni (Eds.), *Encyclopedia of knowledge management* (2nd ed., pp. 650–659). Hershey, PA: Information Science Reference; doi:10.4018/978-1-59904-931-1.ch063

Fink, K. (2011). Process model for knowledge potential measurement in SMEs. In M. Jennex & S. Smolnik (Eds.), *Strategies for knowledge management success: Exploring organizational efficacy* (pp. 91–105). Hershey, PA: Information Science Reference; doi:10.4018/978-1-60566-709-6.ch006

Fink, K., & Ploder, C. (2011). Knowledge management toolkit for SMEs. In M. Jennex (Ed.), *Global aspects and cultural perspectives on knowledge management: Emerging dimensions* (pp. 49–63). Hershey, PA: Information Science Reference; doi:10.4018/978-1-60960-555-1.ch004

Flynn, R., & Marshall, V. (2014). The four levers for change in knowledge management implementation. In Y. Al-Bastaki & A. Shajera (Eds.), *Building a competitive public sector with knowledge management strategy* (pp. 227–245). Hershey, PA: Business Science Reference; doi:10.4018/978-1-4666-4434-2.ch010

Fortier, J., & Kassel, G. (2011). Organizational semantic webs. In D. Schwartz & D. Te'eni (Eds.), *Encyclopedia of knowledge management* (2nd ed., pp. 1298–1307). Hershey, PA: Information Science Reference; doi:10.4018/978-1-59904-931-1.ch124

Framinan, J. M., & Molina, J. M. (2010). An overview of enterprise resource planning for intelligent enterprises. In *Business information systems: Concepts, methodologies, tools and applications* (pp. 60–68). Hershey, PA: Business Science Reference; doi:10.4018/978-1-61520-969-9.ch005

Franco, M., Di Virgilio, F., & Di Pietro, L. (2014). Management of group knowledge and the role of E-WOM for business organizations. In M. Chilton & J. Bloodgood (Eds.), *Knowledge management and competitive advantage: Issues and potential solutions* (pp. 71–89). Hershey, PA: Information Science Reference; doi:10.4018/978-1-4666-4679-7.ch005

Franke, U. J. (2000). The knowledge-based view (KBV) of the virtual web, the virtual corporation and the net-broker. In Y. Malhotra (Ed.), *Knowledge management and virtual organizations* (pp. 20–42). Hershey, PA: Idea Group Publishing; doi:10.4018/978-1-930708-65-5.ch002

Freivalds, D., & Lush, B. (2012). Thinking inside the grid: Selecting a discovery system through the RFP process. In M. Popp & D. Dallis (Eds.), *Planning and implementing resource discovery tools in academic libraries* (pp. 104–121). Hershey, PA: Information Science Reference; doi:10.4018/978-1-4666-1821-3.ch007

Frieß, M. R., Groh, G., Reinhardt, M., Forster, F., & Schlichter, J. (2012). Context-aware creativity support for corporate open innovation.[IJKBO]. *International Journal of Knowledge-Based Organizations, 2*(1), 38–55. doi:10.4018/ijkbo.2012010103

Fuller, C. M., & Wilson, R. L. (2011). Extracting knowledge from neural networks. In D. Schwartz & D. Te'eni (Eds.), *Encyclopedia of knowledge management* (2nd ed., pp. 320–330). Hershey, PA: Information Science Reference; doi:10.4018/978-1-59904-931-1.ch031

Furquim, T. D., & do Amaral, S. A. (2011). Knowledge management practices in brazilian software organizations: The case of SERPRO. In M. Al-Shammari (Ed.), *Knowledge management in emerging economies: Social, organizational and cultural implementation* (pp. 213–226). Hershey, PA: Information Science Reference; doi:10.4018/978-1-61692-886-5.ch013

Gaál, Z., Szabó, L., Obermayer-Kovács, N., Kovács, Z., & Csepregi, A. (2011). Knowledge management profile: An innovative approach to map knowledge management practice. In A. Eardley & L. Uden (Eds.), *Innovative knowledge management: Concepts for organizational creativity and collaborative design* (pp. 253–263). Hershey, PA: Information Science Reference; doi:10.4018/978-1-60566-701-0.ch016

Ganguly, A., Mostashari, A., & Mansouri, M. (2013). Measuring knowledge management/knowledge sharing (KM/KS) efficiency and effectiveness in enterprise networks. In M. Jennex (Ed.), *Dynamic models for knowledge-driven organizations* (pp. 318–336). Hershey, PA: Business Science Reference; doi:10.4018/978-1-4666-2485-6.ch019

Gaumand, C., Chapdaniel, A., & Dudezert, A. (2012). Strategic knowledge management system framework for supply chain at an intra-organizational level. In I. Boughzala & A. Dudezert (Eds.), *Knowledge management 2.0: Organizational models and enterprise strategies* (pp. 142–163). Hershey, PA: Information Science Reference; doi:10.4018/978-1-61350-195-5.ch008

Ghazali, R., & Zakaria, N. H. (2013). Knowledge management processes in enterprise systems: A systematic literature review. In M. Nazir Ahmad, R. Colomb, & M. Abdullah (Eds.), *Ontology-based applications for enterprise systems and knowledge management* (pp. 1–24). Hershey, PA: Information Science Reference; doi:10.4018/978-1-4666-1993-7.ch001

Ghosh, B. (2011). Cross-cultural knowledge management practices to support offshore outsourcing. In M. Al-Shammari (Ed.), *Knowledge management in emerging economies: Social, organizational and cultural implementation* (pp. 249–260). Hershey, PA: Information Science Reference; doi:10.4018/978-1-61692-886-5.ch015

Gohil, U., Carrillo, P., Ruikar, K., & Anumba, C. (2013). Development of a business process model for a project-based service organisation.[IJKBO]. *International Journal of Knowledge-Based Organizations*, *3*(1), 37–56. doi:10.4018/ijkbo.2013010103

Goldsmith, R. E., & Pillai, K. G. (2011). Knowledge calibration and knowledge management. In D. Schwartz & D. Te'eni (Eds.), *Encyclopedia of knowledge management* (2nd ed., pp. 497–505). Hershey, PA: Information Science Reference; doi:10.4018/978-1-59904-931-1.ch048

Gomes de Andrade, F., & Baptista, C. D. (2013). An ontology-based approach to support information discovery in spatial data infrastructures. In C. Rückemann (Ed.), *Integrated information and computing systems for natural, spatial, and social sciences* (pp. 369–387). Hershey, PA: Information Science Reference; doi:10.4018/978-1-4666-2190-9.ch018

Gonçalo, C. R., & Jacques, E. J. (2010). Best practices of knowledge strategy in hospitals: A contextual perspective based on the implementation of medical protocols. In D. Harorimana (Ed.), *Cultural implications of knowledge sharing, management and transfer: Identifying competitive advantage* (pp. 180–202). Hershey, PA: Information Science Reference; doi:10.4018/978-1-60566-790-4.ch009

Górniak-Kocikowska, K. (2011). Knowledge management and democracy: A critical review of some moral issues and social dilemmas. In G. Morais da Costa (Ed.), *Ethical issues and social dilemmas in knowledge management: Organizational innovation* (pp. 28–44). Hershey, PA: Information Science Reference; doi:10.4018/978-1-61520-873-9.ch003

Gottschalk, P. (2014). Police knowledge management strategy. In M. Chilton & J. Bloodgood (Eds.), *Knowledge management and competitive advantage: Issues and potential solutions* (pp. 202–220). Hershey, PA: Information Science Reference; doi:10.4018/978-1-4666-4679-7.ch011

Goudos, S. K., Peristeras, V., & Tarabanis, K. (2010). Application of semantic web technology in e-business: Case studies in public domain data knowledge representation. In *Business information systems: Concepts, methodologies, tools and applications* (pp. 1223–1233). Hershey, PA: Business Science Reference; doi:10.4018/978-1-61520-969-9.ch075

Govindarajan, M., & Chandrasekaran, R. (2012). A hybrid multilayer perceptron neural network for direct marketing.[IJKBO]. *International Journal of Knowledge-Based Organizations, 2*(3), 63–73. doi:10.4018/ijkbo.2012070104

Grant, J., & Minker, J. (2011). Logic and knowledge bases. In D. Schwartz & D. Te'eni (Eds.), *Encyclopedia of knowledge management* (2nd ed., pp. 1022–1033). Hershey, PA: Information Science Reference; doi:10.4018/978-1-59904-931-1.ch097

Green, A. (2011). Engineering business reasoning, analytics and intelligence network (E-BRAIN): A new approach to intangible asset valuation based on Einstein's perspective. In B. Vallejo-Alonso, A. Rodriguez-Castellanos, & G. Arregui-Ayastuy (Eds.), *Identifying, measuring, and valuing knowledge based intangible assets: New perspectives* (pp. 232–253). Hershey, PA: Business Science Reference; doi:10.4018/978-1-60960-054-9.ch011

Greenaway, K. E., & Vuong, D. C. (2010). Taking charities seriously: A call for focused knowledge management research.[IJKM]. *International Journal of Knowledge Management, 6*(4), 87–97. doi:10.4018/jkm.2010100105

Greenaway, K. E., & Vuong, D. C. (2012). Taking charities seriously: A call for focused knowledge management research. In M. Jennex (Ed.), *Conceptual models and outcomes of advancing knowledge management: New technologies* (pp. 333–344). Hershey, PA: Information Science Reference; doi:10.4018/978-1-4666-0035-5.ch017

Gunjal, B., Gaitanou, P., & Yasin, S. (2012). Social networks and knowledge management: An explorative study in library systems. In I. Boughzala & A. Dudezert (Eds.), *Knowledge management 2.0: Organizational models and enterprise strategies* (pp. 64–83). Hershey, PA: Information Science Reference; doi:10.4018/978-1-61350-195-5.ch004

Habhab-Rave, S. (2010). Knowledge management in SMEs: A mixture of innovation, marketing and ICT: Analysis of two case studies. In E. O'Brien, S. Clifford, & M. Southern (Eds.), *Knowledge management for process, organizational and marketing innovation: Tools and methods* (pp. 183–194). Hershey, PA: Information Science Reference; doi:10.4018/978-1-61520-829-6.ch011

Habicht, H., Möslein, K. M., & Reichwald, R. (2012). Open innovation maturity.[IJKBO]. *International Journal of Knowledge-Based Organizations*, *2*(1), 92–111. doi:10.4018/ijkbo.2012010106

Hamburg, I., & Hall, T. (2010). Readiness for knowledge management, methods and environments for innovation. In E. O'Brien, S. Clifford, & M. Southern (Eds.), *Knowledge management for process, organizational and marketing innovation: Tools and methods* (pp. 1–15). Hershey, PA: Information Science Reference; doi:10.4018/978-1-61520-829-6.ch001

Hamza, S. E. (2011). Capturing tacit knowledge from transient workers: Improving the organizational competitiveness. In M. Jennex (Ed.), *Global aspects and cultural perspectives on knowledge management: Emerging dimensions* (pp. 172–188). Hershey, PA: Information Science Reference; doi:10.4018/978-1-60960-555-1.ch012

Harorimana, D. (2010). Knowledge, culture, and cultural impact on knowledge management: Some lessons for researchers and practitioners. In D. Harorimana (Ed.), *Cultural implications of knowledge sharing, management and transfer: Identifying competitive advantage* (pp. 48–59). Hershey, PA: Information Science Reference; doi:10.4018/978-1-60566-790-4.ch003

Hasan, H. (2011). Formal and emergent standards in KM. In D. Schwartz & D. Te'eni (Eds.), *Encyclopedia of knowledge management* (2nd ed., pp. 331–342). Hershey, PA: Information Science Reference; doi:10.4018/978-1-59904-931-1.ch032

He, G., Xue, G., Yu, K., & Yao, S. (2013). Business process modeling: Analysis and evaluation. In Z. Lu (Ed.), *Design, performance, and analysis of innovative information retrieval* (pp. 382–393). Hershey, PA: Information Science Reference; doi:10.4018/978-1-4666-1975-3.ch027

Heiman, B. A., & Hurmelinna-Laukkanen, P. (2010). Problem finding and solving: A knowledge-based view of managing innovation. In P. López Sáez, G. Castro, J. Navas López, & M. Delgado Verde (Eds.), *Intellectual capital and technological innovation: Knowledge-based theory and practice* (pp. 105–130). Hershey, PA: Information Science Reference; doi:10.4018/978-1-61520-875-3.ch005

Hendriks, P. H. (2011). Organizational structure. In D. Schwartz & D. Te'eni (Eds.), *Encyclopedia of knowledge management* (2nd ed., pp. 1308–1318). Hershey, PA: Information Science Reference; doi:10.4018/978-1-59904-931-1.ch125

Hercheui, M. D. (2012). KMS for fostering behavior change: A case study on Microsoft Hohm. In I. Boughzala & A. Dudezert (Eds.), *Knowledge management 2.0: Organizational models and enterprise strategies* (pp. 214–232). Hershey, PA: Information Science Reference; doi:10.4018/978-1-61350-195-5.ch011

Hipkin, I. (2011). Perceptions of factors influencing knowledge-based technology management in conflict areas. In M. Al-Shammari (Ed.), *Knowledge management in emerging economies: Social, organizational and cultural implementation* (pp. 294–307). Hershey, PA: Information Science Reference; doi:10.4018/978-1-61692-886-5.ch018

Hofer, F. (2011). Knowledge transfer between academia and industry. In D. Schwartz & D. Te'eni (Eds.), *Encyclopedia of knowledge management* (2nd ed., pp. 977–986). Hershey, PA: Information Science Reference; doi:10.4018/978-1-59904-931-1.ch093

Holjevac, I. A., Crnjar, K., & Hrgovic, A. V. (2013). Knowledge management and quality in Croatian tourism. In S. Buckley & M. Jakovljevic (Eds.), *Knowledge management innovations for interdisciplinary education: Organizational applications* (pp. 178–192). Hershey, PA: Information Science Reference; doi:10.4018/978-1-4666-1969-2.ch009

Holsapple, C. W., & Joshi, K. D. (2011). Knowledge management ontology. In D. Schwartz & D. Te'eni (Eds.), *Encyclopedia of knowledge management* (2nd ed., pp. 704–711). Hershey, PA: Information Science Reference; doi:10.4018/978-1-59904-931-1.ch068

Holsapple, C. W., & Oh, J. (2014). Reactive and proactive dynamic capabilities: Using the knowledge chain theory of competitiveness. In M. Chilton & J. Bloodgood (Eds.), *Knowledge management and competitive advantage: Issues and potential solutions* (pp. 1–19). Hershey, PA: Information Science Reference; doi:10.4018/978-1-4666-4679-7.ch001

Huang, A., Xiao, J., & Wang, S. (2013). A combined forecast method integrating contextual knowledge. In G. Yang (Ed.), *Multidisciplinary studies in knowledge and systems science* (pp. 274–290). Hershey, PA: Information Science Reference; doi:10.4018/978-1-4666-3998-0.ch019

Huff, C. (2011). What does knowledge have to do with ethics? In G. Morais da Costa (Ed.), *Ethical issues and social dilemmas in knowledge management: Organizational innovation* (pp. 17–27). Hershey, PA: Information Science Reference; doi:10.4018/978-1-61520-873-9.ch002

Hürster, W., Wilbois, T., & Chaves, F. (2010). An integrated systems approach for early warning and risk management systems.[IJITSA]. *International Journal of Information Technologies and Systems Approach*, *3*(2), 46–56. doi:10.4018/jitsa.2010070104

Iyer, S. R., Sharda, R., Biros, D., Lucca, J., & Shimp, U. (2011). Organization of lessons learned knowledge: A taxonomy and implementation. In M. Jennex (Ed.), *Global aspects and cultural perspectives on knowledge management: Emerging dimensions* (pp. 190–209). Hershey, PA: Information Science Reference; doi:10.4018/978-1-60960-555-1.ch013

Jacobson, C. M. (2011). Knowledge sharing between individuals. In D. Schwartz & D. Te'eni (Eds.), *Encyclopedia of knowledge management* (2nd ed., pp. 924–934). Hershey, PA: Information Science Reference; doi:10.4018/978-1-59904-931-1.ch088

Jakovljevic, M. (2013). A conceptual model of creativity, invention, and innovation (MCII) for entrepreneurial engineers. In S. Buckley & M. Jakovljevic (Eds.), *Knowledge management innovations for interdisciplinary education: Organizational applications* (pp. 66–87). Hershey, PA: Information Science Reference; doi:10.4018/978-1-4666-1969-2.ch004

Jasimuddin, S. M., Connell, N., & Klein, J. H. (2011). Understanding organizational memory. In D. Schwartz & D. Te'eni (Eds.), *Encyclopedia of knowledge management* (2nd ed., pp. 1536–1544). Hershey, PA: Information Science Reference; doi:10.4018/978-1-59904-931-1.ch146

Jennex, M. E. (2010). Do organizational memory and information technology interact to affect organizational information needs and provision? In *Ubiquitous developments in knowledge management: Integrations and trends* (pp. 1–20). Hershey, PA: Information Science Reference; doi:10.4018/978-1-60566-954-0.ch001

Jennex, M. E. (2010). Knowledge sharing model of 24-hour knowledge factory. In *Ubiquitous developments in knowledge management: Integrations and trends* (pp. 141–154). Hershey, PA: Information Science Reference; doi:10.4018/978-1-60566-954-0.ch009

Jennex, M. E. (2010). Operationalizing knowledge sharing for informers. In *Ubiquitous developments in knowledge management: Integrations and trends* (pp. 319–340). Hershey, PA: Information Science Reference; doi:10.4018/978-1-60566-954-0.ch020

Jennex, M. E. (2010). Qualitative pre-processing for semantic search of unstructured knowledge. In *Ubiquitous developments in knowledge management: Integrations and trends* (pp. 252–263). Hershey, PA: Information Science Reference; doi:10.4018/978-1-60566-954-0.ch016

Jennex, M. E. (2010). A specialized evaluation and comparison of sample data mining software. In *Ubiquitous developments in knowledge management: Integrations and trends* (pp. 300–318). Hershey, PA: Information Science Reference; doi:10.4018/978-1-60566-954-0.ch019

Jennex, M. E. (2010). Using soft systems methodology to reveal socio-technical barriers to knowledge sharing and management: A case study from the UK national health service. In *Ubiquitous developments in knowledge management: Integrations and trends* (pp. 215–235). Hershey, PA: Information Science Reference; doi:10.4018/978-1-60566-954-0.ch014

Jennex, M. E. (2011). Knowledge management success models. In D. Schwartz & D. Te'eni (Eds.), *Encyclopedia of knowledge management* (2nd ed., pp. 763–771). Hershey, PA: Information Science Reference; doi:10.4018/978-1-59904-931-1.ch074

Jennex, M. E., & Olfman, L. (2011). A model of knowledge management success. In M. Jennex & S. Smolnik (Eds.), *Strategies for knowledge management success: Exploring organizational efficacy* (pp. 14–31). Hershey, PA: Information Science Reference; doi:10.4018/978-1-60566-709-6.ch002

Jennex, M. E., Smolnik, S., & Croasdell, D. (2011). Towards a consensus knowledge management success definition. In M. Jennex & S. Smolnik (Eds.), *Strategies for knowledge management success: Exploring organizational efficacy* (pp. 1–13). Hershey, PA: Information Science Reference; doi:10.4018/978-1-60566-709-6.ch001

Jewels, T. (2013). Teaching enterprise information systems in the United Arab Emirates. In F. Albadri (Ed.), *Information systems applications in the Arab education sector* (pp. 322–337). Hershey, PA: Information Science Reference; doi:10.4018/978-1-4666-1984-5.ch022

Jolly, R., & Wakeland, W. (2011). Using agent based simulation and game theory analysis to study knowledge flow in organizations: The KMscape. In M. Jennex (Ed.), *Global aspects and cultural perspectives on knowledge management: Emerging dimensions* (pp. 19–29). Hershey, PA: Information Science Reference; doi:10.4018/978-1-60960-555-1.ch002

Joshi, S. (2014). Web 2.0 and its implications on globally competitive business model. In M. Pańkowska (Ed.), *Frameworks of IT prosumption for business development* (pp. 86–101). Hershey, PA: Business Science Reference; doi:10.4018/978-1-4666-4313-0.ch007

Judge, R. (2011). A simulation system for evaluating knowledge management system (KMS) implementation strategies in small to mid-size enterprises (SME). In M. Jennex (Ed.), *Global aspects and cultural perspectives on knowledge management: Emerging dimensions* (pp. 92–112). Hershey, PA: Information Science Reference; doi:10.4018/978-1-60960-555-1.ch007

Kalid, K. S. (2011). Transfer knowledge using stories: A Malaysian university case study. In M. Al-Shammari (Ed.), *Knowledge management in emerging economies: Social, organizational and cultural implementation* (pp. 186–198). Hershey, PA: Information Science Reference; doi:10.4018/978-1-61692-886-5.ch011

Kamau, C. (2010). Strategising impression management in corporations: Cultural knowledge as capital. In D. Harorimana (Ed.), *Cultural implications of knowledge sharing, management and transfer: Identifying competitive advantage* (pp. 60–83). Hershey, PA: Information Science Reference; doi:10.4018/978-1-60566-790-4.ch004

Kamthan, P., & Fancott, T. (2011). A knowledge management model for patterns. In D. Schwartz & D. Te'eni (Eds.), *Encyclopedia of knowledge management* (2nd ed., pp. 694–703). Hershey, PA: Information Science Reference; doi:10.4018/978-1-59904-931-1.ch067

Kamthan, P., & Pai, H. (2011). Knowledge representation in pattern management. In D. Schwartz & D. Te'eni (Eds.), *Encyclopedia of knowledge management* (2nd ed., pp. 893–904). Hershey, PA: Information Science Reference; doi:10.4018/978-1-59904-931-1.ch085

Kane, G. C., Schwaig, K. S., & Storey, V. C. (2011). Information privacy: Understanding how firms behave online. In K. Siau (Ed.), *Theoretical and practical advances in information systems development: Emerging trends and approaches* (pp. 81–100). Hershey, PA: Information Science Reference; doi:10.4018/978-1-60960-521-6.ch005

Kankanhalli, A., Tan, B. C., & Wei, K. (2011). Knowledge producers and consumers. In D. Schwartz & D. Te'eni (Eds.), *Encyclopedia of knowledge management* (2nd ed., pp. 867–877). Hershey, PA: Information Science Reference; doi:10.4018/978-1-59904-931-1.ch083

Karagiannis, D., Woitsch, R., & Hrgovcic, V. (2010). Industrialisation of the knowledge work: The knowledge conveyer belt approach. In E. O'Brien, S. Clifford, & M. Southern (Eds.), *Knowledge management for process, organizational and marketing innovation: Tools and methods* (pp. 79–94). Hershey, PA: Information Science Reference; doi:10.4018/978-1-61520-829-6.ch005

Karlsson, F., & Ågerfalk, P. J. (2011). Towards structured flexibility in information systems development: Devising a method for method configuration. In K. Siau (Ed.), *Theoretical and practical advances in information systems development: Emerging trends and approaches* (pp. 214–238). Hershey, PA: Information Science Reference; doi:10.4018/978-1-60960-521-6.ch010

Karna, A., Singh, R., & Verma, S. (2010). Knowledge management for an effective sales and marketing function. In M. Russ (Ed.), *Knowledge management strategies for business development* (pp. 324–337). Hershey, PA: Business Science Reference; doi:10.4018/978-1-60566-348-7.ch015

Kassim, A. M., & Cheah, Y. (2013). SEMblog: An ontology-based semantic blogging tool for knowledge identification, organization, and reuse. In M. Nazir Ahmad, R. Colomb, & M. Abdullah (Eds.), *Ontology-based applications for enterprise systems and knowledge management* (pp. 210–223). Hershey, PA: Information Science Reference; doi:10.4018/978-1-4666-1993-7.ch012

Kayakutlu, G. (2010). Knowledge worker profile: A framework to clarify expectations. In K. Metaxiotis, F. Carrillo, & T. Yigitcanlar (Eds.), *Knowledge-based development for cities and societies: Integrated multi-level approaches* (pp. 162–178). Hershey, PA: Information Science Reference; doi:10.4018/978-1-61520-721-3.ch010

Kettunen, J., & Chaudhuri, M. R. (2011). Knowledge management to promote organizational change in India. In M. Al-Shammari (Ed.), *Knowledge management in emerging economies: Social, organizational and cultural implementation* (pp. 308–324). Hershey, PA: Information Science Reference; doi:10.4018/978-1-61692-886-5.ch019

Khalil, O. E., & Seleim, A. (2012). Culture and knowledge transfer capacity: A cross-national study. In M. Jennex (Ed.), *Conceptual models and outcomes of advancing knowledge management: New technologies* (pp. 305–332). Hershey, PA: Information Science Reference; doi:10.4018/978-1-4666-0035-5.ch016

Khasawneh, R., & Alazzam, A. (2014). Towards customer knowledge management (CKM): Where knowledge and customer meet. In M. Chilton & J. Bloodgood (Eds.), *Knowledge management and competitive advantage: Issues and potential solutions* (pp. 109–121). Hershey, PA: Information Science Reference; doi:10.4018/978-1-4666-4679-7.ch007

Kim, J. (2014). Big data sharing among academics. In W. Hu & N. Kaabouch (Eds.), *Big data management, technologies, and applications* (pp. 177–194). Hershey, PA: Information Science Reference; doi:10.4018/978-1-4666-4699-5.ch008

Kim, S., Felan, J., & Kang, M. H. (2011). An ontological approach to enterprise knowledge modeling in a shipping company.[IJKM]. *International Journal of Knowledge Management*, *7*(4), 70–84. doi:10.4018/jkm.2011100105

Kim, S., Felan, J., & Kang, M. H. (2013). An ontological approach to enterprise knowledge modeling in a shipping company. In M. Jennex (Ed.), *Dynamic models for knowledge-driven organizations* (pp. 351–363). Hershey, PA: Business Science Reference; doi:10.4018/978-1-4666-2485-6.ch021

King, W. R. (2011). Knowledge transfer. In D. Schwartz & D. Te'eni (Eds.), *Encyclopedia of knowledge management* (2nd ed., pp. 967–976). Hershey, PA: Information Science Reference; doi:10.4018/978-1-59904-931-1.ch092

Kivijärvi, H., Piirainen, K., & Tuominen, M. (2010). Sustaining organizational innovativeness: Advancing knowledge sharing during the scenario process.[IJKM]. *International Journal of Knowledge Management, 6*(2), 22–39. doi:10.4018/jkm.2010040102

Kivijärvi, H., Piirainen, K., & Tuominen, M. (2012). Sustaining organizational innovativeness: Advancing knowledge sharing during the scenario process. In M. Jennex (Ed.), *Conceptual models and outcomes of advancing knowledge management: New technologies* (pp. 99–117). Hershey, PA: Information Science Reference; doi:10.4018/978-1-4666-0035-5.ch006

Knyazhansky, M., & Plotkin, T. (2012). Knowledge bases over algebraic models: Some notes about informational equivalence.[IJKM]. *International Journal of Knowledge Management, 8*(1), 22–39. doi:10.4018/jkm.2012010102

Kong, E. (2014). The role of social intelligence in acquiring external knowledge for human capital development, organisational learning, and innovation. In M. Chilton & J. Bloodgood (Eds.), *Knowledge management and competitive advantage: Issues and potential solutions* (pp. 53–70). Hershey, PA: Information Science Reference; doi:10.4018/978-1-4666-4679-7.ch004

Kor, A., & Orange, G. (2011). A survey of epistemology and its implications on an organisational information and knowledge management model. In A. Eardley & L. Uden (Eds.), *Innovative knowledge management: Concepts for organizational creativity and collaborative design* (pp. 95–124). Hershey, PA: Information Science Reference; doi:10.4018/978-1-60566-701-0.ch006

Kostrzewa, A., Laaksoharju, M., & Kavathatzopoulos, I. (2011). Management of moral knowledge and ethical processes in organizations. In G. Morais da Costa (Ed.), *Ethical issues and social dilemmas in knowledge management: Organizational innovation* (pp. 199–214). Hershey, PA: Information Science Reference; doi:10.4018/978-1-61520-873-9.ch012

Kraaijenbrink, J., & Wijnhoven, F. (2011). External knowledge integration. In D. Schwartz & D. Te'eni (Eds.), *Encyclopedia of knowledge management* (2nd ed., pp. 308–319). Hershey, PA: Information Science Reference; doi:10.4018/978-1-59904-931-1.ch030

Kraft, T. A., & Steenkamp, A. L. (2012). A holistic approach for understanding project management. In F. Stowell (Ed.), *Systems approach applications for developments in information technology* (pp. 25–39). Hershey, PA: Information Science Reference; doi:10.4018/978-1-4666-1562-5.ch003

Kulkarni, U., & Freeze, R. (2011). Measuring knowledge management capabilities. In D. Schwartz & D. Te'eni (Eds.), *Encyclopedia of knowledge management* (2nd ed., pp. 1090–1100). Hershey, PA: Information Science Reference; doi:10.4018/978-1-59904-931-1.ch104

Kumar, A. S., Alrabea, A., & Sekhar, P. C. (2013). Temporal association rule mining in large databases. In *Data mining: Concepts, methodologies, tools, and applications* (pp. 586–602). Hershey, PA: Information Science Reference; doi:10.4018/978-1-4666-2455-9.ch029

Laihonen, H., & Koivuaho, M. (2011). Knowledge flow audit: indentifying, measuring and managing knowledge asset dynamics. In B. Vallejo-Alonso, A. Rodriguez-Castellanos, & G. Arregui-Ayastuy (Eds.), *Identifying, measuring, and valuing knowledge-based intangible assets: New perspectives* (pp. 22–42). Hershey, PA: Business Science Reference; doi:10.4018/978-1-60960-054-9.ch002

Land, F., Amjad, U., & Nolas, S. (2011). Knowledge management processes. In D. Schwartz & D. Te'eni (Eds.), *Encyclopedia of knowledge management* (2nd ed., pp. 719–727). Hershey, PA: Information Science Reference; doi:10.4018/978-1-59904-931-1.ch070

Lavanderos, L. P., & Fiol, E. S. (2011). Production cognitive capital as a measurement of intellectual capital. In B. Vallejo-Alonso, A. Rodriguez-Castellanos, & G. Arregui-Ayastuy (Eds.), *Identifying, measuring, and valuing knowledge-based intangible assets: New perspectives* (pp. 112–132). Hershey, PA: Business Science Reference; doi:10.4018/978-1-60960-054-9.ch006

Lavoué, É., George, S., & Prévôt, P. (2011). A knowledge management tool for the interconnection of communities of practice.[IJKM]. *International Journal of Knowledge Management, 7*(1), 55–76. doi:10.4018/jkm.2011010104

Lee, H., Chan, K., & Tsui, E. (2013). Knowledge mining Wikipedia: An ontological approach. In G. Yang (Ed.), *Multidisciplinary studies in knowledge and systems science* (pp. 52–62). Hershey, PA: Information Science Reference; doi:10.4018/978-1-4666-3998-0.ch005

Leung, N. K. (2011). A re-distributed knowledge management framework in help desk. In D. Schwartz & D. Te'eni (Eds.), *Encyclopedia of knowledge management* (2nd ed., pp. 1374–1381). Hershey, PA: Information Science Reference; doi:10.4018/978-1-59904-931-1.ch131

Li, Y., Guo, H., & Wang, S. (2010). A multiple-bits watermark for relational data. In K. Siau & J. Erickson (Eds.), *Principle advancements in database management technologies: New applications and frameworks* (pp. 1–22). Hershey, PA: Information Science Reference; doi:10.4018/978-1-60566-904-5.ch001

Lin, C. Y. (2013). Intellectual capital explains a country's resilience to financial crisis: A resource-based view. In P. Ordóñez de Pablos, R. Tennyson, & J. Zhao (Eds.), *Intellectual capital strategy management for knowledge-based organizations* (pp. 52–75). Hershey, PA: Business Science Reference; doi:10.4018/978-1-4666-3655-2.ch005

Lin, Y., & Dalkir, K. (2012). Factors affecting KM implementation in the Chinese community. In M. Jennex (Ed.), *Conceptual models and outcomes of advancing knowledge management: New technologies* (pp. 1–23). Hershey, PA: Information Science Reference; doi:10.4018/978-1-4666-0035-5.ch001

Lindsey, K. L. (2011). Barriers to knowledge sharing. In D. Schwartz & D. Te'eni (Eds.), *Encyclopedia of knowledge management* (2nd ed., pp. 49–61). Hershey, PA: Information Science Reference; doi:10.4018/978-1-59904-931-1.ch006

Liu, K., Tan, H. B., & Chen, X. (2013). Aiding maintenance of database applications through extracting attribute dependency graph.[JDM]. *Journal of Database Management, 24*(1), 20–35. doi:10.4018/jdm.2013010102

Liu, K., Tan, H. B., & Chen, X. (2013). Automated insertion of exception handling for key and referential constraints.[JDM]. *Journal of Database Management, 24*(1), 1–19. doi:10.4018/jdm.2013010101

Locuratolo, E., & Palomäki, J. (2013). Ontology for database preservation. In M. Nazir Ahmad, R. Colomb, & M. Abdullah (Eds.), *Ontology-based applications for enterprise systems and knowledge management* (pp. 141–157). Hershey, PA: Information Science Reference; doi:10.4018/978-1-4666-1993-7.ch008

López-Nicolás, C., & Meroño-Cerdán, Á. L. (2010). A model for knowledge management and intellectual capital audits. In M. Russ (Ed.), *Knowledge management strategies for business development* (pp. 115–131). Hershey, PA: Business Science Reference; doi:10.4018/978-1-60566-348-7.ch006

Luck, D. (2010). The implications of the development and implementation of CRM for knowledge management. In M. Russ (Ed.), *Knowledge management strategies for business development* (pp. 338–352). Hershey, PA: Business Science Reference; doi:10.4018/978-1-60566-348-7.ch016

Lukovic, I., Ivancevic, V., Celikovic, M., & Aleksic, S. (2014). DSLs in action with model based approaches to information system development. In *Software design and development: Concepts, methodologies, tools, and applications* (pp. 596–626). Hershey, PA: Information Science Reference; doi:10.4018/978-1-4666-4301-7.ch029

Luna-Reyes, L. F., & Gil-Garcia, J. R. (2012). Government and inter-organizational collaboration as strategies for administrative reform in Mexico. In T. Papadopoulos & P. Kanellis (Eds.), *Public sector reform using information technologies: Transforming policy into practice* (pp. 79–101). Hershey, PA: Information Science Reference; doi:10.4018/978-1-60960-839-2.ch005

Lungu, C. I., Caraiani, C., & Dascalu, C. (2013). Sustainable intellectual capital: The inference of corporate social responsibility within intellectual capital. In P. Ordóñez de Pablos, R. Tennyson, & J. Zhao (Eds.), *Intellectual capital strategy management for knowledge-based organizations* (pp. 156–173). Hershey, PA: Business Science Reference; doi:10.4018/978-1-4666-3655-2.ch009

Ma, Z. M. (2011). Engineering design knowledge management. In D. Schwartz & D. Te'eni (Eds.), *Encyclopedia of knowledge management* (2nd ed., pp. 263–269). Hershey, PA: Information Science Reference; doi:10.4018/978-1-59904-931-1.ch025

Maier, R., & Hadrich, T. (2011). Knowledge management systems. In D. Schwartz & D. Te'eni (Eds.), *Encyclopedia of knowledge management* (2nd ed., pp. 779–790). Hershey, PA: Information Science Reference; doi:10.4018/978-1-59904-931-1.ch076

Maria, E. D., & Micelli, S. (2010). SMEs and competitive advantage: A mix of innovation, marketing and ICT—The case of "made in Italy". In M. Russ (Ed.), *Knowledge management strategies for business development* (pp. 310–323). Hershey, PA: Business Science Reference; doi:10.4018/978-1-60566-348-7.ch014

Mariano, S., & Simionato, N. (2010). Where are we looking? A practical approach to managing knowledge captured from eye-tracking experiments: The experience of gulf air. In E. O'Brien, S. Clifford, & M. Southern (Eds.), *Knowledge management for process, organizational and marketing innovation: Tools and methods* (pp. 216–227). Hershey, PA: Information Science Reference; doi:10.4018/978-1-61520-829-6.ch013

Marques, M. B. (2014). The value of information and information services in knowledge society. In G. Jamil, A. Malheiro, & F. Ribeiro (Eds.), *Rethinking the conceptual base for new practical applications in information value and quality* (pp. 134–161). Hershey, PA: Information Science Reference; doi:10.4018/978-1-4666-4562-2.ch007

Masrom, M., Mahmood, N. H., & Al-Araimi, A. A. (2014). Exploring knowledge types and knowledge protection in organizations. In M. Chilton & J. Bloodgood (Eds.), *Knowledge management and competitive advantage: Issues and potential solutions* (pp. 271–280). Hershey, PA: Information Science Reference; doi:10.4018/978-1-4666-4679-7.ch016

Masterson, F. (2013). Knowledge management in practice: Using wikis to facilitate project-based learning. In S. Buckley & M. Jakovljevic (Eds.), *Knowledge management innovations for interdisciplinary education: Organizational applications* (pp. 385–401). Hershey, PA: Information Science Reference; doi:10.4018/978-1-4666-1969-2.ch019

Mattmann, C. A., Hart, A., Cinquini, L., Lazio, J., Khudikyan, S., & Jones, D. ... Robnett, J. (2014). Scalable data mining, archiving, and big data management for the next generation astronomical telescopes. In W. Hu, & N. Kaabouch (Eds.) Big data management, technologies, and applications (pp. 196-221). Hershey, PA: Information Science Reference. doi:10.4018/978-1-4666-4699-5.ch009

Maule, R. W. (2011). Military knowledge management. In D. Schwartz & D. Te'eni (Eds.), *Encyclopedia of knowledge management* (2nd ed., pp. 1125–1135). Hershey, PA: Information Science Reference; doi:10.4018/978-1-59904-931-1.ch108

Mavridis, I. (2011). Deploying privacy improved RBAC in web information systems. [IJITSA]. *International Journal of Information Technologies and Systems Approach*, *4*(2), 70–87. doi:10.4018/jitsa.2011070105

Mavridis, I. (2012). Deploying privacy improved RBAC in web information systems. In F. Stowell (Ed.), *Systems approach applications for developments in information technology* (pp. 298–315). Hershey, PA: Information Science Reference; doi:10.4018/978-1-4666-1562-5.ch020

McLaughlin, S. (2011). Assessing the impact of knowledge transfer mechanisms on supply chain performance. In M. Jennex (Ed.), *Global aspects and cultural perspectives on knowledge management: Emerging dimensions* (pp. 157–171). Hershey, PA: Information Science Reference; doi:10.4018/978-1-60960-555-1.ch011

Medina, J. M., & Spinola, M. D. (2011). Understanding the behavior of knowledge management pathways: The case of small manufacturers of footwear in Peru and Brazil. In M. Al-Shammari (Ed.), *Knowledge management in emerging economies: Social, organizational and cultural implementation* (pp. 261–271). Hershey, PA: Information Science Reference; doi:10.4018/978-1-61692-886-5.ch016

Meloche, J. A., Hasan, H., Willis, D., Pfaff, C. C., & Qi, Y. (2011). Cocreating corporate knowledge with a wiki. In M. Jennex (Ed.), *Global aspects and cultural perspectives on knowledge management: Emerging dimensions* (pp. 126–143). Hershey, PA: Information Science Reference; doi:10.4018/978-1-60960-555-1.ch009

Melzer, S. (2013). On the relationship between ontology-based and holistic representations in a knowledge management system. In M. Nazir Ahmad, R. Colomb, & M. Abdullah (Eds.), *Ontology-based applications for enterprise systems and knowledge management* (pp. 292–323). Hershey, PA: Information Science Reference; doi:10.4018/978-1-4666-1993-7.ch017

Mendes, E., & Baker, S. (2013). Using knowledge management and aggregation techniques to improve web effort estimation. In S. Saeed & I. Alsmadi (Eds.), *Knowledge-based processes in software development* (pp. 64–85). Hershey, PA: Information Science Reference; doi:10.4018/978-1-4666-4229-4.ch005

Metaxiotis, K. (2011). Healthcare knowledge management. In D. Schwartz & D. Te'eni (Eds.), *Encyclopedia of knowledge management* (2nd ed., pp. 366–375). Hershey, PA: Information Science Reference; doi:10.4018/978-1-59904-931-1.ch035

Mikolajuk, Z. (2013). Community-based development of knowledge products. In M. Jennex (Ed.), *Dynamic models for knowledge-driven organizations* (pp. 268–281). Hershey, PA: Business Science Reference; doi:10.4018/978-1-4666-2485-6.ch016

Mischo, W. H., Schlembach, M. C., Bishoff, J., & German, E. M. (2012). User search activities within an academic library gateway: Implications for web-scale discovery systems. In M. Popp & D. Dallis (Eds.), *Planning and implementing resource discovery tools in academic libraries* (pp. 153–173). Hershey, PA: Information Science Reference; doi:10.4018/978-1-4666-1821-3.ch010

Mishra, B., & Shukla, K. K. (2014). Data mining techniques for software quality prediction. In *Software design and development: Concepts, methodologies, tools, and applications* (pp. 401–428). Hershey, PA: Information Science Reference; doi:10.4018/978-1-4666-4301-7.ch021

Moffett, S., Walker, T., & McAdam, R. (2014). Best value and performance management inspired change within UK councils: A knowledge management perspective. In Y. Al-Bastaki & A. Shajera (Eds.), *Building a competitive public sector with knowledge management strategy* (pp. 199–226). Hershey, PA: Business Science Reference; doi:10.4018/978-1-4666-4434-2.ch009

Mueller, C. E., & Bradley, K. D. (2011). Utilizing the Rasch model to develop and evaluate items for the tacit knowledge inventory for superintendents (TKIS). In M. Jennex (Ed.), *Global aspects and cultural perspectives on knowledge management: Emerging dimensions* (pp. 264–284). Hershey, PA: Information Science Reference; doi:10.4018/978-1-60960-555-1.ch017

Muhammed, S., Doll, W. J., & Deng, X. (2011). Impact of knowledge management practices on task knowledge: An individual level study.[IJKM]. *International Journal of Knowledge Management*, *7*(4), 1–21. doi:10.4018/jkm.2011100101

Muhammed, S., Doll, W. J., & Deng, X. (2011). Measuring knowledge management outcomes at the individual level: Towards a tool for research on organizational culture. In M. Jennex (Ed.), *Global aspects and cultural perspectives on knowledge management: Emerging dimensions* (pp. 1–18). Hershey, PA: Information Science Reference; doi:10.4018/978-1-60960-555-1.ch001

Muhammed, S., Doll, W. J., & Deng, X. (2013). Impact of knowledge management practices on task knowledge: An individual level study. In M. Jennex (Ed.), *Dynamic models for knowledge-driven organizations* (pp. 282–301). Hershey, PA: Business Science Reference; doi:10.4018/978-1-4666-2485-6.ch017

Murata, K. (2011). Knowledge creation and sharing in Japanese organisations: A socio-cultural perspective on ba. In G. Morais da Costa (Ed.), *Ethical issues and social dilemmas in knowledge management: Organizational innovation* (pp. 1–16). Hershey, PA: Information Science Reference; doi:10.4018/978-1-61520-873-9.ch001

Murphy, P. (2013). Systems of communication: Information, explanation, and imagination. In G. Yang (Ed.), *Multidisciplinary studies in knowledge and systems science* (pp. 63–78). Hershey, PA: Information Science Reference; doi:10.4018/978-1-4666-3998-0.ch006

Nach, H. (2013). Structuring knowledge for enterprise resource planning implementation through an ontology. In M. Nazir Ahmad, R. Colomb, & M. Abdullah (Eds.), *Ontology-based applications for enterprise systems and knowledge management* (pp. 25–42). Hershey, PA: Information Science Reference; doi:10.4018/978-1-4666-1993-7.ch002

Nah, F. F., Hong, W., Chen, L., & Lee, H. (2010). Information search patterns in e-commerce product comparison services.[JDM]. *Journal of Database Management*, *21*(2), 26–40. doi:10.4018/jdm.2010040102

Nah, F. F., Hong, W., Chen, L., & Lee, H. (2012). Information search patterns in e-commerce product comparison services. In K. Siau (Ed.), *Cross-disciplinary models and applications of database management: Advancing approaches* (pp. 131–145). Hershey, PA: Information Science Reference; doi:10.4018/978-1-61350-471-0.ch006

Natarajan, R., & Shekar, B. (2011). Knowledge patterns in databases. In D. Schwartz & D. Te'eni (Eds.), *Encyclopedia of knowledge management* (2nd ed., pp. 842–852). Hershey, PA: Information Science Reference; doi:10.4018/978-1-59904-931-1.ch081

Nelson, R. E., & Hsu, H. S. (2011). A social network perspective on knowledge management. In D. Schwartz & D. Te'eni (Eds.), *Encyclopedia of knowledge management* (2nd ed., pp. 1470–1478). Hershey, PA: Information Science Reference; doi:10.4018/978-1-59904-931-1.ch140

Neto, R. C., & Souza, R. R. (2010). Knowledge management as an organizational process: From a theoretical framework to implementation guidelines. In E. O'Brien, S. Clifford, & M. Southern (Eds.), *Knowledge management for process, organizational and marketing innovation: Tools and methods* (pp. 16–35). Hershey, PA: Information Science Reference; doi:10.4018/978-1-61520-829-6.ch002

Newell, S. (2011). Understanding innovation processes. In D. Schwartz & D. Te'eni (Eds.), *Encyclopedia of knowledge management* (2nd ed., pp. 1525–1535). Hershey, PA: Information Science Reference; doi:10.4018/978-1-59904-931-1.ch145

Nikabadi, M. S., & Zamanloo, S. (2012). A multidimensional structure for describing the influence of supply chain strategies, business strategies, and knowledge management strategies on knowledge sharing in supply chain.[IJKM]. *International Journal of Knowledge Management*, *8*(4), 50–70. doi:10.4018/jkm.2012100103

Nissen, M. (2014). Cyberspace and cloud knowledge. In *Harnessing dynamic knowledge principles in the technology-driven world* (pp. 193–204). Hershey, PA: Information Science Reference; doi:10.4018/978-1-4666-4727-5.ch012

Nissen, M. (2014). Social media knowledge. In *Harnessing dynamic knowledge principles in the technology-driven world* (pp. 219–227). Hershey, PA: Information Science Reference; doi:10.4018/978-1-4666-4727-5.ch014

Nissen, M. E. (2014). Harnessing knowledge power for competitive advantage. In M. Chilton & J. Bloodgood (Eds.), *Knowledge management and competitive advantage: Issues and potential solutions* (pp. 20–34). Hershey, PA: Information Science Reference; doi:10.4018/978-1-4666-4679-7.ch002

Nissen, M. E., & Levitt, R. E. (2011). Knowledge management research through computational experimentation. In D. Schwartz & D. Te'eni (Eds.), *Encyclopedia of knowledge management* (2nd ed., pp. 728–737). Hershey, PA: Information Science Reference; doi:10.4018/978-1-59904-931-1.ch071

Nisula, A. (2014). Developing organizational renewal capability in the municipal (city) organization. In Y. Al-Bastaki & A. Shajera (Eds.), *Building a competitive public sector with knowledge management strategy* (pp. 151–172). Hershey, PA: Business Science Reference; doi:10.4018/978-1-4666-4434-2.ch007

Niu, B., Martin, P., & Powley, W. (2011). Towards autonomic workload management in DBMSs. In K. Siau (Ed.), *Theoretical and practical advances in information systems development: Emerging trends and approaches* (pp. 154–173). Hershey, PA: Information Science Reference; doi:10.4018/978-1-60960-521-6.ch008

Nobre, F. S., & Walker, D. S. (2011). A dynamic ability-based view of the organization.[IJKM]. *International Journal of Knowledge Management, 7*(2), 86–101. doi:10.4018/jkm.2011040105

O'Brien, J. (2014). Lessons from the private sector: A framework to be adopted in the public sector. In Y. Al-Bastaki & A. Shajera (Eds.), *Building a competitive public sector with knowledge management strategy* (pp. 173–198). Hershey, PA: Business Science Reference; doi:10.4018/978-1-4666-4434-2.ch008

Omari, A. (2013). Supporting companies management and improving their productivity through mining customers transactions. In *Data mining: Concepts, methodologies, tools, and applications* (pp. 1519–1533). Hershey, PA: Information Science Reference; doi:10.4018/978-1-4666-2455-9.ch079

Onwubiko, C. (2014). Modelling situation awareness information and system requirements for the mission using goal-oriented task analysis approach. In *Software design and development: Concepts, methodologies, tools, and applications* (pp. 460–478). Hershey, PA: Information Science Reference; doi:10.4018/978-1-4666-4301-7.ch023

Orth, A., Smolnik, S., & Jennex, M. E. (2011). The relevance of integration for knowledge management success: Towards conceptual and empirical evidence. In M. Jennex & S. Smolnik (Eds.), *Strategies for knowledge management success: Exploring organizational efficacy* (pp. 238–261). Hershey, PA: Information Science Reference; doi:10.4018/978-1-60566-709-6.ch013

Othman, A. K., & Abdullah, H. S. (2011). The influence of emotional intelligence on tacit knowledge sharing in service organizations. In M. Al-Shammari (Ed.), *Knowledge management in emerging economies: Social, organizational and cultural implementation* (pp. 171–185). Hershey, PA: Information Science Reference; doi:10.4018/978-1-61692-886-5.ch010

Pagallo, U. (2011). The trouble with digital copies: A short KM phenomenology. In G. Morais da Costa (Ed.), *Ethical issues and social dilemmas in knowledge management: Organizational innovation* (pp. 97–112). Hershey, PA: Information Science Reference; doi:10.4018/978-1-61520-873-9.ch007

Palte, R., Hertlein, M., Smolnik, S., & Riempp, G. (2013). The effects of a KM strategy on KM performance in professional services firms. In M. Jennex (Ed.), *Dynamic models for knowledge-driven organizations* (pp. 16–35). Hershey, PA: Business Science Reference; doi:10.4018/978-1-4666-2485-6.ch002

Pańkowska, M. (2014). Information technology prosumption acceptance by business information system consultants. In M. Pańkowska (Ed.), *Frameworks of IT prosumption for business development* (pp. 119–141). Hershey, PA: Business Science Reference; doi:10.4018/978-1-4666-4313-0.ch009

Pankowski, T. (2011). Pattern-based schema mapping and query answering in peer-to-peer XML data integration system. In L. Yan & Z. Ma (Eds.), *Advanced database query systems: Techniques, applications and technologies* (pp. 221–246). Hershey, PA: Information Science Reference; doi:10.4018/978-1-60960-475-2.ch009

Papoutsakis, H. (2010). New product development based on knowledge creation and technology education. In E. O'Brien, S. Clifford, & M. Southern (Eds.), *Knowledge management for process, organizational and marketing innovation: Tools and methods* (pp. 148–163). Hershey, PA: Information Science Reference; doi:10.4018/978-1-61520-829-6.ch009

Paquette, S. (2011). Applying knowledge management in the environmental and climate change sciences. In D. Schwartz & D. Te'eni (Eds.), *Encyclopedia of knowledge management* (2nd ed., pp. 20–26). Hershey, PA: Information Science Reference; doi:10.4018/978-1-59904-931-1.ch003

Paquette, S. (2011). Customer knowledge management. In D. Schwartz & D. Te'eni (Eds.), *Encyclopedia of knowledge management* (2nd ed., pp. 175–184). Hershey, PA: Information Science Reference; doi:10.4018/978-1-59904-931-1.ch017

Parker, K. R., & Nitse, P. S. (2011). Competitive intelligence gathering. In D. Schwartz & D. Te'eni (Eds.), *Encyclopedia of knowledge management* (2nd ed., pp. 103–111). Hershey, PA: Information Science Reference; doi:10.4018/978-1-59904-931-1.ch011

Páscoa, C., & Tribolet, J. (2014). Maintaining organizational viability and performance: The organizational configuration map. In G. Jamil, A. Malheiro, & F. Ribeiro (Eds.), *Rethinking the conceptual base for new practical applications in information value and quality* (pp. 266–283). Hershey, PA: Information Science Reference; doi:10.4018/978-1-4666-4562-2.ch012

Paukert, M., Niederée, C., & Hemmje, M. (2011). Knowledge in innovation processes. In D. Schwartz & D. Te'eni (Eds.), *Encyclopedia of knowledge management* (2nd ed., pp. 570–580). Hershey, PA: Information Science Reference; doi:10.4018/978-1-59904-931-1.ch055

Pawlak, P. (2011). Global "knowledge management" in humanist perspective. In G. Morais da Costa (Ed.), Ethical issues and social dilemmas in knowledge management: Organizational innovation (pp. 45-62). Hershey, PA: Information Science Reference. doi:10.4018/978-1-61520-873-9.ch004

Perry, M. (2013). Strategic knowledge management: A university application. In S. Buckley & M. Jakovljevic (Eds.), *Knowledge management innovations for interdisciplinary education: Organizational applications* (pp. 132–144). Hershey, PA: Information Science Reference; doi:10.4018/978-1-4666-1969-2.ch007

Pessoa, C. R., Silva, U. P., & Cruz, C. H. (2014). Information management in industrial areas: A knowledge management view. In G. Jamil, A. Malheiro, & F. Ribeiro (Eds.), *Rethinking the conceptual base for new practical applications in information value and quality* (pp. 378–395). Hershey, PA: Information Science Reference; doi:10.4018/978-1-4666-4562-2.ch017

Peter, H., & Greenidge, C. (2011). An ontology-based extraction framework for a semantic web application.[IJKBO]. *International Journal of Knowledge-Based Organizations*, *1*(3), 56–71. doi:10.4018/ijkbo.2011070104

Peter, H., & Greenidge, C. (2013). An ontology-based extraction framework for a semantic web application. In J. Wang (Ed.), *Intelligence methods and systems advancements for knowledge-based business* (pp. 231–246). Hershey, PA: Information Science Reference; doi:10.4018/978-1-4666-1873-2.ch013

Pham, Q. T., & Hara, Y. (2011). KM approach for improving the labor productivity of Vietnamese enterprise.[IJKM]. *International Journal of Knowledge Management*, *7*(3), 27–42. doi:10.4018/jkm.2011070103

Pham, Q. T., & Hara, Y. (2013). KM approach for improving the labor productivity of Vietnamese enterprise. In M. Jennex (Ed.), *Dynamic models for knowledge-driven organizations* (pp. 206–219). Hershey, PA: Business Science Reference; doi:10.4018/978-1-4666-2485-6.ch012

Philpott, E., & Beaumont-Kerridge, J. (2010). Overcoming reticence to aid knowledge creation between universities and business: A case reviewed. In D. Harorimana (Ed.), *Cultural implications of knowledge sharing, management and transfer: Identifying competitive advantage* (pp. 355–368). Hershey, PA: Information Science Reference; doi:10.4018/978-1-60566-790-4.ch016

Pike, S., & Roos, G. (2011). Measuring and valuing knowledge-based intangible assets: Real business uses. In B. Vallejo-Alonso, A. Rodriguez-Castellanos, & G. Arregui-Ayastuy (Eds.), *Identifying, measuring, and valuing knowledge-based intangible assets: New perspectives* (pp. 268–293). Hershey, PA: Business Science Reference; doi:10.4018/978-1-60960-054-9.ch013

Pineda, J. L., Zapata, L. E., & Ramírez, J. (2010). Strengthening knowledge transfer between the university and enterprise: A conceptual model for collaboration. In D. Harorimana (Ed.), *Cultural implications of knowledge sharing, management and transfer: Identifying competitive advantage* (pp. 134–151). Hershey, PA: Information Science Reference; doi:10.4018/978-1-60566-790-4.ch007

Platonov, V., & Bergman, J. (2013). Cross-border cooperative network in the perspective of innovation dynamics. In J. Wang (Ed.), *Intelligence methods and systems advancements for knowledge-based business* (pp. 150–169). Hershey, PA: Information Science Reference; doi:10.4018/978-1-4666-1873-2.ch009

Poels, G. (2013). Understanding business domain models: The effect of recognizing resource-event-agent conceptual modeling structures. In K. Siau (Ed.), *Innovations in database design, web applications, and information systems management* (pp. 72–106). Hershey, PA: Information Science Reference; doi:10.4018/978-1-4666-2044-5.ch004

Poels, G., Decreus, K., Roelens, B., & Snoeck, M. (2013). Investigating goal-oriented requirements engineering for business processes.[JDM]. *Journal of Database Management*, *24*(2), 35–71. doi:10.4018/jdm.2013040103

Pomares-Quimbaya, A., & Torres-Moreno, M. E. (2013). Knowledge management processes supported by ontology technologies. In M. Nazir Ahmad, R. Colomb, & M. Abdullah (Eds.), *Ontology-based applications for enterprise systems and knowledge management* (pp. 125–140). Hershey, PA: Information Science Reference; doi:10.4018/978-1-4666-1993-7.ch007

Ponis, S. T., Vagenas, G., & Koronis, E. (2010). Exploring the knowledge management landscape: A critical review of existing knowledge management frameworks. In D. Harorimana (Ed.), *Cultural implications of knowledge sharing, management and transfer: Identifying competitive advantage* (pp. 1–25). Hershey, PA: Information Science Reference; doi:10.4018/978-1-60566-790-4.ch001

Powers, S. M., & Salmon, C. (2010). Management of learning space. In D. Wu (Ed.), *Temporal structures in individual time management: Practices to enhance calendar tool design* (pp. 210–219). Hershey, PA: Business Science Reference; doi:10.4018/978-1-60566-776-8.ch015

Pretorius, A. B., & Coetzee, F. P. (2011). Model of a knowledge management support system for choosing intellectual capital assessment methods. In B. Vallejo-Alonso, A. Rodriguez-Castellanos, & G. Arregui-Ayastuy (Eds.), *Identifying, measuring, and valuing knowledge-based intangible assets: New perspectives* (pp. 336–359). Hershey, PA: Business Science Reference; doi:10.4018/978-1-60960-054-9.ch016

Pullinger, D. (2011). Mobilizing knowledge in the UK public sector: Current issues and discourse. In G. Morais da Costa (Ed.), *Ethical issues and social dilemmas in knowledge management: Organizational innovation* (pp. 232–249). Hershey, PA: Information Science Reference; doi:10.4018/978-1-61520-873-9.ch014

Rabaey, M. (2013). Complex adaptive systems thinking approach for intelligence base in support of intellectual capital management. In P. Ordóñez de Pablos, R. Tennyson, & J. Zhao (Eds.), *Intellectual capital strategy management for knowledge-based organizations* (pp. 122–141). Hershey, PA: Business Science Reference; doi:10.4018/978-1-4666-3655-2.ch007

Rabaey, M., & Mercken, R. (2013). Framework of knowledge and intelligence base: From intelligence to service. In *Data mining: Concepts, methodologies, tools, and applications* (pp. 474–502). Hershey, PA: Information Science Reference; doi:10.4018/978-1-4666-2455-9.ch023

Radziwill, N. M., & DuPlain, R. F. (2010). Quality and continuous improvement in knowledge management. In M. Russ (Ed.), *Knowledge management strategies for business development* (pp. 353–363). Hershey, PA: Business Science Reference; doi:10.4018/978-1-60566-348-7.ch017

Rahman, B. A., Saad, N. M., & Harun, M. S. (2010). Knowledge management orientation and business performance: The Malaysian manufacturing and service industries perspective. In K. Metaxiotis, F. Carrillo, & T. Yigitcanlar (Eds.), *Knowledge-based development for cities and societies: Integrated multi-level approaches* (pp. 315–328). Hershey, PA: Information Science Reference; doi:10.4018/978-1-61520-721-3.ch019

Randles, T. J., Blades, C. D., & Fadlalla, A. (2012). The knowledge spectrum.[IJKM]. *International Journal of Knowledge Management*, *8*(2), 65–78. doi:10.4018/jkm.2012040104

Real, J. C., Leal, A., & Roldan, J. L. (2011). Measuring organizational learning as a multidimensional construct. In D. Schwartz & D. Te'eni (Eds.), *Encyclopedia of knowledge management* (2nd ed., pp. 1101–1109). Hershey, PA: Information Science Reference; doi:10.4018/978-1-59904-931-1.ch105

Rech, J., & Bogner, C. (2010). Qualitative analysis of semantically enabled knowledge management systems in agile software engineering.[IJKM]. *International Journal of Knowledge Management*, *6*(2), 66–85. doi:10.4018/jkm.2010040104

Rech, J., & Bogner, C. (2012). Qualitative analysis of semantically enabled knowledge management systems in agile software engineering. In M. Jennex (Ed.), *Conceptual models and outcomes of advancing knowledge management: New technologies* (pp. 144–164). Hershey, PA: Information Science Reference; doi:10.4018/978-1-4666-0035-5.ch008

Reis, R. S., & Curzi, Y. (2011). Knowledge integration in the creative process of globally distributed teams. In M. Al-Shammari (Ed.), *Knowledge management in emerging economies: Social, organizational and cultural implementation* (pp. 47–65). Hershey, PA: Information Science Reference; doi:10.4018/978-1-61692-886-5.ch003

Remli, M. A., & Deris, S. (2013). An approach for biological data integration and knowledge retrieval based on ontology, semantic web services composition, and AI planning. In M. Nazir Ahmad, R. Colomb, & M. Abdullah (Eds.), *Ontology-based applications for enterprise systems and knowledge management* (pp. 324–342). Hershey, PA: Information Science Reference; doi:10.4018/978-1-4666-1993-7.ch018

Reychav, I., Stein, E. W., Weisberg, J., & Glezer, C. (2012). The role of knowledge sharing in raising the task innovativeness of systems analysts.[IJKM]. *International Journal of Knowledge Management*, *8*(2), 1–22. doi:10.4018/jkm.2012040101

Reychav, I., & Weisberg, J. (2011). Human capital in knowledge creation, management, and utilization. In D. Schwartz & D. Te'eni (Eds.), *Encyclopedia of knowledge management* (2nd ed., pp. 389–401). Hershey, PA: Information Science Reference; doi:10.4018/978-1-59904-931-1.ch037

Rhoads, E., O'Sullivan, K. J., & Stankosky, M. (2011). An evaluation of factors that influence the success of knowledge management practices in US federal agencies. In M. Jennex & S. Smolnik (Eds.), *Strategies for knowledge management success: Exploring organizational efficacy* (pp. 74–90). Hershey, PA: Information Science Reference; doi:10.4018/978-1-60566-709-6.ch005

Ribière, V. M. (2011). The effect of organizational trust on the success of codification and personalization KM approaches. In M. Jennex & S. Smolnik (Eds.), *Strategies for knowledge management success: Exploring organizational efficacy* (pp. 192–212). Hershey, PA: Information Science Reference; doi:10.4018/978-1-60566-709-6.ch011

Ribière, V. M., & Román, J. A. (2011). Knowledge flow. In D. Schwartz & D. Te'eni (Eds.), *Encyclopedia of knowledge management* (2nd ed., pp. 549–559). Hershey, PA: Information Science Reference; doi:10.4018/978-1-59904-931-1.ch053

Ricceri, F., Guthrie, J., & Coyte, R. (2010). The management of knowledge resources within private organisations: Some European "better practice" illustrations. In E. O'Brien, S. Clifford, & M. Southern (Eds.), *Knowledge management for process, organizational and marketing innovation: Tools and methods* (pp. 36–61). Hershey, PA: Information Science Reference; doi:10.4018/978-1-61520-829-6.ch003

Riss, U. V. (2011). Pattern-based task management as means of organizational knowledge maturing.[IJKBO]. *International Journal of Knowledge-Based Organizations, 1*(1), 20–41. doi:10.4018/ijkbo.2011010102

Riss, U. V. (2013). Pattern-based task management as means of organizational knowledge maturing. In J. Wang (Ed.), *Intelligence methods and systems advancements for knowledge-based business* (pp. 1–23). Hershey, PA: Information Science Reference; doi:10.4018/978-1-4666-1873-2.ch001

Roos, G. (2013). The role of intellectual capital in business model innovation: An empirical study. In P. Ordóñez de Pablos, R. Tennyson, & J. Zhao (Eds.), *Intellectual capital strategy management for knowledge-based organizations* (pp. 76–121). Hershey, PA: Business Science Reference; doi:10.4018/978-1-4666-3655-2.ch006

Rothberg, H. N., & Klingenberg, B. (2010). Learning before doing: A theoretical perspective and practical lessons from a failed cross-border knowledge transfer initiative. In D. Harorimana (Ed.), *Cultural implications of knowledge sharing, management and transfer: Identifying competitive advantage* (pp. 277–294). Hershey, PA: Information Science Reference; doi:10.4018/978-1-60566-790-4.ch013

Ruano-Mayoral, M., Colomo-Palacios, R., García-Crespo, Á., & Gómez-Berbís, J. M. (2012). Software project managers under the team software process: A study of competences based on literature. In J. Wang (Ed.), *Project management techniques and innovations in information technology* (pp. 115–126). Hershey, PA: Information Science Reference; doi:10.4018/978-1-4666-0930-3.ch007

Russell, S. (2010). Knowledge management and project management in 3D: A virtual world extension. In E. O'Brien, S. Clifford, & M. Southern (Eds.), *Knowledge management for process, organizational and marketing innovation: Tools and methods* (pp. 62–78). Hershey, PA: Information Science Reference; doi:10.4018/978-1-61520-829-6.ch004

Ryan, G., & Shinnick, E. (2011). Knowledge and intellectual property rights: An economics perspective. In D. Schwartz & D. Te'eni (Eds.), *Encyclopedia of knowledge management* (2nd ed., pp. 489–496). Hershey, PA: Information Science Reference; doi:10.4018/978-1-59904-931-1.ch047

Sabetzadeh, F., & Tsui, E. (2013). Delivering knowledge services in the cloud. In G. Yang (Ed.), *Multidisciplinary studies in knowledge and systems science* (pp. 247–254). Hershey, PA: Information Science Reference; doi:10.4018/978-1-4666-3998-0.ch017

Sáenz, J., & Aramburu, N. (2011). Organizational conditions as catalysts for successful people-focused knowledge sharing initiatives: An empirical study.[IJKBO]. *International Journal of Knowledge-Based Organizations, 1*(2), 39–56. doi:10.4018/ijkbo.2011040103

Sáenz, J., & Aramburu, N. (2013). Organizational conditions as catalysts for successful people-focused knowledge sharing initiatives: An empirical study. In J. Wang (Ed.), *Intelligence methods and systems advancements for knowledge-based business* (pp. 263–280). Hershey, PA: Information Science Reference; doi:10.4018/978-1-4666-1873-2.ch015

Sakr, S., & Al-Naymat, G. (2011). Relational techniques for storing and querying RDF data: An overview. In L. Yan & Z. Ma (Eds.), *Advanced database query systems: Techniques, applications and technologies* (pp. 269–285). Hershey, PA: Information Science Reference; doi:10.4018/978-1-60960-475-2.ch011

Salem, P. J. (2013). The use of mixed methods in organizational communication research. In M. Bocarnea, R. Reynolds, & J. Baker (Eds.), *Online instruments, data collection, and electronic measurements: Organizational advancements* (pp. 24–39). Hershey, PA: Information Science Reference; doi:10.4018/978-1-4666-2172-5.ch002

Salisbury, M. (2011). A framework for managing the life cycle of knowledge in global organizations. In M. Jennex (Ed.), *Global aspects and cultural perspectives on knowledge management: Emerging dimensions* (pp. 64–80). Hershey, PA: Information Science Reference; doi:10.4018/978-1-60960-555-1.ch005

Salleh, K. (2014). Drivers, benefits, and challenges of knowledge management in electronic government: Preliminary examination. In Y. Al-Bastaki & A. Shajera (Eds.), *Building a competitive public sector with knowledge management strategy* (pp. 135–150). Hershey, PA: Business Science Reference; doi:10.4018/978-1-4666-4434-2.ch006

Salleh, K., Ikhsan, S. O., & Ahmad, S. N. (2011). Knowledge management enablers and knowledge sharing process: A case study of public sector accounting organization in Malaysia. In M. Al-Shammari (Ed.), *Knowledge management in emerging economies: Social, organizational and cultural implementation* (pp. 199–211). Hershey, PA: Information Science Reference; doi:10.4018/978-1-61692-886-5.ch012

Saunders, C. (2011). Knowledge sharing in legal practice. In D. Schwartz & D. Te'eni (Eds.), *Encyclopedia of knowledge management* (2nd ed., pp. 935–945). Hershey, PA: Information Science Reference; doi:10.4018/978-1-59904-931-1.ch089

Scarso, E., & Bolisani, E. (2011). Knowledge intermediation. In D. Schwartz & D. Te'eni (Eds.), *Encyclopedia of knowledge management* (2nd ed., pp. 601–611). Hershey, PA: Information Science Reference; doi:10.4018/978-1-59904-931-1.ch058

Scarso, E., & Bolisani, E. (2011). Managing professions for knowledge management.[IJKM]. *International Journal of Knowledge Management*, *7*(3), 61–75. doi:10.4018/jkm.2011070105

Scarso, E., & Bolisani, E. (2013). Managing professions for knowledge management. In M. Jennex (Ed.), *Dynamic models for knowledge-driven organizations* (pp. 238–253). Hershey, PA: Business Science Reference; doi:10.4018/978-1-4666-2485-6.ch014

Scarso, E., Bolisani, E., & Padova, A. (2011). The complex issue of measuring KM performance: Lessons from the practice. In B. Vallejo-Alonso, A. Rodriguez-Castellanos, & G. Arregui-Ayastuy (Eds.), *Identifying, measuring, and valuing knowledge-based intangible assets: New perspectives* (pp. 208–230). Hershey, PA: Business Science Reference; doi:10.4018/978-1-60960-054-9.ch010

Schumann, C., & Tittmann, C. (2010). Potentials for externalizing and measuring of tacit knowledge within knowledge nodes in the context of knowledge networks. In D. Harorimana (Ed.), *Cultural implications of knowledge sharing, management and transfer: Identifying competitive advantage* (pp. 84–107). Hershey, PA: Information Science Reference; doi:10.4018/978-1-60566-790-4.ch005

Schwartz, D. (2011). An Aristotelian view of knowledge for knowledge management. In D. Schwartz & D. Te'eni (Eds.), *Encyclopedia of knowledge management* (2nd ed., pp. 39–48). Hershey, PA: Information Science Reference; doi:10.4018/978-1-59904-931-1.ch005

Senaratne, S., & Victoria, M. F. (2014). Building a supportive culture for sustained organisational learning in public sectors. In Y. Al-Bastaki & A. Shajera (Eds.), *Building a competitive public sector with knowledge management strategy* (pp. 118–134). Hershey, PA: Business Science Reference; doi:10.4018/978-1-4666-4434-2.ch005

Shah, A., Singhera, Z., & Ahsan, S. (2011). Web services for bioinformatics. In M. Al-Mutairi & L. Mohammed (Eds.), *Cases on ICT utilization, practice and solutions: Tools for managing day-to-day issues* (pp. 28–46). Hershey, PA: Information Science Reference; doi:10.4018/978-1-60960-015-0.ch003

Shajera, A., & Al-Bastaki, Y. (2014). Organisational readiness for knowledge management: Bahrain public sector case study. In Y. Al-Bastaki & A. Shajera (Eds.), *Building a competitive public sector with knowledge management strategy* (pp. 104–117). Hershey, PA: Business Science Reference; doi:10.4018/978-1-4666-4434-2.ch004

Sharma, A. K., Goswami, A., & Gupta, D. (2011). An extended relational model & SQL for fuzzy multidatabases. In L. Yan & Z. Ma (Eds.), *Advanced database query systems: Techniques, applications and technologies* (pp. 185–219). Hershey, PA: Information Science Reference; doi:10.4018/978-1-60960-475-2.ch008

Sharma, R., Banati, H., & Bedi, P. (2012). Building socially-aware e-learning systems through knowledge management.[IJKM]. *International Journal of Knowledge Management*, *8*(3), 1–26. doi:10.4018/jkm.2012070101

Sharma, R. S., Chandrasekar, G., & Vaitheeswaran, B. (2012). A knowledge framework for development: Empirical investigation of 30 societies. In M. Jennex (Ed.), *Conceptual models and outcomes of advancing knowledge management: New technologies* (pp. 244–265). Hershey, PA: Information Science Reference; doi:10.4018/978-1-4666-0035-5.ch013

Shaw, D. (2011). Mapping group knowledge. In D. Schwartz & D. Te'eni (Eds.), *Encyclopedia of knowledge management* (2nd ed., pp. 1072–1081). Hershey, PA: Information Science Reference; doi:10.4018/978-1-59904-931-1.ch102

Sheluhin, O. I., & Atayero, A. A. (2013). Principles of modeling in information communication systems and networks. In A. Atayero & O. Sheluhin (Eds.), *Integrated models for information communication systems and networks: Design and development* (pp. 1–15). Hershey, PA: Information Science Reference; doi:10.4018/978-1-4666-2208-1.ch001

Sheluhin, O. I., & Garmashev, A. V. (2013). Numerical methods of multifractal analysis in information communication systems and networks. In A. Atayero & O. Sheluhin (Eds.), *Integrated models for information communication systems and networks: Design and development* (pp. 16–46). Hershey, PA: Information Science Reference; doi:10.4018/978-1-4666-2208-1.ch002

Siau, K., Long, Y., & Ling, M. (2010). Toward a unified model of information systems development success.[JDM]. *Journal of Database Management*, *21*(1), 80–101. doi:10.4018/jdm.2010112304

Siau, K., Long, Y., & Ling, M. (2012). Toward a unified model of information systems development success. In K. Siau (Ed.), *Cross-disciplinary models and applications of database management: Advancing approaches* (pp. 80–102). Hershey, PA: Information Science Reference; doi:10.4018/978-1-61350-471-0.ch004

Simard, A. J., & Jourdeuil, P. (2014). Knowledge manageability: A new paradigm. In Y. Al-Bastaki & A. Shajera (Eds.), *Building a competitive public sector with knowledge management strategy* (pp. 1–52). Hershey, PA: Business Science Reference; doi:10.4018/978-1-4666-4434-2.ch001

Simonette, M. J., & Spina, E. (2014). Enabling IT innovation through soft systems engineering. In M. Pańkowska (Ed.), *Frameworks of IT prosumption for business development* (pp. 64–72). Hershey, PA: Business Science Reference; doi:10.4018/978-1-4666-4313-0.ch005

Sivaramakrishnan, S., Delbaere, M., Zhang, D., & Bruning, E. (2012). Critical success factors and outcomes of market knowledge management: A conceptual model and empirical evidence. In M. Jennex (Ed.), *Conceptual models and outcomes of advancing knowledge management: New technologies* (pp. 165–185). Hershey, PA: Information Science Reference; doi:10.4018/978-1-4666-0035-5.ch009

Small, C. T., & Sage, A. P. (2010). A complex adaptive systems-based enterprise knowledge sharing model. In D. Paradice (Ed.), *Emerging systems approaches in information technologies: Concepts, theories, and applications* (pp. 137–155). Hershey, PA: Information Science Reference; doi:10.4018/978-1-60566-976-2.ch009

Smedlund, A. (2011). Social network structures for explicit, tacit and potential knowledge. In M. Jennex (Ed.), *Global aspects and cultural perspectives on knowledge management: Emerging dimensions* (pp. 81–90). Hershey, PA: Information Science Reference; doi:10.4018/978-1-60960-555-1.ch006

Smith, A. D. (2013). Competitive uses of information and knowledge management tools: Case study of supplier-side management.[IJKBO]. *International Journal of Knowledge-Based Organizations*, *3*(1), 71 87. doi:10.4018/ijkbo.2013010105

Smith, P., & Coakes, E. (2011). Exploiting KM in support of innovation and change. In A. Eardley & L. Uden (Eds.), *Innovative knowledge management: Concepts for organizational creativity and collaborative design* (pp. 242–252). Hershey, PA: Information Science Reference; doi:10.4018/978-1-60566-701-0.ch015

Smith, T. A., Mills, A. M., & Dion, P. (2010). Linking business strategy and knowledge management capabilities for organizational effectiveness.[IJKM]. *International Journal of Knowledge Management*, *6*(3), 22–43. doi:10.4018/jkm.2010070102

Smith, T. A., Mills, A. M., & Dion, P. (2012). Linking business strategy and knowledge management capabilities for organizational effectiveness. In M. Jennex (Ed.), *Conceptual models and outcomes of advancing knowledge management: New technologies* (pp. 186–207). Hershey, PA: Information Science Reference; doi:10.4018/978-1-4666-0035-5.ch010

Smuts, H., van der Merwe, A., & Loock, M. (2011). Key characteristics relevant for selecting knowledge management software tools. In A. Eardley & L. Uden (Eds.), *Innovative knowledge management: Concepts for organizational creativity and collaborative design* (pp. 18–39). Hershey, PA: Information Science Reference; doi:10.4018/978-1-60566-701-0.ch002

Soffer, P., & Kaner, M. (2013). Complementing business process verification by validity analysis: A theoretical and empirical evaluation. In K. Siau (Ed.), *Innovations in database design, web applications, and information systems management* (pp. 265–288). Hershey, PA: Information Science Reference; doi:10.4018/978-1-4666-2044-5.ch010

Soffer, P., Kaner, M., & Wand, Y. (2012). Assigning ontological meaning to workflow nets. In K. Siau (Ed.), *Cross-disciplinary models and applications of database management: Advancing approaches* (pp. 209–244). Hershey, PA: Information Science Reference; doi:10.4018/978-1-61350-471-0.ch009

Sohrabi, B., Raeesi, I., & Khanlari, A. (2010). Intellectual capital components, measurement and management: A literature survey of concepts and measures. In P. López Sáez, G. Castro, J. Navas López, & M. Delgado Verde (Eds.), *Intellectual capital and technological innovation: Knowledge-based theory and practice* (pp. 1–38). Hershey, PA: Information Science Reference; doi:10.4018/978-1-61520-875-3.ch001

Sohrabi, B., Raeesi, I., Khanlari, A., & Forouzandeh, S. (2011). A comprehensive model for assessing the organizational readiness of knowledge management. In M. Jennex (Ed.), *Global aspects and cultural perspectives on knowledge management: Emerging dimensions* (pp. 30–48). Hershey, PA: Information Science Reference; doi:10.4018/978-1-60960-555-1.ch003

Sparrow, J. (2011). Knowledge management in small and medium sized enterprises. In D. Schwartz & D. Te'eni (Eds.), *Encyclopedia of knowledge management* (2nd ed., pp. 671–681). Hershey, PA: Information Science Reference; doi:10.4018/978-1-59904-931-1.ch065

Stam, C. D. (2011). Making sense of knowledge productivity. In B. Vallejo-Alonso, A. Rodriguez-Castellanos, & G. Arregui-Ayastuy (Eds.), *Identifying, measuring, and valuing knowledge-based intangible assets: New perspectives* (pp. 133–155). Hershey, PA: Business Science Reference; doi:10.4018/978-1-60960-054-9.ch007

Stamkopoulos, K., Pitoura, E., Vassiliadis, P., & Zarras, A. (2012). Accelerating web service workflow execution via intelligent allocation of services to servers. In K. Siau (Ed.), *Cross-disciplinary models and applications of database management: Advancing approaches* (pp. 385–416). Hershey, PA: Information Science Reference; doi:10.4018/978-1-61350-471-0.ch016

Sterling, L. (2011). Applying agents within knowledge management. In D. Schwartz & D. Te'eni (Eds.), *Encyclopedia of knowledge management* (2nd ed., pp. 12–19). Hershey, PA: Information Science Reference; doi:10.4018/978-1-59904-931-1.ch002

Su, S., & Chiong, R. (2011). Business intelligence. In D. Schwartz & D. Te'eni (Eds.), *Encyclopedia of knowledge management* (2nd ed., pp. 72–80). Hershey, PA: Information Science Reference; doi:10.4018/978-1-59904-931-1.ch008

Su, W. B., Li, X., & Chow, C. W. (2012). Exploring the extent and impediments of knowledge sharing in Chinese business enterprise. In M. Jennex (Ed.), *Conceptual models and outcomes of advancing knowledge management: New technologies* (pp. 266–290). Hershey, PA: Information Science Reference; doi:10.4018/978-1-4666-0035-5.ch014

Subramanian, D. V., & Geetha, A. (2012). Application of multi-dimensional metric model, database, and WAM for KM system evaluation.[IJKM]. *International Journal of Knowledge Management, 8*(4), 1–21. doi:10.4018/jkm.2012100101

Surendran, A., & Samuel, P. (2013). Knowledge-based code clone approach in embedded and real-time systems. In S. Saeed & I. Alsmadi (Eds.), *Knowledge-based processes in software development* (pp. 49–62). Hershey, PA: Information Science Reference; doi:10.4018/978-1-4666-4229-4.ch004

Takahashi, Y. (2011). The importance of balancing knowledge protection and knowledge interchange. In G. Morais da Costa (Ed.), *Ethical issues and social dilemmas in knowledge management: Organizational innovation* (pp. 180–198). Hershey, PA: Information Science Reference; doi:10.4018/978-1-61520-873-9.ch011

Talet, A. N., Alhawari, S., & Alryalat, H. (2012). The outcome of knowledge process for customers of Jordanian companies on the achievement of customer knowledge retention. In M. Jennex (Ed.), *Conceptual models and outcomes of advancing knowledge management: New technologies* (pp. 45–61). Hershey, PA: Information Science Reference; doi:10.4018/978-1-4666-0035-5.ch003

Talet, A. N., Alhawari, S., Mansour, E., & Alryalat, H. (2011). The practice of Jordanian business to attain customer knowledge acquisition.[IJKM]. *International Journal of Knowledge Management, 7*(2), 49–67. doi:10.4018/jkm.2011040103

Tanner, K. (2011). The role of emotional capital in organisational KM. In D. Schwartz & D. Te'eni (Eds.), *Encyclopedia of knowledge management* (2nd ed., pp. 1396–1409). Hershey, PA: Information Science Reference; doi:10.4018/978-1-59904-931-1.ch133

Tauber, D., & Schwartz, D. G. (2011). Integrating knowledge management with the systems analysis process. In D. Schwartz & D. Te'eni (Eds.), *Encyclopedia of knowledge management* (2nd ed., pp. 431–441). Hershey, PA: Information Science Reference; doi:10.4018/978-1-59904-931-1.ch041

Tavana, M., Busch, T. E., & Davis, E. L. (2011). Modeling operational robustness and resiliency with high-level Petri nets.[IJKBO]. *International Journal of Knowledge-Based Organizations, 1*(2), 17–38. doi:10.4018/ijkbo.2011040102

Taxén, L. (2010). Aligning business and knowledge strategies: A practical approach for aligning business and knowledge strategies. In M. Russ (Ed.), *Knowledge management strategies for business development* (pp. 277–308). Hershey, PA: Business Science Reference; doi:10.4018/978-1-60566-348-7.ch013

Te'eni, D. (2011). Knowledge for communicating knowledge. In D. Schwartz & D. Te'eni (Eds.), *Encyclopedia of knowledge management* (2nd ed., pp. 560–569). Hershey, PA: Information Science Reference; doi:10.4018/978-1-59904-931-1.ch054

Toiviainen, H., & Kerosuo, H. (2013). Development curriculum for knowledge-based organizations: Lessons from a learning network.[IJKBO]. *International Journal of Knowledge-Based Organizations, 3*(3), 1–18. doi:10.4018/ijkbo.2013070101

Tran, B. (2014). The human element of the knowledge worker: Identifying, managing, and protecting the intellectual capital within knowledge management. In M. Chilton & J. Bloodgood (Eds.), *Knowledge management and competitive advantage: Issues and potential solutions* (pp. 281–303). Hershey, PA: Information Science Reference; doi:10.4018/978-1-4666-4679-7.ch017

Tsamoura, E., Gounaris, A., & Manolopoulos, Y. (2011). Optimal service ordering in decentralized queries over web services.[IJKBO]. *International Journal of Knowledge-Based Organizations, 1*(2), 1–16. doi:10.4018/ijkbo.2011040101

Tsamoura, E., Gounaris, A., & Manolopoulos, Y. (2013). Optimal service ordering in decentralized queries over web services. In J. Wang (Ed.), *Intelligence methods and systems advancements for knowledge-based business* (pp. 43–58). Hershey, PA: Information Science Reference; doi:10.4018/978-1-4666-1873-2.ch003

Tull, J. (2013). Slow knowledge: The case for savouring learning and innovation. In S. Buckley & M. Jakovljevic (Eds.), *Knowledge management innovations for interdisciplinary education: Organizational applications* (pp. 274–297). Hershey, PA: Information Science Reference; doi:10.4018/978-1-4666-1969-2.ch014

Turner, G., & Minonne, C. (2013). Effective knowledge management through measurement. In S. Buckley & M. Jakovljevic (Eds.), *Knowledge management innovations for interdisciplinary education: Organizational applications* (pp. 145–176). Hershey, PA: Information Science Reference; doi:10.4018/978-1-4666-1969-2.ch008

Uden, L., & Eardley, A. (2011). Knowledge sharing in the learning process: Experience with problem-based learning. In A. Eardley & L. Uden (Eds.), *Innovative knowledge management: Concepts for organizational creativity and collaborative design* (pp. 215–229). Hershey, PA: Information Science Reference; doi:10.4018/978-1-60566-701-0.ch013

Upadhyaya, S., Rao, H. R., & Padmanabhan, G. (2011). Secure knowledge management. In D. Schwartz & D. Te'eni (Eds.), *Encyclopedia of knowledge management* (2nd ed., pp. 1429–1437). Hershey, PA: Information Science Reference; doi:10.4018/978-1-59904-931-1.ch136

Urbancová, H., & Königová, M. (2013). The influence of the application of business continuity management, knowledge management, and knowledge continuity management on the innovation in organizations. In S. Buckley & M. Jakovljevic (Eds.), *Knowledge management innovations for interdisciplinary education: Organizational applications* (pp. 254–273). Hershey, PA: Information Science Reference; doi:10.4018/978-1-4666-1969-2.ch013

Van Canh, T., & Zyngier, S. (2014). Using ERG theory as a lens to understand the sharing of academic tacit knowledge: Problems and issues in developing countries – Perspectives from Vietnam. In M. Chilton & J. Bloodgood (Eds.), *Knowledge management and competitive advantage: Issues and potential solutions* (pp. 174–201). Hershey, PA: Information Science Reference; doi:10.4018/978-1-4666-4679-7.ch010

Vat, K. H. (2011). Knowledge synthesis framework. In D. Schwartz & D. Te'eni (Eds.), *Encyclopedia of knowledge management* (2nd ed., pp. 955–966). Hershey, PA: Information Science Reference; doi:10.4018/978-1-59904-931-1.ch091

Vert, S. (2012). Extensions of web browsers useful to knowledge workers. In C. Jouis, I. Biskri, J. Ganascia, & M. Roux (Eds.), *Next generation search engines: Advanced models for information retrieval* (pp. 239–273). Hershey, PA: Information Science Reference; doi:10.4018/978-1-4666-0330-1.ch011

Wagner, L., & Van Belle, J. (2011). Web mining for strategic competitive intelligence: South African experiences and a practical methodology. In M. Al-Shammari (Ed.), *Knowledge management in emerging economies: Social, organizational and cultural implementation* (pp. 1–19). Hershey, PA: Information Science Reference; doi:10.4018/978-1-61692-886-5.ch001

Wautelet, Y., Schinckus, C., & Kolp, M. (2010). Towards knowledge evolution in software engineering: An epistemological approach.[IJITSA]. *International Journal of Information Technologies and Systems Approach, 3*(1), 21–40. doi:10.4018/jitsa.2010100202

Weiß, S., Makolm, J., Ipsmiller, D., & Egger, N. (2011). DYONIPOS: Proactive knowledge supply. In M. Jennex & S. Smolnik (Eds.), *Strategies for knowledge management success: Exploring organizational efficacy* (pp. 277–287). Hershey, PA: Information Science Reference; doi:10.4018/978-1-60566-709-6.ch015

Welschen, J., Todorova, N., & Mills, A. M. (2012). An investigation of the impact of intrinsic motivation on organizational knowledge sharing.[IJKM]. *International Journal of Knowledge Management, 8*(2), 23–42. doi:10.4018/jkm.2012040102

Wickramasinghe, N. (2011). Knowledge creation. In D. Schwartz & D. Te'eni (Eds.), *Encyclopedia of knowledge management* (2nd ed., pp. 527–538). Hershey, PA: Information Science Reference; doi:10.4018/978-1-59904-931-1.ch051

Wickramasinghe, N. (2011). Knowledge management: The key to delivering superior healthcare solutions. In A. Eardley & L. Uden (Eds.), *Innovative knowledge management: Concepts for organizational creativity and collaborative design* (pp. 190–203). Hershey, PA: Information Science Reference; doi:10.4018/978-1-60566-701-0.ch011

Wijnhoven, F. (2011). Operational knowledge management. In D. Schwartz & D. Te'eni (Eds.), *Encyclopedia of knowledge management* (2nd ed., pp. 1237–1249). Hershey, PA: Information Science Reference; doi:10.4018/978-1-59904-931-1.ch118

Williams, R. (2011). A Knowledge Process Cycle. In D. Schwartz & D. Te'eni (Eds.), *Encyclopedia of knowledge management* (2nd ed., pp. 853–866). Hershey, PA: Information Science Reference; doi:10.4018/978-1-59904-931-1.ch082

Wilson, R. L., Rosen, P. A., & Al-Ahmadi, M. S. (2011). Knowledge structure and data mining techniques. In D. Schwartz & D. Te'eni (Eds.), *Encyclopedia of knowledge management* (2nd ed., pp. 946–954). Hershey, PA: Information Science Reference; doi:10.4018/978-1-59904-931-1.ch090

Wimmer, H., Yoon, V., & Rada, R. (2013). Integrating knowledge sources: An ontological approach. [IJKM]. *International Journal of Knowledge Management, 9*(1), 60–75. doi:10.4018/jkm.2013010104

Woods, S., Poteet, S. R., Kao, A., & Quach, L. (2011). Knowledge dissemination in portals. In D. Schwartz & D. Te'eni (Eds.), *Encyclopedia of knowledge management* (2nd ed., pp. 539–548). Hershey, PA: Information Science Reference; doi:10.4018/978-1-59904-931-1.ch052

Worden, D. (2010). Agile alignment of enterprise execution capabilities with strategy. In M. Russ (Ed.), *Knowledge management strategies for business development* (pp. 45–62). Hershey, PA: Business Science Reference; doi:10.4018/978-1-60566-348-7.ch003

Wu, D. (2010). Who are effective time managers? Bivariate correlation analysis and hypotheses testing. In D. Wu (Ed.), *Temporal structures in individual time management: Practices to enhance calendar tool design* (pp. 116–138). Hershey, PA: Business Science Reference; doi:10.4018/978-1-60566-776-8.ch009

Wu, J., Du, H., Li, X., & Li, P. (2010). Creating and delivering a successful knowledge management strategy. In M. Russ (Ed.), *Knowledge management strategies for business development* (pp. 261–276). Hershey, PA: Business Science Reference; doi:10.4018/978-1-60566-348-7.ch012

Wu, J., Liu, N., & Xuan, Z. (2013). Simulation on knowledge transfer processes from the perspectives of individual's mentality and behavior. In G. Yang (Ed.), *Multidisciplinary studies in knowledge and systems science* (pp. 233–246). Hershey, PA: Information Science Reference; doi:10.4018/978-1-4666-3998-0.ch016

Wu, J., Wang, S., & Pan, D. (2013). Evaluation of technological influence power of enterprises through the enterprise citation network. In G. Yang (Ed.), *Multidisciplinary studies in knowledge and systems science* (pp. 34–44). Hershey, PA: Information Science Reference; doi:10.4018/978-1-4666-3998-0.ch003

Wu, S. T. (2011). Innovation in new technology and knowledge management: Comparative case studies of its evolution during a quarter century of change. In A. Eardley & L. Uden (Eds.), *Innovative knowledge management: Concepts for organizational creativity and collaborative design* (pp. 77–93). Hershey, PA: Information Science Reference; doi:10.4018/978-1-60566-701-0.ch005

Xiao, L., & Pei, Y. (2013). A task context aware physical distribution knowledge service system. In G. Yang (Ed.), *Multidisciplinary studies in knowledge and systems science* (pp. 18–33). Hershey, PA: Information Science Reference; doi:10.4018/978-1-4666-3998-0.ch002

Xu, D., & Wang, H. (2011). Integration of knowledge management and e-learning. In D. Schwartz & D. Te'eni (Eds.), *Encyclopedia of knowledge management* (2nd ed., pp. 442–451). Hershey, PA: Information Science Reference; doi:10.4018/978-1-59904-931-1.ch042

Yaniv, E., & Schwartz, D. G. (2011). Organizational attention. In D. Schwartz & D. Te'eni (Eds.), *Encyclopedia of knowledge management* (2nd ed., pp. 1270–1279). Hershey, PA: Information Science Reference; doi:10.4018/978-1-59904-931-1.ch121

Yeung, C. L., Cheung, C. F., Wang, W. M., & Tsui, E. (2013). A study of organizational narrative simulation for decision support. In G. Yang (Ed.), *Multidisciplinary studies in knowledge and systems science* (pp. 179–192). Hershey, PA: Information Science Reference; doi:10.4018/978-1-4666-3998-0.ch013

Yigitcanlar, T. (2013). Moving towards a knowledge city? Brisbane's experience in knowledge-based urban development. In J. Wang (Ed.), *Intelligence methods and systems advancements for knowledge-based business* (pp. 114–131). Hershey, PA: Information Science Reference; doi:10.4018/978-1-4666-1873-2.ch007

Yigitcanlar, T., & Martinez-Fernandez, C. (2010). Making space and place for knowledge production: Socio-spatial development of knowledge community precincts. In K. Metaxiotis, F. Carrillo, & T. Yigitcanlar (Eds.), *Knowledge-based development for cities and societies: Integrated multi-level approaches* (pp. 99–117). Hershey, PA: Information Science Reference; doi:10.4018/978-1-61520-721-3.ch006

Yıldırım, A. A., Özdoğan, C., & Watson, D. (2014). Parallel data reduction techniques for big datasets. In W. Hu & N. Kaabouch (Eds.), *Big data management, technologies, and applications* (pp. 72–93). Hershey, PA: Information Science Reference; doi:10.4018/978-1-4666-4699-5.ch004

Yoon, K. S. (2012). Measuring the influence of expertise and epistemic engagement to the practice of knowledge management.[IJKM]. *International Journal of Knowledge Management*, *8*(1), 40–70. doi:10.4018/jkm.2012010103

Yusof, Z. M., & Ismail, M. B. (2011). Factors affecting knowledge sharing practice in Malaysia: A preliminary overview. In M. Al-Shammari (Ed.), *Knowledge management in emerging economies: Social, organizational and cultural implementation* (pp. 157–170). Hershey, PA: Information Science Reference; doi:10.4018/978-1-61692-886-5.ch009

Zapata-Cantú, L., Ramírez, J., & Pineda, J. L. (2011). HRM adaptation to knowledge management initiatives: Three Mexican cases. In M. Al-Shammari (Ed.), *Knowledge management in emerging economies: Social, organizational and cultural implementation* (pp. 273–293). Hershey, PA: Information Science Reference; doi:10.4018/978-1-61692-886-5.ch017

Zarri, G. P. (2011). Knowledge representation. In D. Schwartz & D. Te'eni (Eds.), *Encyclopedia of knowledge management* (2nd ed., pp. 878–892). Hershey, PA: Information Science Reference; doi:10.4018/978-1-59904-931-1.ch084

Zarri, G. P. (2011). RDF and OWL for knowledge management. In D. Schwartz & D. Te'eni (Eds.), *Encyclopedia of knowledge management* (2nd ed., pp. 1355–1373). Hershey, PA: Information Science Reference; doi:10.4018/978-1-59904-931-1.ch130

Zhang, Y., Wang, Y., Colucci, W., & Wang, Z. (2013). The paradigm shift in organizational research. In J. Wang (Ed.), *Intelligence methods and systems advancements for knowledge-based business* (pp. 60–74). Hershey, PA: Information Science Reference; doi:10.4018/978-1-4666-1873-2.ch004

Zhang, Z. J. (2011). Managing customer knowledge with social software. In D. Schwartz & D. Te'eni (Eds.), *Encyclopedia of knowledge management* (2nd ed., pp. 1046–1053). Hershey, PA: Information Science Reference; doi:10.4018/978-1-59904-931-1.ch099

Zyngier, S. (2011). Governance of knowledge management. In D. Schwartz & D. Te'eni (Eds.), *Encyclopedia of knowledge management* (2nd ed., pp. 354–365). Hershey, PA: Information Science Reference; doi:10.4018/978-1-59904-931-1.ch034

Zyngier, S. (2011). Knowledge management: Realizing value through governance.[IJKM]. *International Journal of Knowledge Management*, *7*(1), 35–54. doi:10.4018/jkm.2011010103

Zyngier, S. (2013). Knowledge management: Realizing value through governance. In M. Jennex (Ed.), *Dynamic models for knowledge-driven organizations* (pp. 36–55). Hershey, PA: Business Science Reference; doi:10.4018/978-1-4666-2485-6.ch003

Compilation of References

Addressing Big Data Security Challenges: The Right Tools for Smart Protection. (2012, September). White Paper. Trend Micro Incorporated. Retrieved from www.trendmicro.com

Agneeswaran, V. (2012). Big-data - Theoretical, engineering and analytics perspective. In Big Data Analytics (LNCS), (vol. 7678, pp. 8-15). Springer Berlin Heidelberg.

Agrawal, D., Das, S., & Abbadi, A. (2011). *Big data and cloud computing.* Paper presented at the 14th International Conference on Extending Database Technology (EDBT/ICDT 2011), Uppsala, Sweden. doi:10.1145/1951365.1951432

Agrawal, R., & Srikant, R. (1994). Fast algorithms for mining association rules in large databases. In *Proceedings of the 20th International Conference on Very Large Data Bases* (VLDB '94). Morgan Kaufmann Publishers Inc.

Agrawal, R., Imieliński, T., & Swami, A. (1993). Mining association rules between sets of items in large databases. *SIGMOD Record*, *22*(2), 207–216. doi:10.1145/170036.170072

Alam, B. (2013). Matrix Multiplication using r-Train Data Structure, 2013 AASRI Conference on Parallel and Distributed Computing Systems. *AASRI Procedia*, *5*, 189-193.

Al-Kouri, A. (2012). Data Ownership, Who Owns my Data? *International Journal of Management & Information, 2*(1).

Almeida, J., Leite, N., & Torres, R. (2012). VISON: VIdeo Summarization for ONline applications. *Pattern Recognition Letters*, *33*(4), 397–409. doi:10.1016/j.patrec.2011.08.007

Anastasia. (2015). *Big data and new product development.* Entrepreneurial Insights. Retrieved from http://www.entrepreneurial-insights.com/big-data-new-product-development/

Andrejevic, M. (2013). *Infoglut: How too much information is changing the way we think and know.* New York, NY: Routledge.

Andreolini, M., Colajanni, M., Pietri, M., & Tosi, S. (2015). Adaptive, scalable and reliable monitoring of big data on clouds. *Journal of Parallel and Distributed Computing*, (0). doi:10.1016/j.jpdc.2014.08.007

Apache Software Foundation. (n.d.a). *Cassandra.* Retrieved January 28, 2016, from http://cassandra.apache.org/

Apache Software Foundation. (n.d.b). *HBase.* Retrieved February 08, 2016, from http://hbase.apache.org/

Aplin, T. (2005). *The ECJ Elucidates the Database Right.* London: Intellectual Property Quarterly.

Arbor Networks Blog. (2014). *Next Generation Incident Response, Security Analytics and the Role of Big Data.* Retrieved from http://www.arbornetworks.com/corporate/blog/5126-next-generation-incident-response-security-analytics-and-the-role-of-big-data-webinar

Arroyo, I., & Woolf, B. P. (2005). Inferring learning and attitudes from Bayesian Network of log file data. In *Proceedings of the 12th International Conference on Artificial Intelligence in Education* (pp. 33-40).

Article 29 Working Party. (2014). *Opinion 06/2014on the notion of legitimate interests of the data controller under Article 7 of Directive 95/46/EC, 9 April 2014,* 844/14/EN WP 217.

Assunção, M. D., Calheiros, R. N., Bianchi, S., Netto, M. A. S., & Buyya, R. (2015). Big Data computing and clouds: Trends and future directions. *Journal of Parallel and Distributed Computing, 79–80*(May), 3–15. doi:10.1016/j.jpdc.2014.08.003

Bailey, J., Ellis, S., Schneider, C., & Vander, T. (2013). *Blended Learning Implementation Guide.* Foundation for Excellence in Education In Association with: Getting Smart DTLN Smart series.

Baker, K. (2013). *Singular Value Decomposition Tutorial.* Retrieved December 26, 2014, from http://www.ling.ohio-state.edu/~kbaker/pubs/Singular_Value_Decomposition_Tutorial.pdf

Baker, R. S., Corbett, A. T., & Koedinger, K. R. (2004). Detecting Student Misuse of Intelligent Tutoring Systems. In *Proceedings of the 7th International Conference on Intelligent Tutoring Systems* (pp. 531-540). Springer Berlin Heidelberg. doi:10.1007/978-3-540-30139-4_50

Baker, R. S. (2007). Modeling and understanding students' off-task behavior in intelligent tutoring systems. In *Proceedings of the SIGCHI conference on Human factors in computing systems* (pp. 1059-1068). ACM. doi:10.1145/1240624.1240785

Baker, R. S. (2010). Mining data for student models. In *Advances in intelligent tutoring systems* (pp. 323–337). Springer Berlin Heidelberg. doi:10.1007/978-3-642-14363-2_16

Baker, R. S. (2014a). Educational data mining: An advance for intelligent systems in education. *IEEE Intelligent Systems, 29*(3), 78–82. doi:10.1109/MIS.2014.42

Baker, R. S., & Inventado, P. S. (2014b). Educational data mining and learning analytics. In *Learning Analytics* (pp. 61–75). Springer New York.

Baker, R., Gowda, S. M., & Corbett, A. T. (2011). Automatically detecting a student's preparation for future learning: Help use is key. In *Proceedings of the 4th international conference on educational data mining.*

Bakhshi, H., Bravo-Biosca, A., & Mateos-Garcia, J. (2014). *Inside the datavores: how data and online analytics affect business performance.* Nesta.

Bakshi, K. (2012). *Considerations for big data: Architecture and approach.* Big Sky, MT: IEEE Aerospace Conference.

Bantouna, A., Poulios, G., Tsagkaris, K., & Demestichas, P. (2014). Network load predictions based on big data and the utilization of self-organizing maps. *Journal of Network and Systems Management, 22*(2), 150–173. doi:10.1007/s10922-013-9285-1

Barker, K. J., D'Amato, J., & Sheridon, P. (2008). Credit card fraud: Awareness and prevention. *Journal of Financial Crime, 15*(4), 398–410. doi:10.1108/13590790810907236

Barney, J. (1991). Firm resources and sustained competitive advantage. *Journal of Management, 17*(1), 99–120. doi:10.1177/014920639101700108

Barr, R. B., & Tagg, J. (1995). From teaching to learning—A new paradigm for undergraduate education. *Change: The Magazine of Higher Learning, 27*(6), 12-26.

Barrie, S., Ginns, P., & Prosser, M. (2005). Early impact and outcomes of an institutionally aligned, student focused learning perspective on teaching quality assurance 1. *Assessment & Evaluation in Higher Education, 30*(6), 641–656. doi:10.1080/02602930500260761

Basho Technologies. (n.d.). *Riak*. Retrieved December 12, 2015, from http://basho.com/riak/

Beaver, D., Kumar, S., Li, H. C., Sobel, J., & Vajgel, P. (2010). *Finding a needle in haystack: Facebook's photo storage*. Paper presented at the 9th USENIX conference on Operating Systems Design and Implementation (OSDI 2010), Berkeley, CA.

Beck, J., Baker, R., Corbett, A., Kay, J., Litman, D., Mitrovic, T., & Ritter, S. (2004). Workshop on Analyzing Student-Tutor Interaction Logs to Improve Educational Outcomes. In *Intelligent Tutoring Systems* (pp. 909-909). Springer Berlin Heidelberg.

Beck, J., & Mostow, J. (2008). How who should practice: Using learning decomposition to evaluate the efficacy of different types of practice for different types of students. In *Proceedings of the 9th International Conference on Intelligent Tutoring Systems*. doi:10.1007/978-3-540-69132-7_39

Bendler, J., Wagner, S., Brandt, T., & Neumann, D. (2014). Taming uncertainty in big data. *Business & Information Systems Engineering*, *6*(5), 279–288. doi:10.1007/s12599-014-0342-4

Benjamins, V. R. (2014). Big data: From hype to reality? In *Proceedings of the 4th International Conference on Web Intelligence, Mining and Semantics (WIMS14)*. ACM.

Berkeley School. (2012). *Lecture 12 -Analyzing Big Data with Twitter: Recommender Systems*. Retrieved February 10, 2014, from http://www.youtube.com/watch?v=NSscbT7JwxY

Berman, J. J. (2013). Principles of Big Data: Preparing, Sharing, and Analyzing Complex Information. Morgan Kaufmann (Elsevier) Publisher.

Berry, M. W., Dumais, S. T., & O'Brien, G. W. (1995). Using linear algebra for intelligent information retrieval. *SIAM Review*, *37*(4), 573–595. doi:10.1137/1037127

Beyer, M. A., Lovelock, J.-D., Sommer, D., & Adrian, M. (2012, October 12). *Big Data Drives Rapid Changes in Infrastructure and $232 Billion in IT Spending Through 2016*. Retrieved June 12, 2013, from http://www.gartner.com/id=2195915

Bhadani, A. (2011). Cloud Computing and Virtualization. Saarbrucken: VDM Verlag Dr. Muller Aktiengesellschaft & Co. KG.

Bhadani, A., & Chaudhary, S. (2010). Performance evaluation of web servers using central load balancing policy over virtual machines on cloud. In *Proceedings of the Third Annual ACM Conference*. Bangalore: ACM. doi:10.1145/1754288.1754304

Big security for big data. (2012, December). Business White Paper. HP.

Birol, F. (2008). *World Energy Outlook 2008*. Academic Press.

Biswas, R. (2015a). Atrain Distributed System (ADS): An Infinitely Scalable Architecture for Processing Big Data of Any 4Vs. In Computational Intelligence for Big Data Analysis Frontier Advances and Applications. Springer International Publishing.

Biswas, R. (2011). r-Train (Train): A New Flexible Dynamic Data Structure. *Information: An International Journal (Japan)*, *14*(4), 1231–1246.

Biswas, R. (2012). Heterogeneous Data Structure "r-Atrain". *Information: An International Journal (Japan)*, *15*(2), 879–902.

Biswas, R. (2013a). Theory of Solid Matrices & Solid Latrices, Introducing New Data Structures MA, MT: For Big Data. *International Journal of Algebra*, *7*(16), 767–789.

Biswas, R. (2013b). *Heterogeneous Data Structure "r-Atrain". In Global Trends in Knowledge Representation and Computational Intelligence*. IGI Global.

Biswas, R. (2014a). Processing of Heterogeneous Big Data in an Atrain Distributed System (ADS) Using the Heterogeneous Data Structure r-Atrain. *International Journal of Computing and Optimization*, *1*(1), 17–45.

Biswas, R. (2014b). Data Structures for Big Data, *Int. Journal of Computing and Optimization*, *1*, 73–93.

Biswas, R. (2014c). Introducing Soft Statistical Measures. *The Journal of Fuzzy Mathematics*, *22*(4), 819–851.

Biswas, R. (2015b). *Is 'Fuzzy Theory' An Appropriate Tool For Large Size Problems?* Heidelberg, Germany: Springer.

Biswas, R. (2015c). *Is 'Fuzzy Theory' An Appropriate Tool For Large Size Decision Problems? In Imprecision and Uncertainty in Information Representation and Processing*. Heidelberg, Germany: Springer.

Biswas, R. (2015d). "Theory of CESFM": A Proposal to FIFA & IFAB for a new 'Continuous Evaluation Fuzzy Method' of Deciding the WINNER of a Football Match that Would Have Otherwise been Drawn or Tied after 90 Minutes of Play. *The Journal of Fuzzy Mathematics*, *23*(4), 991–1008.

Biswas, R. (2016in Press). Introducing 'NR-Statistics': A New Direction in "Statistics". In S. J. John (Ed.), *Generalized and Hybrid Set Structures and Applications for Soft Computing*. IGI Global. doi:10.4018/978-1-4666-9798-0.ch023

Bizer, C., Boncz, P., Brodie, M. L., & Erling, O. (2011). The Meaningful Use of Big Data: Four Perspectives - Four Challenges. *SIGMOD*, *4*(4), 56 – 60. Retrieved from http://www.sigmod.org/publications/sigmod-record/1112/pdfs/10.report.bizer.pdf

Bloor Research. (2012). *Big Data Analytics with Hadoop and Sybase IQ*. London: Bloor.

Blount, M., Ebling, M., Eklund, J., James, A., McGregor, C., Percival, N., & Sow, D. et al. (2010). Real-time analysis for intensive care: Development and deployment of the Artemis analytic system. *IEEE Engineering in Medicine and Biology Magazine*, *29*(2), 110–118. doi:10.1109/MEMB.2010.936454 PMID:20659848

Bollier, D., & Firestone, C. M. (2010). *The promise and peril of big data*. Washington, DC: Aspen Institute.

Bonomi, F., Milito, R., Natarajan, P., & Zhu, J. (2014). Fog computing: A platform for internet of things and analytics. In *Big Data and Internet of Things: A Roadmap for Smart Environments* (pp. 169–186). Springer. doi:10.1007/978-3-319-05029-4_7

Bonomi, F., Milito, R., Zhu, J., & Addepalli, S. (2012). Fog computing and its role in the internet of things.*Proceedings of the first edition of the MCC workshop on Mobile cloud computing* (pp. 13-16) ACM. doi:10.1145/2342509.2342513

Borghi, M., & Karapapa, S. (2013). *Copyright & Mass Digitisation*. Oxford, UK: Oxford University Press.

Boriboonsomsin, K., Barth, M. J., Zhu, W., & Vu, A. (2012). Eco-routing navigation system based on multisource historical and real-time traffic information. *Intelligent Transportation Systems IEEE Transactions on*, *13*(4), 1694–1704.

Boyaci, A., Ozpinar, A., Ozturk, E., & Yarkan, S. (2015). EV2C: Extended Vehicle-to-Cloud Model and Conceptual Implementation for Big Data.*IEEE Sixth International Conference on Modeling, Simulation and Applied Optimization (ICMSAO'15)*.

Boyd, D., & Crawford, K. (2011). Six provocations for big data. In *A Decade in Internet Time:Symposium on the Dynamics of the Internet and Society*.

Boyd, D., & Crawford, K. (2012). Critical questions for big data. *Information Communication and Society*, *15*(5), 662–679. doi:10.1080/1369118X.2012.678878

Bradji, L., & Boufaida, M. (2011). Open User Involvement in Data Cleaning for Data Warehouse Quality. *International Journal of Digital Information and Wireless Communications, 1*(2), 536–544.

Bransford, J. D., Brown, A. L., & Cocking, R. R. (1999). *How people learn: brain, mind, experience, and school.* Washington, DC: National Academy Press.

Breiman, L. (2001). Statistical modeling: The two cultures. *Statistical Science, 16*(3), 199–231. doi:10.1214/ss/1009213726

Brewer, E. A. (2000). Towards robust distributed systems (abstract). In *Proceedings of the Nineteenth Annual ACM Symposium on Principles of Distributed Computing (PODC '00).* ACM. doi:10.1145/343477.343502

Brown, B., Chui, M., & Manyika, J. (2011). Are you ready for the era of big data? *McKinsey Quarterly.* Retrieved from http://www.mckinsey.com/insights/strategy/areyoureadyfortheeraofbigdata

Browning, V., So, K. K. F., & Sparks, B. (2013). The influence of online reviews on consumers' attributions of service quality and control for service standards in hotels. *Journal of Travel & Tourism Marketing, 30*(1/2), 23–40. doi:10.1080/10548408.2013.750971

Brynjolfsson, E., Hitt, L., & Kim, H. H. (2011). Strength in numbers: how does data-driven decision making affect firm performance? MIT - Sloan School of Management.

Buck, C., Horbel, C., Kesseler, T., & Christian, C. (2014). Mobile consumer apps: Big data brother is watching you. *Marketing Review St. Gallen, 31*(1), 26–35. doi:10.1365/s11621-014-0318-2

Burns, R. (2015). Rethinking big data in digital humanitarianism: Practices, epistemologies, and social relations. *GeoJournal, 80*(4), 477–490. doi:10.1007/s10708-014-9599-x

Buros, W. M. (2013). *Understanding Systems and Architecture for Big Data.* IBM Research Report. Retrieved December 23, 2014 from http://cnf-labs.org/pdf/research-report-ibm.html#

Butler, D. (2013). When Google got the flu wrong. *Nature, 494*(7436), 155–156. doi:10.1038/494155a PMID:23407515

Cardenas, A., Chen, Y., Fuchs, A., Lane, A., Lu, R., Manadhata, P., . . . Sathyadevan, S. (2012, November). *Top Ten Big Data security and Privacy Challenges.* White Paper, Cloud Security Alliance. Retrieved from http://www.cloudsecurityalliance.org/

Casey, E. (2014). *Scalable Collaborative Filtering Recommendation Algorithms on Apache Spark.* (Unpublished Senior Thesis). Claremont Mckenna College, USA.

Cavallo, A. (2012). Online and official price indexes: Measuring Argentina's inflation. *Journal of Monetary Economics, 60*(2), 152–165. doi:10.1016/j.jmoneco.2012.10.002

CCC. (2011a). *Computing Community Consortium. Advancing Discovery in Science and Engineering.* CCC.

CCC. (2011b). *Computing Community Consortium. Advancing Personalized Education.* CCC.

CCC. (2011c). *Computing Community Consortium. Smart Health and Wellbeing.* CCC.

CCC. (2011d). *Computing Community Consortium. A Sustainable Future.* CCC.

Chang, L., Ranjan, R., Xuyun, Z., Chi, Y., Georgakopoulos, D., & Jinjun, C. (2013). *Public auditing for big data storage in cloud computing.* Paper presented at the 2013 IEEE 16th International Conference on Computational Science and Engineering (CSE 2013), Sydney, Australia.

Chang, E. Y., Bai, H., & Zhu, K. (2009). Parallel Algorithms for Mining Large Scale Rich Media Data.*ACM International Conference on Multimedia.* doi:10.1145/1631272.1631451

Chauhan, J. (n.d.). *Penetration Testing, Web Application Security*. Available at: http://www.ivizsecurity.com/blog/penetration-testing/top-5-big-data-vulnerability-classes/

Chawla, N. V., Bowyer, K. W., Hall, L. O., & Kegelmeyer, W. P. (2002). SMOTE: Synthetic minority over-sampling technique. *Journal of Artificial Intelligence Research*, *16*, 321–357. doi: 10.1613/jair.953

Chen, J., Chen, Y., Du, X., Li, C., Lu, J., Zhao, S., & Zhou, X. (2013). Big Data Challenge: A data management perspective. *Frontiers of Computer Science*, *7*(2), 157-164. Retrieved from http://iir.ruc.edu.cn/~jchchen/FCSBigData.pdf

Chen, Q., Wang, L., & Shang, Z. (2008). *MRGIS: A MapReduce-enabled high performance workflow system for GIS*. Paper presented at the 2008 IEEE 4th International Conference on eScience (eScience 2008), Indianapolis, IN. doi:10.1109/eScience.2008.169

Chen, H., Chiang, R. H., & Storey, V. C. (2012). Business intelligence and analytics: From big data to big impact. *Management Information Systems Quarterly*, *36*, 1165–1188.

Chen, M., Mao, S., & Liu, Y. (2014). Big data: A survey. *Mobile Networks and Applications*, *19*(2), 171–209. doi:10.1007/s11036-013-0489-0

Chen, Z., Lu, Y., Xiao, N., & Liu, F. (2014). A hybrid memory built by SSD and DRAM to support in-memory big data analytics. *Knowledge and Information Systems*, *41*(2), 335–354. doi:10.1007/s10115-013-0727-6

Chih-Wei, L., Chih-Ming, H., Chih-Hung, C., & Chao-Tung, Y. (2013). *An improvement to data service in cloud computing with content sensitive transaction analysis and adaptation*. Paper presented at the 2013 IEEE 37th Annual Computer Software and Applications Conference Workshops (COMPSACW 2013), Kyoto, Japan.

Chiky, R., Ghisloti, R., & Aoul, Z. K. (2012). Development of a distributed recommender system using the Hadoop Framework. In *Proceedings of EGC 2012* (pp. 495 – 500).

Choi, H., & Varian, H. (2012). Predicting the present with Google Trends. *Economic Inquiry*, *88*, 2–9.

Cloudera & Teradata. (2011). *Hadoop and the Data Warehouse: When to Use Which*. Cloudera, Inc. and Teradata Corporation.

Cohen, J. (2016). The Regulatory State in the Informational Age. *Theoretical Inquiries in Law, 17*(2).

Conati, C., & Maclaren, H. (2009). Empirically building and evaluating a probabilistic model of user affect. *User Modeling and User-Adapted Interaction*, *19*(3), 267–303. doi:10.1007/s11257-009-9062-8

Cook, T. D. (2014). "Big data" in research on social policy. *Journal of Policy Analysis and Management*, *33*(2), 544–547. doi:10.1002/pam.21751

Corbett, A. (2001). Cognitive computer tutors: Solving the two-sigma problem. In *User Modeling 2001* (pp. 137–147). Springer Berlin Heidelberg. doi:10.1007/3-540-44566-8_14

Corbett, A., & Anderson, J. (1995). Knowledge traching: Modeling the acquisition of procedural knowledge. *User Modeling and User-Adapted Interaction*, *4*(4), 253–278. doi:10.1007/BF01099821

Cottrell, L. (2016). *Network Monitoring Tools*. Retrieved from: http://www.slac.stanford.edu/xorg/nmtf/nmtf-tools.html

Coumaros, J., de Roys, S., Chretien, L., Buvat, J., Clerk, V., & Auliard, O. (2014). *Big data alchemy: How can banks maximize the value of their customer data?* Capgemini Consulting White Paper. Retrieved from https://www.capgemini.com/resources/big-data-customer-analytics-in-banks

Crawford, K., Miltner, K., & Gray, M. (2014). Critiquing Big Data: Politics, Ethics, Epistemology. *International Journal of Communication*, *8*, 1663.

Crouch, C. H., & Mazur, E. (2001). Peer instruction: Ten years of experience and results. *American Journal of Physics*, *69*(9), 970–977. doi:10.1119/1.1374249

CSIRO. (2015). *Commonwealth Scientific and Industrial Research Organisation*. CSIRO.

Cukier, K. (2010). Data, data everywhere: A special report on managing information. *The Economist*. Retrieved 15 June 2015 from: http://www.economist.com/node/15557443

Cumbley, R., & Church, P. (2013). Is big data creepy? *Computer Law & Security Report*, *29*(5), 601–609. doi:10.1016/j.clsr.2013.07.007

Curran, J. (2013). Big data or "big ethnographic data"? Positioning big data within the ethnographic space. *Ethnographic Praxis in Industry Conference Proceedings, 2013*(1), 62–73.

Curry, Kirda, Sy, Stemberg, Schwartz, Stewart, & Yoran. (2013, January). *Big Data Fuels Intelligence-driven Security*. RSA Security Brief.

Cuzzocrea, A., Song, I.-Y., & Davis, K. C. (2011). Analytics over large-scale multidimensional data: the big data revolution! In *Proceedings of the ACM 14th International workshop on Data Warehousing and OLAP* (DOLAP '11). ACM. doi:10.1145/2064676.2064695

D'mello, S. K., Craig, S. D., Witherspoon, A., Mcdaniel, B., & Graesser, A. (2008). Automatic detection of learner's affect from conversational cues. *User Modeling and User-Adapted Interaction*, *18*(1-2), 45–80. doi:10.1007/s11257-007-9037-6

da Silva, A., Falcão, A., & Magalhães, L. (2011). Active learning paradigms for CBIR systems based on optimum-path forest classification. *Pattern Recognition*, *44*(12), 2971–2978. doi:10.1016/j.patcog.2011.04.026

Dan, C., Zhixin, L., Lizhe, W., Minggang, D., Jingying, C., & Hui, L. (2013). Natural disaster monitoring with wireless sensor networks: A case study of data-intensive applications upon low-cost scalable systems. *Mobile Networks and Applications*, *18*(5), 651–663. doi:10.1007/s11036-013-0456-9

Databricks. (2014). *Intro to Apache Spark*. Retrieved October 24, 2014, from http://stanford.edu/~rezab/sparkclass/slides/itas_workshop.pdf

de Monjoye, Y.-A., Shmueli, E., Wang, S. S., & Pentland, A. S. (2014). Open PDS: Protecting the Privacy of Metadata through SafeAnswers. *PLoS ONE*, *10*, 1371.

Dean, J., & Ghemawat, S. (2008). MapReduce: Simplified data processing on large clusters. *Communications of the ACM*, *51*(1), 107–113. doi:10.1145/1327452.1327492

Dean, J., & Ghemawat, S. (2010). MapReduce: A flexible data processing tool. *Communications of the ACM*, *53*(1), 72–77. doi:10.1145/1629175.1629198

Debortoli, S., Müller, O., & vom Brocke, J. (2014). Comparing business intelligence and big data skills. *Business & Information Systems Engineering*, *6*(5), 289–300. doi:10.1007/s12599-014-0344-2

Department for Business & Innovation Skills. (2011). *The Midata Vision of Consumer Empowerment*. Retrieved from https://www.gov.uk/government/news/the-midata-vision-of-consumer-empowerment

Dhar, V. (2013). Data science and prediction. *Communications of the ACM*, *56*(12), 64–73. doi:10.1145/2500499

Dietz-Uhler, B., & Hurn, J. E. (2013). Using learning analytics to predict (and improve) student success: A faculty perspective. *Journal of Interactive Online Learning, 12*(1), 17–26.

Dijcks, J. (2013, June). *Big Data for the Enterprise*. Oracle White Paper. Oracle Corporation.

Dittrich, J., & Ruiz, J. A. Q. (2012). Efficient Big Data Processing in Hadoop MapReduce. In *Proceedings of VLDB Endowment* (pp. 2014-2015). VLDB Endowment. doi:10.14778/2367502.2367562

Dobre, C., & Xhafa, F. (2014). Parallel programming paradigms and frameworks in big data era. *International Journal of Parallel Programming, 42*(5), 710–738. doi:10.1007/s10766-013-0272-7

Docs.oracle.com. (2014). *Data Warehousing Concepts*. Retrieved from: http://docs.oracle.com/cd/B10500_01/server.920/a96520/concept.htm

Domingos, P., & Hulten, G. (2000). Mining High Speed Data Streams.*ACM SIGKDD International Conference on Knowledge Discovery and Data Mining.*

d'Orey, P. M., & Ferreira, M. (2014). ITS for sustainable mobility: A survey on applications and impact assessment tools. *Intelligent Transportation Systems. IEEE Transactions on, 15*(2), 477–493.

Duggal, P. S., & Paul, S. (2013). Big Data Analysis: Challenges and Solutions.*International Conference on Cloud, Big Data and Trust.*

Eberhardt, F., & Scheines, R. (2007). Interventions and causal inference. *Philosophy of Science, 74*(5), 981–995. doi:10.1086/525638

Eberly, D. (1999). Distance between point and triangle in 3D. *Magic Software.* Retrieved from http://www. magic-software. com/Documentation/pt3tri3. pdf

Edelman, B. (2015, April). How to launch your digital platform. *Harvard Business Review.*

Eduventures, Inc. (2013). *Predictive Analysis in Higher Education, Data Driven Decision Making for the Student Life Cycle.* Boston: Eduventures, Inc. Retrieved from http://www.eduventures.com/wp-content/uploads/2013/02/Eduventures_Predictive_Analytics_White_Paper1.pdf

E-LEARNING, Concepts, Trends, Applications. (2014). San Francisco, CA: Epignosis LLC.

El-Hussein, M. O. M., & Cronje, J. C. (2010). Defining Mobile Learning in the Higher Education Landscape. *Journal of Educational Technology & Society, 13*(3), 12–21.

Elkan, C. (2001). *The foundations of cost–sensitive learning*. Paper presented at the 17th International Joint Conference on Artificial Intelligence (IJCAI 2001), Seattle, WA.

Elseberg, J., Borrmann, D., & Nüchter, A. (2013). One billion points in the cloud–an octree for efficient processing of 3D laser scans. *ISPRS Journal of Photogrammetry and Remote Sensing, 76*, 76–88. doi:10.1016/j.isprsjprs.2012.10.004

Erwin, K., & Pollari, T. (2013). Small packages for big (qualitative) data. *Ethnographic Praxis in Industry Conference Proceedings, 2013*(1), 44–61.

Esposti, S. (2014). *When big data meets dataveillance: The hidden side of analytics*. Paper presented at the Annual Meeting of the Society for Social Studies of Science (4S), San Diego, CA.

Facebook. (2015). Retrieved 20 February 2016 from: http://www.statisticbrain.com/facebook-statistics/

Falakmasir, M. H., & Habibi, J. (2010). *Using Educational Data Mining Methods to Study the Impact of Virtual Classroom in E-Learning.* Pittsburgh, PA: EDM.

Faltesek, D. (2013). Big argumentation? TripleC: Communication, capitalism & critique. *Journal for a Global Sustainable Information Society, 11*(2), 402–411.

Fang, Z., Fan, X., & Chen, G. (2014). A study on specialist or special disease clinics based on big data. *Frontiers of Medicine, 8*(3), 376–381. doi:10.1007/s11684-014-0356-9 PMID:25186249

Fanning, C. (2015). Research talent in the big data age. *Research World, 2015*(50), 40–41.

Fanning, K., & Drogt, E. (2014). Big data: New opportunities for M&A. *Journal of Corporate Accounting & Finance, 25*(2), 27–34. doi:10.1002/jcaf.21919

Fanning, K., & Grant, R. (2013). Big data: Implications for financial managers. *Journal of Corporate Accounting & Finance, 24*(5), 23–30. doi:10.1002/jcaf.21872

Fan, W., & Bifet, A. (2012). Mining Big Data: Current Status, and Forecast to the Future. *SIGKDD Explorations, 14*(2), 1–5. doi:10.1145/2481244.2481246

Fayyad, U. M. (2012). Big Data Everywhere, and No SQL in sight. *SIGKDD Explorations, 14*(2), 1–2. Retrieved from http://www.sigkdd.org/sites/default/files/issues/14-2-2012-12/V14-02-01-editorial.pdf

Feinleib, D. (2013). Big Data Demystified: How Big Data Is Changing The Way We Live, Love And Learn. The Big Data Group Publisher, LLC.

Feng, M., & Heffernan, N. T. (2007). Towards live informing and automatic analyzing of student learning: Reporting in assessment system. *Journal of Interactive Learning Research, 18*(2), 207.

Fernandes, H., Maldague, X., Batista, M., & Barcelos, C. A. Z. (2011). *Suspicious event recognition using infrared imagery.* Paper presented at the 2011 IEEE International Conference on Systems, Man, and Cybernetics (SMC 2011), Anchorage, AK. doi:10.1109/ICSMC.2011.6084001

Finch, B. J. (1999). Internet discussions as a source for consumer product customer involvement and quality information: An exploratory study. *Journal of Operations Management, 17*(5), 535–556. doi:10.1016/S0272-6963(99)00005-4

Fisher, D., DeLine, R., Czerwinski, M., & Drucker, S. (2012). Interactions with big data analytics. *Interaction, 19*(3), 50–59. doi:10.1145/2168931.2168943

Flood, M., Jagadish, H. V., Kyle, A., Olken, F., & Raschid, L. (2011). Using data for systemic financial risk management. In *Proc. 5th Biennial Conf. InnovativeData Systems Research.* Gartner Group. Retrieved from http://www.gartner.com/it/page.jsp?id=1731916

Fond, G., Brunel, L., Leboyer, M., & Boyer, L. (2014). Do the treasures of "big data" combined with behavioural intervention therapies contain the key to the mystery of large psychiatric issues? *Acta Psychiatrica Scandinavica, 130*(5), 406–407. PMID:25131263

Forsyth, C. (2012). *For big data analytics there's no such thing as too big.* Cisco White paper. Retrieved 20 February 2015 from: http://www.cisco.com/en/US/solutions/ns340/ns517/ns224/big data wp.pdf

Forsyth, J., & Boucher, L. (2015). Why big data is not enough. *Research World, 2015*(50), 26–27.

Foster, I., Zhao, Y., Raicu, I., & Lu, S. (2008). Cloud computing and grid computing 360-degree compared. In Grid Computing Environments Workshop, 2008 (GCE '08).

Fotopoulou, A. (2014). *Tracking Biodata: Sharing and Ownership.* Report on Research Placement funded by the RCUK Digital Economy NEMODE Network.

Fromholz, J. (2000). The European Union Data Privacy Directive. *Berk. Tech. LJ*, *15*, 461.

Fung, B. C. M., Wang, K., Chen, R., & Yu, P. S. (2010). Privacy-preserving data publishing: A survey on recent developments. *ACM Computing Surveys, 42*(4), 14:1–14:53.

Gaff, B. M., Smedinghoff, T. J., & Sor, S. (2012). Privacy and Data Security. *Computer*, (3), 8–10.

Gandomi, A., & Haider, M. (2015). Beyond the hype: Big data concepts, methods, and analytics. *International Journal of Information Management*, *35*(2), 137–144. doi:10.1016/j.ijinfomgt.2014.10.007

Gantz, J., & Reinsel, D. (2011). *Extracting value from chaos. Tech. rep.* IDC.

García, S., Derrac, J., Cano, J., & Herrera, F. (2012). Prototype selection for nearest neighbor classification: Taxonomy and empirical study. *IEEE Transactions on Pattern Analysis and Machine Intelligence*, *34*(3), 417–435. doi:10.1109/TPAMI.2011.142 PMID:21768651

Garlasu, D., Sandulescu, V., Halcu, I., Neculoiu, G., Grigoriu, O., Marinescu, M., & Marinescu, V. (2013). A big data implementation based on grid computing. In *11th Roedunet International Conference (RoEduNet)*. Sinaia. doi:10.1109/RoEduNet.2013.6511732

Gartner-Research Firm. (n.d.). Retrieved from https://www.gartner.com

George, G., Haas, M. R., & Pentland, A. (2014). Big data and management. *Academy of Management Journal*, *57*(2), 321–326. doi:10.5465/amj.2014.4002

Gervais, D. J. (2007). The *Protection of Databases Kent L. Rev.*, *82*, 1109.

Ghazanfar, M. A., & Bennett, A. P. (2012). The advantage of Careful imputation source in sparse data-environment of recommender systems: generating improved SVD-based recommendations. *Informatica, 37*, 61-92. Retrieved from http://citeseerx.ist.psu.edu/viewdoc/download?doi=10.1.1.368.2112&rep=rep1&type=pdf

Ghose, A., & Ipeirotis, P. G. (2011). Estimating the helpfulness and economic impact of product reviews: Mining text and reviewer characteristics. *IEEE Transactions on Knowledge and Data Engineering*, *23*(10), 1498–1512. doi:10.1109/TKDE.2010.188

Ghoting, A., & Pednault, E. (2009). Hadoop-ML: An Infrastructure for the Rapid Implementation of Parallel Reusable Analytics.*Proc. Large Scale Machine Learning Workshop.*

Gilbert, S., & Lynch, N. (2002). Brewer's conjecture and the feasibility of consistent, available, partition-tolerant web services. *SIGACT News*, *33*(2), 51–59. doi:10.1145/564585.564601

Gillick, D., Faria, A. & DeNero, J. (2006). *MapReduce: Distributed Computing for Machine Learning*. Academic Press.

Gobbetti, E., & Marton, F. (2004). Layered point clouds: A simple and efficient multiresolution structure for distributing and rendering gigantic point-sampled models. *Computers & Graphics*, *28*(6), 815–826. doi:10.1016/j.cag.2004.08.010

Gong, S., Ye, H., & Dai, Y. (2009.) Combining Singular Value Decomposition and Item-based Recommender in Collaborative Filtering.*Second International Workshop on Knowledge discovery and data mining*, (pp. 769-722). doi:10.1109/WKDD.2009.132

González, M. C., Hidalgo, C. A., & Barabási, A.-L. (2008). A-L.Understanding individual human mobility patterns. *Nature*, *453*(7196), 779–782. doi:10.1038/nature06958 PMID:18528393

Goswami, P., Erol, F., Mukhi, R., Pajarola, R., & Gobbetti, E. (2013). An efficient multi-resolution framework for high quality interactive rendering of massive point clouds using multi-way kd-trees. *The Visual Computer*, *29*(1), 69–83. doi:10.1007/s00371-012-0675-2

Gower, S. (2014). *Netflix prize and SVD*. Retrieved December 20, 2014, from http://buzzard.ups.edu/courses/2014spring/420projects/math420-UPS-spring-2014-gower-netflix-SVD.pdf

Greenfield, P. M., & Calvert, S. L. (2004). Electronic media and human development: The legacy of Rodney R. Cocking. *Journal of Applied Developmental Psychology*, *25*(6), 627–631. doi:10.1016/j.appdev.2004.09.001

Grossman, R. L., & Siegel, K. (2014). Organizational models for big data and analytics. *Journal of Organization Design*, *3*(1), 20–25. doi:10.7146/jod.9799

Gundert, L. (2013). *Big Data in Security – Part I: TRAC Tools.* Retrieved from: *http*://blogs.cisco.com/security/big-data-in-security-part-i-trac-tools/

Guo, H., Wang, L., Chen, F., & Liang, D. (2014). Scientific big data and Digital Earth. *Chinese Science Bulletin*, *59*(35), 5066–5073. doi:10.1007/s11434-014-0645-3

Guo, K., Pan, W., Lu, M., Zhou, X., & Ma, J. (2015). An effective and economical architecture for semantic-based heterogeneous multimedia big data retrieval. *Journal of Systems and Software*, *102*, 207–216. doi:10.1016/j.jss.2014.09.016

Haddadi, H., & Brown, I. (2014). *Quantified Self and the Privacy Challenge*. Technology Law Futures.

Hamalainen, W., & Vinni, M. (2010). Classifiers for educational data mining. In Handbook of Educational Data Mining. Chapman & Hall / CRC Press.

Hamdan, N., McKnight, P. E., McKnight, K., & Arfstrom, K. M. (2013). *A review of Flipped Learning. Flipped Learning Network*. Pearson.

Han, J. E. H., Le, G., & Du, J. (2011). Survey on NoSQL database. *The 6th International Conference on Pervasive Computing and Applications (ICPCA 2011)*, (pp. 363-366).

Han, L. X., Liew, C. S., Hemert, J. V., & Atkinson, M. (2011). A generic parallel processing model for facilitating data mining and integration. *Parallel Computing*, *37*(3), 157–171. doi:10.1016/j.parco.2011.02.006

Hashem, I. A. T., Yaqoob, I., Anuar, N. B., Mokhtar, S., Gani, A., & Khan, S. U. (2015). The rise of "big data" on cloud computing: Review and open research issues. *Information Systems*, *47*, 98–115. doi:10.1016/j.is.2014.07.006

Heffetz, O., & Ligett, K. (2014). Privacy and data-based research. *The Journal of Economic Perspectives*, *28*(2), 75–98. doi:10.1257/jep.28.2.75

Helfert, M. & Herrmann, C. (2002). *Proactive data quality management for data warehouse systems*. Academic Press.

He, Q., Wang, H., Zhuang, F., Shang, T., & Shi, Z. (2015). Parallel sampling from big data with uncertainty distribution. *Fuzzy Sets and Systems*, *258*, 117–133. doi:10.1016/j.fss.2014.01.016

Hernandez, M. & Stolfo, S. (1995). *The merge/purge problem for large databases*. Academic Press.

Hernandez, M., & Stolfo, S. (1998). Real-world data is dirty: Data cleansing and the merge/purge problem. *Data Mining and Knowledge Discovery*, *2*(1), 9–37. doi:10.1023/A:1009761603038

Hijazi, S. T., & Naqvi, R. S. M. M. (2006). Factors affecting student's performance: A Case of Private Colleges. *Bangladesh e- Journal of Sociology (Melbourne, Vic.)*, *3*(1).

Hoffmann, A., & Birnbrich, C. (2012). The impact of fraud prevention on bank-customer relationships. *International Journal of Bank Marketing*, *30*(5), 390–407. doi:10.1108/02652321211247435

Honavar, V. G. (2014). The promise and potential of big data: A case for discovery informatics. *Review of Policy Research*, *31*(4), 326–330. doi:10.1111/ropr.12080

Hortonworks. (2012). *Apache Hadoop: The Big Data Refinery.* Hortonworks.

Hsu, C., Zeng, B., & Zhang, M. (2014). A novel group key transfer for big data security. *Applied Mathematics and Computation*, *249*, 436–443. doi:10.1016/j.amc.2014.10.051

Huang, X., & Du, X. (2014). Achieving Big Data Privacy via Hybrid Cloud. In *Proceedings of IEEE INFOCOM Workshop on Security and Privacy in Big Data*, (pp. 512-517). doi:10.1109/INFCOMW.2014.6849284

Hurlburt, G. F., & Voas, J. (2014). Big Data, Networked Worlds. *Computer*, (April): 84–87.

IBM. (n.d.). *SPSS Statistics*. Retrieved from: http://www.ibm.com/software/security/

IDC. (2012, March 7). *IDC Releases First Worldwide Big Data Technology and Services Market Forecast, Shows Big Data as the Next Essential Capability and a Foundation for the Intelligent Economy*. Retrieved May 4, 2013, from http://www.idc.com/getdoc.jsp?containerId=prUS23355112

IEA. (2014). *CO_2 Emissions from Fuel Combustion Highlights Organization for Economic Cooperation.* IEA.

Jaspe, A., Mures, O. A., Padrón, E. J., & Rabuñal, J. R. (2014). *A Multiresolution System for Managing Massive Point Cloud Data Sets. Technical Report*. University of A Coruña.

Jeong, Y. S., & Shin, S. S. (2015). An efficient authentication scheme to protect user privacy in seamless big data services. *Wireless Personal Communications*, *86*(1), 7–19. doi:10.1007/s11277-015-2990-1

Ji, C., Li, Y., Qiu, W., Awada, U., & Li, K. (2012). *Big data processing in cloud computing environments*. Paper presented at the 2012 IEEE 12th International Symposium on Pervasive Systems, Algorithms and Networks (ISPAN 2012), San Marcos, TX. doi:10.1109/I-SPAN.2012.9

Jiang, C., Ding, Z., Wang, J., & Yan, C. (2014). Big data resource service platform for the Internet financial industry. *Chinese Science Bulletin*, *59*(35), 5051–5058. doi:10.1007/s11434-014-0570-5

Jiang, H., Chen, Y., Qiao, Z., Weng, T. H., & Li, K. C. (2015). Scaling up MapReduce-based big data processing on multi-GPU systems. *Cluster Computing*, *18*(1), 369–383. doi:10.1007/s10586-014-0400-1

Jiménez, G. S., Ongena, S., Peydro, J. L., & Saurina, J. (2014). Hazardous times for monetary policy: What do 23 million loans say about the impact of monetary policy on credit risk-taking. *Econometrica*, *82*, 463–505. doi:10.3982/ECTA10104

Jin, X., Wah, B. W., Cheng, X., & Wang, Y. (2015). Significance and challenges of big data research. *Big Data Research*, 2(2), 59–64. doi:10.1016/j.bdr.2015.01.006

Jothimani, D., Bhadani, A. K., & Shankar, R. (2015). Towards Understanding the Cynicism of Social Networking Sites: An Operations Management Perspective. *Procedia: Social and Behavioral Sciences*, *189*, 117–132. doi:10.1016/j.sbspro.2015.03.206

Kabore, S. C. (2012). *Design and implementation of a recommender system as a module for Liferay portal*. (Unpublished master dissertation). University Polytechnic of Catalunya (UPC), Spain.

Kaisler, S., Armour, F., Espinosa, J., & Money, W. (2013). Big data: Issues and challenges moving forward. In *46th Hawaii International Conference on System Sciences (HICSS)*. doi:10.1109/HICSS.2013.645

Kaplan, R. M., Chambers, D. A., & Glasgow, R. E. (2014). Big data and large sample size: A cautionary note on the potential for bias. *Clinical and Translational Science*, *7*(4), 342–346. doi:10.1111/cts.12178 PMID:25043853

Karr, A., Sanil, A. & Banks, D. (2003). *Data Quality: A Statistical Perspective*. Academic Press.

Kasemsap, K. (2014). The role of social networking in global business environments. In P. Smith & T. Cockburn (Eds.), Impact of emerging digital technologies on leadership in global business (pp. 183–201). Hershey, PA: IGI Global. doi:10.4018/978-1-4666-6134-9.ch010

Kasemsap, K. (2015f). Implementing business intelligence in contemporary organizations. In A. Haider (Ed.), Business technologies in contemporary organizations: Adoption, assimilation, and institutionalization (pp. 177–192). Hershey, PA: IGI Global. doi:10.4018/978-1-4666-6623-8.ch008

Kasemsap, K. (2015a). The role of data mining for business intelligence in knowledge management. In A. Azevedo & M. Santos (Eds.), *Integration of data mining in business intelligence systems* (pp. 12–33). Hershey, PA: IGI Global. doi:10.4018/978-1-4666-6477-7.ch002

Kasemsap, K. (2015b). The role of cloud computing adoption in global business. In V. Chang, R. Walters, & G. Wills (Eds.), *Delivery and adoption of cloud computing services in contemporary organizations* (pp. 26–55). Hershey, PA: IGI Global. doi:10.4018/978-1-4666-8210-8.ch002

Kasemsap, K. (2015c). The role of cloud computing in global supply chain. In N. Rao (Ed.), *Enterprise management strategies in the era of cloud computing* (pp. 192–219). Hershey, PA: IGI Global. doi:10.4018/978-1-4666-8339-6.ch009

Kasemsap, K. (2015d). Implementing enterprise resource planning. In M. Khosrow-Pour (Ed.), *Encyclopedia of information science and technology* (3rd ed.; pp. 798–807). Hershey, PA: IGI Global. doi:10.4018/978-1-4666-5888-2.ch076

Kasemsap, K. (2015e). The role of customer relationship management in the global business environments. In T. Tsiakis (Ed.), *Trends and innovations in marketing information systems* (pp. 130–156). Hershey, PA: IGI Global. doi:10.4018/978-1-4666-8459-1.ch007

Kasemsap, K. (2015g). The role of business analytics in performance management. In M. Tavana & K. Puranam (Eds.), *Handbook of research on organizational transformations through big data analytics* (pp. 126–145). Hershey, PA: IGI Global. doi:10.4018/978-1-4666-7272-7.ch010

Kasemsap, K. (2016a). The roles of information technology and knowledge management in global tourism. In A. Nedelea, M. Korstanje, & B. George (Eds.), *Strategic tools and methods for promoting hospitality and tourism services* (pp. 109–138). Hershey, PA: IGI Global. doi:10.4018/978-1-4666-9761-4.ch006

Kasemsap, K. (2016b). Examining the roles of virtual team and information technology in global business. In C. Graham (Ed.), *Strategic management and leadership for systems development in virtual spaces* (pp. 1–21). Hershey, PA: IGI Global. doi:10.4018/978-1-4666-9688-4.ch001

Keen, J., Calinescu, R., Paige, R., & Rooksby, J. (2013). Big data + politics = open data: The case of health care data in England. *Policy & Internet*, *5*(2), 228–243. doi:10.1002/1944-2866.POI330

Kelly, J., Floyer, D., Vellante, D., & Miniman, S. (2013, April 17). *Big Data Vendor Revenue and Market Forecast 2012-2017*. Retrieved May 22, 2013, from http://wikibon.org/wiki/v/Big_Data_Vendor_Revenue_and_Market_Forecast_2012-2017

Kemp, R. (2014). Legal aspects of managing Big Data. *Computer Law & Security Report*, *30*(5), 482–491. doi:10.1016/j.clsr.2014.07.006

Khan, N., Yaqoob, I., & Hashem, I. A. T. (2014). Big Data: Survey, Technologies, Opportunities, and Challenges. The Scientific World Journal.

Khan, H. (2014, December). NoSQL: A database for cloud computing. *International Journal of Computer Science and Network*, *3*(6), 498–501.

Kitchin, R. (2014). *The data revolution: Big data, open data, data infrastructures and their consequences*. London, United Kingdom: Sage Publications.

Kluver, D., & Konstan, J. A. (2014). Evaluating Recommender Behavior for New Users. *RecSys*, *14*, 121–128.

Kobrix Software. (n.d.). *HyperGraphDB*. Retrieved February 14, 2016, from http://hypergraphdb.org/index

Kolodziej, J., & Xhafa, F. (2012). Integration of task abortion and security requirements in GA-based meta-heuristics for independent batch Grid scheduling. *Computers & Mathematics with Applications (Oxford, England)*, *63*(2), 350–364. doi:10.1016/j.camwa.2011.07.038

Kruschwitz, N. (2011). First look: The second annual new intelligent enterprise survey. *MIT Sloan Management Review*, *52*, 87–89.

Kruse, A., & Pongsajapan, R. (2012). Student-centered learning analytics. *CNDLS Thought Papers*, 1-9.

Kshetri, N. (2013). Privacy and security issues in cloud computing: The role of institutions and institutional evolution. *Telecommunications Policy, 37*(4-5), 372-386. doi:10.1016/j.telpol.2012.04.011

Kshetri, N. (2014). Big data's impact on privacy, security and consumer welfare. *Telecommunications Policy*, *38*(11), 1134–1145. doi:10.1016/j.telpol.2014.10.002

Kuder, M., Šterk, M., & Žalik, B. (2013). Point-based rendering optimization with textured meshes for fast LiDAR visualization. *Computers & Geosciences*, *59*(0), 181–190. doi:10.1016/j.cageo.2013.05.012

Kuiler, E. W. (2014). From big data to knowledge: An ontological approach to big data analytics. *Review of Policy Research*, *31*(4), 311–318. doi:10.1111/ropr.12077

Kulik, C. L. C., & Kulik, J. A. (1991). Effectiveness of computer-based instruction: An updated analysis. *Computers in Human Behavior*, *7*(1), 75–94. doi:10.1016/0747-5632(91)90030-5

Kwon, O., Lee, N., & Shin, B. (2014). Data quality management, data usage experience and acquisition intention of big data analytics. *International Journal of Information Management*, *34*(3), 387–394. doi:10.1016/j.ijinfomgt.2014.02.002

Lambrecht, A., & Skiera, B. (2006). Paying too much and being happy about it: Existence, causes, and consequences of tariff-choice biases. *JMR, Journal of Marketing Research*, *43*(2), 212–223. doi:10.1509/jmkr.43.2.212

Lambrecht, A., & Tucker, C. (2013). When does retargeting work? Information specificity in online advertising. *JMR, Journal of Marketing Research*, *50*(5), 561–576. doi:10.1509/jmr.11.0503

Laney, D. (2001). *3D data management: Controlling data volume, velocity and variety*. META Group Research Note, 6.

Laney, D. (2001). *3D data management: Controlling data volume, velocity and variety*. Tech. Rep. 949. META Group.

Langham, B. A. (2009). The achievement gap: What early childhood educators need to know. *Texas Child Care Quarterly*. Retrieved from https://www.collabforchildren.org/sites/default/files/downloads/achievegap09.pdf

Lazar, D., et al. (2009). Computational social science. *Science, 323*(5915), 721–723.

Lazer, D., Kennedy, R., King, G., & Vespignani, A. (2014). The parable of Google Flu: Traps in big dataAnalysis. *Science, 343*(6176), 1203–1205. doi:10.1126/science.1248506 PMID:24626916

Lee, C. R., & Chang, Y. F. (2013). Enhancing Accuracy and Performance of Collaborative Filtering Algorithm by Stochastic SDV and Its MapReduce Implementation. *2013 IEEE 27th International Symposium on Parallel & Distributed Processing Workshops and PhD Forum*, (pp. 1869-1878).

Lee, M., Lu, H., Ling, T., & Ko, Y. (1999). Cleansing data for mining and warehousing. Academic Press.

Leonardi, L., Orlando, S., Raffaeta, A., Roncato, A., Silvestri, C., Andrienko, G., & Andrienko, N. (2014). A general framework for trajectory data warehousing and visual OLAP. *GeoInformatica, 18*(2), 273–312. doi:10.1007/s10707-013-0181-3

Levin, A., & Nicholson, M. J. (2005). Privacy Law in the United States, the EU and Canada: The Allure of the Middle Ground. *U of Ottawa Law & Technology Journal, 2*(2), 362.

Levoy, M., & Whitted, T. (1985). *The use of points as a display primitive.* University of North Carolina, Department of Computer Science.

Li, H., & Lu, X. (2014). Challenges and trends of big data analytics. In *Ninth International Conference onP2P, Parallel, Grid, Cloud and Internet Computing* (3PGCIC). doi:10.1109/3PGCIC.2014.136

Li, C., Chen, J., Jin, C., Zhang, R., & Zhou, A. (2014). MR-tree: An efficient index for MapReduce. *International Journal of Communication Systems, 27*(6), 828–838. doi:10.1002/dac.2619

Li, H., Wei, X., Fu, Q., & Luo, Y. (2014). MapReduce delay scheduling with deadline constraint. *Concurrency and Computation, 26*(3), 766–778. doi:10.1002/cpe.3050

Lin, W., Dou, W., Zhou, Z., & Liu, C. (n.d.). A cloud-based framework for Home-diagnosis service over big medical data. *Journal of Systems and Software.* doi:10.1016/j.jss.2014.05.068

Liu, F., Tong, J., Mao, J., Bohn, R., Messina, J., Badger, L. et al. (2011). *NIST cloud computing reference architecture.* NIST special publication, 500, 292.

Liu, H., & Motoda, H. (2007). *Computational methods offeature selection.* Boca Raton, FL: Chapman and Hall/CRC Press.

Liu, L., Li, Z., & Delp, E. (2009). Efficient and low-complexity surveillance video compression using backward-channel aware Wyner-Ziv video coding. *IEEE Transactions on Circuits and Systems for Video Technology, 19*(4), 452–465.

Liu, Z., Jiang, B., & Heer, J. (2013). *imMens*: Real-time visual querying of big data. *Computer Graphics Forum, 32*(3pt4), 421–430. doi:10.1111/cgf.12129

Lohr, S. (2012, February 11). The Age of Big Data. *New York Times.* Retrieved from http://www.nytimes.com/2012/02/12/sunday-review/big-datasimpact-in-the-world.html

López, V., del Río, S., Benítez, J. M., & Herrera, F. (2015). Cost-sensitive linguistic fuzzy rule based classification systems under the MapReduce framework for imbalanced big data. *Fuzzy Sets and Systems, 258*, 5–38. doi:10.1016/j.fss.2014.01.015

López, V., Fernández, A., García, S., Palade, V., & Herrera, F. (2013). An insight into classification with imbalanced data: Empirical results and current trends on using data intrinsic characteristics. *Information Sciences, 250*, 113–141. doi:10.1016/j.ins.2013.07.007

López, V., Fernández, A., Moreno-Torres, J. G., & Herrera, F. (2012). Analysis of preprocessing vs. cost-sensitive learning for imbalanced classification. Open problems on intrinsic data characteristics. *Expert Systems with Applications*, *39*(7), 6585–6608. doi:10.1016/j.eswa.2011.12.043

Lu, T., Guo, X., Xu, B., Zhao, L., Peng, Y., & Yang, H. (2013). Next Big Thing in Big Data: the Security of the ICT Supply Chain. In *Proceedings of the IEEE SocialCom/PASSAT/BigData/EconCom/BioMedCom*, (pp. 1066-1073). doi:10.1109/SocialCom.2013.172

Lu, J. (2004). Personalized e-learning material recommender system. In *International conference on information technology for application* (pp. 374-379).

Madden, S. (2012). From databases to big data. *IEEE Internet Computing*, *16*(3), 4–6. doi:10.1109/MIC.2012.50

Maletic, J., & Marcus, A. (2000). Data cleansing: Beyond integrity analysis. In *Proceedings of the Conference on Information Quality (IQ2000)*.

Manaei-Bidgoli, B., Kashy, D. A., Kortmeyer, G., & Punch, W. (2003). Predicting student performance: An application of data mining methods with an educational web-based system (LON-CAPA). In *ASEE/IEEE Frontiers in Education Conference*. IEEE.

Manovich, L. (2011). Trending: the promises and the challenges of big social data. In *Debates in the Digital Humanities*. The University of Minnesota Press. Retrieved 15 July 2015 from: http://www.manovich.net/DOCS/Manovich_trending_paper.pdf

Manyika, J., Chui, M., Brown, B., Bughin, J., Dobbs, R., Roxburgh, C., & Byers, A. H. (2011). *Big data: The next frontier for innovation, competition, and productivity*. McKinsey Global Institute.

Marx, V. (2013). The big challenges of big data. *Nature*, *498*(7453), 255–260. doi:10.1038/498255a PMID:23765498

Maslow, A. H. (1943). A theory of human motivation. *Psychological Review*, *50*(4), 370–396. doi:10.1037/h0054346

Mathew, P. A., Dunn, L. N., Sohn, M. D., Mercado, A., Custudio, C., & Walter, T. (2015). Big-data for building energy performance: Lessons from assembling a very large national database of building energy use. *Applied Energy*, *140*, 85–93. doi:10.1016/j.apenergy.2014.11.042

Matti, M., & Kvernvik, T. (2012). *Applying Big-data technologies to Network Architecture*. Ericsson Review.

Ma, Y., Liu, B., Wong, C. K., Yu, P. S., & Lee, S. M. (2000, August). Targeting the right students using data mining. In *Proceedings of the sixth ACM SIGKDD international conference on Knowledge discovery and data mining* (pp. 457-464). ACM. doi:10.1145/347090.347184

Mayer-Schoenberger, V., & Cukier, K. (2013). *Big Data: A Revolution That Will Transform How We Live, Work and Think*. J Murray.

Mayer-Schönberger, V., & Cukier, K. (2013). BIG DATA: A Revolution That Will Transform How We Live, Work, and Think, Eamon Dolan/Houghton Mifflin Harcourt Publisher.

Mayer-Schönberger, V., & Cukier, K. (2013). *Big data: A revolution that will transform how we live, work, and think*. New York, NY: Houghton Mifflin Harcourt.

Mazur, E., & Hilborn, R. C. (1997). Peer Instruction: A User's Manual. Physics Today, 50(4), 65.

Mazur, E., (2009). Farewell, lecture. *Science, 323*(5910), 50-51

McAfee, A., Brynjolfsson, E., Davenport, T. H., Patil, D., & Barton, D. (2012). Big data. The management revolution. *Harvard Business Review*, *90*, 61–67. PMID:23074865

McCormick, T. H., Ferrell, R., Karr, A. F., & Ryan, P. B. (2014). Big data, big results: Knowledge discovery in output from large-scale analytics. *Statistical Analysis and Data Mining: The ASA Data Science Journal*, *7*(5), 404–412. doi:10.1002/sam.11237

McGuire, T., Manyika, J., & Chui, M. (2012). Why big data is the new competitive advantage. *Ivey Business Journal*, *76*, 1–4.

McLuhan, M. (1994). *Understanding media: The extensions of man*. MIT Press.

McNeely, C. L., & Hahm, J. O. (2014). The big (data) bang: Policy, prospects, and challenges. *Review of Policy Research*, *31*(4), 304–310. doi:10.1111/ropr.12082

Mcquiggan, S. W., Mott, B. W., & Lester, J. C. (2008). Modeling self-efficacy in intelligent tutoring systems: An inductive approach. *User Modeling and User-Adapted Interaction*, *18*(1-2), 81–123. doi:10.1007/s11257-007-9040-y

Meek, T. (2015). Big data in retail: How to win with predictive analytics. *Forbes*. Retrieved 27 May 2015 from: http://www.forbes.com/sites/netapp/2015/02/18/big-data-in-retail/

Meijer, E. (2011). The world according to LINQ. *ACM Communications*, *54*(10), 45–51. doi:10.1145/2001269.2001285

Mell, P., & Grance, T. (2011). *The NIST definition of cloud computing*. Retrieved from Computer Security Division, Information Technology Laboratory, National Institute of Standards and Technology Gaithersburg. doi:10.6028/NIST.SP.800-145

Melville, M., & Sindhwani, V. (2010). Recommender Systems. In *Encyclopedia of Machine Learning* (pp. 829-838). http://vikas.sindhwani.org/recommender.pdf

Merceron, A., & Yacef, K. (2010). Measuring correlation of strong symmetric association rules in educational data. In Handbook of Educational Data Mining. Boca Raton, FL: CRC Press. doi:10.1201/b10274-20

Messelodi, S., Modena, C. M., Zanin, M., De Natale, F. G. B., Granelli, F., Betterle, E., & Guarise, A. (2009). Intelligent extended floating car data collection. *Expert Systems with Applications*, *36*(3, Part 1), 4213–4227. doi:10.1016/j.eswa.2008.04.008

Mian, A., Rao, K., & Sufi, A. (2013). Household balance sheets, consumption and economic slump. *The Quarterly Journal of Economics*, *128*(4), 1687–1726. doi:10.1093/qje/qjt020

Mian, A., & Sufi, A. (2009). The consequences of mortgage credit expansion: Evidence from the U.S. mortgage default crisis. *The Quarterly Journal of Economics*, *124*(4), 1449–1496. doi:10.1162/qjec.2009.124.4.1449

Microsoft. (2015). *ASP.NET*. Retrieved February 13, 2016, from http://www.asp.net

Miller, H. G., & Mork, P. (2013). From data to decisions: A value chain for big data. *IT Professional*, *15*(1), 57–59. doi:10.1109/MITP.2013.11

Minelli, M., Chambers, M., & Dhiraj, A. (2013). Big Data, Big Analytics: Emerging Business Intelligence and Analytic Trends for Today's Businesses. Wiley Publishing.

Minelli, M., Chambers, M., & Dhiraj, A. (2013). *Big data, big analytics: Emerging business intelligence and analytic trends for today's businesses*. Hoboken, NJ: John Wiley & Sons. doi:10.1002/9781118562260

Monge, A., Elkan, C., & Associates. (1996). The Field Matching Problem: Algorithms and Applications. Academic Press.

mongoDB, Inc. (n.d.). *mongoDB*. Retrieved October 07, 2015, from http://www.mongodb.org/

Moore, G. E. (1998). Cramming more components onto integrated circuits. *Proceedings of the IEEE*, *86*(1), 82–85. doi:10.1109/JPROC.1998.658762

Moore, J. L., Dickson-Deane, C., & Galyen, K. (2011). e-Learning, online learning, and distance learning environments: Are they the same? *The Internet and Higher Education*, *14*(2), 129–135. doi:10.1016/j.iheduc.2010.10.001

Mor, Y. (2014). Big data and law enforcement: Was 'minority report' right? *Wired*. Retrieved from http://www.wired.com/2014/03/big-data-law-enforcement-minority-report-right/

Moreno-Torres, J. G., Raeder, T., Aláiz-Rodríguez, R., Chawla, N. V., & Herrera, F. (2012). A unifying view on dataset shift in classification. *Pattern Recognition*, *45*(1), 521–530. doi:10.1016/j.patcog.2011.06.019

Morris, B. T., Tran, C., Scora, G., Trivedi, M. M., & Barth, M. J. (2012). Real-time video-based traffic measurement and visualization system for energy/emissions. *Intelligent Transportation Systems IEEE Transactions on*, *13*(4), 1667–1678.

Mukherjee, A., Pal, A., & Misra, P. (2012). Data analytics in ubiquitous sensor-based health information systems. In *6th International Conference on Next Generation Mobile Applications, Services and Technologies (NGMAST)*. doi:10.1109/NGMAST.2012.39

Muller, H., & Freytag, J. (2003). *Problems*. Methods, and Challenges in Comprehensive Data Cleansing.

Mun, M., Hao, S., Mishra, N., Shilton, K., Burke, J., & Govindan, R. et al. (2010). *Personal Data Vaults: A Locus of Control for Personal Data Streams*. ACM CoNext.

Mures, O. A. (2014). *ToView point cloud visualizer*. Retrieved from https://youtu.be/cyeOUs0PyNw

Nafus, D., & Sherman, J. (2014). This One Does Not Go Up to 11: The Quantified Self Movement as an Alternative Big Data Practice. *International Journal of Communication*, *8*, 1784–1794.

National Science and Technology. (2011). *Council*. Materials Genome Initiative for Global Competitiveness.

Needham, J. (2013). *Disruptive Possibilities: How Big Data Changes Everything*. O'Reilly Publisher.

Neo4j Technology Inc. (n.d.). *Neo4j*. Retrieved January 22, 2016, from http://neo4j.com/download/

Nickerson, D., & Rogers, T. (2014). Political campaigns and "big data". *The Journal of Economic Perspectives*, *28*(2), 51–74. doi:10.1257/jep.28.2.51

Novotny, A., & Spiekermann, S. (2013). Personal Information Markets AND Privacy: A New Model to Solve the Controversy.*11th International Conference on Wirtschaftsinformatik*, Leipzig, Germany.

O'Leary, D. E. (2013). Artificial intelligence and big data. *IEEE Intelligent Systems*, *28*(2), 96–99. doi:10.1109/MIS.2013.39 PMID:25505373

Odersky, M., Spoon, L., & Venner, B. (2008). *A Scalable Language*. Retrieved December 15, 2014, from http://www.artima.com/scalazine/articles/scalable-language.html

Oracle Corporation. (n.d.). *Oracle NoSQL Database*. Retrieved from November 03, 2015, from http://www.oracle.com/technetwork/database/database-technologies/nosqldb/overview/index.html

Owen, S. (2012). *Mahout in Action*. New York: Manning Publications.

Pagare, R., & Patil, S. A. (2013). Study of Collaborative Filtering Recommendation Algorithm – Scalability Issue. *International Journal of Computers and Applications*, *67*(25), 10–15. doi:10.5120/11742-7305

Papagelis, M., Rousidis, L., Plexousakis, D., & Theoharppoulous, E. (2005). Incremental Collaborative Filtering for Highly-Scalable Recommendation Algorithms. In M. Said Hacid, N. V. Murray, Z. W. Ras, & S. Tsumoto (Eds.), *Foundations of Intelligent System*. New York: Springer Berlin Heidelberg.

Paper, W. (n.d.). *Gettting Real About Security Management And Big Data: A Roadmap for Big Data in Security Analytics*. White Paper, RSAs and EMC Corporation. Retrieved from www.EMC.com/rsa

ParAccel Inc. (2012). *Hadoop's Limitations for Big Data Analytics*. ParAccel; doi:10.1007/11425274_57

ParAccel. (2012). *Hadoops limitations for big data analytics*. ParAccel White Paper. Retrieved from: http://www.paraccel.com/resources/Whitepapers/Hadoop-Limitations-for-Big-Data-ParAccel-Whitepaper.pdf

Pariser, E. (2011). *The Filter Bubble: What the Internet Is Hiding From You*. Penguin Press.

Park, J., Baek, Y. M., & Cha, M. (2014). Cross-cultural comparison of nonverbal cues in emoticons on Twitter: Evidence from big data analysis. *Journal of Communication*, *64*(2), 333–354. doi:10.1111/jcom.12086

Park, J., Kim, H., Jeong, Y. S., & Lee, E. (2014). Two-phase grouping-based resource management for big data processing in mobile cloud computing. *International Journal of Communication Systems*, *27*(6), 839–851. doi:10.1002/dac.2627

Park, S. T., Kim, Y. R., Jeong, S. P., Hong, C. I., & Kang, T. G. (2016). A case study on effective technique of distributed data storage for big data processing in the wireless Internet environment. *Wireless Personal Communications*, *86*(1), 239–253. doi:10.1007/s11277-015-2794-3

Parks, M. R. (2014). Big data in communication research: Its contents and discontents. *Journal of Communication*, *64*(2), 355–360. doi:10.1111/jcom.12090

Parry, M. L. (2007). Climate Change 2007: impacts, adaptation and vulnerability: contribution of Working Group II to the fourth assessment report of the Intergovernmental Panel on Climate Change (4th ed.). Cambridge University Press.

Pavlik, P. I. Jr, Cen, H., & Koedinger, K. R. (2009). Performance Factors Analysis--A New Alternative to Knowledge Tracing. In *Proceedings of the 14th international conference on artificial intelligence in education*.

Philip, T. M., Schuler-Brown, S., & Way, W. (2013). A framework for learning about big data with mobile technologies for democratic participation: Possibilities, limitations, and unanticipated obstacles. *Technology. Knowledge and Learning*, *18*(3), 103–120. doi:10.1007/s10758-013-9202-4

Pirog, M. A. (2014). Data will drive innovation in public policy and management research in the next decade. *Journal of Policy Analysis and Management*, *33*(2), 537–543. doi:10.1002/pam.21752

Porter, M. (1980). *Competitive Strategy: Techniques for Analyzing Industries and Competitors*. New York: The Free Press.

Prabha, S. L., & Shanavas, D. A. M. (2014). Educational data mining applications. *Operations Research and Applications: An International Journal*, *1*(1).

Prensky, M. (2008). The role of technology in teaching and the classroom. *Educational Technology*. Retrieved from http://www.marcprensky.com/writing/Prensky-The_Role_of_Technology-ET-11-12-08.pdf

Prins, J. E. (2004). The propertization of personal data and identities. *Electronic Journal of Comparative Law*, *8*(3).

Purcell, B. M. (2013). *Big data using cloud computing*. Holy Family University working paper.

Purtova, N. (2011). *Property Rights in Personal Data: A European Perspective*. Kluwer.

Pyle, D. (1999). *Data preparation for data mining*. San Francisco, CA: Morgan Kaufmann Publishers.

Qas.com. (2014). *Contact Data Management Software and Services | Experian Data Quality*. Retrieved from: http://Qas.com

Qian, J., Lv, P., Yue, X., Liu, C., & Jing, Z. (2015). Hierarchical attribute reduction algorithms for big data using MapReduce. *Knowledge-Based Systems*, *73*, 18–31. doi:10.1016/j.knosys.2014.09.001

Qin, S. J. (2014). Process data analytics in the era of big data. *AIChE Journal. American Institute of Chemical Engineers*, *60*(9), 3092–3100. doi:10.1002/aic.14523

Quora. (2011). *LinkedIn Recommendations: How does LinkedIn's recommendation system work?* Retrieved April 28, 2014, from http://www.quora.com/LinkedIn-Recommendations/How-does-LinkedIns-recommendation-system-work

Rahm, E., & Do, H. (2000). Data cleaning: Problems and current approaches. *IEEE Data Eng. Bull.*, *23*(4), 3–13.

Rai, D., & Beck, J. (2011). *Exploring user data from a game-like math tutor: a case study in causal modeling*. EDM.

Ranjan, R., Harwood, A., & Buyya, R. (2012). Coordinated load management in peer-to-peer coupled federated grid systems. *The Journal of Supercomputing*, *61*(2), 292–316. doi:10.1007/s11227-010-0426-y

Ranjan, R., Mitra, K., & Georgakopoulos, D. (2013). MediaWise cloud content orchestrator. *Journal of Internet Services and Applications*, *4*(1), 1–14.

Reichman, J., & Samuelson, P. (1997). Intellectual Property Rights in Data. *Vand. L. Rev., 50.*

Rendie, A. (2011). *Aggregation: Demystifying Database Rights*. Taylor Wessing.

Ricci, F., Rokach, L., & Shapira, B. (2011). Introduction to Recommender Systems Handbook. In F. Ricci et al. (Eds.), *Recommender Systems Handbook*. New York: Springer. doi:10.1007/978-0-387-85820-3_1

Romero, C., & Ventura, S. (2007). Educational data mining: A survey from 1995 to 2005. *Expert Systems with Applications*, *33*(1), 135–146. doi:10.1016/j.eswa.2006.04.005

Romero, C., & Ventura, S. (2013). Data mining in education. *Wiley Interdisciplinary Reviews: Data Mining and Knowledge Discovery*, *3*(1), 12–27.

Romero, C., Ventura, S., & Bra, P. D. (2004). Knowledge discovery with genetic programming for providing feedback to courseware author. *User Modeling and User-Adapted Interaction: The Journal of Personalization Research*, *14*(5), 425–464. doi:10.1007/s11257-004-7961-2

Romero, C., Ventura, S., Pechenizkiy, M., & Baker, R. S. J. d. (Eds.). (2010). *Handbook of Educational Data Mining*. CRC Press. doi:10.1201/b10274

Rosen, J. (2012). The Right to be Forgotten. *Stanford Law Review*, *64*, 88.

Sagiroglu, S., & Sinanc, D. (2013). Big Data. *RE:view*, 42–47. PMID:23577548

Sarwar, B. (2000). Application of Dimensionality Reduction in Recommender System -- A Case Study. *ACM WebKDD 2000 (Web-mining for Ecommerce Workshop)*. Retrieved from http://files.grouplens.org/papers/webKDD00.pdf

Sarwar, B. (2001). Item-based Collaborative Filtering Recommendation Algorithms. In *Proceedings of the 10th International Conference on World Wide Web* (pp. 285-295). New York: ACM.

Sarwar, B. (2002). Incremental Singular Value Decomposition Algorithms for Highly Scalable Recommender Systems. In *Proceedings of Fifth International Conference on Computer and Information Science* (pp. 27- 28).

Schaller, R. R. (1997). Moore's law: past, present and future. *Spectrum, IEEE, 34*(6), 52-59. Retrieved from IEEE.

Schelter, S., & Owen, S. (2012). Collaborative Filtering with Apache Mahout. RecSysChallenge. Dublin: ACM. Retrieved from http://ssc.io/pdf/cf-mahout.pdf

Scheuer, O., & McLaren, B. M. (2011). Educational data mining. In *The Encyclopedia of the Sciences of Learning*. New York, NY: Springer.

Schilling, P. L., & Bozic, K. L. (2014). The big to do about "big data". *Clinical Orthopaedics and Related Research*, *472*(11), 3270–3272. doi:10.1007/s11999-014-3887-0 PMID:25141846

Schintler, L. A., & Kulkarni, R. (2014). Big data for policy analysis: The good, the bad, and the ugly. *Review of Policy Research*, *31*(4), 343–348. doi:10.1111/ropr.12079

Schmitt, C., Shoffner, M., Owen, P., Wang, X., Lamm, B., Mostafa, J., . . . Fecho, K. (2013, November). *Security and Privacy in the Era of Big Data*. White Paper. ARENCI/National Consortium for Data Science. ARENCI White Paper Series.

Schönberger, V. M., & Cukier, K. (2013). *Big Data: A revolution that will transform how we live, work, and think*. New York: Houghton Mifflin Harcourt.

Schroeck, M., Shockley, R., Smart, J., Romero-Morales, D., & Tufano, P. (2012). *Analytics: The real-world use of big data. How innovative enterprises extract value from uncertain data*. Retrieved from http://www-03.ibm.com/systems/hu/resources/the real word use of big data.pdf

Schroeder, R. (2014). Big Data: Towards a More Scientific Social Science and Humanities. In M. Graham & W. H. Dutton (Eds.), *Society and the Internet: How Networks of Information are Changing our Lives*. Oxford, UK: Oxford University Press.

Schultz, J. R. (2014). Big data are, after all, just data. *Performance Improvement*, *53*(5), 20–25. doi:10.1002/pfi.21411

Schumaker, R. P., & Chen, H. (2009). Textual analysis of stock market prediction using breaking financial news: The AZFin text system. *ACM Transactions on Information Systems*, *27*(2), 1–19. doi:10.1145/1462198.1462204

Security, V. (n.d.). *Big Data, Meet Enterprise Security*. White Paper. Retrieved from http://www.voltage.com/solution/enterprise-security-for-big-data/

Segal, I., & Whinston, M. (2012). Property Rights: Handbook of Organizational Economics. Princeton University Press.

Seguin, K. (2013). *The Little MongoDB Book*. Retrieved January 08, 2016, from http://openmymind.net/mongodb.pdf

Servin, O., Boriboonsomsin, K., & Barth, M. (2006). An energy and emissions impact evaluation of intelligent speed adaptation. *Intelligent Transportation Systems Conference* (pp. 1257-1262) IEEE. doi:10.1109/ITSC.2006.1707395

Shah, T., Rabhi, F., & Ray, P. (2015). Investigating an ontology-based approach for big data analysis of inter-dependent medical and oral health conditions. *Cluster Computing*, *18*(1), 351–367. doi:10.1007/s10586-014-0406-8

Shin, D. (2014). A socio-technical framework for internet-of-things design: A human-centered design for the Internet of Things. *Telematics and Informatics*, *31*(4), 519–531. doi:10.1016/j.tele.2014.02.003

Shin, D. H., & Choi, M. J. (2015). Ecological views of big data: Perspectives and issues. *Telematics and Informatics*, *32*(2), 311–320. doi:10.1016/j.tele.2014.09.006

Shovan, P. (2013, October 23). *Connecting MongoDB with ASP.NET*. Retrieved November 03, 2015, from http://www.codeproject.com/Chapters/656093/Connecting-MongoDB-with-ASP-NET

Shute, V. J. (1995). SMART: Student modeling approach for responsive tutoring. *User Modeling and User-Adapted Interaction*, *5*(1), 1–44. doi:10.1007/BF01101800

Siemens, G., & Baker, R. S. (2012). Learning analytics and educational data mining: towards communication and collaboration. In *Proceedings of the 2nd international conference on learning analytics and knowledge* (pp. 252-254). ACM. doi:10.1145/2330601.2330661

Singh, R., & Singh, K. et al. (2010). A descriptive classification of causes of data quality problems in data warehousing. *International Journal of Computer Science Issues*, *7*(3), 41–50.

Skoric, M. M. (2014). The implications of big data for developing and transitional economies: Extending the triple helix? *Scientometrics*, *99*(1), 175–186. doi:10.1007/s11192-013-1106-5

Smith, V. C., Lange, A., & Huston, D. R. (2012). Predictive modeling to forecast student outcomes and drive effective interventions in online community college courses. *Journal of Asynchronous Learning Networks*, *16*(3), 51–61.

Soft Layer. (2014). *Big Data Hosting*. Retrieved December 30, 2013, from: http://www.softlayer.com/solutions/big-data/

Song, J., Guo, C., Wang, Z., Zhang, Y., Yu, G., & Pierson, J. M. (2015). HaoLap: A Hadoop based OLAP system for big data. *Journal of Systems and Software*, *102*, 167–181. doi:10.1016/j.jss.2014.09.024

Spark 1.2.0. (2014). *Spark Programming Guide.* Retrieved October 24, 2014, from: http://spark.apache.org/docs/latest/programming-guide.html

Spark Summit. (2014). *Spark Summit 2014*. Retrieved October 16, 2014, from: http://spark-summit.org/2014

Steinbrook, R. (2008). Personally Controlled Online Health Data – The Next Big Thing In Medical Care?' (2008). *The New England Journal of Medicine*, *358*, 16.

Stough, R., & McBride, D. (2014). Big data and U.S. public policy. *Review of Policy Research*, *31*(4), 339–342. doi:10.1111/ropr.12083

Swan, M. (2013). *The Quantified Self: Fundamental Disruption in Big Data Science and Biological Discovery* (Vol. 1). Big Data.

Szlezák, N., Evers, M., Wang, J., & Pérez, L. (2014). The role of big data and advanced analytics in drug discovery, development, and commercialization. *Clinical Pharmacology and Therapeutics*, *95*(5), 492–495. doi:10.1038/clpt.2014.29 PMID:24642713

Tambe, P. (2014). Big data investment, skills and firm value. *Management Science*, *60*(6), 1452–1469. doi:10.1287/mnsc.2014.1899

Tatebe, O., Hiraga, K., & Soda, N. (2010). Gfarm grid file system. *New Generation Computing*, *28*(3), 257–275. doi:10.1007/s00354-009-0089-5

Techopedia.com. (2014a). *What is Data Purging? - Definition from Techopedia*. Retrieved from: http://www.techopedia.com/definition/28042/data-purging

Techopedia2.com. (2014b). *What is Data Transformation? - Definition from Techopedia.* Retrieved from: http://www.techopedia.com/definition/6760/data-transformation

TechTarget. (n.d.). *Commercial and open source vulnerability management tools.* Retrieved from: *http*://searchitchannel.techtarget.com/feature/Commercial-and-open-source-vulnerability-management-tools

Tekiner, F., & Keane, J. A. (2013). Big Data Framework. In *Proceedings of IEEE International Conference on Systems, Man, and Cybernetics.*

Thangavel, S. K., Thampi, N. S. & I, J. C. (2013). Performance Analysis of Various Recommendation Algorithm Using Apache Hadoop and Mahout. *International Journal of Scientific and Engineering Research, 4*(12), 279-287. Retrieved from http://www.ijser.org/researchpaper%5CPerformance-Analysis-of-Various-Recommendation-Algorithms.pdf

The Big Data Security Gap: Protecting the Hadoop Cluster. (2013). A White Paper. Zettaset Company.

The Economist. (2011). *Drowning in numbers – Digital data will flood the planet and help us understand it better*. Retrieved from http://www.economist.com/blogs/dailychart/2011/11/big-data-0

The Heartbleed Bug. (2014). Retrieved from: http://heartbleed.com/

The White House. (2012, March 29). *Obama Administration Unveils "Big Data" Initiative: Announces $200 Million in New R&D Investments*. Retrieved February 13, 2013, from http://www.whitehouse.gov/sites/default/files/microsites/ostp/big_data_press_release_final_2.pdf

Tielert, T., Killat, M., Hartenstein, H., Luz, R., Hausberger, S., & Benz, T. (2010). The impact of traffic-light-to-vehicle communication on fuel consumption and emissions. *Internet of Things*, *2010*, 1–8.

Tien, J. M. (2013). Big data: Unleashing information. *Journal of Systems Science and Systems Engineering*, *22*(2), 127–151. doi:10.1007/s11518-013-5219-4

Tinati, R., Halford, S., Carr, L., & Pope, C. (2014). Big data: Methodological challenges and approaches for sociological analysis. *Sociology*, *48*(4), 663–681. doi:10.1177/0038038513511561

Triguero, I., Derrac, J., García, S., & Herrera, F. (2012). A taxonomy and experimental study on prototype generation for nearest neighbor classification. *IEEE Transactions on Systems, Man and Cybernetics. Part C, Applications and Reviews*, *42*(1), 86–100. doi:10.1109/TSMCC.2010.2103939

Triguero, I., Peralta, D., Bacardit, J., García, S., & Herrera, F. (2015). MRPR: A MapReduce solution for prototype reduction in big data classification. *Neurocomputing*, *150*, 331–345. doi: 10.1016/j.neucom.2014.04.078

Trivedi, S., Pardos, Z. A., Sarkozy, G. N., & Heffernan, N. T. (2011). *Spectral Clustering in Educational Data Mining*. EDM.

TutorialsPoint. (2014). *Scala Tutorial*. Retrieved December 22, 2014, from: http://www.tutorialspoint.com/scala/scala_pdf_version.htm

Ullman, J. D. (2012). *Designing Good MapReduce Algorithms*. Retrieved May 5, 2014, from: http://xrds.acm.org/article.cfm?aid=2331053

Valvåg, S. V., Johansen, D., & Kvalnes, Å. (2013). Cogset: A high performance MapReduce engine. *Concurrency and Computation*, *25*(1), 2–23. doi:10.1002/cpe.2827

Van Alstyne, M., Brynjolfsson, E., & Madnick, S. (1995). Why Not One Big Database? Principles for Data Ownership. *Decision Support Systems*, *15*(4), 267–284.

Van Genderen, J. (2011). Airborne and terrestrial laser scanning. *International Journal of Digital Earth*, *4*(2), 183–184. doi:10.1080/17538947.2011.553487

Varian, H. (2014). "Big data": New tricks for econometrics. *The Journal of Economic Perspectives*, *28*(2), 3–28. doi:10.1257/jep.28.2.3

Vellido, A., Castro, F., & Nebot, A. (2010). *Clustering educational data. In Handbook of Educational Data Mining* (pp. 75–92). Chapman and Hall/CRC Press. doi:10.1201/b10274-8

Vellido, A., Castro, F., & Nebot, A. (2011). *Clustering Educational Data. Handbook of Educational Data Mining*. Boca Raton, FL: Chapman and Hall/CRC Press.

Victor, J. M. (2013). The EU General Data Protection Regulation: Toward a Property Regime for Protecting Data Privacy. *The Yale Law Journal*, 513.

Villa, A. (2012). *Transfering Big Data Across the Globe*. University of New Hampshire Durham.

Vitolo, C., Elkhatib, Y., Reusser, D., Macleod, C. J. A., & Buytaert, W. (2015). Web technologies for environmental big data. *Environmental Modelling & Software*, *63*, 185–198. doi:10.1016/j.envsoft.2014.10.007

Vozalis, M. G., & Margaritis, K. G. (2006). Applying SVD on generalized Item-based filtering. *International Journal of Computer Science & Application, 3*(3), 27-51. Retrieved from http://www.tmrfindia.org/ijcsa/v3i34.pdf

Walonoski, J. A., & Heffernan, N. T. (2006). Detection and analysis of off-task gaming behavior in intelligent tutoring systems. In *International Conference on Intelligent Tutoring Systems*, (pp. 382-391). Springer Berlin Heidelberg. doi:10.1007/11774303_38

Walunj, S. & Sadafale, K. (2013a). Price based Recommendation System. *International Journal of Research in Computer Engineering and Information Technology, 1*(1).

Walunj, S., & Sadafale, K. (2013b). An Online Recommendation System for E-commerce Based on Apache Mahout Framework. In *Proceedings of the 2013 annual conference on Computers and people research* (pp. 153-158). New York: ACM. doi:10.1145/2487294.2487328

Wang, J., Liu, Z., Zhang, S., & Zhang, X. (2014). Defending collaborative false data injection attacks in wireless sensor networks. *Information Sciences*, *254*, 39–53. doi:10.1016/j.ins.2013.08.019

Wang, L., Chen, D., & Huang, F. (2011). Virtual workflow system for distributed collaborative scientific applications on Grids. *Computers & Electrical Engineering*, *37*(3), 300–310. doi:10.1016/j.compeleceng.2011.01.004

Wang, L., Chen, D., Hu, Y., Ma, Y., & Wang, J. (2013). Towards enabling cyberinfrastructure as a service in clouds. *Computers & Electrical Engineering*, *39*(1), 3–14. doi:10.1016/j.compeleceng.2012.05.001

Wang, L., Chen, D., Zhao, J., & Tao, J. (2012). Resource management of distributed virtual machines. *International Journal of Ad Hoc and Ubiquitous Computing*, *10*(2), 96–111. doi:10.1504/IJAHUC.2012.048261

Wang, L., Kunze, M., Tao, J., & Laszewski, G. (2011). Towards building a cloud for scientific applications. *Advances in Engineering Software*, *42*(9), 714–722. doi:10.1016/j.advengsoft.2011.05.007

Wang, L., Zhan, J., Shi, W., & Liang, Y. (2012). In cloud, can scientific communities benefit from the economies of scale? *IEEE Transactions on Parallel and Distributed Systems*, *23*(2), 296–303. doi:10.1109/TPDS.2011.144

Ward, J. S., & Barker, A. (2013). *Unified By Data: A Survey of Big Data Definitions*. Retrieved December 15, 2014, from: http://arxiv.org/pdf/1309.5821v1.pdf

Washington, A. L. (2014). Government information policy in the era of big data. *Review of Policy Research*, *31*(4), 319–325. doi:10.1111/ropr.12081

Wasikowski, M., & Chen, X. W. (2010). Combating the small sample class imbalance problem using feature selection. *IEEE Transactions on Knowledge and Data Engineering*, *22*(10), 1388–1400. doi:10.1109/TKDE.2009.187

Wei, L., Zhu, H., Cao, Z., Dong, X., Jia, W., & Chen, Y. (2014). Security and privacy for storage and computation in cloud computing. *Information Sciences*, *258*(0), 371–386. doi:10.1016/j.ins.2013.04.028

Wenzel, K., Rothermel, M., Fritsch, D., & Haala, N. (2014b). *An out-of-core octree for massive point cloud processing.* Paper presented at the Iqmulus 1st Workshop On Processing Large Geospatial Data.

Wenzel, K., Rothermel, M., Fritsch, D., & Haala, N. (2014a). Filtering of point clouds from photogrammetric surface reconstruction. *International Archives of the Photogrammetry. Remote Sensing and Spatial Information Sciences, 1*, 615–620.

White, P., & Breckenridge, R. S. (2014). Trade-offs, limitations, and promises of big data in social science research. *Review of Policy Research, 31*(4), 331–338. doi:10.1111/ropr.12078

White, T. (2011). *Hadoop: The definitive Guide.* O'Reilly Media.

Wigan, M., & Clarke, R. (2013). Big data's big unintended consequences. *IEEE Computer, 46*(6), 46–53. doi:10.1109/MC.2013.195

Windham, C. (2005). The student's perspective. In Educating the Next Generation. Educause.

Woniak, M., Graña, M., & Corchado, E. (2014). A survey of multiple classifier systems as hybrid systems. *Information Fusion, 16*, 3–17. doi:10.1016/j.inffus.2013.04.006

Woo, J. (2013). Market basket analysis algorithms with MapReduce. *Wiley Interdisciplinary Reviews: Data Mining and Knowledge Discovery, 3*(6), 445–452. doi: 10.1002/widm.1107

Worster, A., Weirich, T. R., & Andera, F. (2014). Big data: Gaining a competitive edge. *Journal of Corporate Accounting & Finance, 25*(5), 35–39. doi:10.1002/jcaf.21970

Wu, L., & Wang, Y. (2010). *The process of criminal investigation based on grey hazy set.* Paper presented at the 2010 IEEE International Conference on Systems, Man, and Cybernetics (SMC 2010), Istanbul, Turkey.

Wu, X. (2002).. . *EC Data Base Directive. Berkeley Tech. LJ, 17*, 571.

Wu, X., Zhu, X., Wu, G. Q., & Ding, W. (2014). Data Mining with Big Data. *IEEE Transactions on Knowledge and Data Engineering, 26*(1), 97–107. doi:10.1109/TKDE.2013.109

Xiang, Z., Schwartz, Z., Gerdes, J. H. Jr, & Uysal, M. (2015). What can big data and text analytics tell us about hotel guest experience and satisfaction? *International Journal of Hospitality Management, 44*, 120–130. doi:10.1016/j.ijhm.2014.10.013

Xin, J., Wang, Z., Qu, L., & Wang, G. (2015). Elastic extreme learning machine for big data classification. *Neurocomputing, 149*, 464–471. doi:10.1016/j.neucom.2013.09.075

Xu, C., Zhang, Y., Zhu, G., Rui, Y., Lu, H., & Huang, Q. (2008). Using webcast text for semantic event detection in broadcast sports video. *IEEE Transactions on Multimedia, 10*(7), 1342–1355. doi:10.1109/TMM.2008.2004912

Xu, Z., Liu, Y., Mei, L., Hu, C., & Chen, L. (2015). Semantic based representing and organizing surveillance big data using video structural description technology. *Journal of Systems and Software, 102*, 217–225. doi:10.1016/j.jss.2014.07.024

Yang, J. J., Li, J. Q., & Niu, Y. (2015). A hybrid solution for privacy preserving medical data sharing in the cloud environment. *Future Generation Computer Systems, 43-44*, 74-86. doi:10.1016/j.future.2014.06.004

Yang, H., & Fong, S. (2015). Countering the concept-drift problems in big data by an incrementally optimized stream mining model. *Journal of Systems and Software, 102*, 158–166. doi:10.1016/j.jss.2014.07.010

Yang, Y., Nie, F., Xu, D., Luo, J., Zhuang, Y., & Pan, Y. (2012). A multimedia retrieval architecture based on semi-supervised ranking and relevance feedback. *IEEE Transactions on Pattern Analysis and Machine Intelligence*, *34*(4), 723–742. doi:10.1109/TPAMI.2011.170 PMID:21844624

Yang, Y., Pan, B., & Song, H. (2014). Predicting hotel demand using destination marketing organization's web traffic data. *Journal of Travel Research*, *53*(4), 433–447. doi:10.1177/0047287513500391

Yan, M., Lizhe, W., Dingsheng, L., Tao, Y., Peng, L., & Wanfeng, Z. (2013). Distributed data structure templates for data-intensive remote sensing applications. *Concurrency and Computation*, *25*(12), 1784–1797. doi:10.1002/cpe.2965

Yuan, C. (2012). *High performance computing for massive LiDAR data processing with optimized GPU parallel programming*. The University of Texas at Dallas.

Yuan, D., Yang, Y., Liu, X., Li, W., Cui, L., Xu, M., & Chen, J. (2013). A highly practical approach towards achieving minimum datasets storage cost in the cloud. *IEEE Transactions on Parallel and Distributed Systems*, *24*(6), 1234–1244. doi:10.1109/TPDS.2013.20

Yu, H., Pedrinaci, C., Dietze, S., & Domingue, J. (2012). Using linked data to annotate and search educational video resources for supporting distance learning. *IEEE Transactions on Learning Technologies*, *5*(2), 130–142. doi:10.1109/TLT.2012.1

Zadeh, L. A. (1965). Fuzzy Sets. *Information and Control*, *8*(3), 338–353. doi:10.1016/S0019-9958(65)90241-X

Zadeh, L. A. (2011). A Note on Z-numbers. *Information Sciences*, *181*(14), 2923–2932. doi:10.1016/j.ins.2011.02.022

Zaïane, O. R. (2002). Building a recommender agent for e-learning systems. In *Computers in Education:Proceedings. International Conference on* (pp. 55-59). IEEE. doi:10.1109/CIE.2002.1185862

Zaki, A. K. (2014, May). NoSQL databases: New millennium database for big data, big users, cloud computing and its security challenges. *International Journal of Research in Engineering and Technology*, *3*(3), 403–409.

Zhang, C., de Sterck, H., Aboulnaga, A., Djambazian, H., & Sladek, R. (2010). *Case study of scientific data processing on a cloud using Hadoop*. Paper presented at the 24th annual High Performance Computing Symposium (HPCS 2010), Toronto, Canada. doi:10.1007/978-3-642-12659-8_29

Zhang, J., & Zhang, B. (2014). Clinical research of traditional Chinese medicine in big data era. *Frontiers of Medicine*, *8*(3), 321–327. doi:10.1007/s11684-014-0370-y PMID:25217972

Zhang, J., Zulkernine, M., & Haque, A. (2008). Random-forests-based network intrusion detection systems. *IEEE Transactions on Systems, Man and Cybernetics. Part C, Applications and Reviews*, *38*(5), 649–659. doi:10.1109/TSMCC.2008.923876

Zhang, X., Liu, C., Nepal, S., Yang, C., Dou, W., & Chen, J. (2013). SaC-FRAPP: A scalable and cost effective framework for privacy preservation over big data on cloud. *Concurrency and Computation*, *25*(18), 2561–2576. doi:10.1002/cpe.3083

Zhang, X., Liu, C., Nepal, S., Yang, C., Dou, W., & Chen, J. (2014). A hybrid approach for scalable sub-tree anonymization over big data using MapReduce on cloud. *Journal of Computer and System Sciences*, *80*(5), 1008–1020. doi:10.1016/j.jcss.2014.02.007

Zhao, J., Wang, L., Tao, J., Chen, J., Sun, W., Ranjan, R., & Georgakopoulos, D. et al. (2014). A security framework in G-Hadoop for big data computing across distributed Cloud data centres. *Journal of Computer and System Sciences*, *80*(5), 994–1007. doi:10.1016/j.jcss.2014.02.006

Zhao, Z. D., & Shang, M. S. (2010). User-based Collaborative-Filtering Recommendation Algorithms on Hadoop. In *Proceedings of Third International Conference on Knowledge Discovery and Data Mining* (pp. 478-481). IEEE.

Zhou, X., He, J., Huang, G., & Zhang, Y. (2012). A personalized recommendation algorithm based on approximating the singular value decomposition (ApproSVD). *2012 IEEE/WIC/ACM International Conferences on Web Intelligence and Intelligent Agent Technology*. IEEE.

Zhou, G. T., Ting, K. M., Liu, F. T., & Yin, Y. (2012). Relevance feature mapping for content-based multimedia information retrieval. *Pattern Recognition*, *45*(4), 1707–1720. doi:10.1016/j.patcog.2011.09.016

Zikopoulos, P., Eaton, C., DeRoos, D., Deutsch, T., & Lapis, G. (2011). *Understanding big data: Analytics for enterprise class Hadoop and streaming data*. New York, NY: McGraw–Hill.

Zikopoulous, P. C. (2012). *Understanding Big Data: Analytics for Enterprise Class; Hadoop and Streaming Data*. New York: McGraw Hill.

Zwicker, M., Pfister, H., Van Baar, J., & Gross, M. (2001). *Surface splatting*. Paper presented at the Proceedings of the 28th annual conference on Computer graphics and interactive techniques.

About the Contributors

Huda Kadhim Al-Jobori was born in 1971 in Baghdad, Iraq. She received her Ph.D. in Computer Science and Information System, from University of Technology, Iraq in 2003. She joined Ahlia University in 2008 as an Assistant Professor. Dr. Huda has a B.Sc. in Computer Science from AL-Nahrain University, Iraq, and a M.Sc. in Computer Science from AL-Nahrain University, Iraq. Her research interest is Information Security, Artificial Intelligence, Computer Networks, Information Hiding, Image Processing, Database. She has published many papers in refereed journals. She participated in the review of many journal and conference papers and supervised many master and undergraduate students.

Khadija Ateya Almohsen was born in 1988 in Bahrain. She received her B.Sc. in Computer Science, from University of Bahrain, in 2011 with G.P.A 4 out of 4. Ms. Khadija joined Ahlia University in 2011 as a Research Assistant while she was studying Master in Information Technology and Computer Science at the same university. She has just finished her studies with G.P.A. 4 and thus got promoted to a Lecturer role. Her research interests are: Big Data, Machine Learning, Database and Algorithms. Prior to joining Ahlia University, she was working in Microcenter, Bahrain as Technical Support Executive and Trainer.

N. G. Bhuvaneswari Amma is a Faculty in the Department of Information Technology, Indian Institute of Information Technology, Srirangam, Tiruchirappalli, Tamilnadu, India. She received the B.E degree in Information Technology from Jayamatha Engineering College, Aralvaimozhi, India in 2004 and the M.E degree in Computer Science and Engineering in 2009 from College of Engineering, Anna University Guindy Campus, Chennai, India. Her research interest includes Data Mining, Soft Computing and Information Security.

Abhay Kumar Bhadani is a doctoral candidate at Bharti School of Telecommunication Technology and Management, Indian Institute of Technology Delhi. He holds Masters in Technology (ICT), Masters in Computer Applications and Bachelors of Computer Applications. He has developed strong interest in Algorithms, Data Mining, Machine Learning, Modeling Business Problems, Decision Making and Big Data Analytics.

Ranjit Biswas guided fourteen Ph.D.s (degrees conferred) and published more than 120 research papers all being in foreign journals of international repute of USA, German, France, UK, Bulgaria, Italy in the field of Computer Science. He is having about 35 years of teaching experience in India and abroad at renowned universities viz. Calcutta University, IIT Kharagpur, Philadelphia University, IGNOU, NIT, etc. He is a Member in Editorial Board of 14 journals of high esteem international repute published from

USA, German, France, UK, Bulgaria, Italy and Asian countries. Presently, he is Professor & Head of the Department of Computer Science & Engineering in Jamia Hamdard University, New Delhi, India.

Kevin Curran, BSc (Hons), PhD, SMIEEE, FBCS CITP, SMACM, FHEA is a Reader in Computer Science at Ulster University and group leader for the Ambient Intelligence Research Group. His achievements include winning and managing UK & European Framework projects and Technology Transfer Schemes. Dr Curran has made significant contributions to advancing the knowledge and understanding of computer networking and systems, evidenced by over 800 published works. He is perhaps most well-known for his work on location positioning within indoor environments, pervasive computing and Internet security. His expertise has been acknowledged by invitations to present his work at international conferences, overseas universities and research laboratories. He is a regular contributor to print, online, radio & TV news on computing & security issues. He was the recipient of an Engineering and Technology Board Visiting Lectureship for Exceptional Engineers and is an IEEE Technical Expert for Internet/Security matters since 2008. He is a member of the EPSRC Peer Review College. He is a fellow of the British Computer Society (FBCS), a senior member of the Association for Computing Machinery (SMACM), a senior member of the Institute of Electrical and Electronics Engineers (SMIEEE) and a fellow of the higher education academy (FHEA). Dr. Curran's stature and authority in the international community is demonstrated by his influence, particularly in relation to the direction of research in computer science. He has chaired sessions and participated in the organising committees for many highly-respected international conferences and workshops. He was the founding Editor in Chief of the International Journal of Ambient Computing and Intelligence and is also a member of numerous Journal Editorial boards and international conference organising committees. He has authored a number of books and is the recipient of various patents. He has served as an advisor to the British Computer Society in regard to the computer industry standards and is a member of BCS and IEEE Technology Specialist Groups and various other professional bodies.

Emile Douilhet received an undergraduate degree in French law from the Université Paris X Nanterre La Défense in 2012 and an LLB in English law from the University of Essex in 2013. After receiving an LLM in Internet Law from the University of Essex in 2014, he started a PhD at the University of Bournemouth in the Regulation of Big Data. His main research interests are privacy law, data profiling, and data protection, with a focus on EU Law.

Anuj Kumar Dwivedi is Assistant Professor and Head, Department of Computer Science, Govt. Vijay Bhusan Singh Deo Girls Degree College, Jashpur Nagar, C.G., INDIA. He received his Ph.D. Degree in Computer Science from Pandit Ravishankar Shukla University, Raipur, C.G., INDIA. He received his M.Phil. Degree from Annamalai University, T.N., INDIA in Computer Science, while received his M.Sc. Degree in Computer Science from M.C.R.P. University, M.P., INDIA. He had published more than 25 research contributions. He is member of International Association of Engineers (IAENG) and Association of Computer Electronics and Electrical Engineers (ACEEE). His current research interests are in Wireless Sensor Networks and next generation heterogeneous wireless networks.

Rafael Hernandez Barros, PhD, Universidad Autonoma de Madrid; MBA, IESE Business School. For more than 20 years, Rafael has been working as Senior Manager in front and back office (consulting, operations and finance) management roles in the financial services industry, and is currently Financial

Support Director at Aon Spain, business support area on financial strategic planning and corporate compliance. As a Professor, He undertakes regular lecturer assignments about Financial Management and Corporate Finance at master's and bachelor's levels at Universidad Complutense de Madrid and Universidad Carlos III de Madrid, and his academic activity includes research in finance and risk management, done in institutions such as IESE Universidad de Navarra, Cass Business School (City University London), Universidad Autónoma de Madrid and Universidad Complutense de Madrid. His recent research work has been published in The Journal of Business Economics and Management, The Geneva Papers on Risk and Insurance or The Operational Risk Journal, among others; and He also serves as board member and editor-in-chief in some other international journals. Rafael is author of the book "Gestión del Riesgo y Fundamentos Prácticos de Solvencia", published by Editorial Complutense. He is also founding partner, adviser and consultant to several organizations and start-ups.

Wen-Chen Hu received a BE, an ME, an MS, and a PhD, all in Computer Science, from Tamkang University, Taiwan, the National Central University, Taiwan, the University of Iowa, Iowa City, and the University of Florida, Gainesville, in 1984, 1986, 1993, and 1998, respectively. He is currently an associate professor in the Department of Computer Science of the University of North Dakota, Grand Forks. He was an assistant professor in the Department of Computer Science and Software Engineering at the Auburn University, Alabama, for years. He is the Editor-in-Chief of the International Journal of Handheld Computing Research (IJHCR), the general chairs of a number of international conferences such as the 2015 International Conference on Big Data, IoT, and Cloud Computing (BIC 2015), and associate editors of several journals like Journal of Information Technology Research (JITR). In addition, he has acted more than 100 positions as editors and editorial advisory/review board members of international journals/books, and track/session chairs and program committee members of international conferences. He has also won a couple of awards of best papers, best reviewers, and community services. Dr. Hu has been teaching for about 20 years at the US universities and over 10 different computer/IT-related courses, and advising/consulting more than 100 graduate students. He has published over 100 articles in refereed journals, conference proceedings, books, and encyclopedias, edited more than 10 books and conference proceedings, and solely authored a book entitled "Internet-enabled handheld devices, computing, and programming: mobile commerce and personal data applications." His current research interests include handheld/mobile/smartphone/spatial/tablet computing, location-based services, web-enabled information system such as search engines and web mining, electronic and mobile commerce systems, and web technologies.

Alberto Jaspe Villanueva is a researcher in the Visual Computing (ViC) group at the Center for Advanced Studies, Research, and Development in Sardinia (CRS4) in Italy. He was awarded of a Marie Curie Fellowship in 2013 from the DIVA Initial Training Network for researching in 3D massive models analysis and render. He holds a M.Sc. degree with honors in Computer Science from the University of A Coruña (UDC) in Spain. Before joining CRS4, he worked as a Computer Graphics developer and researcher for RNASA and VideaLAB groups in the same university, where he contributed to projects in the fields of Virtual Reality, Architecture Visualization, Terrain and Point Clouds Analysis and Rendering, and Natural Interaction. He also has experience in the industry, as he started and managed for two years the R&D department of CEGA Audiovisuals, a company focused on interactive audio and video installations.

Dhanya Jothimani is a Ph.D. scholar in the Department of Management Studies at IIT Delhi, India. She received her Bachelors of Technology (B.Tech.) from National Institute of Technology, Tiruchirappalli, India, and Masters of Technology (M.Tech.) from IIT Kharagpur, India. Her research interests include Financial Analytics, Data Mining, and Operations Research. She is a member of Institute for Operations Research and Management Science (INFORMS), American Finance Association (AFA), Decision Science Institute (DSI) and Association of Information Systems (AIS).

Argyro Karanasiou is an Associate Professor (Senior Lecturer) specialising in IT and Media Law, affiliated with the Centre for Intellectual Property, Policy & Management (CIPPM) and with the Data Science Institute (DSI) at Bournemouth University, UK. She is also affiliate faculty staff of Harvard Law School (2014-2015), delivering the course CopyrightX:CIPPM in the United Kingdom. Currently, Argyro is also involved in media related projects with the Council of Europe (Regional Expert on online media and reconciliation in South Eastern Europe) and with the OSCE Representative on Freedom of the Media. In 2013 she was awarded an Internet Society IGF Ambassadorship and in 2014 she was named a PbD Ambasssador by the Information and Privacy Commissioner in Ontario, Canada. Her research discusses techno-legal conceptual frameworks for decentralised internet regulation with a particular focus on free speech, media ownership and user empowerment. Her current projects span a wide range of topics from IoT/wearable tech to smart cities and mesh networks. Argyro tweets @ArKaranasiou on all things tech and occassionally blogs on internet and media related policies (The International Forum for Responsible Media Blog), LSE Media Project Blog, protagon.gr).

Kijpokin Kasemsap received his BEng degree in Mechanical Engineering from King Mongkut's University of Technology Thonburi, his MBA degree from Ramkhamhaeng University, and his DBA degree in Human Resource Management from Suan Sunandha Rajabhat University. He is a Special Lecturer at Faculty of Management Sciences, Suan Sunandha Rajabhat University based in Bangkok, Thailand. He is a Member of International Association of Engineers (IAENG), International Association of Engineers and Scientists (IAEST), International Economics Development and Research Center (IEDRC), International Association of Computer Science and Information Technology (IACSIT), International Foundation for Research and Development (IFRD), and International Innovative Scientific and Research Organization (IISRO). He also serves on the International Advisory Committee (IAC) for International Association of Academicians and Researchers (INAAR). He has numerous original research articles in top international journals, conference proceedings, and book chapters on business management, human resource management, and knowledge management published internationally.

Naeem Ahmed Mahoto received his M.E. from MUET, Pakistan. He was awarded Ph.D. scholarship under UESTPs Project for higher studies and received his Ph.D. from Politecnico Di Torino, Italy in 2013. He is currently working an Assistant Professor at MUET Pakistan. Naeem is author of several research articles published in national as well as international journals. He works in the field of data mining and bioinformatics and his research interests are focused on pattern extraction, classification of electronic records in the medical domain and software engineering.

Nigel McKelvey is a lecturer in Computing at the Letterkenny Institute of Technology and specialises in teaching secure programming techniques at both undergraduate and postgraduate level. Other areas of interest include ethical gaming, performance based programming and digital forensics. Nigel is currently completing a Doctorate in Education focusing on adopting heuristic programming techniques within the classroom.

Areej Fatemah Meghji is an Assistant Professor in the Department of Software Engineering at Mehran.U.E.T, Pakistan. She received her M.E working on Social Networking Analysis from Mehran.U.E.T, Pakistan and is presently pursuing her PhD working on Predictive Analysis of Big Data emerging from the sector of Higher Education. Her research interests include Knowledge Management, Data Mining, Natural Language Processing, Artificial Intelligence and Big Data Analytics.

Omar A. Mures holds a BSc in Computer Science and a MSc in High Performance Computing from the University of A Coruña (Spain), where he works as pre-doctoral research associate since 2012. His main research interests include Computer Vision and Computer Graphics.

Alper Ozpinar has obtained his PhD degree in Mechanical Engineering from Yildiz Technical University. He also holds an MS degree in Systems Engineering from Yeditepe University and BS degree in Chemical Engineering from Bogazici University, all located in Istanbul Turkey. His field of expertise include, application of various computer and information systems to different fields of engineering, especially energy, demand side management, environmental health and safety, renewable energy sources, industrial automation and control, automatic data collection systems, systems modeling and simulation. He has seventeen years of experience in computer and software applications last twelve years of which has been focused on environmental and energy field. Served as a consultant and project manager for government organizations like Ministry of Forestry and Environment, Greater Municipality of Istanbul moreover international companies like ABB, Toyota, Bosch, Siemens. He has also worked part time and full time as instructor at different universities and departments given courses related with Cloud Computing, Computer Networks, Programming with different programming languages such as ASP.NET, VB.NET, C++, Java, Numerical Analysis, Artificial Intelligence and Database Systems. He has a vast experience in artificial intelligence applications such as smart grids, artificial neural networks, artificial intelligence, fuzzy logic, genetic algorithm applications. He has worked on neural networks, energy applications, active and passive RFID tags, readers and controllers, RFID technology expert especially on electronic vehicle identification. He has developed numerous projects and software applications with MS Azure, MsAccess, Visual Basic, C# & ASP & VB.Net in Automative, Textiles, Services Sector, Health Sector and various fields of engineering. He is a full time Asst. Prof. Dr. in the Department of Mechatronics in Istanbul Commerce University.

R. Vijaya Prakash works as Associate Professor in Department of Computer Science and Engineering, SR Engineering College, Warangal from the last 10 years. He completed his Masters degree from Punjabi University, Patiala and PhD from Kakatiya University, Warangal. His area of Interest are Data Mining, Artificial Intelligence.

Luke Toland is a graduate of Letterkenny Institute of Technology with Bachelor of Science (Honours) in Applied Computing. Luke has an active interest in Big Data with a particular reference to analytics and warehousing.

Marta Vidal has a BSc and MBA from ESADE Business School, Phd student in Management at Complutense University, and is an Assistant Professor of Management at European University of Madrid.

Javier Vidal-García is an Assistant Professor of Finance, University of Valladolid, Spain. The author has a BSc in Management from Queen´s University Belfast, MSc in Finance from Aston Business School, MSc in Accounting from Complutense University of Madrid, MA in Economics from Autonomous University of Madrid, PhD in Financial Economics from Complutense University of Madrid and has been a researcher at Cass Business School in London, and postdoctoral fellow at the Harvard Business School.

Serhan Yarkan received the B.S. and M.Sc. degrees in computer science from Istanbul University, Istanbul, Turkey, in 2001 and 2003, respectively, and the Ph.D. degree from the University of South Florida, Tampa, FL, USA, in 2009. He was a Post-Doctoral Research Associate with the Department of Computer and Electrical Engineering, Texas A&M University, College Station, TX, USA, from 2010 to 2012. Since 2012, he has been an Assistant Professor with the Department of Electrical-Electronics Engineering, Istanbul Commerce University, Istanbul. His current research interests include statistical signal processing, cognitive radio, wireless propagation channel measurement and modeling, cross-layer adaptation and optimization, and interference management in next-generation wireless networks.

Index

G

H

I

J

K

L

M

N

O

P

Q

R

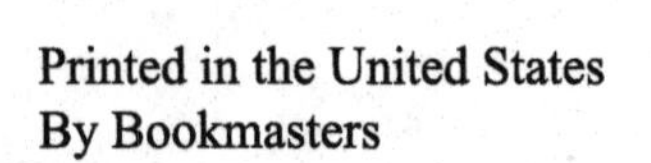
Printed in the United States
By Bookmasters